Islamic Political Movement

Islamic Political Movement

N Farukh

MD Publications Pvt Ltd
New Delhi
www.mdppl.com

Published by :

MD Publications Pvt Ltd
"MD House", 11, Darya Ganj,
New Delhi - 110 002
Phone : +91-11- 45355555
E-mail : contact@mdppl.com
Website: www.mdppl.com

ISBN : 978-81-7533-318-5

Published and Printed by Mr. Pranav Gupta on behalf of **MD Publications Pvt Ltd** at Repro India Limited.

Preface

Islam is a religion that has existed for over fourteen centuries. As such, diverse political movements in many different contexts have used the banner of Islam to lend legitimacy to their causes. Not surprisingly, practically every aspect of Islamic politics is subject to much disagreement and contention between different interpretations, particularly between traditional Islamists and westernization movements within Islam.

Islamism is a set of ideologies holding that Islam is not only a religion but also a political system; that modern Muslims must return to their roots of their religion, and unite politically. Islamist or Islamic parties exist in almost every democracy with a Muslim majority. This term has many different meanings which this article will explore, along with links to other political trends. Islam's involvement with politics dates back to its beginnings with the founding of a community-state in Medina by Muhammad in the 7th century AD.

Islamists claim that the origins of Islam as a political movement are to be found in the life and times of Islam's prophet, Muhammad and his successors, (depending on the Islamist). In 622 CE, in recognition of his claims to prophethood, Muhammad was invited to rule the city of Medina. At the time the local Arab tribes of Aus and Khazraj dominated the city, and were in constant conflict. Medinans saw in Muhammad an impartial outsider who could resolve the conflict. Muhammad and his followers thus moved to Medina, where Muhammad drafted the Medina Charter. This document made Muhammad the ruler, and recognized him as the Prophet of Allah. The laws Muhammad established during his rule, based on the revelations of the Quran and doing of Muhammad, are considered by Muslims to be Sharia or Islamic law, which Islamic movements seek to replicate in the present day. Muhammad gained a widespread following and an army, and his rule expanded first to the city of Mecca and then spread through the Arabian Peninsula through a combination of diplomacy and military conquest.

It was largely through reactive measures that the movement that is labeled Islamist came to be visible to the West, where it was labeled as being a distinct movement from Islam, pan-Arabism and resistance to colonization. The legitimacy of this kind of distinction is very much in doubt. Olivier Roy holds that the primary motive of all of this activity is resistance to colonialism and control of the Islamic World by outsiders. In this view, the movement called Islamist is wholly reactive and incidental, just a convenient rationale used to justify what is in fact resistance of a cultural and economic sort.

I am very grateful to Mr. Pranav Gupta, Director of MD Publications Pvt Ltd, New Delhi, for his kind cooperation and support for this book.

N Farukh

CONTENTS

1

Strategies of Cultural Survival

Islamic culture has been almost universally successful in erasing and overlaying the past traditions of the converted masses in the conquered territories. However, it is the case for Islam as it is for other historical instances of conquest that the cultural imperatives and national aspirations of conquered and submerged ethnicities do not easily vanish. Sometimes their languages continue to survive for long periods of time and even influence the conquerors' speech. Even where the conquered population adopts the tongue of the ruling group, their customs may still persist. Perhaps few overt customs of the vanquished remain, however an examination of otherwise unrecorded folklore shows traces of the previous culture. The assertion of older traditions may find expression in a religious guise. In the case of the Muslim conquests even where the pre-Islamic religions have been largely replaced, dissident or heretical Islamic sects or varieties of mystical and occult teachings within Islam may become the means of national expression for submerged populations. Hitti summarizes the means by which three vanquished groups asserted their cultural distinctiveness under the Arab yoke.

> The sons of Iran were ever mindful of their ancient national glory and never reconciled themselves entirely to the new regime. The Berbers vaguely expressed their tribal feeling and sense of difference by their readiness to embrace any schismatic movement. The people of Syria long expected the rise of a Sufyani to deliver them from the Abbasid yoke.

The continued existence of distinctive pre-Islamic local traditions and regional patriotisms, even where the Islamic faith prevailed, served the important function of braking and diverting the expansion of Islam.

The Persians had, undoubtedly, more success in reasserting their ancient traditions than any other group that fell under the yoke of Islam's nomadic vanguards. They did so by adopting Islam and eventually modifying it to suit their peculiar worldview. Other conquered national groups, in addition to the Persians, adopted Islam as a strategy to preserve something of their national distinctiveness although with less success. The closely related Kurds are one such group. The Berbers also quickly adopted the triumphant faith but had only partial success in avoiding Arabization. In Syria and Iraq the remnants of national consciousness was expressed by the rise of various schismatic groups, the most successful being the Shiites of Iraq.

Another region with a relatively successful record of preserving its previous culture was Spain. There, Christianity persisted in remote and rural regions and in the cities converted natives formed the nucleus of social discontent. "Secret Christianity" was widespread. These schismatic tendencies were perhaps stronger in Spain than elsewhere due to the persistence of Christian ruled enclaves in the north, paving the way for the ultimate end of Islamic rule in Spain. However, that was not the case for the other areas in the west of the Dar-al-Islam. It is generally true that "in the eastern part of the Islamic world, the coming of Islam did not submerge the consciousness of the past to the same extent as it did in the west."

The persistence of pre-Islamic civilization expressed itself strongly in the survival of ancient religious traditions which entered into local versions of Islam:

Springs, trees and stones which had been regarded as places of intercession or healing since before the rise of Islam or even of Christianity were sometimes holy to adherents of different faiths. Some examples of this have been noted in modern times: in Syria, the khidr, the mysterious spirit identified with St. George, was revered in springs and other sanctified places; in Egypt, Copts and Muslims alike celebrated the day of St. Damiana ...

These also survived in a more visible physical form. As Vryonis points out, the genetic markers of the different conquered populations differentially altered the racial character of the conquering warrior elite in the many areas conquered by the nomadic armies:

> The physiognomy of the tribesmen evidently set them off as sharply from the indigenous population as did their peculiar society. It is quite probable that fusion with other groups such as the Kurds, or later with Christians and converts, gradually altered the physical type in many areas ...

IRAN

As indicated above, Iran was the area in which the indigenous population most successfully asserted their national distinctiveness. It is the case that although "Islam has become the dominant cultural force, yet Iranian identity, rooted in its Zoroastrian past, has never quite conceded defeat." As biologist and physical anthropologist C. D. Darlington observes:

> The Persians, who resisted hybridization, preserved their language. ... The subtle intelligence of the defeated Persians overwhelmed the political strength of their Arab conquerors and gave a new twist to their artistic invention and also their religious enthusiasm. ... The intelligence of the Persians expressed itself in the coming centuries in the characteristic art of the country. But it also expressed itself in their attitude to religion.

If the Persians were to preserve something of their ancient culture they, unlike their longtime Byzantine rivals, had no alternative to working within the matrix of Islam. For "in the former Byzantine countries, prominent citizens had been able to flee to Constantinople and from there to redeem their captive compatriots, while the Iranians ... whose country was entirely occupied, had little chance of flight nor had they a state at their disposal to ransom their people." Elements of the

Iranian ruling class from very early in the era of Arab occupation converted to the religion of the conquerors. This was especially true in Iraq where "Iranians being an upper class minority of foreign origin before the Arab conquest, had less resistance to conversion than they had in Iran proper, presumably because joining the Arabs was a way of continuing a degree of social superiority over the Aramaic speaking majority of the population."

However, under the Umayyads, these Persian converts found the barriers to admission into the ruling class high. Continued discrimination in the first century of the conquest, as Karsh points out led to considerable resentment among the converts:

Even the pious caliph Umar II (717-20), who attempted to equalize the Mawali's standing, was reputed to have taken a dim view of Muslims and Mawali intermarrying, and forbade Mawali from selling their lands to Muslims. Little wonder that this state of affairs turned the Mawali into an embittered and disgruntled group whose actions were to shake the empire to its core before too long.

In the Persian regions, this resentment served to fuel the Abbasid revolution. In fact the Abbasid emissary and commanding general was "a man of obscure origin, probably of an Iranian family, Abu Muslim."

The Persians, having made the concession of adopting Islam were able, following the Abbasid revolution, to co-opt the machinery of the Muslim empire and turn it into an instrument to advance Persian culture into central Asia, India and, most of all, into the lands of their ancient Byzantine rivals. Under the Abbasids "Arab Islam succumbed to Persian influence; the caliphate became more a revival of Iranian despotism and less an Arabian sheikhdom. Gradually Persian titles, Persian wines and wives, Persian mistresses, Persian songs, as well as Persian ideas and thought won the day." Persian culture soon became the norm among the Arab population of the Abbasid regime. "With the intensification of interaction between conqueror and conquered, the Arabs adopted indigenous - especially Iranian - habits, manners and ways of life."

Even the bloodline of the Abbasid rulers became part Persian. Under the caliph al-Ma'mun Persian triumphalism reached new heights:

The Khurasanians accepted Abbasid al-Ma'mun as one of their own and because his mother was an Iranian, called him 'son of our sister'. The rebellion of Rafi', which had begun because the distant government in Baghdad would not respond to protests against misrule in Khurasan had now lost its point and in 810 he surrendered himself to al-Ma'mun who pardoned him. The poets ... soon began to represent al-Ma'mun and his vizier al-Fadl b. Sahl, a Zoroastrian until 806 as opponents of Arabs, and by extension, of Islam itself. One poet said of al-Ma'mun, 'A power continuing that of Chosroes and his religion has gathered and the Muslims are humbled.'

But while the Persians rose to positions of prominence as officials, scholars and even rulers of local dynasties, they were soon superseded in the Islamic world by tribesmen of more primitive culture and ferocious disposition. "Only with the accession in 833 of al-Mu'tasim did the Persian element in the caliphal armies take second place to newer groups, most prominent amongst which were Turks". It was the latter who, proving diligent students of their Persian teachers, carried Iranian-Islamic culture into India and into Byzantium ultimately conquering the capital of the Persians ancient enemy, Constantinople. In the words of historian of Iran Richard Frye, "though it was the Arabs who brought Iran and Central Asia together, the Turks were the principal agents for spreading ... the Iranian version of Islamic culture to the west, even to Constantinople."

Despite the success certain elements of the Iranian elite achieved by adopting Islam, which then culminated in the Abbasid revolt, dissatisfaction with the new Islamic order festered for some time finding "expression in a series of religious movements in different parts of Persia". In 749 an ex-Zoroastrian, Bihafarid assumed the mantle of Prophethood.

Sonpadh, who was a Mazdaki associate of the Abbasid mastermind Abu Muslim, rose in revolt in 755. Ustad Sis led a revolt of Zoroastrians in Badghis and although he was executed in 768 there was continuing unrest among his followers. Following Ustad, Yusuf ibn Ibrahim, executed in 778, led the Khurramdin sect which was characterized by a combination of Muslim and Zoroastrian doctrines. Murqanna, who claimed to be a reincarnation of Abu Muslim, seized Bokhara in 776; he was defeated and killed in 783.

The centers of Iranian nationalism and continued anti-Muslim sentiment were the mountainous regions bordering the Caspian Sea. In this area the ancient religion of Zoroaster continued to seize the popular imagination. Apostasy was rife and when Islam finally secured a foothold in Tabaristan "sections of the local population emphasized their continued differentiation by adopting heterodox forms of the new faith". In Tabaristan as early as 700 the local ruler, the Ispahbad "under the pressure of new Arab attacks ... agreed to pay tribute but succeeded in keeping the Muslims out of the country. When the 'Abbasid revolutionary army reached Ray in 748 the Ispahbad Khurshid readily followed the invitation of Abu Muslim to transfer his allegiance and pay tribute to the new power." In 781 the rulers of Tabaristan, Tukharistan and Miyandurud "led a dangerous anti Muslim rebellion."

The following century saw further rebellion in the Caspian region by adherents of a Khurrami leader by the name of Babak. Zoroastrianism ultimately gave way to heretical Shi'ism as the expression of the Persian national spirit. The province of Dailam, in the remote Elburz Mountains which was home to many of Babak's followers became a focus of revolutionary Zaidi Shi'ism. Revolution against Islam turned into revolution within Islam. Another follower of Babak, Mazyar, King of Tabaristan and a converted Muslim led a revolt which became a social revolution against Islamicized landholders in 839. The caliph al-Mu'tasim "now recognized the danger of this rebellion to Islam" and cooperated with the Tahirids to put down the revolt. Another Babaki rebel leader following Mazyar was Mankjur who was also executed in 841. These rebels were accused "of apostasy from Islam and of a desire to see the Arabs and Turks abased and the ancient glories of Persia restored." The rulers of Tabaristan revived the use of ancient Persian titles. The adoption of titles such as Ispahbad "among the rulers seems ... to attest the survival of Persian national sentiments". As late as the 10th century, Zoroastrian sentiments could still spark revolts in the Caspian region:

> Mardavij ibn Ziyar, a potentate from the Caspian Sea province of Daylam ... claimed to be none other than the biblical King Solomon ... and spoke openly about reconstituting a great Zoroastrian Iranian empire. This grandiose plan failed to materialize as he was murdered by his Turkish mercenaries in 935.

Thus was extinguished the last Zoroastrian hope of taking back Iran. So it was that Iranians became reconciled to the permanence of the Islamic religion and sought within the context of orthodox and eventually of heretical Islam to restore their national pride. Iranians made good use of their talents as poets in constructing pro-Persian and anti-Arab propaganda. One such propagandist was the notable Persian dissident, Bashhar ibn Burd, the son of an enslaved Persian aristocrat who was charged with heresy and imprisoned. He was an accomplished poet and "did not miss an opportunity to glorify the memories of ancient Iran. He did not have a high opinion of the Arabs."

With the advent of the late ninth century Saffarid dynasty "Persian panegyric poetry containing imagery drawn from the imperial Iranian past" first appeared. It was under the subsequent Samanid dynasty that the Persian of the Sasanids, once again became the language of court life. Persian epic poetry chronicling the glorious days of the pre-Islamic shahs was once more cultivated under the patronage of high Samanid officials. These epic historical poems were finalized in the Shahname by Firdawsi before the year 999. This remarkable re naissance marked the Iranians as almost unique among Muslim peoples "in having a strong, conscious link with its pre Islamic past."

Still another way that the "Persians saved their national pride" was by "claiming that the Prophet's grandson Husayn married ... a daughter of ... the last Sasanian king of Persia." This is one more indication of the determination of the Persians to preserve their ancient culture. It distinguishes them from many other converts in the conquered territories who were busy inventing fake Arab genealogies for themselves. The Buyid sultans, an Iranian dynasty who wielded power in Baghdad over a puppet Abbasid caliph during the tenth century, carried this national resurgence forward another step by restoring Persian court ceremonial. And in an interesting historical sequel, their Seljuk Turk replacements became willing students of the Iranian traditions of their defeated Buyid rivals. As Bulliet observes:

> The innovation of the Buyids was the use of the imperial regalia of the Sassanid Empire. A royal crown, the title Shahanshah ... all these and more were utilized by the rude Buyid princes to legitimize their regime. ... From that time onward Iran's imperial past became wedded to her Islamic present to such a degree that the two titles adopted simultaneously by the Seljuk Turks when they conquered Iran were Sultan and Shahanshah.

Thus, the Iranians made the best of the Islamic conquest. They burrowed in and managed to insinuate themselves into the fabric of Islam, thereby, preserving much of their national tradition. Moreover, they even managed to take advantage of the Islamic tide to spread their ancient culture beyond the old borders of the Sasanian Empire. In fact, it was the conquests of the Arabs that "brought the various Iranian speaking peoples together in one political unit." Indeed under the aegis of Islam "Sasanian, as well as Arab, influences came to Central Asia." And it was in Central Asia that "the first great flowering of Islamic Iranian culture occurred."

In addition to advancing Persian culture, the Iranian national revival shielded the other indigenous traditions of central Asia. By impeding the advance of Arab culture the Persian revivalists enabled other peoples of inner Asia to retain elements of their own culture in defiance of Arabism and even of some strictures of orthodox Islam. According to Lapidus in Inner Asia "Muslim spirituality ... was tempered by a lively folk culture, which included secular entertainments by musicians, dancers, acrobats, jugglers, and gypsies. The populace also enjoyed tobacco, tea, and wine."

The logic of Persian cultural distinctiveness inevitably led to the triumph of schismatic Islamic doctrines in Iranian territory. In the 16th and 17th centuries, under the Safavid dynasty, Shi'ism emerged as the dominant sect in Iran.

The singular regard that ordinary Iranians have for their ancient pre-Islamic past survives to this day. In 1994 classical historian and documentary filmmaker Michael Wood followed in the path taken by Alexander the Great as he conquered an empire stretching from Greece to India. Wood entered Iran during the festival of Ashura, the time of lamentation when the streets were jammed with parades and passion plays. Carnival floats of figures from Iranian history were present in abundance; among them like a "fairy tale villain" was Iskender (Alexander). Wood noted that Iranians still quote the thousand year old words of the poet Firdawsi describing how Alexander crushed Iran. "The great defeat by Alexander has never been forgotten here...In few countries is the sense of the wounds of history so alive." As he travels through the site where Alexander forced his way through a pass known as the Persian gates Wood observed that "the story of the battle is still told by the local people here; how the Persian hero Ariobarzanes tricked Alexander." He has the following conversation with one of his local guides:

Wood: "How do you know these stories, Zavoreh?"

Zavoreh: "It's a tale as they say here that has been passed from chest to chest."

Wood: "So this is a story that has been handed down from grandfather to father to son; is it in these parts?"

Zavoreh: "Yes."

Wood notes that even the guides are impressed by Alexander's audacity. But then, chillingly, Zavoreh adds the following: "But if I had Alexander here now, I'd like to chop him into little pieces for what he did to Iran." It is also striking, though unsurprising, that the Iranians view Alexander as a devil, whereas in many Arabic and Turkish speaking regions, he is viewed as a romantic figure. This may be a survival of the legend of Alexander which was passed down to both, converted Muslims among the once Greek speaking conquered people, and to conquering nomads of the steppes who had a natural admiration for a renowned warrior. In Afghanistan, some tribes even believe that they are descended from Alexander's Macedonians.

One additional effect of Iranian national assertiveness should be noted. It was one of a number of factors and events that impeded the advance of Islam; and this despite Islam's adoption by the Persians. There can be no doubt that Persian cultural assertiveness slowed down the spread of triumphal Arabism into Asia during those crucial early centuries of the Arab conquests. Also, the schism within Islam and the dynastic rivalries spurred by Iranianism sapped the energy and diverted the resources that would otherwise have gone into further extensions of Islamic territorial conquests.

IRAQ AND SYRIA

In the territories of Iraq and Syria, expressions of the older national traditions were present, although in a much weaker form than in Iran. The Semitic speaking masses had been ruled for many centuries by elites speaking Persian in Iraq and Greek in greater Syria. Furthermore, the affinity of most of the population with the closely related Arab culture facilitated the adoption of Arabic language and mores. However, the ancient cultures were not totally consigned to oblivion. Iraq was subject to a series of revolts by schismatic Islamic sects which found strong support among the indigenous population. One such was Kharijism:

> Iraq was visited by a steady succession of Khariji revolts ... The Kharijis came into existence as a political movement in the 670s, and uprisings were still reported as late as 796 in more remote northern Iraq. Kharijism ... is a variety of Islam and

Arabs unquestionably predominated in these revolts. Nevertheless, mawali were also drawn to Kharijism...

Later on "the Qarmati movement ... sprang up at roughly the same time in eastern Arabia, southern Iraq, northern Iraq and Syria. As with the earlier Khariji revolts, a problem is posed by the mixture of Arab tribesmen and non-Arab peasants in the same movement, but the latter element was particularly evident in southern Iraq." The position of the Muslims as a small minority of the population motivated them to maintain their solidarity and cohesiveness in the first centuries. However, Bulliet contends that once Islam was well entrenched, this solidarity vanished. In the case of Iraq "following the point of 50 percent conversion in 882, there are again parallels with Iran. Instead of independent local dynasties, one encounters a progressive deterioration in the central governments ability to control the countryside."

In Syria, as in Iraq, submerged local nationalism found an expression, not only in the survival of Christianity, but more importantly in the emergence of highly unorthodox and even syncretistic Islamic sects. In fact, the number of dissenting Islamic movements was greater in the relatively small Syrian province than in many larger Muslim territories. The mountains of the Syrian coast and of Lebanon provided a convenient refuge in which both Christian and heretical Muslim sectarians were able to attain considerable autonomy. The mountainous redoubts in Syria is one example of the many cases where heterodox Islamic sects have frequently made their strongest appeal to isolated populations previously unconverted or only nominally converted to Islam. The Zaidis in the mountains of northern Iran, the Fatimids in the mountains of western Tunisia, and the Almohads in the mountains of Morocco followed this line of development. Moreover, such heterodox sects not infrequently incorporated practices of non-Muslim origin to make them more appealing to the potential convert. The Bektashis in Anatolia and the pseudo-Muslim Berber religions of the Barghwata and of the prophet Ha-Mim in Morocco and Algeria afford examples of this tendency.

Furthermore with specific reference to Syria:

In short, considering the Christian tone of some Druze and Nusairi beliefs, it is far more likely that the proselytizing efforts that produced these sects were deliberately aimed at a largely unconverted Christian population in the mountains of coastal Syria than that converts were made primarily among Muslims who subsequently took refuge in the mountains."

Cultural assertiveness in Syria also took on a decidedly political coloration. After the Abbasid revolution, Syrian nationalism expressed itself in loyalty to the recently deposed Umayyads who had made their capital in the province and, undoubtedly, incorporated many local Syrian particularities into their outlook. The otherwise orthodox Sunni Umayyad faction even developed a peculiar apocalyptic religious outlook based on their deposed dynasty. "In 752 a rising in Syria took place in support of the deposed Umayyad dynasty to which that province for long retained its loyalty. ... the pro-Umayyad party began to speak of a Messianic figure of the Umayyad House who would ... return to this world and establish a reign of justice." It did not take the ruthless Abbasid dynasty long to crush their opposition. The Syrian national revolt was subsequently transferred to Spain where the Syrian Muslims formed an important part of the Muslim elite; and these Syrian Muslims paved the way for the accession of the Spanish Umayyad dynasty.

EGYPT AND NORTH AFRICA

In Egypt the local Christian Copts were a population more racially and culturally distinct from their Arab masters than were the indigenous populations of Syria and Iraq. So it was that Copts clinging for a long period of time to their Christian religion were the main guardians of the ancient pre-Arab culture. The first century of Abbasid rule witnessed frequent Coptic rebellions. However, these revolts were usually in alliance with better equipped and more warlike Arabs with grievances against their Abbasid overlords. Unfortunately for the rebels Egypt, by virtue of its geography and unlike Iran and Syria, had no redoubts where carriers of the old nationalism, non-Muslims and Muslim heretics could hold out.

West of Egypt, the Arabs encountered more formidable opponents. The tribal Berbers resisted Arabisation, although, like their more civilized Persian counterparts they adopted Islam and enlisted in the armies of their Arab masters. They were less successful than the Persians in preserving their ancient traditions, possibly because they had no high culture or ancient glories to protect. However, their continued resistance also, undoubtedly, was one of the factors in constraining Arab expansion and keeping the Muslim hold on Spain weaker than it was elsewhere. Modern Arab historian Abun-Nasr points out that, "the countryside Berber remained the dominant language, and Islamic heterodox or even heretical doctrines had a special appeal as a means of rejecting the legitimacy of Arab rule". Indeed, although "some of the Berber population resisted the coming of Islamic rule ... when they did become Muslims Khariji ideas spread among them."

SPAIN

In Spain the assertion of submerged national identity was carried on by a series of Christian martyrs who deliberately courted death by publicly blaspheming Islam. There were also a series of separatist revolts in the provinces led by neo-Muslims "who posed as nationalist champions". One of them a "Moslem descendant of a Visigothic count" ultimately apostatized to the Christian faith of his ancestors. The independent Christian kingdoms of the north gave assistance to all such rebels whether Christian or Muslim.

ANATOLIA

Despite the slow and painful Turkish conquest and the shifting of borders back and forth, Anatolia shows numerous pre-Islamic survivals among its large, once Byzantine, converted population. One expression of the Anatolian cultural spirit was in the peculiar syncretistic forms of Islam prevailing in many parts of the territory. By the time of the Turkish migrations Islam had lost completely its Arab ethnic exclusivity and enthusiastic proselytism was the order of the day. "The great extent of religious syncretism in Anatolian volksreligion is in part to be explained by the desire of the dervishes to convert the Christians." Some Christians "were prepared for assimilation ... by the religious syncretism that tended to equate Islamic practices and saints with those of Christians." Sufi sects were notably active in spreading the word of Islam to the conquered Byzantines. In turn, their own teachings inevitably absorbed many Christian practices. In the Bektashi Sufi order and many doctrines and practices are similar to those of the Christians ... It is difficult to avoid the conclusion that similar practices and doctrines existed because of the entrance of Christians into the order, and because of the close relations between Bektashis and Christians. ... This syncretism which facilitated the conversion from Christianity to Islam recalls the religious syncretism that had accelerated the transition from paganism to Christianity a thousand years earlier in Anatolia.

Mawlawi dervishes were also active in converting non-Muslims and made members of the clergy a particular target. "The conversion of monks and priests was of critical importance, as they were the very bulwark of the Christian element against the eroding process of Islamization. Efflaki speaks of the conversion of monks ... and of Jewish rabbis." The account of Mawlawi founder Rumi's funeral "indicates quite clearly that a powerful process of religious syncretism was in dynamic motion by which Christians and Jews were accommodating themselves to this particular Muslim religious fraternity. The very syncretism and mutual accommodation of dervishes and Christians would eventually result in the absorption of a great many Christians through conversion."

As in other Islamic territories these unorthodox sects were occasionally foci of rebellion and unrest and even verged on the edge of complete apostasy. There was a rising in western Anatolia ca 1416 by Badr-al-Din and his followers who, among other things preached a communistic doctrine "and went even further by declaring the Christian and Muslim religions to be equally valid." Even centuries later at the height of the Ottoman Empire the authorities would find it necessary to take action against such dangerous Muslim-Christian syncretisms. One such "heretical sect was the Khubmesihis, who taught that

Jesus was superior to Muhammad and seem to have been centered in Istanbul in the seventeenth century. ... The sect was said to be inspired by the heretic Kabid who held similar views and was executed in 1527."

There were Byzantines who adopted Turkish customs and language but retained their ancestral Christianity. These Turkish speaking Anatolian Christians were known as Karamanlidhes. "The Karamanlidhes, like the Mozarabs who imitated the Arabs, often had Turkish names, and imitated Turkish customs".

Language was another area of significant Byzantine survivals. The Greek language "has left important philological traces, via loan words in both the Turkish Hochsprache and the Turkish dialects of Anatolia." In rural Anatolia, even up to the present day "the Greek influence becomes readily apparent in the significant substratum of Greek loan words in the spoken Anatolian of modern Turkey." The importance of Greek speaking craftsmen and technicians in the newly conquered lands is reflected by many Greek words and expressions relating to economic activity. This is particularly apparent in the maritime industry where as Vryonis states "Byzantine naval life has left an indelible impression in the Turkish language by virtue of the large number of termini technici which were passed from Greek ... into Turkish."

Turkish political and social institutions are replete with vestiges from Byzantium. Vryonis details numerous instances of Byzantine survival in the administrative, military, fiscal and ceremonial institutions under the Seljuk, Ottoman and other Anatolian Turkish states. Another probable Byzantine relic "the Anatolian guild-futuwwa complex possibly reflects both a direct and an indirect Byzantine influence. All this points to strong similarities in Byzantine and Seljuk-Ottoman urban life and towns."

Anatolian folk culture has significant pre-Islamic elements. Vryonis gives many examples of survivals within folk culture: cuisine, religious, marriage and family practices, folk religion including continuing reverence paid to Christian saints and shrines and baptism, ancient pagan survivals that continued under Christianity and was passed on to the Muslims, and folk literature. Vryonis summarizes the major impacts, both obvious and hidden that pre-Islamic culture had on Turkish ruled Anatolia:

> ...the Islamized Byzantine population brought with it a great part of its popular culture and consequently 'Byzantinized,' partially, the emerging society on the folk level. Inasmuch as the formal culture was Islamic and the language Turkish, this Byzantine ingredient is not immediately apparent, but a detailed examination of Anatolian society reveals its presence in all major aspects of life.

SOUTHEAST ASIA

In Southeast Asia, a region initially converted by peaceful means, the survival of pre-Muslim culture is to be expected. And, indeed, here "village culture was in fact compounded of animist, Hindu, and Islamic elements. ... Islam was ... assimilated to a village religious mentality that focused on belief in a world of spirits, demons, and powers of nature." Southeast Asian Islamic culture exemplifies the cultural experience of other areas where Islam first entered by non-military means. West Africa was similar in that "the process of conversion was slow ... The result was not the formation of a uniform Islamic culture but of a plethora of local variations upon Islamic practice."

One pre-Islamic survival that became attached to the societies established by the violent and free-spirited Muslim Arabs and Turks was that of oriental despotism. Such despotism, possibly originating among the ancient Assyrians and Egyptians passed into both Persia and Byzantium. However, despotism conformed so well to the Islamic ideology of submission that its ultimate emulation by the conquerors of those empires was inevitable.

2

Phases of Political Development

Islamic societies, generally, pass through three phases of political development. The first phase, the "egalitarian" or "republican" follows the initial invasion of the nomadic carriers of Islam or the founding of trading outposts by Muslim merchants. This political tendency is dominant during the early history of a conquered territory; the tribal "republican" tradition is still strong in these early years. The ruler is regarded as simply the first among equals in the warrior caste. Of course, this egalitarianism has nothing to do with rights for *dhimmis*, women or other lesser groups such as Muslims already residing in the conquered territory; all of which may be subject to massacre, enslavement or oppressive tribute. In those instances where Islam is established through the conversion of an existing ruler or elite, as in Indonesia, this phase may be absent altogether.

The following phase may be termed the "liberal despotic". The term liberal is strongly qualified; it simply means that there is a majority or at least large numbers of non-Muslims; Islam has not yet "hardened". The restoration of peace and incorporation of the territory into a larger acumen along with the many *dhimmis* and nominal Muslims in the population engenders a great increase in intellectual activity, architecture, and construction of an infrastructure and communication network. Moreover the rulers and aristocrats tend to be worldly, irreligious or heretical. The Muslims are self confident, as shown by the example of the Byzantine vassal emperor Manuel who was allowed to engage in a religious disputation with Muslim scholars in an atmosphere of relative freedom. However, the state exists in the form of a monarchical despotism. This is often based on Persian or Byzantine models where there is a remote and absolute monarch. While the monarch in this period is often impious or unbelieving, he may, in a Machiavellian manner, cynically make use of Islam to expand his territory, appease the Muslim ulama or eliminate rivals. He may, if he finds it politically expedient, employ fanatical Muslim troops to enslave, slaughter or oppress conquered non-Muslim or even Muslim populations. He may, paradoxically, implement persecutions to obtain favor with the ulama, while simultaneously patronizing favored *dhimmi* intellectuals and advisors. Or, on the contrary, he may be strong enough to protect useful *dhimmi* populations.

The final phase is the "repressive despotic". This usually means the establishment of an absolute theocratic state in which the only curb on the activities of the monarch is that of, a frequently, even more fanatical clergy. Islam has been long established and become hardened and inflexible. Intellectual activity outside of Islamic law and tradition is now discouraged. This is often accompanied by economic depression and stagnation. The ruler may be paradoxically both weak and tyrannical; often he is a fanatical Islamic bigot. Persecution and oppression of non-Muslims is endemic. The two forms of despotism, liberal and despotic, may alternate with each other for long periods, but in the end, it is invariably the repressive despotic imperative that triumphs.

The early rugged individualism of the Arabs was preserved through an elective caliphate. The Arabs formed the electoral class in a type of aristocratic republic. However, the ancient despotic tradition of the conquered masses, that of Persia and Egypt, reasserted itself and combined with the Islamic doctrine of submission. The process began with the Umayyad caliphate in 661and reached its final form in the succeeding Abbasid dynasty. The template for all succeeding Islamic despotisms was set in place.

These three contending political imperatives were in conflict with each other. The egalitarian tribal formation, which tended to dominate at the beginning of each nomadic expansion, inevitably gave way to despotism. At first, this despotism was usually pragmatic, worldly or even tolerant; but the end result was always an intolerant theocracy. This conflict was present from the earliest Islamic times. The tendency toward despotism was one of the factors that propelled the growth of empire.

While Muhammad held to the traditional forms of Arab tribal society with its consultations and councils, in reality, he as Prophet was effectively an autocrat. His immediate successors followed his example. The very expansion of Arab Muslim rule, first in Arabia and later throughout the Middle East was facilitated by caliphs becoming more absolute in power. Karsh contends that "by substituting absolutist rule for the pluralistic system of traditional tribal organization, based as it was on a series of agreements among equals, the *umma* created a powerful drive for expansion."

The result of this despotic imperative was that, although Islam developed a "welfare state", a powerful military-religious ideology and a series of enormous empires, it never developed the concepts of liberty and secular government that arose in Europe. Ironically this was, in part, due to the more rigid class structure that developed in the West. In Islam there was no aristocracy independent of the monarch; religion and the state were also intertwined. In Europe there was rivalry between the Monarch, Church and feudal aristocracy which, in a few places at least, notably Britain, developed into checks on despotic central authority and to the rise of the urban bourgeoisie who were able to restore ancient republican institutions in many major western cities. Kinross, referring to the Ottoman Empire, gives an example of this difference between Islam and Europe:

> ...this Ottoman system of land tenure through military fiefs differed essentially from the feudal system in Europe, in that the landholdings were small and above all seldom hereditary. For all land was the property of the state. ... The sultans retained absolute ownership of the soil they conquered.

Thus, in Islamic society, there were not the divisions and rivalries within the aristocracy that characterized Western Europe; members of all classes from lowest to highest were regarded as "slaves" of an increasingly autocratic Caliph or Sultan and there was no well developed independent religious institution serving as a check on the Monarch. Hence, while Islamic society stagnated, it was the West that pioneered modern concepts of science, technology, government and secularism.

EGALITARIAN PHASE

The term "egalitarian" refers only to members of the conquering military elite and not to the conquered multitudes. The latter, in fact, often received better treatment under the liberal despots. Although the rule of the early caliphs became increasingly arbitrary, they openly espoused the traditional Arab tribal "republicanism". The caliphs found it necessary, to appease their followers by maintaining, at least the appearance, of the old tribal councils and consultative institutions. Moreover, all "four caliphs of this first period were chosen in some manner by their predecessors or colleagues; none succeeded by hereditary right. ... Thereafter the caliphate became, in practice even if not in theory, hereditary".

Appearances, however, were one thing; reality could be something else entirely as pointed out by Karsh:

Uthman vested all key posts in the hands of his family members ... The Medinese elite resented its growing marginalization in the running of the empire, while the provincial leadership was incensed by Uthman's efforts to increase the central government's share in the distribution of local revenues...

Thus, from earliest times there was conflict between the centralizing absolutist tendencies of the ruler and the jealous clinging to their privileges on the part of the traditional tribal elite. The Medinese and provincial elite represented the Arab aristocratic republican imperative while the Caliph and his court upheld the idea of a more arbitrary and despotic form of government. Hitti specifically refers to the reign of the first four caliphs as the 'republican period'. "With the death of Ali (661) what may be termed the republican period of the caliphate, which began with abu-Bakr (632) came to an end. ... The hereditary principle was hereby introduced into the caliphal succession". The idea of Arab egalitarian republicanism persisted into the Umayyad dynasty and the first Umayyad caliphs felt obliged to give to it at least token deference.

A significant token of the hold which democratic Arabian tribal custom had upon the Umayyads is that notice of the appointment [of Caliph Yazid's son as his successor] was sent to the governors of the provinces, who almost everywhere obtained promises of adherence to the arrangement.

An extreme pole of the egalitarian republican viewpoint, at that time, was represented by the Kharijites who opposed arbitration between the caliph Ali and his rival Mu'awiya since they believed that the choice of the caliph was with "Allah alone", thereby denying any form of hereditary dynastic rule legitimacy. The triumph of Mu'awiya established the despotic principle when he "presided over the foundation of Islam's first imperial dynasty by having his son, Yazid succeed him to the throne."

The early Ottomans provide another example of the egalitarianism and republicanism of the nomadic warrior tradition. "The first Ottoman rulers were tribal chiefs who maintained their position and succession by the approval of their warriors". Kinross notes that the "warrior companions" of the early Ottoman sultan Orkhan regarded him "less as a master than as a unifying force and a rallying point among them as brothers-in-arms." In general, viewing the tribal leader as a "brother-in-arms" was characteristic of nomadic tribal societies. When Babur crossed into India to found the Mogul dynasty, he was certainly not looked upon by his companions as if he were a Persian king.

Anarchy and disorder were unfortunate characteristics of the egalitarian phase. The rule of the first four caliphs and the first years of the Umayyad dynasty were marked by disputes regarding the succession which culminated in civil war, assassinations and inter-tribal conflict. Each additional eruption of nomadic Turks into Anatolia was accompanied by warfare and social disruption. The same can be said of the Arab raids into the Sudan, the early Moors in Spain and the Muslim waves crashing into India. The admirable liberty and social equality enjoyed by individual tribesmen came at a great cost to the settled parts of society, and particularly to non-Muslims.

LIBERAL DESPOTIC PHASE

Islamic societies enter upon the "liberal despotic" phase after the initial incursion with its attendant wars and disorder has ended. The end comes when the tribesmen and the population on which they have preyed has reached a point of exhaustion. An accommodation is reached, whereby the victor in one of the civil wars or inter-tribal conflicts is recognized as ruler. At that point a process of recovery can commence. The periods of disorder and recovery can last for decades and even for a century. The establishment of peace is followed by a period of economic security and expansion, and often by an artistic and intellectual renaissance. What was once a besieged territory drained by perpetual Muslim assaults is now part of the greater Islamic acumen? New ideas and technical developments drawn from far-flung territories pour in. Most of the population still consists of *dhimmis* or the descendants of recent converts with the skills and outlook of the older culture. The new rulers maintain order by replacing the tribal organization with an increasingly powerful centralized state along with the splendors and rituals of monarchy.

Although the early Umayyad caliphs made a show of deference to egalitarian Arab tribal forms, despotism soon appeared quite openly. "In 705 Walid, brother of 'Abd-al-Malik, succeeded him on the caliphal throne, for that is what the caliphate has become, a change from a tribal organization to an empire." In fact under most of the Umayyads the "liberal" despotic tendency was uppermost. The religious imperative under this dynasty "was largely a façade that concealed what was effectively a secular and increasingly absolutist rule. The

Umayyad caliphs adopted a lax attitude toward Islamic practices and mores. They were said to have set aside special days for drinking ... Little wonder that Islamic tradition tends to decry the Umayyads for having perverted the caliphate into a 'kingdom', with the implicit connotation of religious digression or even disbelief." Such disregard for religious sensibilities is a common characteristic of liberal despotism.

In addition to personal expressions of impiety, such rulers also granted favors to and cultivated friendship with members of the *dhimmi* community. Under some of the Umayyad caliphs, before the hardening of Islamic attitudes, tolerance, favor and even high office was extended to members of the still majority Christian population of Syria. The Christian physician of Mu'awiyah, the first Umayyad caliph was "made financial administrator of the province of Hims". Al-Akhtal, the Umayyad poet laureate "would enter the caliphal palace with a cross dangling from his neck and recite his poems to the delight of the Moslem caliph and his entourage." Of course, such kingly munificence was extended only to the Arab ruling military aristocracy and a few favored upper-class educated *Dhimmi*s.

This liberal tendency was to recur frequently under the Abbasids and subsequent sultanates, emirates and caliphates. However, such impiety was often masked by the freethinking, dissolute or heretical rulers who, cynically, sought to mollify the religious zealots by instituting various forms of persecution against *dhimmi*s or by sponsoring invasions and raids into non-Muslim lands.

The impious Umayyad munificence affected even the two holy cities of Mecca and Medina, both of which became centers of "worldly pleasure and song." More shocking yet to pious Muslim sensibilities was the assertiveness of aristocratic Umayyad ladies. "Al-Madinah boasted under the early Marwanids the proud and beautiful Sayyidah Sukaynah (ca 735), daughter of the martyred al-Husayn." This liberated woman ran a salon for poets and jurists, pioneered new fashion and "made complete freedom of action a condition precedent to marriage." Her rival, 'Aishah bint-Talbah, grand daughter of the caliph abu-Bakr, "combined with noble descent a rare beauty and a proud and lofty spirit." She refused under any condition to veil herself. The rival Abbasids turned such open impiety into a useful weapon aimed at the Umayyad dynasty. For example, "so widely spread was the cultivation of the musical art under the last Umayyads that it provided their enemies, the Abbasid faction with an effective argument in their propaganda to undermine the house of 'ungodly usurpers'." One of the main factions supporting the Abbasid rebellion, the Shi'ites, embodied an early form of repressive despotism, or at least despotism in a more theocratic form. They enshrined the dynastic principle in the family of the Prophet and contended that "the *umma* should be headed by a prodigious spiritual leader, or imam, possessing superhuman religious knowledge and interpretive powers, who would act as the community's political leader".

Liberal despotism, however, was frequently accompanied with periods of ruthless repression. Despotism took on a particularly brutal form in Iraq under the ruthless governor Hajjaj (694-714) who instituted a reign of terror against Muslim dissidents in a manner reminiscent of modern Iraqi dictators. On the other hand, he, like some of his modern Iraqi counterparts, was not a fanatical religious zealot when it came to the *dhimmi* population under his rule. On the contrary, to protect his revenues, he "took draconian measures to discourage conversion and to drive the new converts back to their villages".

The Abbasids exemplified the tendency toward despotism to a greater extent than did any of the Umayyad caliphs. "The incoming dynasty [Abbasid] depended upon force in the execution of its policies. For the first time in the history of Islam the leathern spread beside the caliph's seat which served as a carpet for the executioner, became a necessary adjunct of the imperial throne." Lewis elaborates on this distinction between the Abbasid caliphs and their predecessors. "Whereas the early Caliphs had been Arabs like the rest whom any man could approach and address by name, the Abbasids surrounded themselves with the pomp and circumstance of an elaborate and hieratic court and could only be approached through a series of chamberlains." Karsh summarizes this evolution toward increasing despotism:

> The growth of monarchical despotism, already noticeable in the days of the Umayyads gained considerable momentum under the Abbasids and was starkly exemplified by the presence of the executioner by the side of the throne. Like the Iranian shahs, the caliph became increasingly inaccessible to his subjects, shielding himself behind a vast cohort of officials, ministers and eunuchs, and leaving the daily running of the empire in the hands of the vizier, a chief executive answerable only to him.

It is striking how this very pattern, down to almost the same exact details, recurs in subsequent Islamic empires. The Iranian Muslim dynasties, the Moguls and, of course the Ottoman Turks exhibit almost identical patterns of despotic monarchical rule. And these occurred at a time when the West was evolving various monarchical forms, from absolute to limited, as well as varieties of parliamentary institutions and even republics with differing degrees of citizen involvement; the republics ranging from aristocratic to petty bourgeois.

Although the Abbasids became increasingly despotic and arbitrary in their government, a number of them partook of the munificence and impiety characteristic of "liberal despotism". The material indulgence of the early Abbasids is well described by Hitti. "Even when stripped of the glow cast by Oriental romance and fancy, enough of the splendor of court life in Baghdad remains to arouse our astonishment." The most splendid of these rulers was the famous Harun al-Rashid. "Harun was the beau ideal of Islamic kingship. Like a magnet, his princely munificence and that of his immediate successors attracted to the capital poets, wits, musicians, singers, dancers ... and others who could interest or entertain." And quickly forgetting the criticism leveled by the rebel Abbasids at the Umayyads, aristocratic women were allowed, once again to flaunt themselves in a most un-Islamic manner. Harun al-Rashid's wife Zubaydah "set the fashion for the smart set and was the first to ornament her shoes with precious stones." Zubaydah had a rival in the sister of Harun, Ullayah "who to cover a blemish on her forehead devised a fillet set with jewels which ... was soon adopted by the world of fashion as the ornament of the day."

Periods of liberal despotism alternated with periods of repressive despotism. It was also the case that rulers, who were otherwise broad-minded, found it politically expedient to keep their *dhimmi* subjects in a state of insecurity. The first Fatimid ruler of Egypt al-Aziz (975-96) "extended to the Christians ... a measure of toleration never enjoyed before" and employed a Christian vizier. However repression began in the very next reign. Al-Hakim the son of al-Aziz "killed several of his vizirs, demolished a number of Christian churches" and was the third caliph to impose the complete stringent measures prescribed for non-Muslims. The reign of al-Aziz illustrates the common occurrence of a minority Muslim sect building coalitions with non-Muslims. His reign and that of his son also shows that the conquest of Muslim territory by a new Muslim dynasty could initiate a period of liberal despotism which, sooner or later, would be followed by repression.

The Fatimids were followed by the Ayyubids (1171-1250), who, although relatively tolerant found it politically useful to keep their upper-class *dhimmis* anxious. When the Ayyubids assumed power in Egypt ...stricter enforcement of the *dhimma* code had already begun. ... By the end of Ayyubid rule, most Jews wore a distinguishing mark on their turbans and cloaks, and most Christians wore a special outer belt. Much of the time, members of the *dhimmi* upper class were still able to evade the requirement, which was considered a mark of humiliation as well as differentiation. Periodic decrees were the way Islamic rulers reminded the upper class *dhimmis* that they should pay for their exemption, which they did.

Of course, as Jewish historian Norman Stillman also observes:

The reimposition of the dress code over a number of years was not an indication of any great tolerance in the interim. Medieval regimes were woefully inefficient when compared with modern totalitarian states in controlling the daily lives and actions of their subjects. Decrees of many sorts had to be reissued from time to time to demonstrate official resolution.

Thus, even in times of liberal Muslim rule ...there was tenuousness in the cordiality of interfaith relationships. The non-Muslim could never entirely disembarrass him of his *dhimmi* status. There was no lack of preachers and religious reformers to remind Muslims and non-Muslims alike that the Pact of Umar was being violated. ... The Muslim community's sense of propriety could be deeply offended when *dhimmis* rose too high or became too conspicuous...

Stillman summarizes the insecurity inherent in the *dhimmi* status even under friendly Muslim rulers. "Even in the best of times, *dhimmis* in all walks of life could suddenly and rudely be reminded of their true status."

Periods of benevolent monarchy, inevitably followed by repression, characterized the non-Arab Muslim dynasties as well. The relatively liberal period of the Seljuk Konya sultanate came to an end with their defeat at the hands of the Mongols in 1243. "By then, ineffectual Mongol governors and a large number of Turkish emirs had destroyed the authority of this kingdom. ... In this period ... justice and security in the kingdom came to an end." The Seljuk state suffered a premature acceleration of the end of the period of benevolent despotism owing to these setbacks.

The transition from nomadic egalitarianism to monarchical despotism and finally to repressive tyranny is well illustrated by the experience of the Seljuk's Ottoman successors. The first Ottoman "sultans had been accessible to their subjects and mixed with them in relative informality. But ... there developed an increasing concern for sacredness of the sovereign, together with a habit of seclusion appropriate to majesty". Mehmed the Conqueror even went so far as to cease sitting with his advisers. "Until now the Sultan had always presided in person over meetings of the council of state ... from the seat on which he sat, as his ancestors from nomadic times had done in their tents. ... But Mehmed ... no longer frequenting the meetings of the Divan", looked down on them, unseen, from behind a screen. Thus, even while restoring order to the Ottoman domains and extending some measure of self government to the Christian church, the Conqueror also began the process of ending the last trappings of the Ottoman tribal 'egalitarian' system. He is quoted as follows by historian Herbert Muller. "It is not my will that any one should eat with my Imperial Majesty; my ancestors used to eat with their ministers, but I have abolished this custom." Under his successors "the ceremonies grew more elaborate, the costumes more ornate, the titles more grandiloquent, the Sultan more inaccessible." And, in the same way as the Abbasids aped the court ritual of the Sasanids, among the Ottomans "... the customs and formalities of the Sultan's court, which in its rigid hierarchy, its pomp and luxury, and its elaborate ceremonial owed much to the Byzantine model".

Despite the increasingly autocratic rule of the sultans, the early empire was relatively benign and forward-looking, a condition that would inevitably change. Stillman describes how the early promise and rapid deterioration of the empire affected its Jewish subjects. The Ottoman realm in the 16th century was "a brief interlude of brightness in the long twilight of the late Islamic Middle Ages for the Jews of Arab lands. The shadows again began appearing toward the end of the century."

Finally, Keay gives an example of how the Muslim rulers in India gradually imposed despotic rule and court ritual on all of their subjects, including their fellow Muslims. Delhi Sultan Balban (1246-65) "influenced by all those royal refugees from the north-west ... introduced into his court an elaborate system of precedence and protocol modeled on the Persian practice. ... Those who would approach the throne must abase themselves ... kissing the ground and ... kissing the royal feet as they advanced."

BENEVOLENT, TOLERANT OR SYNCRETISTIC MUSLIM RULERS

Given the autocratic and absolutist nature of all mature Islamic states, the well-being of the *Dhimmi* population was, to a large extent, dependent on the character of the ruler. Certain Muslim rulers were relatively benevolent to the *Dhimmi* populations whether for reasons of pragmatism, a compassionate nature transcending Islamic religious imperatives, freethinking, or even secret sympathies with, or interest in, other traditions.

Umayyad caliphs were notorious among their Muslim subjects as being deficient in proper religious attitudes. The most reprehensible, from the Muslim point of view was Caliph Walid II who "is said to have stuck the Koran onto a lance and shot it to pieces with arrows". It is, therefore, no surprise that Walid irritated the ulama by showing an interest in un-Islamic ideas while leading a merry existence. "An intensively cultivated man, he surrounded himself with poets, dancing girls, and musicians, and lived the merry life of the libertine, with no interest in religion."

The Abbasids came to power promising to rid Islam of Umayyad impiety. However, as seen above, their personal conduct did not always conform to such high ideals. Caliph Ma'mun even showed a quite un-Muslim interest in comparative religion. During his reign Farruxzatan a Mazdaean religious leader held a disputation with a Muslim convert and also "summoned Jews and Christians to take part in the argument. The Caliph Ma'mun, as is known, favoured such rhetorical jousts". Such disputations were allowed to take place under a number of Muslim rulers. It would appear that, once Islam was established and the danger of overthrow ended, certain rulers of a less rigid and more inquiring frame of mind could afford to patronize such conferences and discourses. Of course, as an Islamic state entered its final repressive phase, such openness became impossible.

Under the Fatimid dynasty in Egypt, many caliphs showed favor toward non-Muslims:

The heterodox Fatimids showed relatively more tolerance toward their *dhimmi* subjects than had most Islamic rulers. Perhaps this was due in part to the fact that the majority of the Fatimid subjects in North Africa, and later in Egypt, were orthodox Muslims who were by and large unfriendly to their Isma'ili overlords.

The Fatimid tolerance was a case of political pragmatism. It was one instance in which a schismatic or upstart ruler might build a political base by showing favor to non-Muslims or to other heretical Muslims. In modern times examples of such political pragmatism are the relative tolerance toward Christians on the parts of the Alawite elite of Syria and of the Sunni Baathists in Iraq.

Saladin, the great founder of the Ayyubid dynasty, despite being a stalwart soldier in the Muslim cause, was widely regarded by friend and foe alike as being an honorable opponent who often showed a mercy that was uncharacteristic of both Muslim and non-Muslim rulers at that time. "Saladin was a brave and capable soldier, a great builder, and a generous and merciful ruler. ... Saladin repeatedly expressed admiration for the piety of Christian pilgrims" and reportedly said "that a bad Muslim could never make a good Christian." Moreover, Saladin's "lieutenants reminded him frequently of the bloody massacres committed by the Crusaders when they first conquered Jerusalem, yet his mercy was widespread."

Saladin's tolerance, however, may also be partly due to the fact that he was rather indifferent to religion; his main interest was in building up his own power:

Reflecting neither a burning spirit of jihad nor an unwavering anti Christian enmity this behavior epitomized Saladin's career. For all his extensive holy-war propaganda, an essential component in a socio-political order based on the principle of religion, Saladin's attitude to the Frankish states was above all derived from his lifelong effort at empire-building. As long as they did not stand in the way of this endeavor he was amenable to leaving them in peace...

Furthermore it was the Ayyubid dynasty founded by Saladin that was later to offer a refuge in Egypt and Syria to Jewish refugees from the persecutions in Almohad Spain. Unfortunately, however, in general few subsequent Muslim rulers lived up to Saladin's example.

In Anatolia, despite the ravages that the nomadic Turks inflicted on the Christian population, a number of Seljuk rulers showed them great benevolence. Such benevolence was shown even in the early years of the Turkish invasion. Sultan Malik

Shah (ca 1090) and Ismail the governor of Armenia are known to have protected churches and monasteries. Tolerant Seljuk rulers also appeared in subsequent centuries. The conditions of the Christians of Melitene "improved considerably in the latter half of the twelfth century thanks to the generosity of Kilidj II Arslan who freed" the church "from paying tribute." Another benevolent Turkish commander was Malik Danishmend who reportedly treated his Christian subjects kindly.

The tolerance shown by the early Turkish leaders may also have had deeper motives owing to the very extensive and early hybridization that characterized the Turkish invaders. Many Muslim Turks, even among the rulers, at that time had Christian parents or in-laws. One such, the Seljuk Sultan Alaeddin, was apparently "not only tolerant of Christianity but sympathetic to it". Another such was the son of the Seljuk sultan Izz-ed-Din who entered the service of the Byzantine Emperor and with "a detachment of his guard remained behind in Constantinople, turned Christian, and formed the nucleus of a corps of Turkish militia".

The succeeding Ottomans, also with an abundance of Christian relatives and Greek ancestry, likewise produced rulers with tolerant dispositions or even syncretistic and heretical outlooks. In particular Mehmed (Muhammad) the Conqueror is said to have an almost heretical interest in Christianity, the Italian Renaissance and Greek philosophy. As a young man Mehmed "caused concern at Adrianople by his apparent support ... of a Persian missionary, leader of a dervish sect which had preached ... an affinity between Islam and Christianity." After the fall of Constantinople there were even "pious hopes that the Sultan might emerge as a potential convert to Christianity. ... Such approaches were never likely to influence the Sultan, seeing himself as ... the heir to the caliphs, thus wedded spiritually and politically to Islam." Mehmed is an example of a frequently occurring case among Muslim leaders. He was an unscrupulous and ruthless ruler and impious by Islamic standards. He was also pragmatic in dealing with his non-Muslim subjects and foreigners. He even had some interest in other religions and heretical syncretistic

Muslim sects. Yet, he was quite content to use the warlike zeal provoked by Islam to further his worldly ambitions and was not about to chance the storm that would arise if he openly showed disrespect for Islam or threatened its monopoly of power.

Mehmed showed some benevolence to cooperative conquered *dhimmis*. He confirmed Gennadius as Patriarch, and established the millet system of self government for the various religious communities. He also "treated the Athenians magnanimously, confirming their civil liberties and exemption from taxes" and "granted privileges to the Orthodox clergy." The Conqueror's treatment of Athens was undoubtedly a result of his interest in the antiquities of the territory over which he ruled; an interest quite uncharacteristic of a Muslim. "After his army captured Athens Fatih went there in 1459 to see the ruined monuments of the ancient city, for his classical studies had imbued him with a deep reverence for classical Greek culture. Kritovoulos calls him a 'Philhellene'". Mehmed's unusual interest in the Greek classics was exhibited on a visit to Troy:

Fatih visited the site of ancient Troy ... which he knew from his reading of Homer. Kritovoulos writes that Fatih's conquest of Byzantium made the sultan feel that he had evened the score with the Greeks for their victory over the 'Asiatics' at Troy, and that he only regretted that he did not have a poet like Homer to extol his deeds.

Once again, this may have been more than just a passing curiosity. In the early days of both Seljuk and Ottoman rule, there appears to have been a consciousness of their pre-Islamic Greek heritage on the part of many members of the Turkish elite who were often of mixed parentage. Such consciousness faded, however, with the hardening of Islamic culture over the centuries.

Mehmed, even after his conquest of Byzantium, continued his interest in Christianity and comparative religion. He ...called on Gennadius ... and in their conversations they ranged widely over Christian theology. Gennadius also wrote a summary of his work and had it translated into Turkish for

Fatih's private study. ... Spandugino, an Italian who lived in Galata early in the sixteenth century, claims that Fatih took to worshipping Christian relics and always kept many candles burning in front of them.

But Fatih's interest in Christianity appears to have been superficial, for he seems to have been basically irreligious, and in his observance of Islam he merely observed the forms of the Muslim faith, as was necessary for him as head of state.

Indeed, his son Prince Beyazit reportedly said that his father did not believe in Muhammad. Mehmed was also a highly atypical Muslim in his interest in the Renaissance that was flowering in Italy during his lifetime. The Venetian Senate sent the artist Gentile Bellini to Constantinople at Mehmed's request. Bellini painted Mehmed's portrait and also decorated his apartments with erotic paintings.

One strange case of syncretism among Ottoman royalty occurred when the purported son of Sultan Ibrahim was captured as a baby, along with his mother a harem favorite, by Christian pirates.

...the child initially captured by the Maltese on the Turkish galley ... was introduced at a certain stage as a possible Ottoman pretender. Now a Catholic priest named Pere Osman, he aspired without success to rally all Ottoman subjects, whether Moslem or Christian, to the cause of a new eastern state, blending the concepts of the Byzantine and the Ottoman empires.

A benevolent Ottoman leader some years later was the Grand Vizier and de facto ruler of the Ottoman Empire Koprulu Ahmed who "relaxed the severity" of his father's regime. "A strict Moslem, he was nonetheless free from fanaticism, tolerating the beliefs of others, protecting Christians and Jews from injustice, and abolishing restrictions on the building of churches."

Muslim Central Asia was the scene of an even more unconventional liberal ruler; one who was not simply a patron of learning but an accomplished scientist in his own right. The grandson of the fearsome Tamerlane, Ulugh Beg (1394-1449), ruler of Transoxiana was "a mathematician and astronomer and ... patron of other scientists". The school he established included scholars from Anatolia, Persia and central Asia.

The community could achieve brilliant results in the exact sciences that still matched those of contemporary Europe, if it was stimulated by an inspired sponsor like Ulugh Beg. Without such support, however, scientists had little institutional framework within which to develop and flourish. Moreover, in Central Asia they had to compete not only with conventional learning represented by the madrassa as a theological seminary, but also with a rising tide of religious fervor...

Ulugh's noted mathematician, Ali Qushchi "ultimately was invited to Istanbul by another enlightened sponsor, the Ottoman sultan Mehmet the Conqueror." The migration of the mathematician Qushchi to newly conquered Byzantium, illustrates how the consolidation of conquered territory and the establishment of peace under a liberal Muslim despot can engender a temporary high period of culture and learning. The inclusion of the once ravaged territory within the larger Muslim world makes it accessible for scholars and promotes a cross fertilization of ideas. Later, however, the inevitable regression inherent in the Islamic meme comes to dominate. It also shows the small renaissance that might occur under enlightened rulers within a territory long under Muslim rule. Rulers such as Ulugh may come to power following the turmoil accompanying the establishment of a new and often heretical dynasty. Such was the case in Fatimid Egypt and in Safavid Persia. In the wake of the violent rise of the unconventional Muslim empire-builder Tamerlane, there occurred a minor Timurid renaissance in Central Asia, which expressed itself in the science of Ulugh and also in literature and art.

The ultimate fate of the enlightened, but unfortunate, scholar-sultan Ulugh Beg exemplifies both the inevitable triumph of repressive despotism and the decay of science under Islam. Ulugh's son Abd al-Latif rebelled and "marched on Samarkand with an army and defeated his father ... Ulugh Beg returned to the city as a ... prisoner of his irate son; worse still, the religious authorities, never fond of the prince-scientist, issued a fatwa mandating his deposition and execution. He was ... beheaded on 27 October 1449." Ulugh's fate also shows how the beginning of repression in one Islamic territory may provide an opportunity for an enlightened neighboring ruler. Thus, the mathematician Qushchi who was close to Ulugh, found a welcome in the Conqueror's domains. A similar welcoming of refugee Jewish intellectuals from Spain by the Ayyubids of Egypt was another such example.

In Muslim India there were a number of instances of tolerant, progressive and even syncretistic rulers. One example, the Khalji Sultan Ala-ud-din (ca 1310), a ruler who verged on the edge of heresy, is described by Keay:

> The sultan was no Islamic bigot: 'there is no instance to show that Ala-ud-din oppressed some people simply because they were Hindus and favored others just because they were Muslims.' Indeed, if one may judge by his reported interest in founding a new religion centred on his own illustrious person, his faith was decidedly unorthodox. ... Like his assumption of the title 'The Second Alexander' on his coinage, it was a case of the megalomaniac getting the better of the Muslim.

Another Muslim ruler, Muhammad bin Tughluq, despite his severity and cruelty, "was comparatively free of religious and ethnic bigotry. Perhaps he was more than any of the sultans glimpsed the potential of an Indo-Islamic accommodation." Nevertheless, despite his dabbling in science and philosophy, Tughluq "killed so many Hindus that there was constantly in front of his royal pavilion ... a mound of dead bodies". In Bengal, Ala-ud-din Husain Shah (1493-1519) "though a Muslim, indeed an Arab, is said to have honoured ... the leader of the Vaishnavire bhakti movement ... In return the Hindus" honored the sultan "as an incarnation of Lord Krishna."

But by far the most daring of all the heretical Muslim rulers was the great Mogul emperor Akbar who exhibited an abiding passion for pursuing religious truth in whatever direction it might lead:

Akbar's curiosity about his subjects and their beliefs also became markedly eclectic. ... he installed a veritable bazaar of disputing divines and presided over their heated debates ... To the Quranic arguments of Sunni, Shia and Ismaili were added ... numerous Sufi orders, the bhakti fervour of Saiva and Vaishnava devotees ... naked Jains, and the varied insights of numerous wandering ascetics, saints and other ... recluses.

Also welcome were ... disciples of Kabir ... and Guru Nanak ... founder of the Sikh faith. ... included ... were Portuguese priests ... from Goa...

In the end "Akbar improvised an ideology based on the only element in which he had complete confidence, his imperial persona." His faith "centred on himself, but whether as God or His representative is not certain." His threat to orthodox Islam led to a major rebellion, but Akbar with considerable Hindu military support managed to crush it. Aided by his Hindu vassals, he also added considerable territory to his domains.

Akbar was the boldest and most successful of all the syncretistic rulers, but, unfortunately even his religious reforms embedded as they were in an Islamic social and political matrix, could not survive his death. The cult of personality he developed in order to carry through his reforms prefigured that which, centuries later, was to be promoted by Ataturk.

A later royal Mogul heretic was Dara Shikoh, Shah Jahan's favorite son and Aurangzeb's rival. Dara Shikoh "inspired deep suspicion amongst orthodox Muslims ... he consorted with Sufis, Hindus and Christians ... translated the Upanishads into Persian ... advanced the idea 'that the essential nature of Hinduism was identical with that of Islam'." After his defeat by Aurangzeb "he was condemned and cut to pieces" and then "paraded through the streets."

On the periphery of the Muslim world, in areas where Islam spread by more peaceful means, relatively tolerant rulers following a more relaxed and syncretistic version of the religion were common. In Indonesia "the stories of the Mahabharata and the Ramayana continued to serve for the aristocracy as a school of chivalry and to be enjoyed by the people. The culture of the Javanese princely courts remained essentially Hinduistic-Javanese up to very recent times." One overtly apostate ruler was Sultan Amangkurat of the Javanese state of Mataram who in 1674 had some six thousand Muslim clerics killed. "Amangkurat ... did not share his father's sentiment toward Islam. He rejected the title of 'sultan' and preferred the Javanese one of 'susuhunan'. He ... restricted the jurisdiction of the religious courts. Thus, his reign constituted a marked reaction against the growing Islamization of Javanese society." Like Dara Shikoh and Ulugh Beg, Amangkurat came to an unfortunate end when his orthodox Muslim enemies rebelled and overthrew him.

West Africa was also the scene of many unconventional rulers who fell short of the strict standards of Muslim orthodoxy. Under the newly converted rulers of Sub Saharan West Africa, many pre-Islamic customs remained intact. "As a good Muslim, there were aspects of life in Mali which Ibn Battuta found shocking - above all, the freedom given to women, who went about unveiled and chose whom they would as their companions." Since the oppression and degradation of women was one of the prime factors in Islam's successful expansion, such freedom would be looked upon as quite egregious by orthodox Muslims.

REPRESSIVE DESPOTIC PHASE

Islamic states invariably, until the era of Western intervention, end up as rigid theocracies ruled by a small class of bigoted officials under an aloof and arbitrary tyrant. As we have seen, in earlier years such repression was often interspersed with intervals of rule by relatively enlightened or tolerant caliphs or sultans. Arab historian Hourani describes how the increasing Islamization of the population inevitably put an end to toleration and cemented the second class status of non-Muslims.

In the early centuries of Islamic rule there appears to have been much social and cultural intercourse between adherents of the three religions. ... As time went on ... the barriers became higher. The conversion ... to Islam turned a majority into a diminishing minority. ... Islam ... developed its own social institutions, within which Muslims could live without interaction with non Muslims.

Pressures upon Jews and Christians may have come mainly from the urban masses, particularly in times of war or economic hardship, when hostility might be directed against the non Muslim officials of the ruler. At such moments, the ruler might respond by enforcing the laws strictly, or dismissing his non Muslim officials...

Persecution of the remaining non-Muslims was accompanied by, and undoubtedly was one of the reasons for, the decline in intellectual accomplishment in general, and the diminishment of freedom even for Muslims. Harbingers of such decline were present at a very early date. The Umayyad caliph Umar II enforced the dress code for Christians and Jews and barred them from holding public office. The, otherwise munificent, Abbasid caliph Harun re-enacted those decrees. Finally, the "stringent regulations against *dhimmis* culminated in the time of al-Mutawakkil, who in 850 and 854 decreed that Christians and Jews should affix wooden images of devils to their houses" among other severe measures. Indeed, the generally tolerant and worldly outlook that marked Umayyad rule became increasingly rare among the Abbasids.

The claim to divine inspiration was exemplified in the strong messianic overtones of the throne names adopted by all Abbasid caliphs and was accompanied by public indulgence of religious figures and institutions. ... The relaxed Umayyad attitude to religious observance gave way to strict public enforcement of religious codes of behavior and zealous persecution of heretics.

To be sure, even under the early Abbasids the two competing models of despotism, the enlightened and the repressive, continued to war with each other despite the religious pretensions of the dynasty. In the same way as "the Umayyads sought often to buttress their credentials through spectacular religious acts, such as the building of the Dome of the Rock", so the "Abbasids complied with the stipulations of ...religious law", but "only to the extent it served their needs". In private they "indulged in the same vices - wine, singing girls, and sexual licence - that had given the Umayyads their bad reputation." Furthermore, "scathing criticism was leveled at Ma'mun and his two immediate successors ... for their endorsement of the philo-Hellenistic Mu'tazilite school of thought ... Yet even when the caliph Mutawakil (847-61) ... reestablished the orthodox dogma; this did not mean greater religious observance at the personal level." Repressive despotism became fairly well entrenched by the time of the Abbasid caliph Qahir (932-34) "who took strict measures against wine-drinkers and singing girls" and this despite the fact that he "was hardly ever sober."

Muslim Spain, despite the propaganda of the proponents of the myth of Andalusia, was subject to the same fall from a tolerant progressive outlook into repressive despotic rule. The Spanish vizier and de facto ruler al-Mansur (ca. 980), "to ingratiate himself with the ulema ... burned all the books in the library of al-Hakam 61-7 dealing with philosophy and other subjects blacklisted by those theologians." This is an example of another common pattern whereby policies of repression and religious reaction are instituted by weak or usurping rulers to curry favor with the ulama.

Following another brief period of liberalism under some of the "party kings", the final stage of repression in Muslim Spain began with the overthrow of the Abbadid dynasty of Seville by the Murabits (Almoravids) in 1090. "Under the Murabits, fresh converts to Islam and heirs to a barbarian legacy not yet dead, an outburst of religious fervour on the part of theological zealots resulted at the beginning of the twelfth century in suffering for many Christians, Jews and even liberal Moslems. Under the devout 'Ali (1106-43) ... al-Ghazzali's works were put on the black list or committed to the flames in Spain and al-Maghrib". Although the succeeding early Muwahhids (Almohads) are described by Hitti as a "Dynasty puritanic in theology but liberal in its patronage of philosophy", they were even more fanatical in the persecution of Christians and Jews.

In Egypt, the liberal phases occurring under the Fatimids and Ayyubids were finally ended by the repression of the Mamluks. Under these "slave" sultans there was strict enforcement of dress and building codes directed against the *dhimmis*. There were also decrees against non-Muslim doctors among "a number of innovative anti-*dhimmi* measures taken in the Mamluk period." Indeed, the "last one hundred years or more of Mamluk rule weighed heavily upon all of the subjects of the empire – Muslim and non-Muslim." The Mamluk Sultan Barsbay (c. 1422) in response to an outbreak of plague regarded it as punishment for the people's sins and "prohibited females from going outdoors and sought to make atonement by fresh exactions from Christians and Jews."

The Seljuk Turkish rulers became increasingly despotic when, in the latter days of the formerly tolerant Konya sultanate, the government came under increasing pressure from nomadic Turkmen and Mongols. As a result the population was plagued by rapacious officials and tax farmers. "The sultan 'Ala al-Din III Kaykubad enacted such fiscal oppression that finances were thrown into confusion and many villagers fled their homes."

The Ottomans inevitably followed in the dolorous footsteps of their Islamic predecessors. One early harbinger of the more repressive despotism to come occurred when Sultan Selim the Grim in 1514 decided "to follow one campaign against Moslem heretics in Anatolia with another designed to force Anatolian Christians to recant or face the sword". He desisted only after the Seyhulislam, the chief judge of Islam, pointed out that payers of the *jizya* had a right to preserve their faiths.

The shift from the liberal to the repressive despotic stage in the Ottoman Empire accelerated after the death of Suleiman's favorite concubine Roxelana. Suleiman "had withdrawn within himself, growing more than ever silent, more melancholy ... more remote from human contacts." At one time his court had been enlivened by music. But as the Sultan grew more fearfully religious "the instruments were thus broken up and consigned to the flames. In response to similar ascetic scruples he took to eating off earthenware instead of silver plate, moreover banned the importation into the city of all wine".

One exemplar of the increasing Ottoman despotic repression was Mehmed III, who although a weakling ...was to have his nineteen brothers strangled by mutes – the largest fratricidal sacrifice in Ottoman history. ... Meanwhile six pregnant slaves, their favourites from the harem, had been sewn up in sacks and thrown into the Bosporus, lest they give birth to claimants to the throne. Later Mehmed put to death his own chosen son Mahmud, a young man of spirit who had begged to be given command of the armies fighting the rebels in Anatolia, and this had inflamed his father's jealous suspicions. His mother and his favourite companions ... suffered the same fate.

Worse still was the very embodiment of the Oriental despot, Murad IV (1623-1640) whose reign of terror, well described by Kinross brought about the end of a period of military anarchy:

His trusted henchmen and well-trained spies scoured the city of Istanbul on his orders, tracking down the known traitors ... executing them on the spot ... flinging their corpses into the Bosporus to be washed up on shore before the populace. Bloodshed similarly swept through the provinces."

Later, to deprive the public of its centers of reunion and possible trouble, he closed all cafes and wineshops in the cities of the Empire – on no temporary basis but for the rest of his reign – and made the smoking of tobacco illegal. Offenders caught at night smoking a pipe, drinking coffee, or flushed with wine might instantly be hanged or impaled, and their bodies thrown out into the street as a warning to the rest.

As time went on Murad became carried away by the thirst for blood. At first his executions were justified by unquestionable guilt; then they grew more sweeping ... eventually he was killing, heedless of any suspicion, for the sake of killing, from wanton caprice or impulsive ill humour.

His cruelties became legendary. Disturbed by the boisterous merriment of a party of women ... he had them all seized and drowned. He murdered one of his own doctors ... He impaled a courier for informing him mistakenly that the Sultana had given birth to a son ... He beheaded his chief musician for singing a Persian air ... In five years it is said that twenty-five thousand men perished at his orders, many of them by his own hand.

In India it was Sultan Aurangzeb who initiated the full repressive despotic phase of the Mogul regime. Keay describes how under his severe rule...dancers, musicians and artists were dismissed from the imperial employ. Their places were taken by bearded jurists and Quranic divines ... The tax on Hindu pilgrims, lifted by Akbar, was reimposed ... revenue endowments enjoyed by temples and brahmans were rescinded; Hindu merchants were penalized ... newly built or rebuilt temples were to be destroyed. ... Finally, in 1679 ... the reimposition of the detested *jizya*...

But even Aurangzeb did not try to force the conversion of non-Muslims. "He was too shrewd; they too numerous."

The Shiite Safavids also, eventually followed the path to repressive Islamic despotism. "In 1656, Shah 'Abbas II granted extensive powers to his wazirs to force Jews to become Muslims. Al-Majlisi persuaded Shah Husayn (1688-1726) to decree the forcible conversion of Zoroastrians."

Paralleling the phases of Islamic political development were the phases of Muslim intellectual life. Islamic "golden ages" followed the re-establishment of peace and security under the auspices of the new regime. The time lag between the conquest and the peak of the golden age varied from a few decades through several centuries in different Muslim lands. However, these golden ages were a result of the parasitic exploitation of the intellectual and economic resources left over from the preceding civilization. When these were exhausted intellectual achievement went into a rapid decline.

3

Parasitic Civilization

Islam's "golden age" and "splendors" is a topic of incessant fascination. It would, of course, be more accurate to speak of Islam's "golden ages" since there were a number of such intellectual and artistic flowerings. The high civilizations of Abbasid Baghdad and of Moorish Spain, as well as the magnificence of the Ottoman and Mogul courts are well-known.

However, the Muslim efflorescence, like the financial underpinning for the Muslim military campaigns, depended on the wealth expropriated from, and on the continuing economic exploitation of, conquered non-Muslim populations. In addition, it must be acknowledged that the Muslim invaders were not, in general, total barbarians; they were not Huns or Mongols or Vandals. They valued the level of civilization that they encountered in their invasions and maintained a cultivated and often comfortable existence.

However, one thing about the historical record is noteworthy; the various golden ages of Islamic civilization always occur early in the first few centuries in which a new territory is occupied. Wherever the various Muslim vanguards invaded, the vast majority of the population was non-Muslim. It would take many years for this population to be converted and assimilated. These non-Muslims or recent converts are the ones who carried on the work which many historians are prone to attribute to "Islamic" civilization. Thus, a distinction must be drawn between the so-called high Islamic civilization and the religion of Islam. Eventually as the process of Islamization proceeds the non-Islamic component of the population becomes a small minority and stagnation sets in. This process is evident in the first centuries of the Arab conquests where the process of Arabization and conversion to Islam took a few centuries to complete; this was the "Arab" golden age, a product of unconverted or recently converted Christians, Jews and Zoroastrians. In Spain the golden age lasted longer, perhaps because the process of Islamization was never as complete in Moorish Spain as in the Arab East.

It is remarkable how closely this pattern was repeated in the subsequent expansions of Islam as a consequence of the Turkish and Mogul conquests. The initial splendors of the Seljuk and Ottoman empires were the result of unconverted or recently converted subjects. When the Islamization of the newly conquered territories was complete intellectual stagnation once again set in. Similarly, an initial flowering as an extension of the ancient Hindu culture followed the Mogul conquest of India.

It must, however, be granted that Islamic civilization did serve a valuable purpose as a bridge between the West and the ancient civilizations of India and China. This resulted in the transmission of science and technology from China and mathematics from India. It must also be noted that, as will be shown below, the so-called Arabic numerals are really Hindu in origin; algebra is a combination of Indian, Greek and pre-Islamic Mesopotamian mathematics. And while it is true that Muslim rulers did enable some of the knowledge of the classical world to be preserved, the importance of this work has been greatly exaggerated. In addition, the actual work of transcribing and preserving this classical knowledge was done by non-Muslims or by recent converts.

PLUNDER AND ECONOMIC EXPLOITATION

The first Muslim invaders were always invariably motivated by the desire for loot and, as we have seen in 7: Culture of the Harem, the lust for concubines. The Prophet himself "skillfully couched his worldly objectives in divine terms" and this "fusion of the sacred and the profitable was endorsed by future generations of Islamic leaders." Thus, Islamic scripture contains explicit promise of, and religious sanction for, plunder from infidels:

> Fight against such of those who have been given the scripture as believe not in Allah nor the Last Day, and forbid not that which Allah hath forbidden by His messenger, and follow not the religion of truth, until they pay the tribute readily, being brought low.
>
> Surah 9:29

> Whoso fighteth in the way of Allah, be he slain or be he victorious, on him we shall bestow a vast reward.
>
> Surah 4:74

With vast territories conquered and large populations subdued, the early Arab leadership found it prudent to regularize and bureaucratize plunder. The caliph Umar instituted a register known as the Diwan "which remunerated the fighters out of the proceeds from the conquered lands and thus allowed them to continue prosecuting war operations without worrying about their subsistence." The necessity for caliphs to keep their supporters happy with a continuing distribution of loot is illustrated by the civil conflict that began in the reign of Caliph Uthman which was "exacerbated by the temporary halt of the conquests in the early 650s and the attendant reduction in the spoils of war."

Plunder also served Muslim rulers, from the time of the early Arabs to the end of the Muslim expansions, as the wherewithal for vast public works. For those rulers with pretensions to intellectual achievement plunder could also be used to attract scholars. Mahmud of Ghazni, for example, employed his plunder in adorning his capital and subsidizing a gathering of scholars at his court but "for Hindus, this paragon of valour and piety would ever be nothing but a monster of cruelty". Successive generations of Muslim ghazis became increasingly addicted to looting, with explosive results when the spigot was turned off as occurred when the Rajput leader Prithviraj had succeeded in bottling up the Muslims in the Punjab. "But this interdiction had served only to increase the pressure for a more decisive encounter. The Ghorids rose to the challenge because for them ... plunder was a necessity."

As the Arab empire expanded and the rate of new conquest slowed, it became necessary for plunder from war to be replaced by the less violent form of plunder known as taxation. The conquering Muslim military elites were, thus, supported by the *dhimmi* populations "who had to pay special taxes" such as the kharaj or land tax and the *jizya* or poll tax. Bat Yeor summarizes the Islamic view of the "collective booty" owed by the *dhimmis* to their conquerors:

> The concept of fay - collective booty reserved for the upkeep of the Islamic community – constituted the legal argument which preserved the religions of the conquered peoples. This economic burden, which devolved on the disarmed vanquished people to the benefit of a warlike community destined to conquer the world, is very clearly set out by the Muslim jurisconsults.

This concept of "fay" became very well entrenched within Muslim tradition, even long after the Arab heyday.

The economic surplus extracted from the vanquished population, on which the Muslim elite depended, did help to preserve infidel religions for many centuries. In many cases it was the *dhimmis* who "did the jobs Arabs were unwilling to do." In early Abbasid times "the agricultural class, who constituted the bulk of he population ... and the chief source of revenue, were the original inhabitants of the land, now reduced to the position of *dhimmis*. The Arab considered it below his dignity to engage in agricultural pursuits. ... In country places and on their farms these *dhimmis* clung to their ancient cultural patterns and preserved their national languages." These were Syriac, Aramaic, Iranian and Coptic. "Many of those who embraced Islam moved to the cities."

In the early days of a newly conquered territory the Muslim rulers found that practicality and efficiency required this system of extortion be administered by native bureaucrats or even by infidel clergy. These punitive exactions, despite the attempts by some officials to mitigate them, would inevitably lead to the decimation of non-Muslim populations.

The caliph entrusted to the patriarch the task of collecting the taxes extorted from his flock, leaving him only with a pittance. The chronicles record in detail these relationships based on money and violence and always involving torture, from the lowest social level to its summit. Equally, one should have few illusions about the appointment of high Christian officials, particularly to the Treasury. Integrated into this Islamic machinery for the destruction of Christendom, they could, by a gesture, temporarily slow it down, temper it, or exacerbate it, but could not abolish it.

However, at some point it must have occurred to the more prescient caliphs, sultans and viziers that non-Muslims were essential as a source of taxes, expertise, and entrepreneurship and as go-betweens and emissaries with non-Muslim states; so conversions were no longer actively sought. These rulers did "endeavor to protect the *dhimmi* peasantry against uncontrolled extortions by governors or local tyrants." Agriculture, being the source of wealth and power, the state was dependent for its revenues "on compulsory work by an abundant workforce." As the number of converts grew the remaining "infidel subjects were more oppressively mulcted and humiliated." Over the objections of the devout, some rulers began to actively discourage conversions since the "treasury of the Sultan had come to depend on the contributions of the unbeliever." In fact, as occurred in Islamic Spain, officials sometimes shut off completely "this escape route from a miserable existence by forbidding Christians and Jews to convert to Islam. Too many converts would destroy the tax base."

In times of disorder when the caliph or the sultan could no longer protect them, the diminishing supply of *dhimmi*s endured further extortion from rebellious nomads. "The wealth-producing *dhimmi* communities became a coveted prize and plunder to warring political forces." Vryonis observes how during the Turkish conquests this competition for the diminishing *dhimmi* resource was a cause of warfare among nomadic tribes.

> The invasions had caused a certain disruption and decline in the Christian population of the Anatolian plateau. As a result ... the various Turkish princes began to raid the land of one another and of the Christians and to carry away entire Christian towns and villages in order to repopulate their own domains.

One enlightened nomad sultan, however, with all the attention to detail of a compulsive greenhouse proprietor, carefully nurtured his valuable stock of *dhimmi* farmers:

> The great care the sultan [Kaykhusraw] lavished upon these Christian colonists is illustrative of the importance the Muslim rulers attached to repopulating their domains with Christian farmers. He had them carefully guarded so none would escape en route, and on arrival ... he gave them land and seed to plant. He bestowed upon them five years tax immunity ... many who heard of the tax exemption migrated to the sultan's domains because of the great disorder that had now enveloped the Byzantine Maeandrian regions.

Nevertheless, despite the best efforts of some far-seeing Muslim rulers, in the long run the Islamic meme followed the logic inherent in its program. And once the *dhimmi* populations were sufficiently depleted through conversion, enslavement and displacement, the natural result was inevitably the stagnation of Islamic society.

BRIEF RENAISSANCE AND PERMANENT DECLINE

After the initial Arab conquests, it required about a century for peace and stability to become commonplace so that civilization could resume its advance. This lag was reinforced by the continuing Arab advance into North Africa and the easternmost territories of the Persians which continued into the eighth century and must have consumed considerable resources. All subsequent Muslim conquests resulted in lags of various lengths during which peace and security was being re-established and the still numerous non-Muslim population could resume the work of civilization. Trifkovic observes that "since dead bodies paid no taxes while the captives were economic assets, once the conquerors' rule was firmly established a degree of normalcy was reestablished at the level of local communities."

THE DHIMMI ROOTS OF EARLY MUSLIM CIVILIZATIONS

The achievements of the civilizations under Muslim rule were substantial. However, almost all of this occurred in the early periods of such rule, once peace and stability had been restored. Furthermore, these high periods of culture were almost exclusively the product of the conquered, and still not completely Islamized native populations. The observations, in this regard of Professor Darlington who looks at society with the eye of a trained biologist, are pertinent:

> But while war accounts for the expansion of Islam it does not account for the sparkling creation of culture which followed the expansion. This ... happened only where there was something valuable before the coming of Islam. And the sparkle in each instance lasted only half a dozen generations. It lasted evidently as long as the conquest of each ancient society brought about the recombination of valuable racial components.
>
> So it was that successively in Damascus and Baghdad, in Cordoba and Marrakesh, in Isfahan and Delhi, we see the characteristic flame of the new hybrid Islamic civilizations always based on a precarious balance between conversion and non-conversion, hybridization and non-hybridization, a balance which Muslim violence was not fitted to sustain. When the conquest ceased ... the intellectual and artistic ... life of Islam came to a standstill. ... When the limits of conquest had been reached ... and new hybridization was excluded, decay set in, slow but everywhere irremediable.

Other students of Islam contend that "Islamic science developed for a while despite Islam." Only in those few areas and times when it was protected by freethinking or unorthodox elites could it flourish. Such times usually occurred early in Muslim rule. Stillman, writing of the early Arab conquests makes the observation, applicable to Muslim polities in general, that Islamic civilizations are extensions of the pre-existing cultures modified for the service of the new faith:

Classical Islamic civilization was not Islam the religion, although the latter was an essential component. Islamic civilization was an amalgam of cultural elements that included Islamic religion, Arabic culture with its strong pre-Islamic roots, Greek humanism, and subtle remnants of the ancient heritage of the Near East.

Hitti echoes these ideas with respect to the early post-conquest Arab dynasties in the east:

What we therefore call 'Arab civilization' was Arabian neither in its origins and fundamental structure nor in its principal ethnic aspects. The purely Arabian contribution in it was in the linguistic and to a certain extent in the religious fields. Throughout the whole period of the caliphate the Syrians, the Persians, the Egyptians and others, as Moslem converts or as Christians and Jews, were the foremost bearers of the torch of enlightenment and learning. ... The Arab Islamic civilization was at bottom the Hellenized Aramaic and the Iranian civilizations as developed under the aegis of the caliphate and expressed through the medium of the Arabic tongue.

It took almost three centuries for most of the vanquished population to convert to Islam and most such conversions were motivated by self interest and not by religious conviction. Islamic culture, thus, developed "on a substratum composed of the heritage of the Syro-Aramaean, Persian and Hellenistic civilizations which had preceded it. With Islam the Near Orient not only recaptured the whole of its former political domain but regained in the realm of culture its ancient intellectual preeminence." However, as we have seen, the price paid by the native non-Muslims for this reassertion of their submerged civilization under Arab domination was a steep one.

In the fields of science and philosophy the contributors were in large majority non-Arab and non-Muslim. As Hitti notes:

When we therefore speak of 'Arab medicine' or 'Arab philosophy' or 'Arab mathematics' we do not mean the medical science, philosophy or mathematics that are necessarily the product of the Arabian mind or developed by people living in the Arabian peninsula, but that body of knowledge enshrined in books written in the Arabic language by men who flourished chiefly during the caliphate and were themselves Persians, Syrians, Egyptians or Arabians, Christian, Jewish or Moslem and who may have drawn some of their material from Greek, Aramaean, Indo-Persian or other sources.

The subjects dominated by Arab Muslims were specifically those that related to the Arabic language and the Islamic religion. Theology, jurisprudence, philology and linguistics were "those intellectual activities evoked by the predilections of the Arabs as Arabs and Moslems." The scholars in this field were mostly of Arab descent "in contrast to the physicians, astronomers, mathematicians and alchemists ... who were of Syrian, Jewish or Persian origin." Even so, the great theologian al-Bukhari was a Persian, while the founder of one of the four orthodox Muslim schools, abu-Hanifah, was the grandson of a Persian and presumably non-Muslim slave. It is also "noteworthy that many of the pioneering grammarians of the Arabic language were themselves non-Arabs." There was one great exception to the general rule that philosophy and science was the domain of the non-Arabs. This was Al-Kindi whose "pure Arabian descent earned him the title 'the philosopher of the Arabs', and indeed he was the first and last example of an Aristotelian student in the Eastern caliphate who sprang from Arabian stock." The acclaim Al-Kindi received from his fellow Arabs highlights the paucity of noteworthy philosophers and scientists of both Arab stock and Muslim religion.

The early Arab rulers were able to capitalize on the different specializations of the conquered groups and there arose a division of labor based largely on ethnicity. It is ironic that in the first years of the conquest mosques were built by Greek-speaking Christians. Greeks and Aramaeans continued to dominate the field of architecture for many years. Although they eventually adopted the Arabic tongue "they continued the style and inherited the mathematics, and the ability to use it, of their Greek or ... of their Babylonian ancestors." Persian, Coptic and Hindu designers found a niche in architectural decoration. When al-Walid built his famous grand mosque in Damascus, he "employed Persian and Indian craftsmen as well as Greek artisans provided by the emperor of Constantinople. Papyri ... show that material and skilled workmen were imported from Egypt."

Jews were valued "for their medical skill and general literacy" and unlike the Greeks and Persians "were able to exert their influence largely without conversion" for a long period of time. Indians were also valued for their medical skills. The Barmakid minister Yahya "paid an Indian scholar called Manka to translate an Indian medical book ... the book of Sasard into Arabic." Hindus were also valued for their skills in astronomy and mathematics. "The same Hindu scholar who brought to the court of al-Mansur the astronomical work Sindhind is credited with having also introduced Hindu arithmetical lore with its numeral system (called in Arabic Hindi) and the zero." Personal tutors usually consisted of practicing Christians or those recent converts adopted by Arab tribes as clients. "After the time of 'Abd-al-Malik the tutor or preceptor, usually a client or Christian became a standing figure in the court."

The maritime trades were dominated by those of Greek or Phoenician descent; a situation that continued under succeeding Muslim rulers for a thousand years. These seamen ...were by origin Phoenician and Greek and by ancestry much hybridized. ... they must have willingly converted ... For so we must understand the fall of Cyprus ... to be followed by Sicily and Sardinia, Crete and Malta. Another Muslim advance in the Mediterranean was delayed until the fifteenth century. Then the annexation of Greece was followed by the incorporation and conversion of the Greek and Dalmatian ... sea-faring populations in the Ottoman Empire.

During the reign of the Umayyad caliphs Abd-al-Malik (685-705) and al-Walid (705-715) the Arabization of the state administration occurred by "changing the language of the public registers from Greek to Arabic in Damascus and from Pahlawi to Arabic in al-Iraq and the eastern provinces and in the creation of an Arabic coinage." However, this caused no end to the state's dependence on the skills of non-Arabs. Under the Abbasids the appointment of non-Muslims to high office continued into the latter half of the ninth century. These appointments occurred even during times of the implementation of stringent regulations against *dhimmis*. Despite these persecutions, caliphs and other high officials were long dependent on non-Muslim expertise.

It was during the Abbasid caliphate that Arab Islamic civilization reached its height. It was at this time that the epoch of the translation of Greek works occurred. The caliphs and the Arab elite of Baghdad, remarkably open to the ideas of classical civilization, subsidized a great explosion of creativity:

The apogee of Greek influence was reached under al-Ma'mun. The rationalistic tendencies of this caliph and his espousal of the Mu'tazilite cause which maintained that religious texts should agree with the judgments of reason, led him to seek justification for his position in the philosophical works of the Greeks.

Hitti observes that the "Abbasid dynasty, like others in Muslim history, attained its most brilliant period of political and intellectual life soon after its establishment." Its height was reached during the reigns of Harun al-Rashid and his son al-Ma'mun (786-833). The primary reason for the early occurrences of Muslim high culture, of course, is the continued existence of a large reservoir of *dhimmis* or of recent converts with specialized skills. Other reasons include the establishment of peace and stability after a long period of strife, the inclusion of newly conquered territories into an empire with expanded trade and the diffusion of ideas, and the need for new dynasties to consolidate their rule by including non-Muslims in the governing coalition.

The fertilization caused by the diffusion of ideas from distant parts of the Arab oecumene is illustrated by the most famous literary composition of the Islamic world. The so-called 'Arabian Nights' "was an old Persian work ... containing several stories of Indian origin. ... As time went on additions were made from numberless sources: Indian, Greek, Hebrew, Egyptian and the like."

The relative paucity of intellectual achievement, under Abbasid rule, in Syria and Egypt as compared to Iraq lends support to the thesis that *dhimmis* or recently converted Muslims were the driving force in intellectual achievement. For in those provinces:

> Administration and secular arts and sciences depended to a very great extent on government employment and favor. In Egypt and Syria such employment and favoritism seems to have been directed more toward the Arab population than toward the indigenous convert community.

Intellectual achievement in the late post-Abbasid Arab dynasties is but a pale reflection of the brilliance in early Baghdad. Under the minority sect Fatimid caliphs of Egypt, who cultivated the support of Christian elements, there was a minor renaissance. Hitti notes that as late as 1125 in Fatimid Egypt the façade of the al-Aqmar mosque "may have been due to some Armenian Christian architect." However, with the decline of Abbasid Baghdad and with the steady decrease in non-Muslim numbers, Islamic science began its terminal decline. Such science as existed was confined to previously peripheral areas, now under independent dynasties, like Syria, Egypt, Persia, central Asia and Spain. In addition these remnants of Islamic science were critically dependent on Mongol rulers, Persian scholars or the few remaining *dhimmi* intellectuals:

> In science there were only two branches wherein the Arabs after the middle of the thirteenth century maintained their leadership: astronomy-mathematics, including trigonometry, and medicine, particularly ophthalmology. But in the first discipline the contribution was made mainly by Arabic-writing Persian scholars whose centre of activity was the Il-Khanid observatory; and library of Maraghah ... It is interesting to find the Syrian Jacobite Catholicos .... (Barhebraeus, 1226-86) known as an

historian and as the last classical author in Syriac literature lecturing there on Euclid in 1268 and on Ptolemy in 1272-3.

There were a large number of significant scholarly figures who were either non-Muslims, converts, or of recent non-Muslim and non-Arab ancestry. There were still others who, although nominally Muslim are reputed to be guilty of various forms of heresy, freethinking or atheism. In the years starting with the first caliphs and extending through the Umayyad dynasty, some of these scholars were as follows. Abdullah ibn Saba (ca 650), a Jewish convert from Yemen was a noted legal scholar. A quarter century later another converted Jew, Wahb ibn Munabbih, was well known as a writer in history. Another converted Jewish historian, Ka'b al-Ahbar, a contemporary of ibn Saba, was from the city of Hims in Syria. The poet al-Akhtal (640-710), a close friend and drinking companion of the caliph Yazid was a Syrian Christian. His fellow poet al-Farazdak was an Arab who was described by Muslims as dissolute and, therefore, likely a freethinker. Another Christian poet at the time was Jamil al-Udhri from Yemen. The city of Kufa in Iraq was the home of another poet, the Persian convert al-Rawiyah (713-72).

Music was an important art form in the early days of the Arab Empire. The Arabian Peninsula, in those early days before the full force of the sharia was felt, was a center of music and song. A surprising number of renowned musicians residing there were non-Arabs. Ibn-Surayj (640-726) was a Turkish convert and freed slave. Musajjah (ca 714) was a black African convert and client member of a Meccan tribe. His contemporary, al-Gharid was originally a half breed Berber slave. Another contemporary, ibn-Muhriz was from Persia and, thus, of recent non-Muslim background. Jamilah, also a contemporary is described as a Medinese freedwoman and therefore, also of probable non-Muslim origin; she is one of very few women in the Islamic world recognized for artistic or intellectual ability. Ma'bad (ca 720) was a Muslim of half African parentage. In this era Hunayn al-Hiri (ca 735) was a well known Christian musician in neighboring Iraq.

Medicine was the only science that was well established in Umayyad times. In the late seventh century ibn-Uthal, a famous Christian physician practiced in Damascus; Tayadhuq, another renowned practitioner in Iraq was a Greek Christian and Masarjawayh, a Persian Jew, was still another well-known Iraqi physician. Finally, there was one important philosopher in late Umayyad times. He was the famous Syrian Christian John Damascene who died in 748.

The early Abbasid dynasty was the high water mark for intellectual accomplishment in the Islamic world. Despite increasing repression, non-Muslim, convert and suspected heretic scholars were present in abundance. Baghdad, in those years, was one of the great centers for the study of astronomy. One famous astronomer was al-Fadl ibn-Nawbakht (ca 815) who was from Persia, and therefore of recent non-Muslim ancestry. His contemporary Isa al-Asturlabi, although described as an Arab Muslim was apparently of recent Christian background. Al-Farghani, who lived some thirty years later, was a Turkish Muslim and, therefore, either a convert or the descendant of recent converts. Abu-Ma'shar, (ca 886), like ibn-Nawbakht, a Persian Muslim, was a well known astrologer. Another Persian Muslim astronomer in the following century was al-Khazin. Sind ibn-'Ali (ca 830) was a converted Jew, who also left his mark in the field of astronomy. Al-Battani (877-918) also a respected astronomer was a Sabian (Mandean). From that obscure monotheistic Sabian religion emerged a famous family of translators specializing in Greek astronomy. The founder was Thabit ibn-Qurrah (836-901) who was followed by his son Sinan, his grandsons Thabit and Ibrahim, and his great grandson abu-al-Faraj.

Another famous family of translators was the Nestorian Christians Hunayn ibn-Ishaq, his son Ishaq and his nephew Hubaysh ibn-al-Hasan who all worked in the mid ninth century translating Greek medical and philosophical texts. Other famous translators were the Christian Thawafil ibn-Tuma (ca 785) who worked in literature, and the Syrian Christian Yuhanna ibn-Masawayh who translated medical texts. The Syrian Christian Qusta ibn-Luqa (ca 922) translated Greek mathematical and philosophical writings. Jacobite Christians Yahya ibn-Adi (893-974) and Isa ibn-Zu'rah (ca 1008) translated works of Greek philosophy. Indeed, according to the historian Franz Rosenthal, almost "all of the translators [from Greek into Syriac or Hebrew or from Greek, Syriac, or Hebrew into Arabic] were Christians." The aforementioned Sabian Thabit family plus a scattering of Jews were exceptions.

Another famous family worked in the field of medicine. These were the Nestorian Christians Jurjis ibn Bakhtishu (ca 771), his son Bakhtishu and grandson Jibril. A converted Christian from Persia, Ali al-Tabari (ca 850), also made his mark as a physician as did the Persian Zoroastrian convert Al-Majusi (ca 994). The eleventh century Christian physicians, Ali ibn-Isa, Ibn-Jazlah and ibn-Butlan also left their mark on the study of medicine. But, perhaps the most famous physician and medical theorist was the Persian Al-Razi (865-925), who although nominally Muslim was notorious as a freethinker condemned by Muslims for blasphemy.

Three additional freethinkers, known as the arch-heretics of Islam, were the Syrian philosophers Al-Rawandi (ca 915), Al-Tawhidi (ca 1023) and Al-Ma'ari (973-1057). Another famous heretic was the Turkish Sufi, Al-Farabi, the student of two Christian scholars, who died in 950. Al-Farabi, who was the model Muslim heretic, is described by Trifkovic as follows:

> Greatly influenced by Baghdad's Greek heritage in philosophy that survived the Arab invasion, and especially the writings of Aristotle, Farabi adopted the view - utterly heretical from a Moslem viewpoint - that reason is superior to revelation. He saw religion as a symbolic rendering of truth, and, like Plato, saw it as the duty of the philosopher to provide guidance to the state. He engaged in rationalistic questioning of the authority of the Koran and rejected predestination. He wrote more than 100 works, notably The Ideas of the Citizens of the Virtuous City. But these unorthodox works no more belong to Islam than Voltaire belongs to Christianity.

Non-Muslims, heretics and converts were also well represented in the natural sciences and geography. Al-Jahiz (ca 868), a member of the rationalist and soon to be declared heretical Mutazilite sect, was a renowned zoologist. A school of geography, dominated by Persians, flourished in the late ninth and early tenth centuries: ibn-Khurdadhbih (ca 912), al-Ya'qubi (ca 891), ibn-Rustah and al-Hamadhani (ca 903), al-Balkhi (ca 934), al-Istakhri and ibn-Hawqal (ca 950) worked in Iraq, Persia and Arabia. All were described as Persian Muslims and, thus, at that early period, presumably of recent non-Muslim family backgrounds. Qudamah (ca 928), a converted Christian also did work in geography.

Another group of Persian Muslims dominated the study of history. Ibn-al-Muqaffa was active in historical studies soon after the Abbasids assumed power. A century later ibn-Qutaybah worked in Baghdad along with his younger contemporaries, al-Baladhuri and ibn-Dawud al-Dinawari. Al-Tabari (838-923) worked in Persia, as did his younger contemporary, Hamzah al-Isfahani. The above-mentioned Ibn-al-Muqaffa was a Persian Zoroastrian convert, whose suspect orthodoxy led to his being burned at the stake. A few years afterward in 783, the poet ibn-Burd, also well known in early Abbasid literary circles, was a Persian heretic, who was also put to death for his Zoroastrian apostasy. Abu-Nuwas, another Persian poet managed to avoid Burd's unfortunate fate.

In the following century, Abu-Tammam, a converted Christian living in Syria also attained renown as a poet. Ibn-Ishaq, who died in 767, the grandson of a Christian slave achieved fame as a biographer. Two non-Arabs of recent non-Muslim family backgrounds achieved success in philology, a subject usually reserved for native Arabs. One was Al-Jawhari (ca 1008), a Turkish Muslim in Baghdad. His contemporary philologist was ibn-Jinni the son of a Greek slave who worked in Syria.

Following the "golden prime" of the early Abbasids, Islamic scholarship fell into a sharp decline. With the steady increase in converts and the decrease in the number of non-Muslims, the primary source of accomplished scholars dried up. With the passage of time, the descendants of earlier converts became far removed from the family and national traditions that promoted and sustained high scholarly achievement. The inner logic of the Islamic meme unfolded creating a climate of anti-intellectualism and a rigid pseudo scholarship; both of which were upheld by an increasingly powerful clerical class. Nevertheless, there were occasional intellectual revivals encouraged by some of the more enlightened rulers of the later local Arab dynasties. Non-Muslims, converts and heretics, once again, played a disproportionate role in these mini-renaissances.

Al-Biruni (973-1050), a famous astronomer in Afghanistan, was a Persian Shi'ite accused of agnostic leanings. Another Persian freethinking astronomer was Umar al-Khayyam (1038-1123) who attained even greater fame as a poet. Two centuries later the Syrian Jacobite Christian, Barhebraeus also did notable work in astronomy. One of the greatest Muslim philosophers also worked in Persia. This was al-Ghazzali, who before he achieved his great eminence was a practicing Sufi.

Two notable scholars worked in late Abbasid Iraq. One was the geographer Yaqut (1179-1229) who was a Greek converted Christian. The other was the historian Sibt ibn-al-Jawzi (1186-1257) the son of a converted Turkish slave.

Under the Fatimid, Ayyubid and Mamluk dynasties, Egypt which had been a scholarly backwater since the Muslim conquest, became the intellectual center of the Arab world. Of course, the minor intellectual flowerings, encouraged by new dynastic rulers, paled in comparison to the earlier Baghdad renaissance. Clearly the flame of Muslim learning was growing dim. The scholar Al-Kindi (d. 971) was described at this late date as an Egyptian and, therefore, was presumably from a family of recently converted Copts; he was noted for his historical works. Another Fatimid intellectual was the Vizier, Ibn-Killis, a converted Jew who established an academic institute. In the late 12th and 13th centuries three Egyptian Jews attained fame as physicians: Jami (ca 1190), his contemporary al-Naqid, and al-Kuhin al-Attar (ca 1260). Al-Khuzai al-Mawsali (ca 1310) was a converted Christian or Jew who achieved some literary eminence under the Mamluks. Finally, in late Mamluk times the noted historian ibn-Taghri-Birdi (1411-69), was the son of a Turkish slave woman.

Islamic Spain has a reputation for intellectual accomplishment almost as great as that of Baghdad at the height of Abbasid rule. But the experience of Islamic Spain is similar to that of Baghdad, with a brief period of creativity following re-establishment of peace and stability after the conquest, followed by a sharp decline. The founder of the Spanish Umayyad dynasty, Abd-al-Rahman, seized control half a century after the Moorish conquest and laid the foundation for the flowering of Andalusian civilization. He diligently strove to "fashion into a national mould Arabians, Syrians, Berbers, Numidians, Hispano-Arabs and Goths ... and in more than one sense did he initiate that intellectual movement which made Islamic Spain from the ninth to the eleventh centuries one of the two centers of world culture."

However, there was a considerable lag until Spanish intellectual achievement reached its apogee. Most of the greatest figures of the Andalusian enlightenment only make their appearance beginning with the eleventh century, some three centuries after the initial conquest and over two centuries after the establishment of an independent dynasty. In the Arab East, on the contrary, the great age of achievement commenced within a century and a half of the conquest. One of the reasons for the Spanish lag was, undoubtedly, the continuing conflicts which plagued a territory that was only partially conquered. It was the continuing Christian resistance by Navarre, Leon and their Frankish allies that "generated Muslim distrust of the Christian majority and resulted in their widespread exclusion from governmental posts." Hence the Muslim rulers of Spain were not, at first, able to fully capitalize on the abilities of their large Christian population. In the Islamic east, on the other hand, the fully subdued non-Muslim population posed no such threat. Furthermore, in Spain "Muslim-Christian tensions were further exacerbated by the bitter enmity between Berbers and Arabs ... as well as by a series of social and religious grievances ... and numerous squabbles among the unruly slave soldiers" and the imported "rivalry between the two great tribal leagues of Qays and Yemen." It was only in the early tenth century that Abd-al-Rahman III temporarily suppressed these conflicts and felt strong enough to proclaim himself caliph. It was during his reign that the first great scholars appeared and began the fabled intellectual flowering of Moorish Spain.

One other reason for the lag may be that the Christians of Spain were at a lower level of learning and culture than were the Eastern Christians. This may well may account for the greater prominence of Jewish scholars in Spain's golden age, as compared with that of the golden age of Baghdad. It was during the caliphates of Abd-al-Rahman III and of his son al-Hakam that "many Jews came from the East" and that "Cordova became the centre of a Talmudic school whose foundation marks the beginning of the flowering of Andalusian Jewish culture." These Jews were instrumental "in the translation process, which brought the fruits of medieval Islamic Hellenism into Europe."

These Jewish migrants illustrate once again a common Islamic pattern whereby the founder of a new dynasty will seek to enhance his prestige by attracting or inviting refugees including many scholars into his domains. Thus, Spain became a repository of high culture at times when various eastern scholars, Syrians, Jews or political refugees were subject to repression or persecution. Darlington notes this diffusion of intellectuals and artists to the periphery of the Islamic world:

> And with the extension of Islam, repeated, under successive races of conquerors, the artisans of Damascus, Muslim or infidel, might be found in later generations practising their skills in Toledo or Samarkand and contributing to the uniform spread of what was now known as Islamic civilization.

One such refugee intellectual was Ziryab who was forced to flee from his enemies at the court of Harun-al-Rashid. Seeking "to make of Cordova a second Baghdad", Abd-al-Rahman welcomed the exiled young Persian minstrel who was also a poet, astronomer and geographer.

Therefore, the relative lag and later efflorescence of intellectual activity in Spain and elsewhere on the Muslim periphery may also be due to the slow migration of artisans and intellectuals out to the Muslim frontier which offered better opportunities for patronage and a refuge from the gathering clouds of persecution in the heartland of Islam. The magnet offered by Umayyad Spain may also partly explain the relative paucity of intellectual achievement in Syria as compared to Iraq under the early Abbasids. This may be the result of the transfer of Syrian high culture to Spain. Under the Abbasids many Syrians would have found a Spain dominated by their kinsmen a more congenial place. Indeed Spain may in that period be regarded as an extension of Syria and its great period of intellectual achievement was partly due to displaced Syrian energy.

The following are significant scholars of non-Muslim origin or of heretical orientation who were from Muslim Spain or the neighboring Maghreb. These are, once again, obtained from Hitti's thorough and authoritative History of the Arabs. The ninth century Cordovan writer Abd-Rabbih (860-940) was reportedly descended from a slave freed about sixty years before his birth. The seminal tenth century saw the rise of a school of philology in Cordova. One of its leading lights was al-Qali (901-67), an immigrant from Baghdad reputedly of Armenian birth. Another was the Jew Judah ben-David who died in 1010. Eleventh century Cordova, the capital of the now declining Umayyad caliphate witnessed a great upsurge in intellectual achievement. The historian Ibn-Hazm (994-1064), the grandson of a converted Christian was active at this time. Astronomical studies were pursued by Al-Majriti (ca 1007) and Al-Karmani (ca 1066), both described as Hispano-Muslims and, therefore, presumably of recent non-Muslim descent. Their contemporary, the astronomer Al-Zarkali, a Jew worked in the city of Seville. Another Jew, Ben-Shaprut (ca 1013), was active in the study of medicine in Cordova during this period.

At the height of the Umayyad caliphate the city of Seville was home to the poet Ibn-Hani (937-73), regarded as a heretic tainted with the opinions of the Greek philosophers. Three centuries later, during the decline of Spanish Islam, that city was home to another distinguished poet, the converted Jew, Ibn-Sahl.

The eleventh and early twelfth centuries witnessed the high point of intellectual activity in Muslim Spain. Beginning with the eleventh century, intellectual activity diffused away from the one-time center, Cordova. Although the relatively tolerant Umayyads and "party" kings were followed by the puritanical Almoravids and Almohads, the latter continued to patronize and tolerate Muslim scholars and philosophers. Non-Muslims, however, experienced a period of intense persecution with a consequent diminishment in scholarship. Before the advent of the fanatical Berber dynasties, the city of Valencia was home to the famous Jewish philosopher Ben-Gabirol (Avicebron) (1021-1058). A few decades later, the avowed atheist philosopher Ibn Bajjah (Avenpace), worked in Granada. One of the most renowned philosophers, the Jewish physician Maimonides was forced by the Almohads to flee to Cairo in 1165. At this time Seville was the site of the astronomer Ibn-Aflah, described as a Hispano-Muslim and presumably of recent non-Muslim background. Another Hispano-Muslim astronomer was Al-Bitruji, who worked a half century later. The Hispano-Muslim botanist Al-Ghafiqi, a contemporary of Ibn-Aflah did his work in the city of Cordova.

After 1150, the Andalusian flowering entered a period of terminal decline. However, while orthodox Muslims largely ceased their scholarly activities the large non-Muslim population joined by a number of heretical Muslims continued their intellectual pursuits in certain localities, notably the city of Seville. The latter location was home to the mystical Sufi philosopher Ibn-Arabi (1165-1240). Another Sufi philosopher, Ibn-Sab'in (1217-1269) worked in the city of Ceuta on the other side of the Strait of Gibraltar. Seville also was the city of the greatest philosopher of the Muslim west. Ibn-Rushd (Averroes) (1126-1198) is widely regarded by orthodox Muslims as a heretic. Averroes is described by Trifkovic as follows:

On the other side of the Empire, in Spain, Averroës exercised much influence on both Jewish and Christian thinkers with his interpretations of Aristotle. While mostly faithful to Aristotle's method, he found the Aristotelian "prime mover" in Allah, the universal First Cause. His writings brought him into political disfavor and he was banished until shortly before his death, while many of his works in logic and metaphysics had been consigned to the flames. He left no school...

Averroes' mentor, Ibn-Tufayl was a follower of the atheist Granadan philosopher Ibn-Bajjah.

A number of scholars from Spain and the Maghreb were patronized or granted refuge by nearby Christian rulers. Constantine the African (ca 1087), apparently a member of the rapidly vanishing Christian community of North Africa brought the medical learning preserved in the Islamic world to Italy. Two centuries later the Jew Faraj ben Salim translated the medical works of the heretic Razi under the auspices of the rulers of Sicily.

The Turkish conquerors also "mined" their non-Muslim population resources for their administrative, technical and intellectual skills. The Seljuk sultans maintained a chancellery manned by Greek bureaucrats with the Byzantine administrative title of notaran. This Greek bureau persisted for centuries following the Seljuk conquests. Greek scribes were "maintained not only in the Seljuk administration but also among some of the emirates that succeeded the Seljuk state." Greeks also appeared as ambassadors, tax collectors and even court musicians. Vryonis observes how the economic institutions of the conquering Turks were formed from those developed by Byzantines. At the height of the Seljuk sultanate "those elements of Christian agrarian, commercial and artisanal population which had remained in Anatolia took an increasingly active part in the expanding economic life of the Muslim portion of the peninsula." Moreover a "substantial element of the farming population, indeed the majority, in the Seljuk domains of the twelfth and thirteenth centuries consisted of Christians." Even into the fifteenth century Christian peasants were apparently still a majority of the rural population in many areas as illustrated by the example of the renowned wine produced by Christian villagers in Begshehhir.

Seljuk art was heavily dependent on, if not actually dominated by, Greek Christians and recent converts. The great

Sufi master Rumi had within his circles the famous painters Kaloyani and 'Ayn al-Dawla Rumi. The latter artist, who was elaborately praised by the Turkish chronicler Eflaki, was personally converted to Islam by Rumi. The textile industry was dominated by Greek, Armenian and Syrian craftsmen. Greeks, as well as Syrian Christians, served as physicians to the Seljuk ruling class. Greek and Armenian technicians dominated the Seljuk mining and metallurgy industries. Greek shipwrights, sailors and navigators dominated both Seljuk and early Ottoman maritime activities. Vryonis observes that,

> Greek mining communities of Anatolia were quite active in Ottoman times... a Greek goldsmith ... taught the craft of jewelry making to the sultan Selim I. It was Greeks who introduced the Turks to maritime life ... It is everywhere discernible, from the first Turkish fleet that was built by Greek Smyrniotes in the eleventh century down to the establishment of the first Ottoman naval arsenal in Europe in the fourteenth century.

It was the field of architecture that was the most important expression of Turkish high culture. By the time of the final Turkish conquests of Byzantium, the Muslim world had fallen behind the Europeans in science, technology and art. The days of the high Arab culture and scholarship were gone. However, architecture was one field in which the now Turkish led Muslim world could still excel. But, as was the case with Arab science, it was non-Muslims or recent converts that were also the driving force in this field. There is substantial "evidence that side by side with Muslim architects there were active certain Christian architects and architects who though Muslims were converts." The Sufi saint Rumi who employed a Greek architect and Greek masons for work on his house provides devastating testimony regarding the superiority of craftsmen of Christian origin over those of Turks. He is quoted, in once instance, explaining "the desirability of using Greek rather than Turkish masons."

There were a number of famous Christian architects in Seljuk and early Ottoman times as detailed by Vryonis. The Greek architect Thyrianus worked in the Seljuk domains in the early 13th century. In 1215 Sebastus rebuilt the walls of

Sinope. Kaloyan al-Qunewi (ca 1270) worked in Konya. At a later date Nikomedianous was prominent in the court of the Ottoman sultan Orhan I. The architect Keluk ibn Abdullah was an Armenian convert.

The Turks were famous for the gulam and devshirme systems, an inventive addition to the existing Muslim institution of slavery. Vryonis notes that much "of the vitality of both the military and the administration derived from the system by which the Ottomans took the cream of the Christian youth, converted them to Islam, and then trained them to wield the sword and the pen." Large numbers of children were confiscated from their families and educated as administrators, artisans and soldiers in the employ of the Sultan's government. "These gulams and devshirmes were fully integrated into the life of Muslim Anatolia, as is witnessed by their tremendous contribution to the military, administrative, religious, and cultural life of Anatolia." The following are some of the gulams of Greek origin who achieved fame and distinction in the 13th century. Karatay held a number of important posts under the Seljuk sultan. He was also a tutor to the royal children, a disciple of the mystic poet Rumi and a patron of architecture and learning. Amin al-Din Mikail was a Seljuk financial administration innovator who was also famous for his general great knowledge. Shams al-Din Hass Oguz was a writer and calligrapher who was renowned for his magnificent literary and artistic style.

Mehmed the conqueror of Constantinople made good use of infidel resources in achieving his great conquests. "The help the Ottomans received from Christian subjects, mercenaries, converts, and technical experts was a theme of repeated lament for the European chroniclers." The Slav troops that Mehmed drafted for the siege of Constantinople included a band of skilled miners. These included Saxon technicians whom Mehmed put to use in tunneling under Constantinople's walls. The Hungarian Orban went to work for Mehmed the conqueror as his chief cannon maker. "The Ottomans were probably already casting guns at Edirne by this time; what Orban brought was the skill to construct the molds and control the critical variables on a far greater scale." The historian of the siege, Crowley, notes the importance of non-Muslims in building the Conqueror's navy:

> The empire had acquired an experienced resource of shipwrights, sailors and pilots, both of Greek and Italian origin, as it rolled up the coasts of the Black Sea and Mediterranean, and this skilled manpower could be brought into play in naval reconstruction.

Bernard Lewis confirms this dependence of the Ottomans on European military technology. It was "the Ottomans among Muslim states" that "made full and effective use of musketry and artillery, but even they ... were dependent on Western technology and, to an increasing extent, relied on Western renegades and mercenaries to equip and direct their artillery."

Once his life's ambition was accomplished through the use of both Islamic fanaticism and infidel greed, the irreligious and cynical Conqueror now saw that the Greeks "could be an asset to his empire, having an aptitude for industry, commerce, and seamanship which the Turks did not share." The relative incapacity of the Turks was, thus, acknowledged by their greatest warrior. When one considers the preponderant amount of Greek and other infidel blood flowing through the veins of Muslim Turks the suspicion naturally arises that this Turkish intellectual incapacity can only be explained as a result of Islam.

Mehmed, aspiring to the role of a Renaissance Italian duke, initiated and patronized a flurry of activity in architecture, painting, and sculpture. He encouraged scholarship and learning which flourished under the early Pax Ottomanica. Many of these scholars and artists were Greek; many others were Italian such as the Venetian artist Gentile Bellini. Medicine was also "largely undeveloped among the Turks, and the Sultan's own medical advisers were for the most part Jews from Italy." One aristocratic captive from Trebizond, George Amirutzes "was a distinguished philosopher and scientist, and he became Fatih's instructor in geography, astronomy and astrology." However, all of the Conqueror's painstaking collecting and scholarly patronage tragically came to naught. "All these works of the Renaissance were to be removed as 'indecent' after Mehmed's death by his iconoclastic son Bayezid II" and most of them vanished except for one portrait of the Conqueror which was, fortuitously, purchased by a Venetian merchant.

The height of Ottoman civilization occurred in the reign of Suleiman the Magnificent who "raised to its peak an oriental civilization deriving from nomadic, tribal and religious origins." Architecture was the expression of this height.

Here was the full flowering of that architectural tradition which Mehmed the Conqueror had first evolved from that of Byzantium ... Providing a link between those two contrasting civilizations, it attained its peak with the work of a man who now ranks ... as one of history's great architects. This was Mir-mar Sinan, the son of a Christian stonemason from Anatolia...

In addition to the great Armenian architect Sinan, other leading lights of Suleiman's court were of recent non-Muslim origin. These include the great admiral-corsair Barbarossa who was Greek. One of his grand viziers was also Greek while another was a Slav.

The history of printing in the Ottoman lands illustrates both the disrepute into which innovation fell and the continuing dependence of progress on the efforts of men of non-Muslim origin. Islamic attitudes inevitably hardened with the passing of the more tolerant or at least more intellectually curious rulers, such as Mehmed. In fact, there were printing presses in the sixteenth century set up by Jewish exiles, Armenians and later Greeks. These were allowed to operate on the condition that they not be used for the sacred Arabic and Turkish languages. However it was left to Ibrahim Muteferrika "a renegade from the Hungarian nobility" who in 1727 brought the first Muslim printing press to Turkey and cajoled or begged the authorities to permit its use. For a brief time "Ibrahim Muteferrika and his press propagated the new ideas and discoveries of European science." However with Muteferrika's death in 1745, printing was once again banned for an additional forty years.

The use of windmills and watermills furnish yet another example of Muslim technological backwardness. Lewis notes how even "primitive" medieval Europe was more technologically sophisticated than many "golden age" Islamic societies. "A comparison between the Domesday Book and the Ottoman imperial registers ... revealed the astonishing fact that there were proportionately more mills in Norman England than in the central Ottoman lands in the days of Suleyman the Magnificent."

In the Seljuk and early Ottoman periods, numerous Christian converts and slaves manned the highest ranks of the administrative bureaucracy. In later Ottoman times power "passed from a ruling institution of renegade Christians to one of predominantly Moslem-born officials" who were rather insular and parochial in outlook. This necessitated the creation of the institution of the dragoman. The high office of Dragoman of the Porte was created in 1669 as a sort of Secretary of State and was reserved for the Sultan's Christian subjects. Around this high official numerous lesser Christian bureaucrats gathered. These Greek Phanariots "were to serve often as ambassadors or as governors of autonomous Christian provinces. Thus, with the passing of the Sultan's Slave Household did the Ottomans continue, without either conscription or enforced conversion, to draw on the abilities of their Christian subjects?"

Early Islamic Persia also had a brilliant cultural flowering fueled by non-Muslims and Muslim heretics. Indeed, as we have seen, Persian infidels or recent converts played a major role in the translation of Greek works in Abbasid Baghdad. There was a similar effort to translate Persian scientific and philosophical works into Arabic:

> The transition from the Sasanian to the Islamic era in the sciences is marked by the period of translation from Graeco-Syriac, Pahlavi and Sanskrit sources into Arabic. In this very important process the majority of translators were Christian and Harranian, but the Persians also had a major role, especially in making available works of Pahlavi in the Arabic

language, which the Persians ... adopted rapidly as the scientific and philosophical language of discourse.

Furthermore, certain powerful families of Persian converts, in particular the Barmakid and Naubakht families, acted as patrons and supporters of the scholars undertaking this work. This work continued at a later time under the native Samanid dynasty. Jaihani the Samanid Prime Minister from 914 to 922 wrote on geography and patronized geographers, astronomers and other scholars. "Jaihani, who had been suspected of harbouring Shi'i beliefs or even Manichaean dualist tendencies ..., was removed from office."

The Muslim rulers of India, eventually found that utilizing the talents of the despised "idol worshippers" was more profitable than slaughtering them. In fact maintaining even a minimal level of civilized life depended on the effective exploitation of Hindus, heretics and recent converts. In the sultanate of Delhi, ca 1330, "most trade, most industry and all financial services remained in Hindu hands." The experience of the Delhi sultans paralleled the situation in the Ottoman Empire where such activities were most effectively carried out by Greeks, Armenians and Jews.

The fragmentation of Muslim authority in India opened up new opportunities for scholars and technicians:

As Delhi's authority declined, aggressive new sultanates on India's Islamic frontier in Bengal, Gujarat, Malwa and the Deccan boosted the market for military personnel and offered even better prospects for plunder... Scholars, jurists and artisans gravitated towards the more generous patronage on offer.

This competition between Indian Muslim states creating a temporary 'boom' in intellectual achievement was similar to the circumstances creating the high level of scholarship that existed in Spain during the Umayyad caliphate. In Spain, the eagerness of the Umayyads to increase their prestige at the expense of their eastern rivals spurred them to collect Muslim, infidel and heretic scholars from all over the Islamic world.

The high civilization that existed under the Mughal sultans depended heavily on non-Muslims. The Mughal "synthesis of Indian and Islamic traditions and their eagerness to enlist the support of Hindu subjects" was crucial to their empire building as well as to their architecture, poetry, painting and music.

PRACTICALITY OF EARLY MUSLIM RULERS

One factor underlying the early accomplishment of Islamic civilizations was the pragmatism of the early conquerors. They were willing and even eager to partake of those ideas and technologies of the vanquished cultures that were of obvious practical use. During the period of translations from the Greek "the criterion of choice was usefulness; they translated what was useful ... medicine, astronomy, chemistry, physics, mathematics, and also philosophy, which at that time was considered useful." Medicine has an obvious use and is valued in all civilizations. The sciences and mathematics have obvious uses in industry, agriculture, architecture, navigation and, of course, warfare. Philosophy was found useful by Muslim scholars for the defense, propagation and reinforcement of Islamic doctrine. However, Greek literature and art had no such use. As Lewis observes:

> ...we find no poets, no dramatists, not even historians. ... you take what is useful from the infidel; but you don't need to look at his absurd ideas or to try and understand his inferior literature, or to study his meaningless history.

Hitti notes that no "close contact was ... established between the Arab mind and Greek drama, Greek poetry and Greek history. In that field Persian influence remained paramount." Yet it is these unpractical subjects that give a culture its spirit and the ideological basis for advances in the more useful arts and sciences. The questions regarding man's place in the universe, his relationship with the gods etc., raised by Greek dramatists and artists are instrumental in shaping the social attitudes that predispose a culture toward scientific and technological endeavors. As the philosopher Jacob Needleman puts it regarding the importance of the poetic impulse in science:

The impulse to understand, to learn the meaning of what is alive, whatever form it takes: surely this is what science once touched in us. Its power in the Western world does not originally come from the benefits of technology, but because it alone ... once called forth this impulse in man to understand the whole of life...

Indeed, it may be conjectured that without the impulse of great writers and artists, there was nothing to counteract the increasing rigidity that Islamic law imposed with the passage of time; a rigidity that ultimately stifled all expressions of Muslim accomplishment. The later Ottomans showed a similar pattern of pragmatism in their translation period from the 16th to the 18th centuries. However, among the Turkish elite philosophy was no longer considered useful and European history was. By the 16th century, Islamic dogma was fully crystallized, so that philosophy was no longer regarded as useful, although a wayward sultan like Mehmed the Conqueror may have at one time indulged himself by dabbling in it. On the other hand, the successful Western counterattack made the study of their history a matter of some urgency.

Muslim scholars and scientists could attain considerable expertise in those fields of great interest and usefulness. "The study of the horse formed one conspicuous exception" to the lack of advancement in zoology "and was developed almost to the rank of a science." The example of such a narrow field of science demonstrates how Muslim curiosity was directed chiefly at utilitarian ends; knowledge of the horse having immediate advantages in warfare and trade. However, even in a subject of such intense interest, Arabs were still largely indebted to the work of non-Muslims. For "although the Arabs since Bedouin days possessed an extensive empirical knowledge of diseases of camels and horses, yet their more systematic knowledge and improved technique must have come from Byzantine sources."

The admission of exiled Jews into the Ottoman realm is an example, par excellence, of Islamic pragmatism. Sultan Bayezid II (1481-1512) was shrewd enough to recognize the benefits provided to his empire by the Jews expelled from Spain. He "welcomed the talented Sefardim into his realm ... Bayezid and his courtiers are said to have considered Ferdinand of Spain a fool for impoverishing his own kingdom while enriching theirs. Some of the Sefardic immigrants ... helped the Turks to produce their own cannon and powder."

MYTH OF THE WESTERN DEBT TO ISLAM

A persistent misconception, the debt western science and scholarship owes to Islam, has afflicted historians for many years, although never more so than at the present time. The historian Herbert Muller, writing at a time when academic candor was still common, debunks the belief in the preservation and transmission of science under Islam, as well as a few other widely cherished myths.

> For the sake of understanding ... I should say flatly that these high-minded apologists for Islam are talking about a fiction or a dream. The religion preached by Mohammed, and thereafter practiced in his name, is quite different from the Islam they describe. The prophet had nothing of the scientific outlook, and demanded absolute obedience to the law that he alone laid down. Islam never produced a democracy or a state in which the people were actually sovereign. In all states, past and present, economic inequality has been glaring. Its holy wars fought on principle, its degradation of women, and its formal acceptance of slavery make nonsense of its theoretical principle of equality, or any profession of universal human brotherhood.

Other historians and philosophers echo Professor Muller's viewpoint. Charles Burnett writing in The Cambridge Companion to Arabic Philosophy refutes the belief that it was the Arabs who re-transmitted Plato's Republic to Europe. "The Republic of Plato, though translated into Arabic, was not subsequently translated into Latin." Frederick Copleston in his History of Philosophy says that "it is a mistake to imagine that the Latin scholastics were entirely dependent upon translations from Arabic or even that translation from the Arabic always preceded translation from the Greek." Moreover, "translation from the Greek generally preceded translation from the Arabic." Another historian of philosophy Peter Dronke concurs:

Note that Latin versions of a number of learned Greek works (Euclid, Ptolemy) came through translations from the Arabic; most of the works of Aristotle, however, were translated directly from the Greek, and only exceptionally by way of an Arabic intermediary...translations from the Arabic must be given their full importance, but not more. Another confirmation comes from Dod, according to whom the following were first translated from Greek: Categories, De interpretatione, Prior Analytics, Posterior Analytics, Topics, Sophistici elenchi, Physics, De generatione et corruptione, Meteorologica (Book IV), De anima, De sensu, De memoria, De somno, De longitudine, De inventute, De respiratione, De morte, De animalibus (De progressu, De motu), Metaphysics, Nicomachean Ethics, Eudemian Ethics, Politics, Oeconomica, Rhetoric, Rhetorica ad Alexandrum, and Poetics. Only the following were first translated from Arabic: De caelo, Meteorologica (Books I-III), and De animalibus (Historia, De partibus, De generatione).

Furthermore, as Franz Rosenthal points out, many of the works translated from the Arabic were not the work of Muslims. "Aristoteles latinus" by Bernard Dod, a of The Cambridge History of Later Medieval Philosophy, provides a comprehensive list of medieval translations of Aristotle from Arabic into Latin, none by Islamic scholars -unless by "Islamic" one means "Christian or Jewish." Indeed, in Islamic Spain it was Jewish scholars who were instrumental in translating Greek knowledge into Latin. Carson sums up the reality of the translation process as follows:

So the great rescue of Greek philosophy by translation into Arabic turns out to mean no rescue of Plato and the transmission of Latin translations of Arabic translations of Greek texts of Aristotle, either directly or more often via Syriac or Hebrew, to a Christendom that already had the Greek texts and had already translated most of them into Latin, with almost all of the work of translation from any of these languages into any other having been done by Christians and Jews and none of it by Muslims.

Moreover, the most important preservers and transmitters of classical knowledge were not Muslims, or even *dhimmis* working in Muslim lands. While much has been made of Muslim Spain as a transmitter of ancient Greek knowledge to the West few have remarked on how the Byzantines transmitted Greek knowledge to Muslims and non-Muslims alike. The 11th century Byzantine scholar Psellus "remarked at the height of his career that Celts, Arabs, Persians and Ethiopians came to Constantinople to hear his lectures." And it was these same Byzantines, who at the time of the tragic destruction of their city brought this knowledge to the West. As the famous historian Steven Runciman observes:

> ...these refugee Greek scholars ... took trouble to collect and copy the Greek manuscripts that Byzantium had preserved. ... It was from these scholars... that the men of the Renaissance learnt most of their philosophy. ... They conserved ancient books ... and transmitted what they had conserved for the benefit of European civilization.

IMPERIAL CONSEQUENCES: PEACE, TRADE AND CROSS FERTILIZATION

The victory of the holy warriors of Islam and the economic recovery of the conquered territory was followed by a resumption of the civilization of the native population under Muslim auspices. In addition, Muslim rulers were able to capitalize on the different specializations of the conquered groups and on a division of labor based largely on ethnicity. Furthermore, the inclusion of the new territory within the trading network of a much larger Muslim empire created a brief period of intellectual and technological advancement due to the cross fertilization of different cultures.

In the case of the Abbasid cultural flowering, Hourani notes that "as the Abbasid caliphate brought the lands of the Indian Ocean and Mediterranean Sea into a single trading area, so too the Greek, Iranian and Indian traditions were brought together, and it has been said that 'for the first time in history, science became international on a large scale. Of course, for this Islam must be given its' due, however, this advancement was caused by the fact that for a while under the Pax Islamica different ideas cross-fertilized each other. It was not due to anything inherent in Muslim civilization itself, but it did give the appearance of a brilliant Islamic civilization for a brief period of time. Social scientist Charles Murray provides additional details regarding the process of this intellectual ferment:

> The extraordinarily rapid rise of the Arabic empire provides a number of reasons for the ignition of the burst of activity. First, the empire brought the neglected raw materials of the ancient world under one roof. In the words of historian Thomas Goldstein, 'A Muslim could study, from records preserved on his own soil, the astronomies of India, Babylon and Egypt; Indian and Persian mathematics; the philosophical concepts of the Greeks; the medicine, geography, astronomy, and mathematics of the Hellenistic age; the botanical, pharmacological, zoological, geological, and geographic lore amassed by the ancient world as a whole.' The trade routes and commercial centers ... of the Arab world made these materials accessible to scholars across the empire and encouraged cross-fertilization of ideas. ... Initially, the Islamic elites engaged the cultures they conquered undefensively, flexibly, and curiously.

Muslim empire builders were not unique in bringing about the cross fertilization of ideas from widely distant cultures. An apt comparison can be made to another extraordinary group of nomadic conquerors, the Mongols:

> The energy and genius of the relatively small number of people who were at the core ... have baffled historians ... just as the effects, ranging from horrifying massacres and devastations to periods of admirable cross-cultural exchange and stimulation, have never ceased repelling and attracting them.

The results of the conquests of these non-Muslim nomads were very similar to the various Islamic conquests. However, no historian would presume to write about the "brilliant Mongol civilization".

It was under the Mongols that a Jewish convert to Islam, Rashid al-Din compiled a universal history at the behest of the khans Ghazan and Oljetu. "He assembled a team of collaborators, including two Chinese scholars, a Buddhist hermit ... a Mongol specialist in tribal tradition, and a Frankish monk, as well as some Persian scholars, and with their aid, he wrote a vast history of the world from England to China."

In addition to the importance of non-Muslims and recent converts, this shows how, once peace was established, the Mongol empire also promoted intellectual advance through cross fertilization of ideas from its many conquered territories. Lewis notes that "the Mongols united, for the first time under one dynasty, the civilizations of the Middle East and of the Far East, with immediate and beneficial effects both for trade and culture." No one, however, attributes these achievements to Mongols or to Mongol culture or ideology.

Furthermore, the vaunted Muslim "tolerance" pales in comparison with that of the bloody-minded Mongol rulers. Jewish and Christian officials served in the Mongol administration. The apogee ... came during the reign of Arghun Khan (1284-91). ... Only a few years before ... the Jewish oculist and philosopher Sa'd b. Kammuna had written a comparative study of Judaism, Christianity, and Islam ... The publication of such a book in Arabic would have been unthinkable when Islam was the ruling faith.Mongol tolerance could survive their savage conquests. But one thing it could not survive was their conversion to Islam. "The Jews and Christians of Iraq and Iran soon returned to their traditional *dhimmi* status when the Ilkhanid dynasty became Muslim once and for all in 1295."

An important spur to the subsequent development of Islamic civilization was the transmission of learning and technology from the distant lands of the East. Chinese technology, obtained through trade or capture, was of great importance. After the Chinese were defeated at Talas, for example, "many captives were brought to Samarkand, where, it is reported, they started a paper making industry."

Of equal or greater importance was the transmission of knowledge from the ancient civilization of India. The most famous and misunderstood example occurs in the field of mathematics. It is casually assumed that algebra and modern number notation were invented by the Arabs. The so-called Arabic numerals were simply systematized from Hindu texts. The famous Arab mathematician al-Khwarizmi wrote two books on arithmetic and algebra ... One of these ... Concerning the Hindu Art of Reckoning ... In this work, based presumably on an Arabic translation of Brahmagupta, al- Khwarizmi gave so full an account of the Hindu numerals that he probably is responsible for the widespread but false impression that our system of numeration is Arabic in origin. ...when subsequently Latin translations of his work appeared in Europe, careless readers began to attribute not only the book but also the numeration to the author. ....ultimately the scheme of numeration making use of the Hindu numerals came to be called ... algorithm, a word ... derived from the name of al-Khwarizmi...

Algebra had a more mixed origin; it was only partly derived from Hindu texts. The word algebra was also obtained from al-Khwarizmi's book Al-jabr wa'l muqabalah. Moreover, in certain respects, the works of al-Khwarizmi were at a lower level than those of his Greek and Hindu predecessors:

...in two respects the works of al-Khwarizmi represented retrogression from that of Diophantus. First it is on a far more elementary level ... and second ... [it] is thoroughly rhetorical, with none of the syncopation found [in the works of Diophantus] ... or in Brahmagupta's work. Even numbers were written out in words rather than symbols! ... Nevertheless, the Al-Jabr comes closer to the elementary algebra of today than the works of Diophantus or Brahmagupta, for the book is not concerned with difficult problems in indeterminate analysis but with a straightforward and elementary exposition of the solution of equations, especially of second degree.

Thus, the Arabs must be credited not with inventing algebra, but with making it more accessible for the solution of simple problems. As for the ultimate origin of modern algebra there are three schools of thought: "one emphasizes Hindu influences, another stresses the Mesopotamian, or Syriac-Persian, tradition, and the third points to Greek inspiration. The truth is probably approached if we combine the three theories." Historians of mathematics Boyer and Merzbach conclude:

> It is probable that al-Khwarizmi typified the Arabic eclecticism that will so frequently be observed in other cases. His system of numeration most likely came from India, his systematic algebraic solution of equations may have been a development from Mesopotamia, and the logical geometric framework for his solutions palpably was derived from Greece.

The example of algebra is an ideal case illustrating the role of cultural cross fertilization in the short-lived period of high civilization under the early Pax Arabica. Algebra was derived from a combination of ideas developed by the oriental culture superseded by Islam, the classical learning of ancient Greece, and an impetus from a far-off land, in this instance India that became accessible due to the vast extent of the Arab empire. And, of course, it reached its full development in a land that still contained a majority population of non-Muslims and recent converts who were well versed in their ancient traditions.

Furthermore, the Hindus had a continuing role in the development of algebra subsequent to al-Khwarizmi as the civilization of the Arabs ossified under the deepening influence of Islam. The "radical sign, and many algebraic symbols" appear to have been invented by the Hindu mathematician Bhaskara in the twelfth century.

Mathematical knowledge was, by no means, the only contribution India made to the golden age of Arab culture. Will Durant notes how the Muslims "took much of this Hindu chemical science and industry to the Near East and Europe; the secret of manufacturing 'Damascus' blades, for example, was taken by the Arabs from the Persians, and by the Persians from India." He also notes that India contributed much medical knowledge to the Arabs. "Haroun-al-Rashid accepted the preeminence of Indian medicine and scholarship and imported Hindu physicians to organize hospitals and medical schools in Baghdad." The technique of vaccination was first developed in India as early as 550 A.D. This practice was adopted by the Muslims and reportedly found its way into Europe from the Ottoman Empire.

There has been much written in certain modern academic circles regarding the "stealing" of ideas by one civilization from another. In no case was this truer than in the wholesale appropriation of India's intellectual treasures by the early Arabs. Keay points out that India's "scientific and mathematical discoveries, though buried amidst semantic dross and seldom released for practical application, were readily appreciated by Muslim scientists and then rapidly appropriated by them. Al-Biruni was a case in point: his scientific celerity in the Arab world would owe much to his mastery of Sanskrit and access to Indian scholarship." It is not a coincidence that the astronomer al-Biruni (973-1050), who worked in Afghanistan and is described as a Persian Shi'ite with agnostic leanings, would be quite open to the study of Hindu works.

4

Muslim Self Sufficiency

From its inception the Muslim community was preoccupied with the Islamic religion in general and the spiritually superior Arab people in particular. Indeed the one undeniable achievement of Islam was the elevation from barbarism of the tribes on the Arabian Peninsula itself; the achievement of which was one of the Prophet's primary goals. As the scholar of comparative religion John Noss observes:

Muhammad gave much thought to the behavior of his followers, and must be said to have legislated for them so comprehensively, and with such a uniform purpose of elevating their morals to a higher level than before – the high level of an inclusive brotherhood instead of the lower level of divisive tribal organization...

There can be no doubt that the "laws prohibiting wine and gambling as well as the regulations covering the relations of the sexes and granting a higher status to women, must have meant to his early followers a considerable change in their way of life." Considering the status of women under Islam, one can surmise that the condition of Arabian women's lives must have been quite oppressive before Islam. From the commandments in the Qu'ran we can infer that female infanticide was widely practiced until prohibited by Muhammad. Unrestricted polygamy must also have been practiced; Muhammad limited this to four wives, required that the husband have sufficient means and that all wives be treated equitably. However, there was no restriction on sexual slavery. He also regularized divorce and granted women the right to at least some fair treatment, presumably correcting the gross abuses that existed until his time. The Arab obsession with their own spiritual and cultural elevation was accompanied by a disdain and disinterest in other traditions, even that of the large numbers of conquered peoples over whom they ruled. For a brief period of time, certain members of the ruling elite patronized scholars to translate and interpret these other traditions, but for the most part this was limited to the immediately practical and useful arts and sciences.

As Lewis notes until "the Mongol conquests, [Muslims] have virtually nothing to say about their neighbors in Asia, Africa, and Europe, and very little even about their own pagan ancestors." This doctrine of Arab supremacy prevented the higher philosophy of the ancient Greeks from becoming truly incorporated into Islamic culture. This was quite different from the attitude of the Romans and later western Europeans who were eager students of the higher Greek wisdom. The Muslims were content with useful technical and scientific knowledge. Some, though by no means all, Muslim schools of theology attempted to co-opt much of Greek philosophy in the service of Islam. A few Muslim rulers, like the quirky Ottoman Conqueror, even engaged Greek scholars in study and discussion. However, while some of the forms might be adopted, Islam had no use for the substance of Greek thought.

The tale of the burning of the Library at Alexandria illustrates Islam's self imposed intellectual isolation. The story that the Library at Alexandria was burned at the orders of the caliph "is one of those tales that make good fiction but bad history. ... Abd-al-Latif al Baghdadi who died as late as A.H. 629 (1231) seems to have been the first to relate the tale. Why he did it we do not know; however, his version was copied and amplified by later authors." The story, though not literal fact, does, however, express an important symbolic truth regarding the attitude the early Arab conquerors had to the accomplishments of earlier civilizations. That may be the reason why it gained such wide currency both within and outside of the Muslim world. Moreover, this early Arab attitude was bequeathed to later Muslim civilizations.

INTELLECTUAL ATROPHY

With the passage of time, and with Islam becoming the dominant majority religion, there began the final phase of Islamic civilization. This phase is characterized by intellectual atrophy leading to economic and technological stagnation. The critic of Islam Robert Spencer is of the opinion that the demise of philosophy and of the rationalist sects such as Mu'tazilism was part of an 'anti-intellectual rage' which afflicted Arab Islam at the end of the golden ages of Baghdad and Andalusia. In addition "the impetus for such a reaction came from the *Qur'an* and Islamic tradition, or it wouldn't have been so strong or long lasting." He theorizes that this reaction is a consequence of fundamental Islamic theology:

> Jews and Christians believe that God created the universe to operate according to reliable, observable laws. While he can suspend those laws, ordinarily he does not do so ... This way of thinking provided a foundation for the edifice of modern science ... But to the Muslim who found all knowledge in the *Qur'an* and suspected philosophers of infidelity, that was tantamount to saying, 'God's hand is chained.' Allah, they argued, could not be thus restricted. ... If one could not rely on the universe to obey observable laws ... science could not flourish.

This view of Islam is echoed by Murray:

> Islam, more than Christianity ... saw God as sustaining the universe on a continuing basis, and as a deity who is not bound by immutable laws. To proclaim scientific truths that applied throughout the universe and throughout time could easily become blasphemy, implying limits to what God could and could not do.

Stillman contends that it was in the thirteenth century that the "secular and humanistic tendencies of Hellenism ... began to wane; at the same time the Islamic religious element in its most rigid form began to wax ever stronger." It would appear, however, that the strengthening of Islam was the cause and not the result of the decline in Hellenism which was the product of the *dhimmi* or recently converted elements in the population. By the thirteenth century those elements had become small minorities in most Arab lands and with the decline in the numbers of non-Muslims the well of Greek thought dried up.

The Islamic scholar G. E. Grunebaum also believed that it was the strengthening of Islam that put an end to the great period of Arab Islamic civilization:

> Islam was never able to accept that scientific research is a means of glorifying God. ... When the religious leadership began to oppose scientific inquiry ... the internalized misgivings of the scientific elites led them to acquiesce. ... During the golden age, the orthodox did not aggressively enforce those aspects of the Faith that discouraged free-flowing inquiry and debate; once they began to do so, Islamic contributions to the sciences effectively ended.

Patai notes the deleterious effects of Islam on the Arab intellect and the premature termination of the Arab golden age:

> The fact remains that under traditional Islam, efforts at human improvement have rarely transcended ineffectuality. In general, the Arab mind, dominated by Islam, has been bent more on preserving than innovating, on maintaining than improving, on continuing than initiating. In this atmosphere, whatever individual spirit of research and inquiry existed in the great age of medieval Arab culture became gradually stifled; by the fifteenth century, Arab intellectual curiosity was fast asleep.

Another factor in Muslim intellectual degeneration was, undoubtedly, the end of imperial expansion. Once the Arab empire reached its maximum extent the temporary bubble in wealth caused by economic expansion, trade, and the flow of technology and expertise, in the early Islamic acumen ceased. Furthermore, considering the extent of the Muslim domains, the wealth expropriated by the Muslim elites, and the number of technologies and variety of ideas available to them, it is remarkable how little in terms of human advancement and accomplishment was achieved by Muslims even at the height of their golden age. Muslim accomplishments were paltry when compared to what was achieved in the small and fragmented cities of Greece, in the divided states of the Indian subcontinent or in parochial and isolated China. Still another factor contributing to Islamic intellectual decline was the tendency toward increasing despotism and the lack of independent centers of power such as church, monarchy, landed aristocracy and urban bourgeoisie typical of many parts of Europe.

The decline in Arab culture occurred quite rapidly. Hitti contends that Arab culture in the eastern Mediterranean was already in decline at the time of the Crusades. The physical sciences ceased to advance once the Abbasid caliphate entered its decline. "The Moslems of today, if dependent on their own books, would have even less than their distant ancestors in the eleventh century." The historical sciences also after the time of the historian Miskawayh (1030) began a rapid decline. There was a simultaneous increase in less intellectually rigorous subjects during this time. "The whole period (11th -12th century) was marked by predominance of humanistic over scientific studies. Intellectually it was a period of decline."

It was the fate of fabled Andalusia that its golden age would be followed, like that of the Abbasids, by intellectual decline. The stage was set when the vizier al-Mansur burned the library of the scholar-caliph al-Hakam in order to please the increasingly powerful and rigidly anti-intellectual Muslim clergy. After another brief period of enlightenment under the party kings, Islamic anti-intellectualism resumed its course under the repressive Almoravids. Not one to be upstaged by the book burnings of al-Mansur, the devout Almoravid 'Ali (1106-43) burned all of al-Ghazzali's works that he could get his hands on in Spain and the Maghreb. The succeeding Almohads were slightly less hostile to scholarly pursuits, but were even more fanatical in driving many Christian and Jewish scholars into exile.

Also inevitable was the decline of the lesser intellectual renaissance that began in Fatimid Egypt, once a center of medical learning. "Egyptian medicine since Ayyubid days was dominated by Jewish physicians carrying on the glorious tradition of ibn-Maymun. But among neither Moslem nor Jewish physicians do we find creative activity." In 1448 the Mamluk Sultan Jaqmaq "prohibited Jewish and Christian physicians from treating Muslim patients. ... Jaqmaq's decree is indicative not only of the decline of the position of non-Muslims in the later Islamic Middle Ages, but also of the waning esteem for Hellenic science and its practitioners." In Muslim North Africa west of Egypt, there were no discernible golden ages at all; only the occasional isolated scholar like ibn-Khaldun or ibn-Battutah. This relative lack of intellectual activity in that part of North Africa was due to the continuing depredations of both Berber and Bedouin nomads and a consequent Islamization of the population that was even deeper than that of Spain or the Arab east.

Both the Seljuk and Ottoman Turks had brief periods of artistic and, to a lesser extent, intellectual glory during the period of stability subsequent to their conquests. However, as Muller notes, Islam was unable to sustain periods of enlightenment for more than a brief time. Their religion made the nomadic Turks a great power ... But it quickens chiefly the military virtues of courage, fortitude, loyalty, and obedience, not so much the qualities that make for sophistication, enlightenment, and creativity. It impedes the continued growth of its converts by the rigidity of its doctrine and discipline. The Ottoman Turks restored an empire to Islam and adorned it with suitable art; but they proved unable to extend or renew its culture, or create a high civilization of their own.

Darlington observes how once the Ottoman Empire's advance was halted, the lack of new *dhimmi* populations to exploit led to its inevitable decline. "As in other Muslim empires no one ever discovered how to organize a process of social promotion that would replace capture and conquest."

One question that remains is why the Ottomans were unable to attain the level achieved during the brilliant albeit brief flowering of Baghdad. To be sure, there was a slight initial efflorescence which expressed itself primarily in architecture and poetry, but few Ottoman subjects reached the level previously attained by many of the scholars of Abbasid Baghdad or Umayyad Spain. This is especially puzzling since the empire of the Ottoman Turks at its height covered an area equivalent in size to that of the early caliphs. One reason may be the chronic and slower nature of the Turkish conquest which exhausted and impoverished the vanquished population. In addition, many of the intellectual elite among the conquered had ample time and opportunity to flee, to the ultimate benefit of Italy and the West. However, the most important reason may be that during the era of the Turkish conquests Islamic thought attained its nadir of rigidity. In the early ages of Baghdad and Andalusia, on the other hand, Islam was still slightly flexible.

In India the high point of Mughal civilization came to an end with the repressive despotism of the bigoted sultan Aurangzeb. Under his intolerant rule discrimination "against Hindus and the active promotion of Islamic values were ... revived." It was no coincidence that during his time "the great tradition of Mughal building virtually ceased."

The inevitable closing of the Muslim mind is symbolized by the ultimate fate of the art collection that was painstakingly accumulated under the patronage of Mehmed the Conqueror. These works were destroyed or sold and dispersed by his pious son Bayezid. That sad event was a repeat of the earlier destruction of the scholarly library of the Umayyad caliph al-Hakam in Cordova at the instigation of the intolerant ulema. Even more tragic was the fate of the unfortunate scientist-sultan Ulugh Beg who, after presiding over a scientific renaissance in Samarkand, was executed at the insistence of the religious authorities. Equally typical of the ultimate fate of Islamic science was the destruction by the Chief Mufti of the great observatory built by Ottoman Sultan Murad III under the direction of the astronomer Taqi al-Din. Another example was the abrupt end of the Mughal renaissance with the death of the tolerant reformer Akbar.

The intellectual deficiency resulting from the Islamic meme continues up to the present day. Thierry Gattuso observes the following with respect to the underachievement of Muslim citizens of Britain:

> The United Kingdom census of 2001 for the first time looked at the nation's religious background. The findings showed that Muslims make up 2.8% of the UK population. Hindus 1%, Sikhs 0.6, Buddhists and Jews both make up 0.5% of the UK population. 31% of Muslims of working age have no qualifications, the highest of any religious group. As in many countries owning your own home is a major achievement and financial responsibility. 82% of Sikhs followed by 78% of Jews own their own home in the UK. Only 52% of Muslims own their own home, the lowest of any religious group. 14% of Muslims are unemployed, compared to 8% of Sikhs and 6% of Hindus. The underachievement of Muslims is even bleaker when you examine where most Muslims, Hindus, Sikhs and Buddhists in the UK come from. 75% of Muslims, 97% of Hindus, 98 % of Sikhs and 69% of Buddhists in the UK are from or have ancestral links to South Asia. Therefore any cultural factors can be largely ruled out when comparing the achievement of Muslims with people from other religious groups. Muslims complain that they have to overcome language difficulties and face discrimination in the UK and state this as a factor in their poor performance. Buddhists, Hindus and Sikhs face the same language and discrimination issues as Muslims, yet their achievements and performance is much better than Muslims.

The underachievement of Muslims should come as no surprise to those of us who understand the true nature of Islam. Everything a Muslim needs to know is in the Koran, Hadith or *Sunnah*. Muslims are not encouraged to seek knowledge and better themselves. Muslims are against progress, modernity and science. Those that control Islam do not want to see Muslims educated as an educated Muslim will apply commonsense and logic to the Koran and see it for what its is, a collection of distorted Bible and Torah stories and in print the mind of a 7th century Bedouin bandit leader.

The following analysis, and that in the next section, assumes a slight knowledge of statistics on the part of the reader. An analysis of IQ data lends support to Gattuso's assertion. The following table compares IQ test data for Turkey, Greece and Bulgaria.

The adjusted scores, which are the result of various studies, show higher scores for Greece and Bulgaria with respect to that of Turkey. The one exception is a study of Greek children from the early 1960s with a score in the middle of the Turkish range. The overall score which is a summary of the studies shows that Turkey lags her European neighbors by two to three points. The use of IQ data from these countries minimizes the effect due to heredity. Genetic factors are unlikely to account for these differences for the following reasons. As we have seen, there was in Turkey extensive hybridization with the Byzantine peoples of Anatolia and a large genetic infusion after the Ottoman conquests from peoples in the Balkans and all along the Black Sea. Similarly, there would have been an inevitable genetic infusion from the Turkish conquerors to the vanquished people of Bulgaria and Greece. The genetic studies of Cavalli-Sforza show the close relationship between modern Turks and adjacent Europeans as shown in his synthetic maps of principal components for Europe and western Asia. Effects due to cultural factors are also minimized. With the exception of religion other aspects of culture and worldview are similar. Music, dance, cuisine, and other traits are likely the remnants of ancient underlying Aegean and Pontic cultures common to all three countries.

Two other observations from the IQ data are of interest. One is the lower scores attained by immigrant Turks as compared to those remaining in Turkey. It appears that immigrant Turks in Europe, who presumably come from smaller cities and rural areas, score somewhat lower than the Turkish population as a whole. Seventy years of Kemalism seems to have raised IQs among a portion of the population up to levels equivalent to those in neighboring Europe. The difference between the immigrant and home populations is noted by Seyran Ates a lawyer for family and criminal law and a women's rights activist in Germany. She observes that the Turkish community in Berlin is very conservative and traditional, much more so than most people in Turkey proper. So there is, among immigrants a regression backwards towards Middle Ages Islam. In addition, IQs in the adjacent countries of Iran and Iraq are lower than that of Turkey. The work of Cavalli-Sforza shows that the genetic distances between Iran, Iraq and Turkey are relatively close. This slight gap may be due to the fact that in both Iran and Iraq Islam has existed many centuries longer than it has in Turkey. Also Turkey has had the benefit of eighty years of enforced secularism.

However, a sample size of three countries is too small to permit rigorous statistical verification. The sample size may be increased by adding those European and Muslim countries bordering or facing each other across the Mediterranean, as well as certain similar adjacent territories. The following table shows the IQs obtained for these countries by a number of studies. These particular countries are chosen to hold genetic and non-religious cultural factors as close as possible. Most of the European and Muslim countries are of Mediterranean racial stock. In almost all of them there has been a long history of genetic interchange. Many of the European countries were partially or completely under Muslim rule for many centuries; others experienced briefer periods of Muslim occupation of or incursions into some of their provinces. In addition, many of the populations of these countries are made up of closely-related racial groups. Some populations are made up of similar Mediterranean racial components. Others have large Turco-Mongolian components in their ancestry: e.g. Bulgaria, Turkey, Iran, and Russia.

The European countries have an average IQ of 94.6 with a standard deviation of 4.89. The Islamic countries have an average IQ of 85.9 with a standard deviation of 2.13. The difference between the two groups, as measured by a standard t test is highly statistically significant. It suggests a difference in IQs due to an Islamic effect of some eight points. This effect might be a result of the fatalistic attitude engendered by Islamic theology in its adherents. It might also result from Muslim child-rearing practices. The long-lasting institution of

Muslim slavery may have left an indelible residue by creating negative attitudes toward work and initiative, including that of intellectual effort. There is the possibility that the greater economic development north of the Mediterranean is the main factor, and if the economic gap narrows the IQ gap will close. However, most of the European countries in the sample are from the least developed parts of the continent, and it is only in the last few decades that they have begun to develop modern economies; a rather short amount of time to produce such a large differential. Of course, these results are only suggestive and further research is warranted.

RISE AND FALL OF ISLAMIC SCHOLARSHIP

Scholarship, science and human accomplishment appear to follow the hypothesized general pattern over time, shown in the following chart, in all Islamic societies.

The general scheme shown above illustrates the changes in the level of civilization in a Muslim conquered territory. Stage A represents the level preceding the Muslim invasion. In stage B the level drops precipitously as the invasion proceeds bringing war, famine, slavery and displacement. In the following stage C, stability is restored under a new Islamic government. The majority of the population consists of non-Muslims and recent converts. The territory becomes part of the larger Islamic community and, with trade and the cross-fertilization of cultures, civilization rises to new heights in a golden age. However, in the following stage D, conversion reduces the non-Muslim population, Islamic law is more rigidly followed, despotism and persecution increase. The Muslim mind closes; the level of civilization declines. In the terminal stage E, there is a general cultural and economic stagnation causing the level of civilization to stabilize at a low level.

To test the above hypothesized path of Islamic intellectual accomplishment, the significant scholarly figures listed in Hitti's authoritative History of the Arabs was compiled. These were arranged by subject matter and time period and it was usually possible to categorize the background of the scholar by the description in the text. The scholarly fields were grouped into the following categories:

i. S: Science, Math, Medicine, Philosophy
ii. H: History, Geography, Social Science
iii. L: Grammar, Literature, Arts
iv. T: Theology, Law

The background of the significant figures fall into the following categories:

i. N: Non-Muslim, Heretic, Sufi, Non-believer, apostate, convert, child of convert
ii. R: Recent: Grandson of Convert or Muslim of Non Arab ethnicity before end of Islamic 3rd century
iii. M: Assumed long family history of Islam or Muslim of Arab ethnicity

The time pattern of numbers of significant figures makes it possible to test the above hypothesis of rise, golden age, decline and stagnation. The background categories measure the impact of non-Muslims, nominal Muslims or heretical Muslims in contributing to Islamic civilization and attainment. In Hitti's terminology when a figure is referred to as, a 'Hispano Muslim', 'Persian Muslim', "Syrian Muslim' etc., this is taken as an indication of relatively recent non-Arab and non-Muslim ancestry, and the figure is placed in category R. Of course, there is no certainty that this is always the case.

However, on the other hand, this is probably balanced in that many of those figures referred to as 'Arab Muslim' or simply as Muslim may well be of non-Arab or recent non-Muslim background; these latter figures are placed in category M. Using this methodology, the following contention is tested:

The handful of famous intellectual figures in Islam, when examined, always turn out to have been either non-Muslim, or a generation or two away from being non-Muslims (so still raised in an intellectual environment of some non-Muslim mental freedom) or if Muslim and from a Muslim family, than very likely a heretic or a freethinker, like ar-Razi.

The analysis is broken into two sets. The first part presents the significant figures from the eastern Arab provinces. Spain and the Maghreb, with their distinct historical experience are analyzed separately. There are 171 significant figures in the Arab east. The following table shows the change in the number of significant figures over time by field.

Literature and the arts peak early; these are heavily concentrated in the first Arab century and then precipitously drop in subsequent centuries. Theology and law are also concentrated in the early years. Undoubtedly this is due to the work on the codification of Muslim law following the death of Muhammad.

The more rigorous sciences peak in the first Abbasid century and continue fairly strong for another two centuries before a steep decline beginning in the second half of the 11th century. History and the social sciences rise more slowly, reach a maximum in the early 10th century and then abruptly drop. Thus, scholarly activity peaks in the 9th through the 11th century.

Significant figures of non-Muslim and recent non-Muslim background make up more than half the total. As indicated above, this result is quite conservative since many of the scholars who are labeled as Arab Muslim, might well be of recent descent from non-Arab converts who were assimilated as clients into Arab tribes. After 1050, with the decline in the non-Muslim population, the number of non-Muslim figures becomes negligible. The table indicates a strong dependence of intellectual achievement on the existence of non-Muslim populations as a source of significant figures.

The following table gives the cross tabulation of background category by field of scholarship. Non-Muslims and recent converts dominate the arts and sciences and constitute almost half of the social sciences. Only theology and law, unsurprisingly, are made up of overwhelming orthodox Muslim percentages.

Restricting the view to the rigorous fields of science and philosophy and to the critical first four centuries yields the following results:

Scientists by Background: First 4 Centuries

N— — — —34

R— — — — —3

M — — — —23

Total — —- 60

Science, math and philosophy in the "golden age" are dominated by non-Muslims or recent Muslims who make up 62% of the total significant figures.

In summary, the above tabulations yield the following conclusions. By the fourth century after the conquest, the number of major intellectuals declines. Non-Muslims or recent Muslims constitute a majority of significant figures until the fifth century. Non-Muslims are a majority in the fields of science/ math/philosophy and arts/humanities and are close to half in the field of history/social sciences. Therefore, the conclusion is that Arab Islamic civilization declines after three centuries as the number of non-Muslims declines and the process of Islamization accelerates. Moreover, this effect is undoubtedly even greater than that shown since many of those categorized as Muslims are likely near descendents of conquered peoples.

Intellectual activity in Spain began with a greater time lag after the conquest than was the case in the Muslim east. This late start may be a consequence of the lower level of pre-Islamic civilization in Spain as compared to that in the East. The golden age beginning in the tenth century was instigated by the establishment of an independent Umayyad caliphate. Two centuries after the inception of the golden age, the fourth century after the conquest, scholarship entered a period of decline which was exacerbated by fanatical Berber dynasties. However, even during the time of the new dynasties and for some years afterward, scholarly achievement was stronger than during the equivalent period in the East. This lateness of the decline in scholarship was likely facilitated by the lower degree of Islamization and the stronger position of *dhimmis* in Muslim Spain. The resistance of the *dhimmi* population in succumbing to Islamization was a result of the continuing existence of the Christian kingdoms that provided a source of refuge for Christian and even Jewish scholars during periods of persecution as well as political pressure and leverage against weakening Muslim rulers. Even so, in the thirteenth century, Islamic civilization in Spain began its terminal decline.

Identifiable non-Muslims, heretics and recent converts number 22 out of 51 significant figures, a proportion somewhat lower than that in the East. However, in Spain it is likely that many more of those who, for lack of further information, must categorized as orthodox Muslims of long standing, are probably of recent non-Muslim descent. In addition, identifiable non-Muslims, heretics and Muslims of recent origin dominate the more rigorous intellectual subjects of science, mathematics and philosophy. Furthermore, the Jewish component of scholars in these fields is greater than that of unconverted Christians; six of the scholars listed are unconverted Jews, while only one is readily identified as an unconverted Christian. This is a much larger percent of Jews than occurs in the East and is another indication of the initial lower level of culture in Christian Spain, as compared to that in the East, at the time of the Muslim conquest.

Syria is quite important in intellectual achievement in the first century when the Damascus based Umayyads were in power. Iraq assumes an overwhelming dominance in achievement during the first centuries of Abbasid rule. Baghdad became the point of concentration for émigré scholars from all over the empire particularly from neighboring Persia. Science/math/philosophy predominated in Iraq. On the other hand, the early numbers in Arabia proper are heavily dominated by poets/musicians. The minor secondary spikes are due to intellectual activity in Egypt and Syria. However, these later spikes in intellectual activity are much dampened. These occur within a century of new dynasties coming to power in those regions.

These secondary spikes are the result of a number of factors. A new dynasty usually improves local conditions after a period of disorder, war or civil strife. These new dynasties are frequently heretical, schismatic, regarded as illegitimate, or of a different ethnic group (Turk, Berber, Kurd, Persian, Caucasus Mamluk etc.) and seek to obtain support from the remaining *dhimmi* population as a counterweight to a hostile orthodox Muslim majority. As we have seen, new locally-based dynasties have a tendency to compete with the Baghdad caliphs in attracting scholars. They also consciously seek to compete in prestige with previous or rival dynasties. Furthermore, they may seek the propaganda value of subsidizing intellectual activity. In addition, a new dynasty may co-opt local talent that would otherwise have flowed to the central government of Baghdad. However, eventually the same pattern of decline sets in for Syria and Egypt following these minor spikes in intellectual achievement. The same effect is also seen in Persia with the native semi-independent dynasties after 850. More recent Persian dynasties and the Turkish dynasties are beyond the scope of Hitti's history.

The inverse relationship between the number of significant figures and the non-Muslim percent of population is evident. Once Muslims pass the fifty percent mark, the number of significant figures per time period drops, never again to approach the Abbasid heights. The following charts show the breakdown of activity in the three provinces of Iraq, Egypt and Syria. Scholarly activity in Iraq, constituting the largest fraction shows clearly the stages of intellectual activity from recovery after the Muslim conquest to peak and inevitable decline. The charts for Egypt and Syria show the later spikes in scholarship under local rulers followed by the same decline. The Fatimids assumed power in Egypt about the year 970. Two centuries later the Ayyubids came to power in both Egypt and Syria followed by the Mamluk dynasty in 1250. The latter, though uncultured and bloodthirsty, had an appreciation for art and architecture. Also clearly shown is the shift in intellectual leadership from Syria to Iraq with the replacement of the Umayyads by the Abbasids in 750.

The conversion curve and significant figures chart for Persia show the minor spike and subsequent decline in scholarly activity resulting from the rise of the native independent Saffarid and Samanid dynasties about the year 875. The numbers of significant figures in the three provinces outside of Iraq are always minuscule and, hence, subject to random fluctuations.

Of course, the absolute number of significant figures does not account for the crucial factor of population size. Increases or decreases in population will affect the number undertaking and succeeding in scholarly endeavors. The following charts show population and significant figures per million for Iraq, Persia, Syria and Egypt.

The rise, peak and decline of the ratio of scholars are obvious for Iraq. The initial decline following the Umayyad overthrow in Syria and the later peaks in the outlying provinces can also be seen.

The following chart shows the rise, peak and decline in the number of significant figures in Iraq and Persia. It encompasses the time period from the early Arab conquests through the rule of the Abbasids and the closely linked local Persian dynasties. Below is a chart of population. The population of the two lands shows almost no variation between 650 and 1250 which is the entire period over which the rise, peak and decline in intellectual achievement occurs. Although the Mongol invasions are often blamed for the destruction of high civilization in these two lands, the number of significant figures declines well before the Mongol depredations of the 1250s caused a drop in population. In fact, population is virtually flat for the four centuries from 800 through 1200. By the year 1200 scholarship had dropped to a lower level than had existed in Umayyad times five centuries before.

The Andalusian golden age commenced about the year 912 when Abdel Rahman III established formal independence by proclaiming himself caliph. Its progress was cut short with the accession of the Almoravids and resumed with the equally fanatical, but somewhat more intellectually curious, Almohads.

The full cycle of Islamic intellectual development in Spain is obscured by the steady decline of Muslim power before the advancing Christians. However, the steady drop in activity beginning with the thirteenth century indicates that the evolution of Islamic civilization in Spain would have closely mirrored that in the eastern provinces.

The largest percent of significant figures occurs in the first few centuries when Muslims were still a minority and begins to decline when the Muslim percent rises above fifty. There is a minor peak after the rise of independent or semi-independent local dynasties, but this is followed by an irreversible decline within two centuries. A linear regression run between the percent of significant figures occurring within centuries and the percent of Muslims in the population shows a strong negative relationship (correlation coefficient 65%) between the two. An increase in conversions of 10% in any century decreases the century's share of significant figures by 1.5%. Regressing the percent of significant figures on the preceding century's percent of Muslims shows an even stronger relationship (correlation of 83%). Pre-Islamic cultural imperatives would be expected to influence a recently converted population.

An increase in conversions of 10% in any century decreases the next century's share of significant figures by almost 1.8%. The most favorable assessment of Muslim civilization that could be made, given these results, is that "Islam provided a sense of purpose and vitality that helped power the achievements of its golden age, but Islam could not accommodate itself to the degree of autonomy required to sustain it."

Two other studies support this general view of Muslim intellectual achievement. The process of rise, peak and decline is also shown in Bulliet's graph which gives the proportional representation of Arab territories in biographical sources. His graph clearly shows the rise and decline of learning in Iraq and Umayyad Syria. And it shows that at the time of new or breakaway dynasties, in Iran, Egypt, Syria, Spain and Anatolia, there was a secondary intellectual impetus. His graph only measures proportions and not absolute numbers of notable figures; it also does not evaluate the importance of these significant figures, so it cannot be used as a real gauge of intellectual accomplishment. Moreover, Bulliet regards the Mongol conquest as an important factor in the decline in scholarly activity, when as seen above, that decline preceded the Mongol invasion.

Another supporting perspective on Islamic intellectual rise and decline occurs in Murray's study of human accomplishment. He presents a graph of numbers of significant figures and index measurements of their achievements for the field of Arabic literature. This graph given for the period 500 to 1300 shows a decline after 1050. "The golden age of classic Arabic literature coincided with the golden age of Arabic culture in general." The peaks in literature occurred in the century from 950 to 1050.

Furthermore, Murray's data permits a comparison of Islamic achievement with that of other civilizations. Given the extraordinary rise in western accomplishment since the Renaissance, a direct comparison of Islamic accomplishment with that of the west would be unable to separate out the general factors involved in western supremacy over the rest of the world, and those factors specifically resulting from Islam. However, additional light can be cast on the pattern of Islamic achievement through a comparison with other civilizations that were also surpassed by the modern west. The following chart shows the percent of significant figures, listed by Murray, occurring in each century between 600 and 1800 for the Islamic world, China, Japan and India. Century percents are used to avoid the complications that would arise by the large variations in population between these territories.

The graph shows that the peak in Islamic civilization occurs in the eleventh century with almost 18% of the total significant figures. The subsequent drop-off is severe. China, after recovering from a low point in the seventh century, has a fairly narrow range of oscillation; the percent drops off toward the end as a result, no doubt, of western pressure. Japan shows a general rise over the centuries prefiguring its entry into western science and technology. India's pattern is of considerable interest. India shows a general downward trend after an early cultural highpoint. It is no coincidence that the decline begins at the time of the Arab invasion of Sind and accelerates in the tenth century with the destructive raids of the Ghaznavids. There is a slight recovery in the eleventh century followed by a new decline, doubtless due to increased Muslim pressure in the late twelfth century with the Ghurid territorial expansion. Finally, the beginning of Mogul rule permits a slight recovery which is greatly accelerated under Akbar's eclectic rule, only to plunge, once again, under Akbar's fanatical successors.

Both the qualitative and quantitative results in this are in conformity with the general pattern of cultural achievement set out in the figure entitled Phases of Islamic Civilization. That pattern is one of recovery from the Islamic jihad, rise, peak and then decline as the *Dhimmi* proportion of the population decreases.

5

The Islamic Reformation

Conventional wisdom holds that the problems brought by Islam to its own adherents and to non-Muslims alike, can only be mitigated through a reformation similar to that which occurred in Christianity beginning in the 16th century. However, the fundamentalist "back to scripture" radical Wahhabi sect is the closest modern Islamic analogue to the Protestant Reformation. And that is certainly not what is meant when the call for reformation is discussed. This contains an outline of those movements in Islamic history which, in one sense or another, have attempted to reform Islam.

KHARIJITES

These separatists, responsible for the assassination of the caliph Ali, viewed "with hostile eyes the political developments occurring behind the scenes among the Moslem leaders" and "concluded that the only sure way of getting the right caliph was to let the whole Moslem world" participate in his election. "It was natural that these fierce puritans" should be slaughtered by the Umayyads. Thus, Kharijitism represented a reaction by Arab grass roots warriors against increasingly remote ruling elite. They embodied the early spirit of tribal "republicanism" against increasing autocracy. Despite the religious fanaticism of this early Wahhabi like group, they in some sense represent the last significant political activity of the free Bedouin spirit.

MU'TAZILITES

In the first centuries following the Arab conquests, increasing numbers of non-Arab converts embraced Islam bringing with them their Hellenistic outlook. Thus, there were spawned within early Islam several movements influenced by pre-Islamic philosophy and theology. The Mu'tazilites "took it for granted that the theological doctrines ... were subject to rational testing. Their reading of translations of works of Greek philosophy made it seem to them a foregone conclusion that no doctrine could be true which did not survive such a test." However, despite a period of support from certain more enlightened rulers, Mu'tazilism could not withstand the inevitable Islamic reaction. Although "the Mu'tazilites did manage to teach the orthodox theologians the value of using a rational method of exposition, the weight of opinion turned against them and the 10th century saw their school come to an end."

The Qadarites were another briefly flourishing movement influenced by pre-Islamic Greek ideas. They "represent a reaction against the harsh pedestinarianism of Islam ... and betray Christian Greek influence."

ISMAILITES

Following the political dispute leading to Shi'ism, a number of extremist Shi'ite sects emerged which presented a challenge to Islamic orthodoxy. These radical Shi'ite mystical movements posed a more enduring attack on orthodox Islam than their rationalist opposites were able to do. These groups often embodied an anti-Arab reaction and a reassertion of Mesopotamian and Persian national aspirations.

Ismail, the first son of the sixth Imam, accused of drunkenness was barred from the succession. His followers, the Ismailites or Seveners remained loyal. They believe that Ismail never died but would return as the Mahdi. "In their fervid belief, Ismail was the very incarnation of God himself, and would soon return." Interpreting the Koran allegorically, they "arrived at an esoteric, hidden doctrine, which was so heretical that they spread it to others only through secret missionary activity."

The Qarmatians were a radical Ismailite offshoot that in the 9th century established a state on the western shore of the Persian Gulf in defiance of the Abbasid caliphate. "Before they finally fell, the Qarmatians set a record of a century of revolutionary violence and bloodshed - all at bottom a kind of vengeance of the Persians upon the Arabs ... a vengeance disguised ... as religious obedience to the will of a divine Imam descended from Muhammad."

Another violent offshoot of the Ismailites was the famous "Assassins" who specialized in political terrorism directed against both Muslims and Crusaders. They now survive as a rather more peaceful sect, half of whose members "have acknowledged as their rightful heads a fabulous line of Khans" including the famous Agha Khan.

SUFIS

Of all the existing Muslim sects, none evokes as much hopeful admiration on the part of non-Muslims as the contemplative and relatively tolerant Sufis. They softened the hard edges of legalistic Islam; many Sufi masters and disciples attempted to humanize Islam's remote and implacable deity. Sufism's vaunted tolerance may be due, in part, to its being a continuance in Islamic guise of older mystical traditions. The modern Sufi popularizer, Idries Shah, contends that Sufism, in a variety of forms long predated the Muslim conquest. "The breakup of the old order in the Near East, according to Sufi tradition, reunited the 'beads of mercury' which were the esoteric schools operating in the Egyptian, Persian and Byzantine empires into the 'stream of quicksilver' which was intrinsic, evolutionary Sufism." Thus, the Sufi "innovation" was a result of the same cross cultural fertilization that resulted in a temporary renaissance of science and technology in the early Muslim empires.

Sufism embodied a number of non-Islamic influences. Neo-Platonism, Gnosticism, Buddhism, and Hinduism provided Sufism with its philosophical foundations. Christian monasticism gave the Sufis a model for organization. Theosophical and pantheistic thought was incorporated into Sufi teachings. Christian teachings influenced Sufism to such an extent that many early Sufis were regarded by orthodox Muslims as crypto-Christians. Besides an almost unseemly affection for the prophet Jesus, the veneration of saints characterized many Sufi orders "especially ... in places where Christians ... embraced Islam more or less superficially."

Such saint worship was in direct conflict with Koranic doctrine. Moreover, the "Sufi eschatological traditions with their Antichrist suggest that the fraternities found many recruits among those newly converted to Islam from the older forms of monotheism." The first great Sufi mystic was Ma'ruf al-Karkhi who before embracing Islam was either a Christian or from the closely related Sabian sect; the Sabians or Mandaeans claimed John the Baptist as their prophet. Another famous early Sufi mystic was "dhu-al-Nun (Man of the fish) al-Misri (the Egyptian), of Nubian parents who died ... in 860." At that time since Nubia was still a Christian land it is likely that al-Misri was also a convert.

The influence of Zoroastrianism, like Christianity, manifested itself in the saint-worship condemned by the orthodox. One famous early Persian Sufi was al-Bistani (ca. 875) whose grandfather was a Zoroastrian priest. Sufi mystical and meditative practices show great similarity to those practiced by Hindu yogis. Buddhist teachings were another school of thought originating in India that was adopted by certain Sufi schools. Al-Bistani, in addition to Zoroastrian influences, brought certain Buddhist doctrines into Sufi thought. "The Aghani has preserved for us at least one portrayal of an unmistakable Buddhistic view of life." The Persian al-Bistani, grandson of a Magian, "probably introduced the doctrine of fana, self-annihilation... a reflection of Buddhist Nirvana." In addition, the school established by an early Sufi of Central Asia, ibn Adham, had "features reminiscent of the asceticism of Buddhist monks."

Since Buddhism was an alien and non-monotheistic religion, those Sufis studying Buddhist ideas were more likely to run afoul of the ulema than were those who stayed with more familiar Christian or Zoroastrian ideas. Noss observes that "a few mystics were not theists. They substituted the realm of truth for Allah; and when the Buddhist influences penetrated Iraq, the Sufis there moved perilously close to atheism ... These and others among the more extreme Sufis were recognized by the Orthodox Moslems as heretics."

At a later time, the Sufism practiced in Anatolia combined Christian teachings with more primitive strains. In Turkey "besides inheriting the old religions of Asia Minor the dervish orders ... have preserved the traces of shamanism which the early Turks brought with them from Central Asia." Sufism in Anatolia also evinced the very opposite tendency. Greek philosophical notions existed alongside the more primal Central Asian shamanism. The famous Bektashi "was a missionary, semiheretical order with Neoplatonic tendencies toward pantheism and mysticism" and "used wine frankly as a means to spiritual intoxication." Their heretical doctrine that was probably most shocking to the orthodox was the unprecedented equality they gave to women.

Syncretism was the inevitable result of the many methods and beliefs that Sufism adopted from other religions and philosophies. This was particularly evident in newly conquered Anatolia. The account of the funeral of the great Sufi saint Rumi "indicates quite clearly that a powerful process of religious syncretism was in dynamic motion by which Christians and Jews were accommodating themselves to this particular Muslim religious fraternity. The very syncretism and mutual accommodation of dervishes and Christians would eventually result in the absorption of a great many Christians through conversion."

In general, Sufism is strongest in those areas where ancient pre-Islamic cultural traits are best preserved. The Sufis continue "to uphold the validity of personal religious response, intuition, the practices of their religious orders, and reverence for sainted leaders. This is true especially in the non-Arab areas and particularly among the Berbers, Persians and Turks." However, Sufism has always been and remains to this day under relentless attack from the champions of orthodoxy. "But even the Sufis have been chastened by Wahhabi Puritanism and orthodoxy; in fact they have abandoned many a practice to which they were once devoted."

A long history of Sufi martyrs attests to the pressure brought to bear by the forces of orthodoxy. The Persian al-Hallaj was executed in 922 for having declared 'I am the truth'. "His crucifixion made him the great Sufi martyr." A later Sufi martyr, al-Suhrawardi, was executed in 1191 at the behest of the normally tolerant Saladin. Apparently, the forbearance of that great Muslim ruler could not extend to someone whose "impassioned prayer" with Neo-Platonic and Christian elements, was regarded by the orthodox as apostasy. A later powerful ruler, Mehmed the Conqueror was unable to save his Persian dervish friend who was burned at the stake by a fanatical crowd instigated by the Mufti. Shortly afterward, the Persian savant's heretical followers were also slaughtered.

One of the most renowned of the Sufi masters was more fortunate, but still barely escaped with his life. Ibn El-Arabi, (ca 1200) despite his outward conformity to Islamic norms was "accused of heresy and worse in Egypt. He narrowly escaped an attempt by a fanatic to murder him."

The history of Sufi persecution demolishes one other myth which passes as conventional wisdom; that being the contention that the official execution of heretics originated under Christianity. As Darlington observes heretics "were crucified by sultans before they were burnt by popes; the first Sufi to die was Al-Hallaj in Baghdad in A.D. 922; and 500 years later there was Badr el-Din" who in 1420 was executed in Konya.

Many Sufi savants and sects eventually accommodated themselves to the implacable forces of orthodox Islam, thereby deflecting persecution. There arose, therefore, what may be termed the other face of Sufism; Sufism has its dark sides. Some Sufi masters with their followers reconciled their mystical doctrines with those of orthodox Islam. Other Sufi sects went beyond simply conforming to theological orthodoxy. Sufis have been generally pacific in contrast to the violent mystical Shi'ite sects. However, certain Sufi sects fully embraced and even exceeded the bellicosity characteristic of Islam in general.

Al-Ghazali was the principal figure who began the redirection of the mystical energies diverted to Sufism into the service of orthodox Islamic scholarship. The masterpiece of this one-time Sufi mystic was Ihya Ulam al-Din. "The mysticism of this work vitalized the law; its orthodoxy leavened the doctrine of Islam." Fundamentally he "employed Greek dialectic to found a pragmatic system and made philosophy palatable to the orthodox school of theologians." Furthermore, in Hitti's view, the "scholastic shell constructed by al-Ash'ari and al-Ghazzali has held Islam to the present day" while western Christendom succeeded in breaking through its own version of scholasticism. However, as shown in a previous the inability of Islam to advance appears to be more fundamental than that of being enclosed in a scholastic shell. As Spencer puts it:

Al-Ghazali's masterwork heralded the beginning of the decline of Islamic philosophy ... Although al-Ghazali himself probably would have disapproved ... The Incoherence of the Philosophers helped reinforce an anti-intellectual strain of thought that was present in Islam from the beginning.

Nevertheless, despite his mystical leanings and his ending the period of creative Islamic philosophy, al-Ghazali became one of the most acclaimed authorities in theology and law. "So successful was this heretic in becoming the virtual father of the Moslem church, that even the most orthodox still call him by the highest academic title known, the Authority of Islam."

Furthermore, al-Ghazali's attitude toward holy war illustrates that not all Sufis were pacific contemplatives:

Indeed, even al-Ghazali (d. 1111), the famous theologian, philosopher, and paragon of mystical Sufism, (who, as noted by the great scholar of Islam W.M. Watt, has been '...acclaimed in both the East and West as the greatest Muslim after Muhammad...”), wrote the following about jihad:

> ‘...one must go on jihad (i.e., warlike razzias or raids) at least once a year...one may use a catapult against them [non-Muslims] when they are in a fortress, even if among them are women and children. One may set fire to them and/or drown them...If a person of the Ahl al-Kitab [People of The Book – Jews and Christians, typically] is enslaved, his marriage is [automatically] revoked...One may cut down their trees...One must destroy their useless books. Jihadists may take as booty whatever they decide...they may steal as much food as they need...’

It was among the Turks that the idea of the warrior Sufi attained its highest development. The ghazis of Anatolia, following the collapse of the Seljuk state were reinforced by “‘holy men,’ sheikhs and dervishes of an unorthodox Moslem persuasion ... and who rekindled Turkish enthusiasm for war against the infidel.” A.E. Vacalopoulos also notes the importance of Sufis both in participating in jihad and in inciting Seljuk and Ottoman ghazis to embark on further conquests:

> ...fanatical dervishes and other devout Muslim leaders...constantly toiled for the dissemination of Islam. They had done so from the very beginning of the Ottoman state and had played an important part in the consolidation and extension of Islam. These dervishes were particularly active in the uninhabited frontier regions of the east. Here they settled down with their families, attracted other settlers, and thus became the virtual founders of whole new villages, whose inhabitants invariably exhibited the same qualities of deep religious fervor. From places such as these, the dervishes or their agents would emerge to take part in new military enterprises for the extension of the Islamic state. In return, the state granted them land and privileges under a generous prescription which required only that the land are cultivated and communications secured.

Under the Ottomans one of the most important dervish

orders, the Bektashi, was particularly "noted for its connection with the Janissaries." However, despite their co-option by orthodox Islam, in some Sufis, even among the militant Bektashis, unconventional views regarding jihad could still be found. One dervish in 1690 went among Ottoman troops on the eve of battle calling them fools for believing in the heavenly rewards promised to jihadists. The story "reflects a widespread suspicion of the dervish orders" and the questioning on the part of the orthodox clergy of Sufism's commitment to basic Islamic doctrine.

HERETICAL MUSLIM SECTS

Some sects have embraced such eccentric theological views that they are regarded by many of the more conventional Muslims as, not merely heretics, but apostates. These sects often provide an expression of the submerged national feelings of peoples conquered by Muslim invaders. Shi'ism has been the source of many of these heretical and apostate movements. Some of these extremist Shi'ite sects are Takhtajis, Qizil-bash and Bektashis of Turkey and the Ali-deifiers of Persia and Turkestan. These sects along with Nusayris, Assassins, Druses and Qarmatians are considered beyond the pale of mainstream Islam even by more conventional Shiites. Some of these Shi'ite sects, like the Sufis, have adopted many doctrines from Christianity. In fact, at least one of these mystical sects, the Bektashi is sometimes regarded as a Sufi fraternity instead of as an independent Shi'ite sect (see above). Other sects add syncretistic elements from Buddhism, Hinduism and shamanism.

The Nusayris or Alawites, "followers of ibn-Nusayr present a remarkable example of a group passing directly from paganism to Isma'ilism." They "consider Ali the incarnation of the deity", possess a liturgy and celebrate a number of Christian festivals particularly that of Christmas and Easter. Another extreme Shi'ite manifestation is represented by the Druses. These began as an "Ismailite sect which originated from the adulation given to the mad Fatimid caliph, Hakim al

Mansur, ... by two of his ministers, who declared him to be a return in the flesh of the hidden Imam, and in fact an incarnation of God himself."

The Ahmadiya, another movement with strong syncretistic elements, regarded as distinctly heretical by the orthodox, was founded by Mirza Ghulam Ahmad who at the end of the 19th century proclaimed himself both Messiah and avatar of the Hindu god Krishna. "But he remained a Moslem in the sense that he said he was not a prophet in himself but only in and through Muhammad." Ahmad rejected the concept of holy war and his followers are both pacifists and "ardent missionaries." The Lahore splinter branch has returned to the Moslem fold by rejecting Ahmad's extreme claims, although they still revere him as a "genuine renewer of religion."

SYNCRETISM

Several religions were founded with certain marked Islamic influences, but are to such a large extent combined with other religious doctrines that they have transcended Islam altogether. Sikhism is a syncretistic religion combining elements of Hinduism and Islam. Sikhism had its start with certain reformers of Hinduism who appeared in India and whose "recurrent efforts of reform were the indirect effects of the severe and militant monotheism of the Moslems." One such was Kabir (1440-1518) who "caught from the Moslems their hatred of idols." Adopting monotheism "he declared that the love of God was sufficient to free anyone of any class or race from the Law of Karma." Kabir was followed by Nanak (1469 - 1538) whose doctrine was "an attempt to combine the insights of two widely differing faiths." He "called his God the True Name, because he meant to avoid any delimiting name ... like Allah, Rama, Shiva or Ganesha." He also removed the Hindu proscription against meat eating. Moreover, although Nanak's sect began as both contemplative and pacific, "yet it was the singular fate of the religion ... to change with the years into a vigorously activist political faith." Under the impetus of Islamic persecution there developed "in full strength a military ardor, a self dedication to the arbitrament of the sword."

Bahaism, a syncretistic offshoot of Ismailism became, like Sikhism, a separate faith. The Persian Mirza Ali Muhammad, calling himself Bab-ud-Din proclaimed that his mission "was to prepare the way for a greater than himself who should come after him and complete the work of reform and righteousness which he had begun." Bab-ud-Din was executed as a heretic in 1850. The next leader, who took the name of Baha'u'Llah, was imprisoned by the Turks. The Bahais "call upon all religions to unite, for every religion contains some truth."

PROSPECTS FOR REFORM

There are, thus, severe impediments to Islamic reform. Following the example of the early Protestants by returning to scriptural roots leads to the rise of fundamentalist sects, such as Wahhabism which are even more fanatically committed to warlike and repressive doctrines. On the other hand, attempts at doctrinal reform seem destined to failure. The movements established by such reformers have either been forced to accommodate themselves to Sunni or Shi'ite orthodoxy, or else have been formally ejected from the main body of Islam as apostasies.

Some of the most troublesome aspects of Islam are deeply embedded within the Islamic meme and, therefore, are very difficult to reform. These include the violence inherent in the doctrine of jihad, the sexual ideology depending on the oppression of women and the intolerance inherent in the doctrine of Muslim supremacy and destiny. There is also the attitude toward labor, the stifling of initiative and innovation and the intellectual atrophy resulting from fatalism, parasitism and slavery. All of these are the very factors responsible for Islam's historical success and growth. Consequently, they have become crystallized in Islamic culture and are, thus, extraordinarily difficult to uproot or to drastically modify.

Perhaps what is needed as a prerequisite of real reform is a rising of consciousness among the masses in the territories conquered by Arabs and their Turkish or Mogul successors which would lead them to embrace with pride the buried and suppressed achievements of their pre-Islamic ancestors. It may be necessary for Muslims to recognize and mourn for the oppression, enslavement, rape and indignities that one fraction of their ancestors imposed on the greater part, often the overwhelmingly greater part, of their ancestral lineage. Secularism and the political disestablishment of Islam would necessarily follow. As Warraq puts it:

> ...this process of historical education ... would lead to a much needed broadening of the intellectual life, a deeper tolerance for other ways of life, a simple expansion of historical knowledge that has remained so limited and narrow. Greater knowledge of the pre-Islamic past can only lead to the lessening of fanaticism. ... The ideas of change and continuity will also have to become a part of the Muslim's consciousness if Muslim societies are to move forward – this will only occur with the recognition of the pre-Islamic past...

Thus far there has been only one Muslim nation, Turkey, where such a program has achieved any real success. Even there, the failure of the Kemalist elite to fully acknowledge their own history and to disestablish Islam in the village culture of Anatolia, may be leading to an Islamic revival. Other secularizing movements, usually established by dictators, have recognized the regressive nature of orthodox Islam on economic and social development. However, the modern personality cults of despots, even fairly benevolent ones like Ataturk, and the superficialities of certain secular elements within the governing and intellectual elite have not, so far, been sufficient for major and lasting reform.

The promoters of change have often recognized that a return to pre-Islamic roots is an essential condition for removing the debilitating effects of Islam. Ataturk and less palatable secularizers like Saddam or Nasser have attempted to undermine Islam by returning to an older pre-Islamic substrate as the basis of a new nationalism. So Ataturk emphasized the Hittite ancestry of the Anatolian Turks; of course he conveniently ignored the more important Greek ancestry because the Greeks were regarded as the current enemy. The Shah held a massive party to celebrate the founding of the Persian Empire by Cyrus the Great. Nasser decorated Cairo with replicas of colossal Egyptian statuary. Saddam fancied himself the reincarnation of Nebuchadnezzar who will, literally, rebuild Babylon. These attempts to uproot and minimize the effects of Islam have, for a number of reasons, seen rather mixed results.

One of the problems with such attempts at reform is that the reformers have always held back from fully acknowledging their history and have been unwilling to confront Islamic attitudes that are firmly rooted in rural villages or urban souls. Thus, the Turks have embraced and mythologized the quite remote history of the Hittites, even claiming against all evidence that the latter were an offshoot of the Central Asian Turkish "sun" people. At the same time, they reject their much more recent Greco-Roman, Byzantine and Armenian heritage. They even refuse to acknowledge their recent history of genocide against Armenian Christians, or their ethnic cleansing of the numerous Greek speaking population of Anatolia which occurred shortly thereafter.

The failures of other secularizing despots have been even greater. Saddam might have seen himself as leading the Babylon of Nebuchadnezzar and Nasser may have thought of himself as carrying on the ancient tradition of the Pharaohs, but neither of them were willing to discard all of the old Arab and Muslim resentments against the western powers and against Christians and Jews. The late Shah may have viewed himself as successor to the ancient Persian emperors, but he was unwilling to accommodate himself to more liberal secular forces and, thereby, helped to bring his radical Shi'ite enemies to power.

Erasure of the pre-Islamic past occurred in almost all conquered lands. It is noteworthy that Muslim peoples, with the partial exception of the Persians, have a singular lack of curiosity regarding the pre-Islamic traditions of their ancestors. This distinguishes Islam from the other supra-national proselytizing religions, Christianity and Buddhism. While the path was sometimes indirect, the last two religions ultimately came to terms with the pre-existing civilizations in the lands in which they triumphed. Islam, however,...adamantly required conquered people to scorn their own past and love their Islamic Arab conquerors by striving to imitate them. More importantly, the Koran is written in Arabic and Islam's sacred places, Mecca and Medina, are in Arabia. It was clear that the conquered and newly converted had to accept the primacy of the Arabic language, Arabic values and above all Arabia itself.

Thus, it may be said that the "vanquished were 'culturally disemboweled,' condemned to the enforced psychosis of renouncing their old and highly developed identities for a crude and violent desert blueprint that regulated the minutest details of their lives."

Iran was the one great exception to this almost complete erasure of the past. As we have seen, the Persians at a very early time endeavored mightily to preserve their national consciousness and even succeeded to a small degree in using Islam as a means of reasserting their culture. Thus, the efforts made by the modern dynasty of Shahs are consistent with the history of Iran under Islam. Basso describes these efforts as follows:

There have been times when Iran has dared to remember its past. In 1926, Reza Khan was crowned the first Pahlavi King of Iran and as part of his reforms he made it clear that he regarded Islam as a foreign imposed faith that should not determine Iran's identity. As part of his attack on Islam, Reza Khan connected his new Iran with the ancient Zoroastrian past. The Farsi language was purged of Arabic words, architecture began to take inspiration from ancient Achaemenian styles and schoolbooks were re-written to enhance an Iranian identity. Cities were renamed with Iranian names; parents were encouraged to give Iranian, and not Arabic, names to their children. In 1935 Persia it was replaced with Iran, as it was known in the days of Cyrus the Great. These reforms were of course reversed after the 1979 Islamic Revolution.

However, these "attempts to restore Persian national pride met only bewilderment and anger. … Rather than evoke pride, this past greatness inspired contempt, as the creation of infidel predecessors." There is one notable exception to the trashing of ancient Iranian history by fanatical Shi'ites. Even the latter still maintain and cultivate the ancient anger and resentment against the West that goes back to Alexander's invasion and the wars with the Romans.

Iranian Shi'ites reversal of the reforms of the Pahlavi dynasty has been matched by a more general fundamentalist reaction against modern secularism; a reaction often directed against the pre-Islamic artifacts cherished by secular nationalists. One example is that of the Pakistani militants who want to use the archaeological site of Mohenjo-Daro, not as a celebration of the achievements of their ancestors, but as a "teaching opportunity" for the truth of Islam triumphing over barbaric idolaters. Even the secular Turks are not exempt from a desire to uproot pre-Islamic culture; in Cyprus "Muslims attempted to use the fourth century monastery of San Makar as a hotel." In Libya Tripoli's Catholic cathedral was recently converted into a mosque. In Afghanistan there was, of course the destruction of the famous Bamiyan Buddhas.

However, for most of Muslim history it was neglect and indifference that played the most significant role in the erasure of the past. The actions of the Ottoman authorities are illustrative. These include the use of the Parthenon as an ammunition storage depot. There was also the permission granted by various Turkish authorities to Europeans to dismantle and export archaeological treasures in exchange for relatively small payments or bribes.

Thus, a true hope for Islamic reforms must wait for actions such as the following throughout most of the Muslim world. One such action might be for a future Iranian regime to resume the secular reforms begun by the Shahs, albeit under more democratic auspices. Another would be for Turkey to acknowledge its Greek and Armenian cultural and genetic heritage. Only by accepting the Hellenic heritage common to western civilization can the Turkish elite truly reach their long desired goal of becoming modern Europeans. The Turks would also do well to acknowledge their past history of jihad, persecution and genocide, and integrate these into their modern national consciousness. Still another such action would be for Egyptians to truly embrace their great past and reject the parochial calls of fanatical Muslim scholars. At the same time they would do well to recognize the Coptic minority as the purest embodiment of that past and cease the persecution to which that group is still subjected. Similarly, true reform can only be achieved in Iraq when all persecution of the Assyrian and Chaldean Christians ceases. Also, reform in Pakistan can only come about with the recognition of their past as part of Indian civilization and an end to discrimination against Hindus and other minorities.

Another requirement for reform would be acknowledging the truth of Islamic history on the part of both Muslim and Western scholars. The next examines some of the myths about that history which are widely believed and disseminated.

6

Myth and Reality

A number of misconceptions regarding Muslim history prevail in the West. Probably the most important of these myths concerns the alleged toleration Muslim society had for practitioners of other faiths. Since it is undeniable that Islam, like other monotheistic religions, is less tolerant than the faiths practiced in India and East Asia, the proponents of this view usually fall back on the idea that, at the very least, Islam is more tolerant than Christianity. This notion of a superior Muslim tolerance as compared to Christianity feeds the legend of peace-loving Muslims victimized by barbaric Christian crusaders. And this idea, in turn, is related to the assertion that at a time that western Europeans led a squalid and brutish existence, Muslims were cultured lovers of learning whose cities were the "ornaments of the world." The myth of Muslim achievement was exposed in a previous , therefore, the relative primitiveness of Dark Ages Europe warrants a closer examination. One additional assertion, which is that of Muslim society being free of racism, has also been effectively refuted in a preceding.

THE MYTH OF MUSLIM TOLERANCE

There are a number of excellent works questioning the prevailing myth of a tolerant Islam, so that the issue will be only briefly dealt with here. Ibn Warraq, for one, gives many examples of persecution of religious dissenters and heretics throughout the Islamic world. Bat Yeor also discusses in depth the intolerant treatment of minority religions at all times in Muslim history. Robert Spencer also examines the question of Muslim tolerance and concludes with the following:

> Did Muslims treat Christians and Jews better than Christians treated Muslims and Jews? ...both sides have a lot to answer for. But this much is clear: the conventional wisdom that religious minorities had a better quality of life in the House of Islam than in Christendom is at least open to question.

The favorable treatment meted out to Jews in Islamic society is one example of tolerance that is often cited. This is, however, contradicted by the documented persecution undergone by such prominent figures as Maimonides. Bostom describes the experience of a less renowned Jewish philosopher:

> Moreover, we cannot ignore the testimony of Isaac b. Samuel of Acre (1270-1350 C.E.), one of the most outstanding Kabbalists of his time. Conversant with Islamic theology and often using Arabic in his exegesis, Isaac nevertheless believed that it was preferable to live under the yoke of Christendom rather than that of Islamdom.
>
> Thus, Isaac b. Samuel fled from the Holy Land to Italy and ultimately to Christian Spain. There he wrote as follows:
>
> The word ziz in Arabic is derogatory, for when they wish to say in that tongue, 'Strike him upon the head,' 'Give him a blow upon the neck,' they say zazzhu ('hit him')...Indeed, on account of our sins they strike upon the head the children of Israel who dwell in their lands and they thus extort money from them by force. For they say in their tongue, mal al-yahudi mubah, 'it is lawful to take money of the Jews.' For, in the eyes of the Muslims, the children of Israel are as open to abuse as an unprotected field. Even in their law and statutes they rule that the testimony of a Muslim is always to be believed against that of a Jew.

All religious minorities were subject to humiliation and extortion. Far worse were the sporadic pogroms and massacres:

The myth of Islamic tolerance is defied by the massacre and extermination of the Zoroastrians in Iran; the million Armenians in Turkey; the Buddhists and Hindus in India; the more than six thousand Jews in Fez, Morocco, in 1033; hundreds of Jews killed in Cordoba between 1010 and 1013; the entire Jewish community of Granada in 1066; the Jews in Marrakesh in 1232; the Jews of Tetuan, Morocco in 1790; the Jews of Baghdad in 1828; and so on ad nauseum.

Even into modern times, Western ambassadors frequently remarked on the persecution suffered by religious minorities in the Ottoman Empire. In the 18th century "Turkey was no interfaith utopia." In 1758, the British ambassador observed the Sultan executing Christians and Jews for violating the *Dhimmi* dress code. Twelve years later "another ambassador reported that Greeks, Armenians and Jews seen outside their homes after dark were hanged. In 1785, a third noted that Muslim mobs had dismantled churches after Christians had secretly repaired them." Bernard Lewis notes that the so-called "golden age of equal rights was a myth, and belief in it was a result, more than a cause" of Jewish sympathy for Islamic societies. Furthermore, the "myth was invented in 19th century Europe as a reproach to Christians - and taken up by Muslims in our own time as a reproach to Jews."

Furthermore, the primary reason for whatever Muslim tolerance may have existed is that it was realized by pragmatic Islamic leaders, following the initial conquests that persecuting the large conquered population would have had a number of unfortunate results. Any attempt by Muslims to forcibly convert or drive out all infidels would have led to mass rebellion and a stiffened military resistance on the part of the yet unconquered population. It would have also destroyed the economic base of the conquered territories which provided Muslim warriors with the resources for further expansion. And, in fact, once enough of the population became Muslim, the possibility of rebellion receded and the economic dependence on non-Muslims lessened. Under these circumstances, Muslim authorities became less accommoda-ting and put increased pressure on the remaining non-Muslims to emigrate or convert.

In addition, the nature of Islamic expansion was quite unlike the history of Christian expansion in Europe. In their rapid conquests Muslims found many different sects of nonbelievers in the conquered population. Muslim leaders found it advantageous to play off one set of infidels against another. They also found it advantageous to cultivate alliances with persecuted sects against the governing authorities in the still unconquered dar-al-harb. This would, naturally, give the illusion that Muslims were more tolerant, when in fact those infidel groups presently favored were simply pawns in a greater political game.

Fabled Andalusia was supposedly the very model of Islamic tolerance. The prevailing view is that "Andalusia under Islamic rule was a proto-multiculturalist paradigm" which is "all the more appealing to modern post-Christian Westerners because this paradise of tolerance was not constructed under the auspices of Christianity, thereby seeming to vindicate their long insistence that all cultures are equal and that some - particularly non-Christian ones - are more equal than others." This myth of "Andalusia" is summed up by Yeor.

Andalusia represents the paradisiacal life of Jews and Christians living under the shari'a in the Moorish caliphate of the early middle Ages. ... Jews and Christians were grateful to be protected and to learn from the achievements of Muslim scholars ... This vision propagates and imposes the theory that only in Islamic lands did science, art and civilization flourish while Christendom was still immersed in barbarism and illiteracy.

Both Spencer and Yeor effectively demolish the myth of the "tolerant Andalusia." Stillman, a specialist in the history of the Jews under Islam provides an additional perspective. In iconic Spain there was a "depth of anti-Jewish sentiment" as seen in "the rabble-rousing poetry of Abu Ishaq of Elvira." Following the assassination of the Jewish vizier Joseph ha-Nagid "a mob went on a rampage in the Jewish quarter of Granada, slaughtering its inhabitants and razing the quarter to the ground." The Almohad rulers ended whatever small degree of toleration of the Jews still remained in Spain. By 1172 the Almohads "tolerated neither Jews nor Christians within their empire. There were mass conversions of Jews to Islam. Many fled over the frontier into Christian Spain, while others made their way to the more tolerant Muslim East. ... Jewish life in ... Islamic Spain ceased to exist altogether." Thus, Jews were expelled from Muslim Spain centuries before their more famous expulsion at the hands of the Christians.

Muslim Spain, therefore, was no paragon of religious toleration for the "peoples of the book". However, the circumstances for Christians and Jews in the Maghreb were far worse. In fact Christianity in the land of St. Augustine ultimately became extinct under Muslim rule. Thus in "contemporary North Africa, however, there were no native Christians to absorb some of the Muslim hostility against nonbelievers." For that reason, the persecution of the Jews of North Africa paralleled that occurring anywhere in medieval Christian Europe. In Almohad North Africa the "urban Jewish population from Tunisia to Morocco had outwardly professed Islam during the height of the Almohad terror. Those communities that resisted were put to the sword." The Almohad regime also dealt the final blow to North African Christianity. "The Jews became the *dhimmi*s par excellence in North African society, for no native Christian population seems to have survived the Almohad persecution."

Muslim persecution of the Jews in the Maghreb, however, eased somewhat under the Merinids of 14th century Morocco who found the Jews to be useful allies and go-betweens with respect to the rising Portuguese power. The Merinids "employed Jews in their service because of the latter's extreme vulnerability and, hence, according to Islamic political psychology, dependability." Christians in conflict with Muslims, of course, were equally capable of playing that game. In 16th century Morocco "most of the Jewish newcomers seem to have preferred living in the Portuguese-held coastal towns rather than the Islamic interior. They joined in the defense of these enclaves against Muslim attacks." The practical-minded

Portuguese were "notably tolerant toward the Jews in their African possessions" long after Jews were expelled from Portugal proper in 1497.

Egypt differed from the rest of North Africa, in that a strong Christian minority survived; the consequence was a slight mitigation in the situation of the Jews. "In the Mamluk Empire, the Jews were not the only infidels. The Copts more frequently and more immediately took the brunt of anti-*dhimmi* persecution." Muslim rulers often found it useful to play one group of *dhimmis* off against another.

THE REAL IMPERIALISM

A fantasy almost unique to modern western intellectuals of a "progressive" outlook is that Muslims are natural allies in the struggle against "imperialism". This conceit ignores the fact that it is Islamic imperialism that was by far the most successful version. "It turns out that the Arabs were the most successful imperialists of all time, since to be conquered by them (and then to be like them) is still, in the minds of the faithful, to be saved."

Muslim imperialism was much more durable and robust than any existing in the ancient world. The ancient Persians conquered a large territory but were content to leave the native cultures in place or even, as in the case of the return of the Jews from exile, to preserve them. The Macedonian Greek conquests were as rapid and extensive as that of the early Arabs. However, their effect on the conquered population was superficial and their empire ephemeral. The Romans also conquered a vast territory. But in contrast to the Arab conquests, the Roman Empire took three centuries to build. Moreover, while Roman culture penetrated all of Western Europe, modern Europeans, even those speaking Latin languages do not regard themselves as 'Roman'. On the other hand, Muslim descendants of Egyptians, Babylonians and Berbers consider themselves Arab:

Arabic penetrated the conquered peoples to such an extent that at the beginning of the eighth century it had evolved into the official imperial language. ... by adopting the Arabic language, the conquered peoples - Iranians, Syrians, Greeks, Copts, Berbers, Jews and Christians - placed their abundant talents and learning at the service of their conquerors ...

The ultimate adoption of the Arabic language and Islamic religion by indigenous populations was accompanied by the neglect and erasure of ancient traditions. A similar process followed the later Turkish conquests. Even where native languages were preserved, the adoption of Islam by the conquered led to the extirpation of much of the pre-existing culture at the hands of the Muslim imperialists.

Five centuries later the Mongols conquered an empire as large as that of the Arabs in a similar short amount of time. However, their imperialism was a failure in comparison. The Mongols wrought much devastation, but the civilization of the vanquished survived; there was no mass adoption of Mongol language or culture.

The modern empires of Western Europe encircled the globe. However, with the exception of certain sparsely populated lands, mostly in North America and Australia, there was no irrevocable displacement of aboriginal cultures. Even in the superficially Christianized lands conquered by the Spaniards the native Aztec, Mayan and Incan outlooks remain strong and have even undergone something of a modern revival. European imperialism was, paradoxically, beneficial to certain native cultures which were under attack by Islam. The British and French put an end to the African slave trade. British rule in India protected many Hindus from further Muslim depredations. And, far from attempting to replace Hindu culture, many Britons became ardent students and popularizers of Indian culture and the Hindu classics.

Furthermore, according to the historian Paul Fregosi, even the recent colonial experience of Islamic lands under European rule was much milder than that of Christian lands conquered by Muslims. When he compares "the Muslim occupation of Christian lands in Europe, the Middle East and North Africa to European colonialism, he finds that the latter was much briefer and less culturally pervasive."

CIVILIZED ARABS AND BARBARIAN EUROPEANS

The apologists for Islam point to the high level of civilization in the Muslim world when compared to that of early medieval Europe. They would be rather more convincing in their assertion, if the Muslim raids and conquests themselves were not a major cause of decline in the civilization of an already beleaguered West.

The effect of the Arab conquests in the Mediterranean and their continued raids and incursions on Western Europe was severe. When the Roman Empire fell into the hands of the barbarians, there was a period of upheaval. Within a short time, however, civilization in the West began to recover. Then for a few centuries beginning with the seventh, new waves of barbarians descended on Europe. From the north seafaring Vikings began their destructive incursions and at the same time Europe was attacked from the east by nomadic horsemen from the steppes. In both of these cases the invaders were eventually contained and then absorbed into the Christian civilization of Europe.

However there was a third wave of invaders from the east and south. These were, of course, the Arabs, whose religion of Islam, was a much more formidable threat and was to constitute a continuing disruptive force to western European civilization and to Byzantium. The almost permanent war, the disruption of trade and the sundering of the Mediterranean were a constant drain on the economy of Europe and retarded the full recovery of western civilization right up to the time of the Renaissance. The noted authority on medieval Europe, Christopher Dawson notes the following regarding the dark ages in Europe.

> But the worst had not yet come. In the seventh century the Arabs conquered Byzantine Africa, the most civilized province of the West ... Early in the eighth century the tide of Moslem invasion swept over Christian Spain and threatened Gaul itself. Christendom had become an island isolated between the Moslem south and the Barbarian north.

The Muslim invasion was, thus, a primary factor in the slow recovery of civilization in Europe after the shock resulting from the fall of Rome. Other distinguished historians also note the importance of continual warfare brought by Muslims in causing the decline of civilization in Europe. According to Henri Pirenne the Arab advance "changed the face of the world." The rapid Arab advance destroyed the classical civilization of Europe and "put an end to the Mediterranean commonwealth in which it had gathered its strength." Historian Walter Kircher asserts that "with the conquests of the Moslems and their domination of Mediterranean trade routes, large-scale commercial activity, and with it the coining and use of money almost ceased in Western Europe."

The Arab assault upon the west continued into later centuries. The navy of the Aghlabids of North Africa (800-909), "harried the coasts of Italy, France, Corsica and Sardinia." They conquered Sicily in 902. "Besides Sicily, Malta and Sardinia were seized mainly by pirates whose raids extended as far as Rome." Moreover, as we have seen, there were continuing raids by Muslim corsairs seeking booty and slaves on the coasts and shipping of Western Europe. Despite this harassment, civilization in the West recovered and eventually far surpassed that of Islam.

Therefore, the temporary superiority of Muslim civilization in the seventh through the tenth century is irrelevant. Islam came into possession of the most advanced and civilized lands in the world. And, as was shown in 11, after a brief period of high culture, Muslims squandered this advantage. At the same time, Muslim predation helped to cause and then to prolong the European dark ages.

Western Europe was not the only region whose civilization was retarded by Islamic aggression. Byzantium was also under constant pressure from Muslims. This may, at least partly, explain the long stagnation of Byzantine civilization. This Byzantine stagnation continued until the later middle ages. The late Byzantine renaissance that then occurred, ironically, may have been due to a deep recognition on the part of cultured Byzantines that their end at the hands of the implacable Muslims was inevitable leading them to devote resources to one final amazing effort. Without the constant Islamic attacks one can only speculate what heights the Byzantine genius might have attained. As it turned out the last Byzantine renaissance was effectively displaced to safer soil in Italy and the West. The unfortunate fate of the ancient Hindu civilization is still another example of the destructive nature of the Islamic meme with respect to adjacent cultures.

In general, any non-Muslim population subject either to razzias or to direct Muslim rule suffered from cultural atrophy. Any intellectual resources arising in such cultures were appropriated, through conversion, slavery or *dhimmitude*, to serve the interests of the Islamic state. In Ottoman ruled Europe there was an absence of any great achievement at the very time that the neighboring European nations were experiencing rapid advancement. The historian A. H. Lybyer notes the disincentive to achievement experienced by populations subjected to Muslim warfare or conquest:

> The Ottoman system took children forever from parents, discouraged family cares among its members through their most active years, allowed them no certain hold upon property, gave them no definite promise that their sons and daughters would profit by their success and sacrifice, raised and lowered them with no regard for ancestry or previous distinction, taught them a strange law, ethics and religion, and ever kept them conscious of a sword raised above their heads which might put an end at any moment to a brilliant career.

That the Balkans, once the site of the last brilliant Byzantine renaissance, "did not produce great art and science under the Ottomans is no mystery."

THE MYTH OF THE CRUSADES

Few things are more certain to put Westerners on the defensive than the mention of the Crusades. "Virtually all Westerners have learned to apologize for the Crusades. Less noted is the fact that these campaigns have an Islamic counterpart for which no one is apologizing and of which few are even aware."

The notion of hordes of violent barbaric Europeans descending on civilized Muslims who had, since time immemorial, lived in peace on their ancestral lands is a fabrication. In the late eleventh century, as we have seen, western Christendom finally imbibed the ideology of holy war from its longtime Muslim adversaries - the speech of Pope Urban at Clermont in 1095 initiating both the crusades and the gathering speed of the Spanish reconquista. Christians were certainly no slackers when it came to warfare and violence, but the condemnation of such actions in the New Testament presented Christian religious leaders with an almost insurmountable obstacle in finding scriptural sanction for unleashing war on distant lands. Trifkovic describes the dilemma:

What the Crusaders did to the Muslim inhabitants of Jerusalem in 1099 was as bad as what the Muslims had done to countless Christian cities before and after that time, but the carnage was less pardonable because, unlike the Muslims', it was not justifiable by Christian religious tenets. From the distance of almost a millennium, however, it is time to see the phenomenon as Christendom's reaction to Muslim aggression. It was a reconquest of something taken by force from its rightful owners ...

This alleged Western aggression was, therefore, simply a retaking of lost Christian territory for if "Westerners had no right to invade these putative Muslim places, and then Muslims had no right to conquer them to begin with." It is, of course, true that ...these sins of the Muslims do not excuse the sins that the Christians committed against them in return. One massacre doesn't cancel out another. But clearly what we now call 'human rights abuses' have not come only from the Western side, and the recent defensiveness of the West before the House of Islam and the world on this issue is hardly justified by the facts.

Furthermore, the Crusades were ineffective in ending Muslim aggression against Christian lands. Long after the Crusades "had become a distant memory in the West, the warriors of jihad continued to press into the heart of Europe."

The fall of the Crusader stronghold of Acre in 1291 put an end to crusading activity in the Muslim east. "Through the next four centuries, however, Muslim armies solidified their hold on southeastern Europe and kept advancing whenever and wherever it was possible to do so."

ISLAM AND CHRISTIANITY

It is one of the delights of modern historians to unfavorably compare Christianity with Islam. Both religions, of course, are the offspring of Judaism. However, their early histories could not be more different. Christianity came to power after centuries as a marginal and often persecuted sect. Islam, after less than a decade of persecution, became a distinct religion at the same time that it assumed political power. Islam from its beginning was always more of a political than a religious movement.

The difference between the two faiths is exemplified by the activities of pious reformers. Pietistic and monastic movements arising within the framework of Christian society were invariably pacific and quietist, seeking a return to the basic New Testament principles. Similar movements within Islam, however, were usually warlike, aggressive and militant in conformity with basic Koranic doctrine. One need only compares and contrasts the activities of St. Francis and his followers with those of the communal military sects of North Africa founded by pious Muslim scholars. Warlike, angry and violent Christians, while marking most of Christian history acted in direct contradiction to the teachings of the founder of the religion. Similar warlike and violent Muslims behaved according to the precepts of their Prophet.

Furthermore, the experience of the newly triumphant Christianity following the conversion of the emperor Constantine contrasts with that of conquering Islam. The early Muslim rulers had to deal with the existence of populations following other higher religions. Christians, on the other hand, were only confronted by an outmoded paganism and a small population of Jews. Muslim rulers, as a practical matter, had to tolerate large non-Muslim populations for many years.

Similarly, as a practical matter, Christian rulers had to tolerate paganism for several centuries after assuming political power. Long afterward, paganism continued to exist in a subterranean manner sometimes surfacing as witchcraft, or as the Neo-Platonism which openly emerged during the Renaissance. Christianity also adopted many pagan practices, as Islam inevitably incorporated beliefs and practices of preceding religions.

While Muslims ruled over both Christian and Jewish *dhimmis*, Christian rulers only had to contend with the existence of Jews as a rival religion. The experience of *dhimmis* under Islam paralleled that of Jews under Christianity. Christian and Jewish *dhimmis* were sometimes persecuted and sometimes protected or even utilized by Muslim rulers. Similarly, Jews in Christian Europe were often persecuted but also often protected or even favored by tolerant or practical secular or religious leaders. Often their talents and international connections were utilized by Christian monarchs as they were by Muslim sultans. There were times that Christian reformers, e.g. Cromwell and the Puritans, showed friendship to Jews as a way of making theological points. Also in some instances, as in Byzantium and Venice, itinerant Muslims were granted some measure of tolerance. Similarly in Reconquista Spain up until the 16th century, various Muslim populations lived under the protection of Christian rulers in a sort of reverse dhimmitude. On the whole, therefore, the experience of other religious groups living under both Christianity and Islam were similar.

Although established Christian and Muslim societies share many common features, with respect to proselytism and conversion, the historical experience of the two religions were quite different. The initial spread of Christianity was peaceful, whereas that of Islam was the result of violence. Walter Brandmüller outlines the different ways that Christianity and Islam began:

For the Christians, conversion was something that must be voluntary and individual, obtained primarily through preaching and example, and this is how Christianity did in fact spread during its first centuries. Obviously, we must immediately note that this conception of early Christianity underwent changes in later eras, connected with the diffusion of a spirit of religious intolerance in Western culture. John Paul II himself acknowledged that in this regard the Church's children 'must return with a spirit of repentance [for] the acquiescence given, especially in certain centuries, to intolerance and even the use of violence in the service of truth.' (Tertio Millennio Adveniente, 35).

But on the part of the Muslims, from the earliest times, even while Mohammed was still alive, conversion was imposed through the use of force. The expansion and extension of Islam's sphere of influence came through war with the tribes that did not accept conversion peacefully, and this went hand in hand with submission to Islamic political authority. Islamism, unlike Christianity, expressed a comprehensive religious, cultural, social, and political strategy. While Christianity spread during its first three centuries in spite of persecution and martyrdom, and in many ways in opposition to Roman domination, introducing a clear separation between the spiritual and political spheres, Islam was imposed through the power of political domination.

Moreover, neither religion had a monopoly on either toleration or persecution of religious minorities. The continued existence of Jews in Europe could not have occurred if there were no philosemitic or at least pragmatic members of the ruling elite. Practical Christian rulers also tolerated Muslims in reconquered territory as was the case in Sicily and early Reconquista Spain and later in Russia and the Balkans. And, of course, mercantile minded Christian rulers as in Constantinople and Venice mandated freedom of worship for Muslim merchants.

Muslims were quite as capable of persecuting Jews as were Christians. The rabbi Isaac b. Samuel (cf. above) wrote the following:

For this reason our rabbis of blessed memory have said, 'Rather beneath the yoke of Edom [Christendom] than that of

Ishmael.' They plead for mercy before the Holy One, Blessed be He, saying, 'Master of the World, either let us live beneath Thy shadow or else beneath that of the children of Edom' (a Talmudic verse)

Thus, Muslims were not always more tolerant of Jews than were Christians nor was the flow of Jewish refugees as between Christian and Muslim lands always one way, as the conventional wisdom would have us believe. Indeed, under the fanatical Almohads the position of both Christians and Jews in Spain became quite untenable.

The succeeding Almohads (1130-1232) wrought tremendous destruction upon both the Jewish and Christian populations in Spain and North Africa. This devastation -massacre, captivity, and forced conversion -was described by the Jewish chronicler Abraham Ibn Daud, and the poet Abraham Ibn Ezra. Suspicious of the sincerity of the Jewish converts to Islam, Muslim "inquisitors" (i.e., antedating their Christian Spanish counterparts by three centuries) removed the children from such families, placing them in the care of Muslim educators. ...

These brutal, discriminatory practices resulted in a massive emigration of Jews and Jewish converts to Islam to the Christian kingdoms of the Iberian Peninsula, from both Muslim-controlled Al-Andalus and the North African Maghreb. During the first half of the 13th century, Jaime I of Aragon, in particular, advanced policies of protecting Jews within his territories, granting safe-conduct and letters of naturalization to all Jews who made their way by land or sea, and established themselves in the states of Majorca, Catalonia, and Valencia. Jewish converts to Islam were permitted to return to Judaism if they wished so. Within 250 years, however, the descendants of these Jews who had escaped the Muslim Almohad depredations would be subjected to the fanatical rage of the Spanish Inquisition, and some of them would find refuge under the suzerainty of the Muslim Ottoman Empire, especially in the region of Salonika, at the end of the 15th century. To complete this morose cycle of persecution, the vacuum filled by Jews fleeing the Spanish Inquisition was created when their co-religionist counterparts -the Jews living under Byzantine (and Venetian) rule in Thrace -were subjected to massacre, pillage, enslavement, and deportation by these same Ottoman conquerors, during their jihad campaigns of the early to mid-15th century.

Both religions zealously persecuted heretics and apostates. However, centuries before the inquisition was institutionalized, Muslim rulers were executing and often burning heretics. In 742 Dja'd Ibn Dirham was put to death for believing in free will and that the Koran was created. Ibn al-Muqaffa, well known for his rational and unorthodox religious views, was burned in 760. Furthermore under the caliph "Mansur's successors, al-Mahdi (775-785 C.E.) and al-Hadi (785-786 C.E.) repression, persecution, and executions were applied with even greater ferocity. Special magistrates were appointed to pursue the heretics, and the whole inquisition was masterminded by the Grand Inquisitor, called the Sahih al-Zanadiqa. It was enough for a simple rumor to be aired for the Inquisitor to take immediate steps to incriminate the suspect." It is noteworthy that the Catholic country where the Inquisition was practiced with the most zeal and greatest effect was Spain, which had been under Muslim rule for centuries. Even the family of the prophet, the Hashimites, was not safe from this early inquisition. "Several members of the family were executed or died in prison." The scholar Al-Sarakhsi was executed in 899 after "he incurred the wrath of the caliph" for his public discussion of heretical doctrines.

As demonstrated by the Crusades, Christianity was also able to mount religious war. Warfare, in general, among Christians was frequent. However, neither "Christianity nor any other religion has ever had a doctrine like jihad. ... Ibn Khaldun acknowledges this ... 'The other religious groups ... did not have a universal mission, and the holy war was not a religious duty to them, save only for purposes of defense.' ... Islam is 'under obligation to gain power over other nations.'" It is an undeniable fact that "the Crusaders who pillaged Jerusalem were transgressing the bounds of their religion in all sorts of ways." However, the Muslim warriors who "murdered, raped, pillaged and enslaved" were following Muhammad's example.

Modern progressives are profuse in their condemnation of the treatment of women in Christian societies. However, the condition of women in Muslim ruled lands is incomparably worse. Bernard Lewis makes the following succinct, but apt, cultural comparison:

The women of Christian Europe were very far from achieving any kind of equality, but they were not subject to polygamy or legal concubinage. Even the limited measure of freedom and participation that they enjoyed never failed to shock a succession of Muslim visitors - all of them male - to Western lands. Western civilization was richer for women's presence; Muslim civilization poorer by their absence.

The institution of Muslim slavery was discussed at length. The difference between Christian and Muslim attitudes toward this institution is also noted by Lewis:

Although it was known in medieval Europe, slavery was of minor importance there, far less significant in the social and economic life of Europe than in pre-Columbian America or in Muslim and non-Muslim Africa. ... The inventiveness and cupidity of Europe, learning from and drawing on the plantation systems and the slave trade of Africa and the Islamic world, found this answer. Colonial slavery and the seaborne slave trade became a major factor in the crisscrossing interchanges between the four shores of the Atlantic - Western Europe, western Africa, North America, and South America.

But it was Europe, too, that first decided to set the slaves free: at home, then in the colonies, and finally in the entire world. Western technology made slavery unnecessary; Western ideas made it intolerable. There have been much slavery, but there has been only one abolition, which eventually shattered even the rooted and ramified slave systems of the Old World.

Moreover, it is of interest to note that the Spanish and Portuguese, the Christians most influenced by Islamic culture, were the first to apply large scale colonial slavery and whose traders introduced it to other western colonial powers.

Anonymous said...

Jehad in Kashmir was nurtured by some very famous doctors like Dr. Guru, Dr. Alaqaband in 1989. The Jehadis got sanctuary in the famed Sheri Kashmir Medical Research Institute. They would kill Hindus and to escape arrest would occupy the patient's beds and pretend to be sick. Soon these very Doctors started getting mid night knocks from these Jehadis. Dr. Alaqaband was horrified to see Jehadis seeking sex with his young girls. He fled the state of Kashmir and took refuge in New Delhi, capital of India, a state against which he had waged Jehad. Seek refuge in Delhi to save your girls from Islamic rape, yet wage war against your saviours. This is creed of Islam as is practiced.

Over all, 18 years later after Jehad in Kashmir began; the Muslims have paid dearly to keep their faith. Jehadis have waged war against the Indian State but sought their wages from the local Muslim population in terms of sex with preferably virgins. Fear of Jehadis and hope of forming Nizame Mustafa has prevented the population from rising against the sexual-jehadi adventures at night and gun battles with Indian police during the day.

The Muslim leaders have turned a Nelosn's eye against the sexcapades of Islamists. They have gained millions of Dollars in the bargain from Pakistan and Saudi Arabia. They have however, taken care to hide their own daughters in the Indian States, against whom back in Kashmir they help wage a war of Jihad.

7

Democracy in Islamic Political Thought

Democracy has preoccupied Arab political thinkers since the dawn of the modern Arab renaissance about two centuries ago. Since then, the concept of democracy has changed and developed under the influence of a variety of social and political developments. The discussion of democracy in Arab Islamic literature can be traced back to Rifa'a Tahtawi, the father of Egyptian democracy according to Lewis Awad, who shortly after his return to Cairo from Paris published his first book, *Takhlis Al-Ibriz Ila Talkhis Bariz*, in 1834. The book summarized his observations of the manners and customs of the modern French, and praised the concept of democracy as he saw it in France and as he witnessed its defence and reassertion through the 1830 Revolution against King Charles X. Tahtawi tried to show that the democratic concept he was explaining to his readers was compatible with the law of Islam. He compared political pluralism to forms of ideological and jurisprudential pluralism that existed in the Islamic experience:

Religious freedom is the freedom of belief, of opinion and of sect, provided it does not contradict the fundamentals of religion... The same would apply to the freedom of political practice and opinion by leading administrators, who endeavour to interpret and apply rules and provisions in accordance with the laws of their own countries. Kings and ministers are licensed in the realm of politics to pursue various routes that in the end serve one purpose: good administration and justice.

One important landmark in this regard was the contribution of Khairuddin At-Tunisi (1810-99), leader of the 19th-century reform movement in Tunisia, who, in 1867, formulated a general plan for reform in a book entitled Aqwam Al-Masalik Fi Taqwim Al-Mamalik (The Straight Path to Reforming Governments). The main preoccupation of the book was in tackling the question of political reform in the Arab world. While appealing to politicians and scholars of his time to seek all possible means in order to improve the status of the community and develop its civility, he warned the general Muslim public against shunning the experiences of other nations on the basis of the misconception that all the writings, inventions, experiences or attitudes of non-Muslims should be rejected or disregarded. Khairuddin further called for an end to absolutist rule, which he blamed for the oppression of nations and the destruction of civilizations.

Ghannouchi believes that neither Khairuddin nor any of the Islamic scholars of his time had intended to cast doubt on Islam or introduce changes to it. They only sought to understand Islam better and explore new means and methods to implement it, relying on the explanations of both ancient and contemporary scholars. They sought to legitimize borrowing from the West on the basis that...wisdom (or knowledge) is a believer's long-cherished objective', that '... religion has been revealed for the benefit of the creation', and that '... [the] Shari'a and the vital interests of the community are fully compatible'. To implement his reform plan, Khairuddin established the As-Sadiqiyah School for teaching modern arts and sciences within an Islamic framework. The purpose of the School, according to the founding declaration, was: 'To teach the *Qur'an*, writing and useful knowledge, i.e. juridical sciences, foreign languages, and the rational sciences that might be of use to Muslims being at the same time not contrary to the faith. The professors must inculcate in the students love of the faith by showing them its beauties and excellence, in telling them the deeds of the Prophet, the miracles accomplished by him, the virtues of the holy men...' Khairuddin At-Tunisi believed that '... kindling the *Umma*'s potential liberty through the adoption of sound administrative procedures and enabling it to have a say in political affairs, would put it on a faster track toward civilization, would limit the rule of despotism, and would stop the influx of European civilization that is sweeping everything along its path.

In his search for the causes of decline in the Muslim world, Jamal ad-Din Al-Afghani (1838-97) diagnosed that it was due to the absence of 'adl (justice) and shura (council) and non-adherence by the government to the constitution. One of his main demands was that the people should be allowed to assume their political and social style by participating in governing through shura and elections. In an article entitled 'The Despotic Government', published in Misr on 14 February 1879, Al-Afghani attributed the decline to despotism which is the reason why thinkers in the Eastern (Muslim) countries could not enlighten the public about the essence and virtues of the 'republican government'. 'For those governed by it', he stresses, 'it is a source of happiness and pride'. He goes further, to insist that '... those governed by a republican form of government, alone deserve to be called human; for a true human being is only subdued by a true law that is based on the foundations of justice and that is designed to govern man's moves, actions, transactions and relations with others in a manner that elevates him to the pinnacle of true happiness.' To Al-Afghani, a republican government is a 'restricted government' that is accountable to the public, and that is thus the antithesis of the absolutist one. It is a government that consults the governed, relieves them of the burdens laid upon them by despotic governments and lifts them from the state of decay to the first level of perfection.

Muhammad Abduh (1849-1905) believed that Islam's relationship with the modern age was the most crucial issue that Islamic communities needed to deal with. In an attempt to reconcile Islamic ideas with Western ones, he suggested that maslaha (interest) in Islamic thought corresponded to manfa'a (utility) in Western thought. Similarly, he equated shura with democracy and ijma' with consensus. Addressing the question of authority, Abduh denied the existence of a theocracy in Islam and insisted that the authority of the hakim (governor) or that of the qadi (judge) or that of the mufti was civil. He strongly believed that ijtihad should be revived because '... emerging priorities and problems, which are new to the Islamic thought, need to be addressed'. He was a proponent of the parliamentary system and defended pluralism, refuting claims that it would undermine the unity of the *umma*. He argued that European nations were not divided by it. 'The reason', he concludes, 'is that their objective is the same. What varies is the method they pursue toward accomplishing it'.

Abdurrahman Al-Kawakibi (1849-1903) wrote two books on the subject, Taba'i' Al-Istibdad (The Characteristics of Tyranny) and Umm Al-Qura (The Mother of Villages). The first is dedicated to defining despotism and explaining the various forms it may take, with much of the discussion focusing on political despotism. The relationship between religion and despotism and what he calls the 'inseparable tie' between politics and religion are also discussed. While stressing that Islam as a religion is not responsible for the forms of despotic government that have emerged and reigned in its name, Al-Kawakibi concludes that 'Allah, the omniwise, has intended nations to be responsible for the actions of those whom they choose to be governed by. When a nation fails in its duty, God causes it to be subdued by another nation that will govern it, just as happens in a court of law when a minor or an incompetent is put under the care of a curator. When, on the other hand, a nation matures and appreciates the value of liberty, it will restore its might; and this is only fair.' The entire book is an attempt to explain the reasons why the Muslim *umma* declined and became easy prey for 19th-century colonial powers. Like Al-Afghani and Abduh, Al-Kawakibi attributed the success of Western nations to '... the adoption of logical and well-practised rules that have become social duties in these advanced nations which are not harmed by what appears to be a division into parties and groups, because such a division is only over the methods of applying the rules and not over them.' In his other book, Al-Kawakibi constructs a series of dialogues involving fictional characters whom he describes as thinkers each belonging to a known town in the Muslim world, all summoned to a conference organized in Makka (Umm al-Qura) during the pilgrimage (hajj) season to discuss the causes of decline of the Muslim *umma*. One character, Al-Baligh Al-Qudsi, says: 'It seems to me that the cause of tepidity is the change in the nature of Islamic politics. It was parliamentary and socialist, that is perfectly democratic. But due to the escalation of internal feuds, after the Guided ones (the first four Caliphs) it was transformed into a monarchy restrained by the basic rules of Shari'a, and then it became almost completely absolute.' Ar-Rumi says: 'The calamity has been our loss of liberty.' In conclusion, Al-Kawakibi stresses that progress is linked to accountability while regress is linked to despotism.

Muhammad Rashid Rida (1865-1935) saw that the reason for the backwardness of the *umma* was that '... the Muslims have lost the truth of their religion, and this has been encouraged by bad political rulers, for the true Islam involves two things, acceptance of the unity of God and consultation in matters of State, and despotic rulers have tried to make Muslims forget the second by encouraging them to abandon the first.' He stressed that the greatest lesson the people of the Orient can learn from Europeans is to know what government should be like. In his book *Al-Khilafa* (The Caliphate) he stresses that Islam is guidance, mercy and social-civic policy. About the latter, which he seems to use as a synonym for politics, he says: 'As for the social-civic policy, Islam has laid its foundations and set forth its rules, and has sanctioned the exertion of opinion and the pursuit of ijtihad in matters related to it because it changes with time and place and develops as architecture and all other aspects of knowledge develop. Its foundations include that authority belongs to the *umma*, that decision-making is through shura, that the government is a form of a republic, that the ruler is not favoured in a court of law to the layman - for he is only employed to implement Shari'a and public opinion, and that the purpose of this policy is to preserve religion and serve the interests of the public...

Nineteenth-century Islamic political thinkers, who were clearly influenced by European democratic thought and practice, tried to establish a resemblance between democracy and the Islamic concept of shura. Faced with a crisis of government augmented by the autocracy and corrupt conduct of Muslim rulers, they sought to legitimize the borrowing of aspects of the Western model they believed were compatible with Islam and capable of resolving the crisis. However, the trend changed in the aftermath of the First World War and following the demise of the khilafa (Caliphate), whose abrogation, in 1924, shocked the Muslims in spite of the fact that many of them had suffered greatly at the hands of some Ottoman rulers.

The khilafa was an administrative legacy that for many centuries represented a moral shield and a political entity. The challenge was no longer despotism. The Muslims had already lost their symbol of unity, which they had been trying to reform. The European democracies, which provided inspiration and were greatly admired by reformists in the East, had colonized much of the Arab world, dividing its territories among them as booties. The Western colonizers' endeavours to westernize the Muslims were viewed as a serious threat to the Arab-Islamic identity, and, thus, liberating Muslim lands from colonialism became a priority. Hence, the call for reform was replaced by one for revival.

During this period, Rashid Rida, Abduh's disciple, published the Al-Manar Journal which attracted a readership of Islamic intellectuals who shared Rida's specific additions to the thoughts of his masters Al-Afghani and Abduh, namely the condemnation of innovations in doctrine and worship and the acceptance of the rights of reason and public welfare in matters of social morality. A young man who frequented Rida's circle and regularly read his Journal, then attempted to carry it on after Rida's death. His name was Hasan Al-Banna (1904-49). Trained by his father Ahmad Al-Banna, a graduate of Al-Azhar University and author of an encyclopaedia of Hadith and Islamic Jurisprudence, young Hasan grew up to become the founder of the largest and first international

Islamic movement in modern times, the al-Ikhwan al-Muslimun (Muslim Brotherhood).

Established as a study circle, known as Madrasat at-Tahdhib (The School of Refinement), in 1928 in the Egyptian port city of Al-Isma'iliyya - the headquarters of the Suez Canal Company and the British forces in Egypt - the group grew rapidly and spread to other parts of the country within a short period of time. Its growth accelerated by the 1936 Anglo-Egyptian Treaty and the Arab Revolt in Palestine against the British Mandate and Zionist colonization; the movement quickly transformed itself into a political entity. By 1939 a series of rasa'il (messages or articles), mostly authored by Al-Banna, were circulated explaining the Ikhwan's mission, clarifying its ideas and underlining its method. In the first of these articles, entitled Bayn al-Ams wa'l-Yawm (Between Yesterday and Today), Hasan Al-Banna diagnosed the situation in the Muslim world as follows:

European power expanded, thanks to discoveries, expeditions, and travels to far and distant lands as far as many of the remote Islamic countries like India, as well as some of the neighbouring Islamic provinces. Europe began to work earnestly at dismembering the powerful and far-flung Islamic state proposing numerous plans toward this end, referring to them at times as 'the Eastern question' and at others as 'dividing up the inheritance of the Sick Man of Europe'. Every state began to seize any opportunity as it arose, adopting the flimsiest of excuses to attack the peaceful yet careless Islamic state, and to reduce its periphery or demolish parts of its integral fabric. This onslaught continued over a long period of time, during which the Ottoman Empire was stripped of much of its Islamic territory which then fell under European domination, e.g., Morocco and North Africa. Many non-Islamic areas previously under Ottoman rule became independent during this time, e.g., Greece and the Balkan States. The final round of this struggle was the First World War, from 1914 to 1918, which ended in the defeat of Turkey and her allies, providing a perfect opportunity for the strongest nations of Europe, (England and France, and under their patronage, Italy).

They laid their hands on the huge legacy left behind by the Islamic nations, imposing their rule over them under the various titles of occupation, colonialism, trusteeship or mandate dividing them up in the following manner: North Africa (Morocco, Algeria, and Tunis) became French colonies lying in between a zone of international influence in Tangier and a Spanish colony in the Rif; Tripoli and Barca became Italian colonies in which Italy did not wish a single trace of Islam to remain. She forced Italian citizenship upon the people giving it the name of 'South Italy' and filling it with thousands of hungry families and wild beasts in human form (Italian outcasts); Egypt and the Sudan fell under English authority, neither one possessing a shred of independent authority; Palestine became an English colony, which England took the liberty of selling to the Jews so that they might establish therein a national Zionist homeland; Syria became a French colony; Iraq became an English colony; the Hijaz (the Western Province of Arabia) possessed a weak, unstable government dependent on charity and clinging to false treaties and worthless covenants; Yemen possessed an outmoded government and a poverty stricken populace exposed to attack anywhere and at any time; the remaining nations of the Arabian peninsula consisted of small emirates whose rulers lived under the wing of the British consuls and who fought one another for the crumbs falling from their tables, their breasts burning with mutual resentment and hatred.

This was the case despite the reassuring promises and binding treaties drawn up by the Allies with the mightiest monarch of the Peninsula, King Hussein, stating that they would help him achieve the Arab independence and support the authority of the Arab Caliphate; Iran and Afghanistan possessed shaky governments beset by power hungry people on every side, they would be under the wing of one nation at one time and under that of another at other times; India was an English colony; Turkistan and the adjoining regions were Russian colonies, subjected to the bitter harshness of the Bolshevik authorities. Apart from these, there were also the Islamic minorities scattered across many countries, knowing no state to whose protection they might have recourse, nor any well armed government to defend their nationality, as, e.g., the Muslims in Ethiopia, China, the Balkans, and the lands of Central, South, East and West Africa. Under such conditions, Europe won in the political struggle, and finally accomplished her goal in dismembering the Islamic empire, annihilating the Islamic state and erasing it politically, from the list of powerful, living nations.

Al-Banna notes that as each of these nations struggled to regain its freedom and the right to exist as an independent entity, concepts of localized nationalism arose, and many states working towards this revival purposely ignored the idea of unity. From that moment the Muslim Brotherhood launched the struggle for the return of the Islamic empire as a unified state embracing the Muslims that had been scattered around the world, raising the banner of Islam and carrying its message. At this stage, the Europeans ceased to be a model. On the contrary, they were blamed for the ills of the Muslim *umma*. 'The Europeans', Hasan Al-Banna wrote:

> ... worked assiduously in trying to immerse (the world) in materialism, with its corrupting traits and murderous germs, to overwhelm those Muslim lands that their hands stretched out to... they were able to alter the basic principles of government, justice, and education, and infuse in the most powerful Islamic countries, their own peculiar political, judicial, and cultural systems. They imported their semi-naked women into these regions, together with their liquors, their theatres, their dance halls, their amusement arcades, their stories, their newspapers, their novels, their whims, their silly games, and their vices.
>
> Here they allowed for crimes intolerable in their own countries and beautified this tumultuous world to the deluded, naive eyes of wealthy Muslims and those of rank and authority. This was not enough for them, so they built schools and scientific cultural institutes, casting doubt and heresy within the hearts of people. They taught them how to demean themselves, to vilify their religion and their homeland, to detach themselves from their beliefs, and to regard anything

Western as sacred, in the belief that only that which is European can be emulated. These schools were restricted to the upper class, the ruling body, the powerful and the future leaders. Those who were unsuccessful in such places were sent abroad to complete their studies. This drastic, well organised social campaign was tremendously successful since it appealed to the mind. It will continue to exert its strong intellectual influence over a long period of time. Thus, it was far more dangerous than any political or military campaign. Some Islamic countries went overboard in their admiration for the European civilisation and their dissatisfaction with the Islamic one, to the point that Turkey declared itself a non-Islamic state, imitating the Europeans in everything that they did. Aman Allah Khan, King of Afghanistan, tried this, but the attempt cost him his throne. In Egypt the manifestations of this mimicry increased and became so serious that one of her intellectual leaders could openly say that the only path to progress was to adopt this civilisation: good or evil, bitter or sweet, praiseworthy or reprehensible. From Egypt it spread with strength and speed into the neighbouring countries, to the extent that it reached Morocco and encircled the holy sanctuaries within the midst of Hijaz.

Explaining that his movement's mission is one of reawakening and deliverance, Al-Banna declared that the goals of his organization were:

1. Freeing the Islamic homeland from all foreign authority, for this is a natural right belonging to every human being which only the unjust oppressor will deny.
2. The establishment of an Islamic state within this homeland, which acts according to the precepts of Islam, applies its social regulations, advocates its sound principles, and broadcasts its mission to all of mankind.

Al-Banna warned the Muslims, in general, and the members of his group, in particular: 'As long as this state does not emerge, every Muslim is sinning and Muslims are responsible before Allah the Almighty for their failure and slackness to establish it. In these bewildering circumstances, it is against the interests of humanity that a state advocating injustice and oppression should arise, while there should be no one at all working for the advent of a state founded on truth, justice, and peace. We want to accomplish these two goals in the Nile Valley and the Arab Kingdom, and in every land which Allah has blessed with the Islamic creed: uniting all the Muslims.'

The leaders of the Muslim Brotherhood took a special interest in stressing that their movement was set up in response to the downfall of the khilafa. 'When the khilafa was brought down', Mustafa Mash-hoor, deputy leader of the Brotherhood explained: 'Imam Hasan Al-Banna rose up and proclaimed the restoration of the khilafa to be a religious duty incumbent upon every single Muslim man and woman.' In a message sent to the heads of Muslim states in June 1947, Hasan Al-Banna demanded that they shoulder their responsibilities and undertake the task of serving the *umma*.

The task, he explained, consisted of two parts: the first, to rid the *umma* of its political shackles so as to achieve its freedom and restore its lost independence and sovereignty; and the second to rebuild the *umma* anew in order to pursue its path among nations and compete with others for the attainment of social perfection. Hence, Hasan Al-Banna's main concern was to mobilize the public against colonialism and its adverse effects on society. He called for the re-establishment of Islamic governance on three foundations: the ruler's accountability to Allah and to the public, the unity of the *umma* within a framework of brotherhood, and respect for the will of the *umma* and its right to check its rulers who are obliged to respect its will and opinions. In his analysis of the causes of European progress, he prognosticated the eventual collapse of Western civilization due to immorality, usury and political divisions.

In his message Bayn al-Ams wa'l-Yawm (Between Yesterday and Today), he cites (political) parties as one of the factors that would lead to European decline. Although he stood for parliamentary elections twice, and while stressing that the parliamentary and constitutional system is in essence compatible with the Islamic system of government, he was adamant in his opposition to political parties. He regarded them as a potential threat to Islamic unity, which he deemed was essential for the re-establishment of the khilafa. 'They (political parties) are this homeland's greatest misdeed, the root of social corruption whose fire is scalding us. They are not genuine parties in the sense by which parties in any other country of the world are known. They are no more than a series of dissension caused by personal disagreements among a number of the children of this *umma*. Whose circumstances necessitated one day that they should speak in its name and demand its national rights...

There is no more room for half solutions and there is no escape from the inevitability of the dissolution of all these parties. The forces of the *umma* ought to be joined in one party that would have to work for the restoration of its independence and freedom, and that would lay down the foundations for general domestic reform. Between the two World Wars, thinkers affiliated with the liberal trend campaigned, like their 19th-century predecessors for total Westernization. Embracing secularism, they called for formulating modern constitutions and legal systems that, just as the Europeans had done, exclude religion and restrict its rule to the private domain. They hoisted the slogan of 'separating state and religion' and blamed Islam for the backwardness of the Arabs.

The abolishment of the khilafa in 1924 aroused a debate among thinkers of the time over its importance. Ali Abd Ar-Raziq (1888-1966), an Al-Azhar graduate who later studied at Oxford, contributed to the debate with a book that turned out to be among the most controversial works in modern Islamic history. Abd Ar-Raziq's theory claimed there were no such things as Islamic political principles. He denied the existence of a political order in Islam and claimed that the Prophet never established one and that it was not part of his mission to found a state.

As Arab societies responded to the challenge of colonialism and rose to restore their freedom in and struggle for their independence, Westernized elites took over the leadership of national movements that originally had Islamic inclinations. Despotic single-party regimes or absolute monarchies replaced the colonial authorities in most of the Arab countries. Throughout the post-independence era, Islam, its culture and its heritage came under savage onslaught in the name of modernization. The Al-Azhar of Egypt was turned into a secular university, the Tunisian Az-Zaytouna Institute was closed down, *awqaf* (endowment) institutions were nationalized, Shari'a courts were either dissolved or marginalized and political parties and groups were banned or outlawed.

The Ikhwan, who had already established branches or strong links in many Arab and Muslim countries, were hit hard by Nassir in Egypt soon after he came to power in 1952. Following the execution of several of their leaders and the imprisonment of hundreds of their followers in 1954, they were driven underground. The challenge had once again changed shape. It was no more the challenge and struggle for independence and freedom, but rather the struggle to resist and defend the *umma* against what was perceived as a pernicious onslaught against Islam and the cultural identity of the *umma* not only by foreign colonial powers but also by post-independence regimes. From then until the early seventies, members of the Islamic movement were influenced mainly by the works of Mawdudi and Nadwi and by the writings of Sayyid Qutb.

Sayyid Qutb (1906-66), who was imprisoned for ten years in 1954 and then executed in 1966, became the leading ideologue of the Muslim Brotherhood from the mid-fifties. His book Milestones, which was written in response to Nassir's persecution of the Ikhwan, acquired a wide acceptance throughout the Arab world after his execution and following the defeat of the Arabs in the 1967 War with Israel.

In it, he put forward the thesis of *jahiliyya* (ignorance, barbarity or idolatry), from which Islam came to deliver the world. Qutb divided social systems into two categories: the order of Islam and the order of *jahiliyya*, which was decadent and ignorant, the type which had existed in Arabia before the Prophet Muhammad received the Word of God, when men revered not God but other men disguised as deities. Muslim society, according to him, was itself divided into two realms, that of Islam and that of *jahiliyya*. This was clearly expressed by Qutb in Milestones as follows: '*Jahiliyya* is now present not only in the capitalist West and the Communist East; it has also infected the world of Islam.

All that is around us is *jahiliyya*. Peoples' imaginings, their beliefs, customs, and traditions, the sources of their culture, their art and literature, their laws and statutes, much even of what we take to be Islamic culture, Islamic authorities, Islamic philosophy, and Islamic thought: all this too is of the making of this *jahiliyya*. Drawing from the theory of Mawdudi (1903-79) that as Islam has reverted to a state of *jahiliyya*, true Muslims find themselves in a state of war against the apostates, Sayyid Qutb concluded that true Muslims, the tali'a (vanguards), are and must be set apart within the ambient infidel society as a sort of 'counter-society'. In his trial statement, Sayyid Qutb declared: 'We are the *ummah* of the believers, living within a *jahili* society. Nothing relates us to state or to society and we owe no allegiance to either. As a community of believers we should see ourselves in a state of war with the state and the society.

However, as far as democracy is concerned Qutb seemed to develop his own theory. In this he went much farther than Mawdudi, rejecting the concept altogether, denouncing it as alien, incompatible and *jahili*. The term *hakimiyya* (sovereignty), which Qutb constantly referred to while arguing against man-made political systems, was originally coined by Mawdudi, who used it to distinguish between Islamic and *jahili* (barbaric) societies. Mawdudi had argued that in a *jahili* situation, the edifice of politics rises on the foundations of *al-hakimiyya* al-bashariya (human sovereignty) whether such sovereignty rests in the hands of an individual, a family or a class or is the sovereignty of the public. 'Legislating in this kind of reign', Mawdudi explained, 'is entirely in the hands of man. All laws are made and replaced according to desires and to experimental interests. So is the case with political plans, which are only drawn or altered as, dictated by the passion for utility and the provision of interests? In such a reign, no word is given precedence and no affair is awarded prevalence except if such were the functions of those who are most cunning, most resourceful and most capable of fabricating lies; those who have reached the pinnacle of deceit, cruelty and guilefulness; and those who have siezed full control and are recognised as leaders in their community where, in their "laws", falsehood becomes truth just because its proponents have power and have the ability to terrorise, and where, in their courts of law, truth becomes falsehood just because it has no supporter or defender. In spite of all of this, Mawdudi still believed that Islam, by virtue of the institution of shura, was democratic. In spite of his reservations about the Western liberal democratic practice, he called for a chance to be given to democracy, one which would allow it to adapt and succeed in Muslim countries. Considering the task of reforming the system of government and administration to be part of the Muslim faith, Mawdudi suggested that the means of achieving such a reform would be to 'displace those who are corrupt and misguided from power and to replace them with those who are fit and righteous. As to how this change could be achieved, Mawdudi stressed:

> There is no other way in a democratic system except to participate in the battle of elections that is by educating the public opinion in the country and changing the people's standard in electing their representatives. We should also reform the election mechanism and cleanse it from theft, deceit and forgery. By doing so, we would be in a position to hand power to righteous men, who are eager to develop the country on the pure basis of Islam.

When asked about the flaws in liberal democracy, he explained to his students that notwithstanding the flaws in any particular form of democracy, the principle that the masses have the right to choose, and to bring to account and replace their government, should always prevail. When asked which method for running the affairs of the people is principally correct, Mawdudi retorted: 'Should those who are in charge of the affairs of the people and who run them on their behalf be appointed by the free will of the people so that they only administer and govern through consultation, and after having obtained the consent of the people, and so that they only remain in power so long as they enjoy the confidence of the public? Or should one person, or a group of persons, impose themselves upon the people, take charge of their affairs and run such affairs according to their own whims, and whose appointment or dismissal, or whose running of the people's affairs, are beyond the will or control of those who are being run by them?

He further explained that any flaws in democratic practice were due to three main reasons:

The first, the assumption that the masses are the source of total power and absolute sovereignty, while in effect, and in any attempt to set up an absolute democracy in the world, the masses come under the control of, and suffer the hegemony, of very few individuals. Mawdudi suggested that Islam had a solution for this problem. 'Islam', he stressed, 'rectifies this flaw at the outset by imposing a siege on democracy derived from a basic law dictated by the Creator, Master and True Sovereign of this universe. This is a law that both the public and those in charge of administering its affairs are obliged to abide by. Thus, the question of absolute independence, which eventually causes democracy to fail, does not arise.

The second and third reasons, Mawdudi argued, pertain to the standard of education and the degree of awareness of the electorate, or what he refers to as the masses. Here too, Islam provides an answer with its emphasis on educating the Muslims, '... preparing them morally and calling on each of them to have a sense of responsibility'. For democracy to yield its fruits and proceed successfully, Mawdudi argued, that much would depend on the existence of a strong and vigilant public opinion. 'Such a public opinion', he explained, 'comes [in] to being when the community comprises righteous individuals who are entered in a social system that is established on [a] sound basis, [one] that is so vivid that evil and those who invite to it do not grow whereas good and those who invite to it do grow.

Reaffirming that Islam may provide all the necessary rules and teachings for such guarantees to be maintained; Mawdudi expressed his conviction that once these guarantees are secured the apparatus of democracy might function successfully. 'It might also be possible', he added, 'that whenever a flaw appears somewhere in this apparatus, mending it would be provided for by a better apparatus. The mechanism of self-correcting, together with progress and development, would suffice for democracy to be given an opportunity and be experimented with, for it is possible through experimentation to develop any deficient apparatus until it become[s], step by step, perfectly sound.

On the other hand, Qutb seems to have been completely opposed to any reconciliation with democracy. In the beginning, he was opposed to the idea of calling Islam democratic and even campaigned for a just dictatorship that would grant political liberties to the virtuous alone. In his *tafsir* (interpretation) of Sura al-Shura (42 of the *Qur'an*) he said: 'Democracy is, as a form of government, already bankrupt in the West; why should it be imported to the Middle East? Sayyid Qutb and his disciples, including Sa'id Hawwa of Syria and Dr. Abdulqadir Abu Faris of Jordan, in their treatment of the issue of democracy took an anti-Western position. Their discourses exhibit a lack of interest in the origin, nature or conditions of democracy or of its compatibility or incompatibility with Islamic values. In all discussions, the abstract democratic concept is confused with the attitude or policies of Western democracies toward the Arab world and Muslim issues. Their rejection of democracy was, understandably, a reaction.

Sa'id Hawwa initially wrote: 'Democracy is a Greek term which signifies sovereignty of the people; the people being the source of legitimacy. In other words it is the people that legislate and rule. In Islam the people do not govern themselves by laws they make on their own as in democracy. Rather, the people are governed by a regime and a set of laws imposed by God.' However, Hawwa seemed to adopt a more moderate position later in life, in fact just before his death, one much more reflective of the changing attitude of the mainstream Islamic movement. He wrote:

> We see that democracy in the Muslim World will eventually produce victory for Islam. Thus, we warn ourselves and our brothers against fighting practical democracy. In fact, we see that asking for more democracy is the practical way to the success of Islam on Islam's territory. Our enemies have realised this fact, and that is why they have assassinated democracy and established dictatorships and other alternatives. Many of the followers of Islam have been unable to see the positive things democracy provides to us; they only looked at the issue from a purely theoretical and ideological perspective, and failed to look at it from the perspective of reality, namely that the majority rules, that the values of such a majority dominate and that in whichever country a Muslim majority exists Islam will prevail. Even when the Muslims are a minority, democracy is mostly in their interest.

In what amounted to a coup against his own previous stand and those of his mentor, Sa'id Hawwa seemed to campaign for, and encourage Islamists to adopt, the democratic alternative. He regretted that the Islamists have failed to benefit from the democratic circumstances that existed in many countries in the Muslim world, insisting that 'democracy in the Muslim World is the most appropriate climate for the success of Islam in the future.' Acknowledging the dilemma, he went on to say: 'The Islamists have fought democracy in the Muslim World because democracy in the Western concept has the right to make things *halal* (permissible) or *haram* (prohibited). It is a well established rule in Islam that no *ijtihad* (opinion) is allowed where a *nass* (sacred text) already exists. However, the problem here is that in the phase of conflict between Islam and other [ideologies] in the Islamic territory, we should know which system is better in order for the battle to be won by Islam.

Hawwa's years of exile from the early 1980s until his death in the Jordanian capital, Amman, in 1988 represented an important transitional period in the thinking of the Mashriqi (eastern) Islamic school of thought away from the rejectionist thought of the earlier decade. The dramatic events of the early 1980s in Syria, particularly the military confrontation between the regime and some Islamist factions, as a consequence of which the government declared an all-out war against all forms of Islamic activity coupled with the destruction of the city of Hama and the wiping out of the organized edifice of the Muslim Brotherhood in the country, had profound and long-term effects on Islamic movements throughout the region. Ironically, it was the leaders and intellectuals of the severely bruised Syrian Islamic Movement that led the trend. The violent means of change had proven disastrous and the radical reform approach was a complete failure.

It was thanks to Hawwa himself, and those who shared his insight, that this transition took place. Criticizing those Islamic writers who stood adamantly against the democratic process, he wrote: 'Undoubtedly, democracy is the most favourable environment in the Muslim world for the battle to be won by Islam. Nevertheless, some people have been found in the Muslim world to fight democracy. The alternative has been military dictatorships and [single] party dictatorships that kept all the ills and prejudices of the Western democracy against Islam and the Islamists and denied Islam and the Islamists the freedom of passage. Democracy, wherever it exists in the Muslim world, means that eventually Islam and the Islamists will win and achieve their objective[s].' Then as if reminding his readers, who at the time were mostly members and supporters of the Muslim Brotherhood in the countries of the Middle East, Hawwa hailed the decision once made by the founder of the movement, Hasan Al-Banna, to participate in parliamentary elections. This was, as admitted by many pro-democracy Islamists, a very significant event in the history of the Islamic movement that for much of the 1960s and the 1970s nobody seemed, or probably wanted, to remember.

Hawwa wrote: 'Al-Banna was wise when he wanted to participate in the parliamentary life, and Al-Hudaybi was wise when he called for the revival of the parliamentary life in Egypt.' Then as if to distinguish between two different trends within the ranks of Islamism, Hawwa declared: 'Participating in the elections to benefit from the democratic life has become a common denominator among the genuine Islamic movements, and thus we ought to be brave and frank in declaring that we do not fear [the emergence of] democracy in the Muslim world but fear for it. Hawwa went so far as to remind the Islamists that they would be committing suicide by rejecting democracy: 'Because they fought democracy and viewed it through its [literal] meaning rather than its implications, the Islamists have killed themselves.

Consequently, they have been governed by the worst regimes that have imposed on them what they had feared from democracy; they have been denied the freedom democracy grants to them.' Then he asked: 'How could the Islamists fear democracy, the fear of which only leads to usurping them their freedom and to the rule of the minority?' They should instead fear for democracy. The human experience has thus far shown that there can be no alternative to democracy other than revolutions, minority conspiracies and violence. All of this is a much greater risk than giving everybody the freedom to choose so that the majority elects those whom it deems fit and capable. It is, however, clear that Hawwa did not think of democracy as an end in itself, but as a means to what he believed to be the noblest end, namely the implementation of Islam. 'Experience has proven that, in the Islamic *ummah*, democracy is the lesser of the two evils and the more moderate of the two damages prior to reaching the state of Islamic government'.

In the meantime, a different school of thought was developing in the Arab Maghreb drawing its inspiration from the 19th-century reform movement of Khairuddin at-Tunisi and the ideas of 'Abduh (who had twice visited Tunis and had a number of associates there), Bin Badis, Ath-Tha'alibi, Al-Taher al-Haddad, 'Allal Al-Fasi and others. Malik Bennabi, however, is credited with having laid the foundations of this modern Maghreb school of thought. An Algerian thinker of French culture, Bennabi (1905-73) believed that the coming of

Europe had enabled the Muslims to escape from their decadence - caused by the emergence of a type of mind incapable of thought and afflicted with moral paralysis - by breaking up their rigid social order and freeing them from belief in occult forces and fantasies. From the early 1950s until his death, he wrote and lectured on what he believed to be the grand issues: namely, civilization, culture, concepts, orientalism and democracy. In a lecture entitled 'Democracy in Islam' delivered in French at the Maghreb Students Club in 1960 - attended then by Rachid Al-Ghannouchi and later on co-translated into Arabic by him - Bennabi attempted to answer the question 'Is there democracy in Islam?' He pointed out that defining the concepts of 'Islam' and 'democracy' in a conventional manner would lead to the conclusion that, with respect to time and location, the connection between the two is non-existent. He suggested that deconstructing the concepts in isolation from their historical connotations and re-defining democracy in its broadest terms, without linguistic derivatives and free from any ideological implications, would lead to a different conclusion.

'Democracy', he said, 'ought to be looked at from three angles: democracy as a sentiment toward the ego, democracy as a sentiment toward the other, and democracy as the combination of the socio-political conditions necessary for the formation and development of such sentiments in the individual.' He went on to say: 'Contrary to the depiction of the romantic philosophy of the era of Jean-Jacques Rousseau, these conditions are not created by nature, nor are they the requisites of natural law, but are the upshot of a specific culture, the crowning of the progress of the humanities and a new appraisal of the value of man; his appraisal of himself and his appraisal of others. Thus, the democratic sentiment is the product of this progress over the centuries and of this twin appreciation of the value of man.'

Citing the French historian Guizot, in his book *Europe from the End of the Roman Empire to the French Revolution*, Bennabi stressed that various stages of progress led to the emergence of democracy in Europe and to the growth of the democratic sentiment in the European countries. He said: 'The great historian explains to us how remote and simple the origins of Western democracy had been before the democratic sentiment slowly formed prior to bursting with the declaration of human rights and citizen rights; the declaration which expressed the new appraisal of man and the legendary and political crowning of the French Revolution.

Thus, 'the European democratic sentiment began to express itself - though not yet ridden of the obscurity that accompanies an object while in the state of making or evolving - through the two grand historical movements, the movement of reform and the movement of renaissance.' Bennabi considers the two movements to be the first expression of the value of the European human in the domain of the soul and in the domain of the mind. He stresses that this is the essence of the Western democratic sentiment when ridden of the fetters of history and politics - since the obscurity is caused by a package composed of phenomena and characteristics peculiar to Western history and which are not found in the history of other races and peoples - and when things are expressed in the terms of psychology and sociology.

In other words, the democratic sentiment in Europe was, according to Bennabi, the product and natural outcome of the reform and renaissance movements. 'This', he stresses, 'is its correct historical meaning, and therefore it cannot simply be severed from the history of Europe so as to be applied to other nations.' However, he reiterates that whether in Europe or anywhere else, the general rule with regard to the nature of the democratic sentiment is that it is the outcome of a specific social continuity. 'In psychological terms', he adds, 'it is the middle position between two ends that are opposed to each other; the end that expresses the psyche of the oppressed slave on the one hand and the end that expresses the psyche of the oppressive master on the other. The free man, or the new man, in whom the values and conditions of democracy are embodied is the positive co-ordinate that is the sum of two negatives that individually negate all such values and conditions: the negative of servitude and the negative of enslavement.'

As for the question of the existence of democracy within Islam, Bennabi argues that this is dependent on the provision of what he earlier refers to as the general conditions of the democratic sentiment. He then puts forward a set of questions: Does Islam provides and guarantees these objective and subjective conditions, in the sense that it creates a sentiment toward the 'ego' and toward the 'other' that is compatible with the democratic sentiment? And does it create the appropriate social circumstances for the development of such a sentiment? Does Islam truly reduce the quantity and intensity of the negative motives and of the anti-democratic tendencies that characterize the conduct of the oppressed and the conduct of the oppressor? He suggests that any project aimed at founding a democracy should be considered an educational enterprise for the whole community, administered through the implementation of a comprehensive curriculum that encompasses psychological, ethical, social and political aspects.

'Democracy', he asserts, 'is not - as is superficially understood by the common usage of its etymology - a mere political process; a process whereby powers are handed over to the masses... But is the generation of a sentiment, and of objective and subjective responses and standards, that collectively lay the foundations upon which democracy, prior to being stated in any constitution, stands in the conscience of the people. The constitution is usually nothing but the formal outcome of the democratic enterprise once transformed into a political reality indicated by a text that is inspired by customs and traditions, and dictated by a sentiment generated in a given circumstance. Such a text will have no meaning if not preceded by the customs and traditions that inspire it, or in other words the historical justifications that necessitate it.' He then warns that the answer to the question 'Is there democracy within Islam?' is not necessarily pertinent to a *fiqh* (jurisprudence) rule deduced from the *Sunna* or the *Qur'an*, but is one which is related to the essence of Islam as a whole. 'In this sense', he argues, 'Islam should be viewed not as a constitution that proclaims the sovereignty of a given community, or that states the rights or liberties of a certain people, but as a democratic enterprise that is the product of an exercise, through which the position of a Muslim vis-a-vis his or her encompassing society is defined, along the path toward accomplishing democratic values and norms provided a Muslim's temporal activity is tied to the general principles endorsed by Islam in the form of a seed sown in the Islamic conscience, and in the form of a general sentiment, and of motives, that constitute the Islamic equilibrium within every member of the community.'

Speaking of models of democracy - 'Western' in Europe, 'popular' in the East and 'new' in China - that differ from one another in the way they express their new symbolic evaluation of man, Bennabi sees that an Islamic model of democracy is attainable. Whereas in the other models the main objective is to endow man with political rights, enjoyed by the 'citizen' in Western countries, or social securities, enjoyed by the 'comrade' in Eastern countries, 'Islam', is distinguishable, according to Bennabi, because it 'endows man with a value that surpasses every political or social value'. He explains that the declaration in the *Qur'anic* verse 70 of 17, (We have honoured the children of Adam), endows man with more than just rights or securities. 'This verse was revealed as if to lay the foundations for a democratic model that is above every other model, where the divine element within man is taken into consideration and not just the human or social aspects as in the other models. Thus, a kind of sanctity is endowed upon man rising his value above whatever value other models give to him.

However, Bennabi is keen to distinguish between what Islam has the potential to offer and the prevalent state of the Muslims. He concludes that democracy exists within Islam, not during the era when Islamic traditions petrify and lose their brilliancy such as nowadays, but during the era of their making and when society is developing, such as during the first 40 years of Islamic history. Bennabi's analysis was revolutionary during his time, when Islamists in much of the Arab world, especially in the Middle East, were influenced by Qutb's thoughts and made an enemy out of democracy without ever understanding it. It was primarily thanks to his disciples such as Rachid Ghannouchi and other North African thinkers that mainstream Islamic movements gradually, though sometimes reluctantly, relinquished old positions on this matter. Malik Bennabi, who according to Ghannouchi, 'undoubtedly represents an element of the Islamic culture of rationalism and particularly a revival of Ibn Khaldun's historical culture of rationalism', had a profound influence on the Tunisian Islamic group. The two men's first encounter came when, on his way back from Paris to Tunis, Ghannouchi travelled by land through Spain, Morocco and Algeria where he visited Bennabi before entering Tunisia.

He had read his books in Damascus when he, as he put it, returned to Islam. Having read *Sayyid Qutb* during his student years in Syria and France, and having been greatly influenced by his thoughts during that initial period of self- searching, he listened attentively to Bennabi as he strongly criticized Qutb. The latter had actually referred to Bennabi in one of his writings without mentioning his name: 'An Algerian writer who writes on Islam believes that Islam is one thing and civilisation is another.' Bennabi was seemingly offended by Qutb's remark which he believed was demeaning. After listening to the critique, Ghannouchi concluded that Bennabi had deeper knowledge and a better understanding of civilization than Qutb.

Bennabi believed that 'whereas civilisation is the transformation of any good idea into a reality, Islam is a set of guidelines, a way of life, or a project, that creates a civilisation only when put into practice; when its adherents carry it and move through the world positively influencing man, material and time. Therefore, a Muslim may be uncivilised just as a non-Muslim may be civilised. On the other hand, Qutb insisted that civility is a synonym of Islam; that a Muslim is civilized and a non-Muslim is not. 'This belief', Ghannouchi comments, 'would inevitably lead to takfir' (that is charging someone with unbelief), and goes on to say, 'Qutb seemed to have borrowed the belief of the Al-Khawarij that a person is not a Muslim unless he or she is sinless and applied it to the question of civility; that is a person is not a Muslim unless he is perfectly civilised, and therefore all those backward Muslims are infidels!

8

Islamic Expansion and Decline

A specter is haunting not just Europe, but, the entire world. The phantom this time is not nationalism or any philosophy with roots in post-enlightenment Europe. It is the escape from confinement of a genie that once aggressively spread war across three continents. This objective of this chapter is to explore certain common factors and tendencies underlying the history of Islam in all of its geographical and ethnic diversity. In particular, to cast light on the remarkably similar phases occurring in all Islamic societies, of expansion and decline, of intellectual achievement followed by stagnation and of political liberalism which inevitably turns into despotism and repression. Moreover, it now appears that history is beginning to repeat itself, not as farce but as renewed tragedy.

There is no claim of expertise in all of the intricacies of Muslim history, theology, law or philosophy. In addition, he has no knowledge of Arabic or of the other languages spoken in the dar-al-Islam. Therefore, heavy reliance is placed upon those historians and social scientists who are recognized authorities both on Islam and within their respective scholarly fields. These sources range from antagonistic to sympathetic in their attitude toward Islam. However, most of the reliance in this study is on authoritative and respected sources.

One of the primary authoritative scholars relied upon is Philip Hitti, especially his massive History of the Arabs. Hitti is a respected historian who appears to be quite sympathetic to the subjects of his research. Hitti accounts for some 16% of the citations, in addition to a compendium of significant intellectuals that form the database for a statistical study of Muslim intellectual accomplishment over time. Albert Hourani, another well regarded historian cited, is also very sympathetic to Arab Muslims. Another authoritative source is the famous historian Bernard Lewis some of whose many works are cited to a large but somewhat lesser extent than those of Hitti. Lewis is regarded as the leading living authority on Islamic history, and while generally objective, shows a marked sympathy, in particular to the Ottoman Turks. Ira Lapidus and Efraim Karsh are two noted authorities in the general history of Islam who are frequently cited. Lapidus appears to be generally sympathetic to Islamic culture, while Karsh can be quite critical.

Numerous sources cited are from authorities specializing in particular Islamic or neighboring lands, or else in particular Muslim ethnic groups. Lord Kinross is a well respected authority on Ottoman Turkish history and, while objective, is also notably sympathetic to the Muslim Turks who are the subjects of his study. Speros Vryonis, an expert in Byzantine civilization and history, provides a wealth of information on the Turkish conquest of the Byzantine Empire. While considerably more critical of Islam and of Turks than is Kinross, he also presents his facts in a fair and objective manner. Almost ten percent of the citations refer to Vryonis' works. A.A. Vasiliev, another authoritative specialist on Byzantium, is cited in several places. He appears to be somewhat friendlier toward Islam than is Vryonis. Also sympathetic to the Turks, in a qualified way, is Herbert Muller, a generalist in world history who did considerable research into the history of Anatolia. Roger Crowley, who takes great pains to be fair to both sides, is a source of much information regarding the fall of Constantinople.

Richard N. Frye, a noted authority on Iranian history is the source of much information on Muslim Iran. He is also an expert on Central Asian history. Another specialist on inner Asia, frequently quoted, is Svat Soucek; both of these authors provide objective and unbiased historical accounts of Islamic rule in Iran and Central Asia. The historian John Keay also provides much objective information on India during and after the Muslim invasions. Will Durant, the famous world historian, adds a rather more chilling perspective to the Indian experience at the hands of the Muslim invaders, as does acclaimed author V. S. Naipaul. Dutch historian Bernard H. M. Vlekke provides a somewhat friendlier account of the spread of Islam from India to Southeast Asia. Arab historians Yusuf Fadl Hasan and Jamil M. Abun-Nasr write of the Arab penetration into Africa. Hasan gives a detailed history of the Arabization of the Sudan, while Abun-Nasr writes of the history of the Maghreb under Islam. Anthropologists Roland Oliver and Brian Fagan also provide quite objective accounts of the Arab penetration into Africa. The specialist in Jewish history, Norman Stillman, provides many details regarding the experience of both Jewish and Christian minorities under Muslim rule.

Two notable social scientists specializing in Islamic societies, frequently cited, are Reuben Levy and Raphael Patai. In the field of comparative religion, two scholars quite sympathetic to Islam, John B. Noss and Huston Smith, provide much material regarding the early history of Islam, Muslim sects and comparisons with other religions. Ignaz Goldziher, a recognized early twentieth century expert on Islamic law also provides information on Islamic law and society. The respected translation of the Koran by the convert Mohammed Pickthall is cited a number of times as background.

Quantitative historian and Islamic specialist, Richard W. Bulliet, provides much material on the process of the conversion of conquered non-Muslims to Islam. In addition, he gives estimates of the progress of that conversion in a series of statistically derived conversion curves. Social scientist and statistician Charles Murray, also working in quantitative history, provides both general background on, and rankings of, significant figures in various civilizations including that of Islam. C. D. Darlington, an evolutionary biologist, brings the perspective of his science to the study of human history. His observations on Islamic history have provided much useful material. Another expert in the field of human genetics, L. Luca Cavalli-Sforza, is briefly cited. The mathematicians Carl B. Boyer and Uta C. Merzbach provide historical perspective on the history of Muslim mathematics, in particular the development of algebra and the Arabic numbers.

Four researchers who are cited a number of times, and whose work must be viewed as having points of view quite unsympathetic to Islam, are Robert Spencer, Serge Trifkovic, Ibn Warraq and Bat Yeor. However, they are cited primarily for the general historical information contained within their works. In addition to the above major authors, a large number of minor sources are also cited with attitudes toward Islam, similarly, ranging from friendly to questioning to hostile. Social commentator Howard Bloom provides some unflattering analyses of the Islamic "meme." The total citations, for both critical views and general historical background, for all writers with an anti-Islamic polemic, amount to about twelve percent.

This study has relatively little to say on the many reports of massacres and atrocities committed by the soldiers of Islam; these are well enumerated in many other sources. It must be stated at the outset that the behavior of Muslims in war was not necessarily worse than that exhibited by most other peoples both before and since the time of Muhammad. However, the scriptural inspired military prowess of Muslim warriors and their consequent success, may have given them many more opportunities for slaughter and atrocity than was the case for non-Muslims. In that, ironically, they are similar to the much vilified contemporary Serbs whose greater military skills gave them an advantage over opponents who would otherwise have happily indulged in equally egregious, though certainly less reported, behavior. Similarly, this paper only briefly treats of the modern legend of Islamic tolerance toward, and compassion for, those of other faiths. This academic myth has also been convincingly debunked by a number of recent authors.

This is not meant to be a comprehensive history of Islam. For one thing it covers only the earlier periods in the history of the various Muslim polities and does not, generally, extend into recent times. Furthermore, it simply endeavors to uncover those common factors facilitating the spread of Islam. Some of these factors are, however, rather obscure and are only implicit in the standard histories; this study seeks to draw these out and make them explicit. By bringing together numerous distinct sources a coherent picture of the similar historical tendencies common to all Islamic societies begins to emerge. It also attempts to show how some of the very factors responsible for the triumph of Islam contribute to its subsequent decline. Furthermore, it illuminates the remarkable similarities in expansion and decline that characterize the different Muslim conquests.

The following is a brief outline of the theory of Islamic expansion and decline. In the first phase, invasion and conquest, Muslims expand into a new territory. The actual work of invasion is commonly carried out by a recently converted nomadic vanguard. In some cases the expansion occurs rapidly through war, in other cases it occurs through a slow process of raiding or infiltration.

Conquest is followed by a period of recovery varying from decades to several centuries. The newly annexed territory is invariably devastated. The new Muslim authorities may attempt to stabilize conditions, if only to turn their new conquest into an economic asset. However, this is frequently disrupted by conflicts within the ranks of the original invaders and by a series of destructive secondary nomadic incursions. Eventually, one faction of invaders succeeds in establishing hegemony and a strong central government capable of re-establishing order. This phase is often characterized by a legacy of tribal egalitarianism, limited, of course, to the ranks of the invading warrior elite.

In many cases the period of recovery is followed by an Islamic golden age. However, this is simply a continuation of the preceding civilization in a new form and is crucially dependent on the work of dhimmis and recent converts. The golden age is made possible by the re-establishment of peace and order, the re-opening of trade routes and the cross-fertilization of ideas and technologies from the many cultures brought into the larger Islamic civilization. The peak of the golden age is marked by the patronage of scholars and architects on the part of a wealthy and powerful elite who are themselves often descended from recent converts. However, the tradition of austere tribal egalitarianism is replaced by increasing oriental despotism and magnificence.

The final stage is invariably one of decline and stagnation. Islamic civilization is characterized by a parasitic dependence on the economic, technological and intellectual resources of the dhimmi population. Eventually that population is reduced to a minority through conversion, polygamy and concubinage, and slavery. With the passing of time Islamic attitudes harden, the pre-Islamic culture is largely forgotten and the Muslim mind closes. The state becomes a repressive theocracy, ruled by increasingly despotic caliphs or sultans, and dominated by a rigid and intolerant clerical class.

A POWERFUL AND DANGEROUS MEME

Ideas, like pathogens may spread in epidemic fashion. An idea or a linked constellation of ideas are subject to natural selection like genes. Religions, philosophies, ideologies are examples of such memes; those adapted to the conditions or circumstances of the time persist and spread. As Howard Bloom remarks:

> Memes are ideas, the snatches of nothingness that leap from mind to mind. ... A melody wells up in the reveries of a solitary songwriter. It seizes the brain of a singer. Then it infects the consciousness of millions. ... But the memes that count the most are the ones that assemble vast arrays of resources in startling new forms. They are the memes that construct social superorganisms.

Islam is one such meme; a particularly formidable one that once besieged much of the world and has now experienced a second birth:

> The modern growth of Islam is the coalescence of a superorganism drawn together by the magnetic attraction of

a meme. But this meme has an advantage: The social body it is trying to pull together has existed as a unified social beast in the past. The old reflexes of solidarity are still there, waiting to be aroused. The meme of the new Islam is not laboring to generate a small and fragile embryo. It is simply attempting to awaken a sleeping giant.

Islam, like other religious traditions taps into some of the deepest yearnings of the human psyche. It gives a meaningful and comprehensive explanation of the universe and ensures fearful believers that piety and acquiescence to the will of the Creator will be rewarded with blissful immortality. In these respects Islam, like the other successful religions is proving itself more robust than the dry utopian ideologies contrived by various 19th century German philosophers; unlike such transient creeds, Islam is forever. In addition, Islam beckons its more zealous followers with material and sensual rewards both in paradise and on earth. Furthermore, the rewards guaranteed to its devotees, particularly its male devotees, by Islam are more full-blooded than the benefits promised by competing religions and more eternal than the, rather thin, gruel offered by the secular ideologies.

It is true that the carriers of the Islamic meme, in the first century of the Arab conquests were rather ambivalent about purveying it to the non-Arab subject peoples. However, at all times and in all lands subject to the Muslim juggernaut the following was true:

In its early years the religion of Muhammad had a swift and terrible spread, often, where resistance occurred to the terrible accompaniment of fire and sword; and so it made an unforgettable impression upon many peoples both of the East and West. In the 1st century of its existence it must have appeared to those who stood in the path of its advance like a devouring fire enlarging from its center, which rushed upon them with remorseless and inexorable speed; before they knew what to do, it was upon them. ... Many, not caring to withstand the New Order, and half convinced already, surrendered themselves and became Moslems. ... Some resisted actively and became dead men, incapable of counter argument.

Islam, in addition to promising material rewards on earth and sensual delights in heaven, enticed potential converts with the lure of theological simplicity. According to the scholar of comparative religions John Noss:

> But though, its severity appalled those who resisted it, its simplicity and clarity appealed to those who bowed to its teaching. ... In general, it does not overburden them with a multitude of scriptures and doctrines and a plethora of abstruse doctrines. It has kept to one basic scripture, preserved from the first in a state of textual purity such that comparatively few variant readings have arisen to confuse the commentators.

The straightforwardness of Islam has an especial appeal to members of more primitive cultures:

> The basic simplicity of Islam and the thoroughness of its discipline make it an attractive and effective religion for primitive peoples.

Professor Reuben Levy referring to the spread of Islam in sub-Saharan Africa observes:

> Ultimately by providing him with a way of life which, though not by any means easy, is yet simple and clearly defined, Islam frees him from the numerous vague terrors inseparable from a primitive state of culture ...

The simplicity of its creed when combined with its legitimation of war, plunder and slavery rendered Islam especially alluring to primitive nomadic tribes steeped in a culture that already glorified raiding and warfare. The most important of such nomadic groups, after the early desert Arabs, the Turks, have been described as follows:

> These were a people driven instinctively by an inherited impulse as nomads to move outward ... in search of pastures new. Since their conversion to Islam, this search was sanctified and further inspired by their religious duty as Ghazis, under the holy law, to seek out and fight the infidel ... to raid and occupy his lands, seize his possessions, kill or carry into captivity his people, and subject their communities to Moslem rule.

Islam which "offers no unattainable ideal, few theological complications and perplexities, no mystical sacraments and no priestly hierarchy involving ordination, consecration and 'apostolic succession'" was a suitable religion for uncultured nomadic peoples of the deserts or steppes, with no cities and often times no permanent habitations or even structures. The Muslim credo "was easily grasped by the nomadic tribes of the desert and, later of the steppe. Especially when the celestial reward was preceded by the tangible loot divinely sanctioned."

Islam is not alone in its muscular orientation toward religious expansion. Nor is it unique in its claim on a monopoly of truth and its insistence that followers must believe in, or at least not openly question, revealed dogma. Its great monotheistic and proselytizing sister religion, Christianity, shares many of the same characteristics. Indeed, even the religions of East Asia with their history of relative tolerance are not immune to religious warfare and persecution:

Sometimes a sternly Confucian or vigorously Taoist emperor would institute widespread persecution; one such ... in 845 A.D. destroyed 45,000 Buddhist buildings, melted down tens of thousands of Buddha images, and sent over 400,000 monks, nuns and temple servitors back into the world.

The religions of Judaism and Hinduism, whose adherents have for the most part avoided proselytizing, have a number of violent episodes recounted in their root sacred books. In the case of early Judaism these tell how the Hebrew tribes had to war against Canaanites, Amorites, Philistines and others in order to establish themselves in the land promised them by God. However the offensive wars described in this quasi-historical account are limited to one territory and a brief historical period. The scriptures do not provide an ongoing justification of these actions for all time and all places. Nor was there any scriptural imperative to conquer and convert other peoples to the Jewish religion.

On the contrary, Judaism has usually discouraged even voluntary conversion. In addition, in the case of Judaism the strict interpretation of the law has been long superseded through rabbinical injunction as it was in Christianity through the personal example of Jesus. Adulterers, homosexuals or apostates may be ostracized or excommunicated but are no longer executed unless the adherents of these faiths violate their religious imperative. In the same way the early Hindu texts describe the tribal warfare that supposedly occurred in ancient India. But they do not promote these methods as a duty incumbent on Hindus as a means of forcing their religion on unbelievers. The same might be said of the root mythology of the ancient Greeks and Romans as described in Homer. Bloody minded though they were, no Greek or Roman would think of using violence to force their conquered subjects to worship Zeus or Athena. Christians, it is true, suffered sporadic persecution, as their religion was regarded as an innovation, a cult dangerous to the stability of the Roman state; Jews and other long established religious minorities were left alone except in times and places of active rebellion.

The case of the Islamic meme is rather different. There are in its root scriptures a constant injunction to spread the rule of Islam by means of violence and coercion. Non-Muslims are required to either convert to Islam or to submit to being ruled by Muslims under conditions of tribute and degradation. Furthermore, warriors who die in war to extend Islam get a free pass into the rather lush Islamic paradise. These injunctions are in the Koran, the basic Muslim testament. Now some of the early Meccan verses enjoin the believers to do good works, and to be charitable and peaceful.

But the peaceful injunctions, at least with respect to infidels, are abrogated by later Medinan verses which were written after Muhammad attained political power. These verses not only require the faithful to take part in war but provide detailed recommendations for strategies, deception when signing treaties or truces and divvying up the booty captured; these also give religious sanction to rape. Now rape occurs in all wars at all times, but Islam is the only world religion that sanctifies it and gives it religious justification as a permanent institution through concubinage and sexual slavery. Furthermore the Hadith (the sayings attributed to Muhammad and his companions) and the Sira (the biography of Muhammad) which are the Muslim equivalents of the Acts and Epistles also give religious sanction to violence, theft, slavery and rape on the part of Muslims when dealing with unbelievers.

It would be useful, at this point, to examine the remarkable career of the founder of the Islamic meme. The next chapter looks closely at the character of the prophet Muhammad.

THE FLAWED PROPHET

To understand the development of the Islamic meme one must consider the character and the historical mission of its founder Muhammad. The Prophet was born in a pre-Islamic Arabia which, for many centuries exhibited a particular resistance to civilizing influences. Christianity was six centuries old and, after its slow absorption of the high civilizations at the center of the Roman Empire, spread with remarkable speed to the inhabitants of the Roman periphery. Then within one or two centuries, most of the barbarian invaders of the empire were converted to one form or another of Christianity. Even in the far off British isles the higher civilization of the Mediterranean world carried by the Christian religion spread, in a remarkably short time to the Celtic tribes beyond the Roman frontier and to the Saxon invaders of eastern Britain. Once the initial depredations of these tribes were exhausted, they showed a remarkable eagerness to engage the civilizing tutelage of wandering monks and formal missions. And within a few decades, these new converts carried Christian civilization deep into the forests of central Europe.

In Arabia, however, the Bedouin way of life resisted the civilizing influence of Mediterranean culture that had been carried for many centuries by wandering Christians as well as migrating Jewish refugees. This stands in stark contrast to the experience in far off Western Europe as well as neighboring Ethiopia just across the Red Sea. It was only in the isolated caravan cities and in more settled Yemen that the ideas of the higher religions penetrated; and even in these areas they were confined to a tiny fraction of the population.

The challenge facing Muhammad was to develop a religious ideology that would appeal to Arab sensibilities while enabling them to participate at the level of the higher civilizations that had surrounded them for millennia. To do so he had to fabricate a religion for Arabs that would transcend the parochialism of local tribes, satisfy their traits of individuality and notions of honor, conform to their code of morality and, at the same time, provide an outlet for channeling their aggressive tendencies. Indeed so successful was the Prophet in carrying out this program that "before his sudden death in 632, he knew he was well on the way to accomplishing his divine mission of unifying the Arab tribes under a theocracy governed by the will of the one and only God, Allah." Although Muhammad may have had a more universal mission in the back of his mind, his fellow Arabs were the focus of his teachings and activities. The claim made that he "wrote to the rulers of other lands, including Heraclius, proposing that they accept Islam ... is now recognized as a later invention without historical foundation."

A number of religious models have developed in various regions. However, the major religions, while differing enormously in doctrine appear to fall into roughly two general types. The first type is that of the tribal/national religions, examples of which are Judaism, Hinduism, Zoroastrianism, Shintoism, Taoism and Confucianism. These sometimes start off as very primitive, violent and warlike creeds as evidenced in the Old Testament of Judaism and in the early Hindu epics, the Mahabharata and Ramayana; which show the clashes of early tribal societies over the possession of land, water, or even livestock.

The second configuration is of the proselytizing religions is comprised of Buddhism, Christianity and Islam. Both Buddhism and Christianity spread slowly and peacefully, at least initially. Both transcended their original national backgrounds almost from their beginning. Both, in fact, have virtually vanished in their respective lands of origin.

The solution Muhammad and his immediate successors developed in order to civilize the Arabs, Islam, is a combination of both a tribal and a proselytizing religion. This gave the new creed some unique advantages. Islam was able to spread rapidly over a vast territory through the sword. However, only long after its initial military success were large numbers of converts accepted into the faith. The territory of its original tribal people, Arabia, remains the most zealous stronghold of the faith.

As one historian observes regarding the benefits to primitive tribal peoples of the religion that was the ultimate outcome of Muhammad's efforts:

> More quickly than any other, the record suggests, it can inspire them with zeal, elevate their moral code, promote their self-respect, and make them a disciplined community.

The violent and martial nature of Islam was present almost from its first days. And while these traits account for the extraordinary success of the faith, they developed as a contingent outcome of its prophet's initial spiritual development; in fact the success of Islam was a consequence not of Muhammad's more uplifting visions, but rather of his ultimate spiritual failings.

To begin with it may be observed that the other great missionary religions, Buddhism and Christianity developed out of existing tribal religions that had undergone many centuries of religious evolution and ethical development. These were mature religions long past their primitive foundations and they were embedded in refined and cosmopolitan societies that had experienced considerable cross-fertilization of ideas with other high cultures. Islam, on the contrary, had its incubation within a primitive pagan tribal culture. The founders of the other religions had very different backgrounds and these inevitably shaped the future course of their new religions. Jesus inherited all of Judaism's spiritual insights and was most likely in direct contact with esoteric sources of wisdom, possibly with the various Essene sects. Gautama was heir to a long tradition of Hindu religious development and had the advantage of studying with a number of Hindu adepts. Muhammad, however, although a man of great spiritual gifts, lacked the benefit of extensive personal contact with genuine existing religious teachings and teachers. He was also isolated in a remote backwater facing conditions similar to that of the early Hebrew prophets with which he shared a similar problem; that of civilizing and uniting a primitive and barbaric people.

The difficulties and the temptations facing the Prophet Muhammad were immense and the spiritual resources he could draw upon were sparse. As the great yogi Vivekananda observed:

> The yogi says that there is a great danger in stumbling upon this state (the superconscious). In a good many cases there is the danger of the brain's being deranged; and as a rule you will find that all those men, however great they were, who stumbled upon this superconscious state without understanding it groped in the dark and generally had, along with their knowledge, some quaint superstitions. They opened themselves to hallucinations. Mohammed claimed that the Angel Gabriel came to him in a cave one day and took him on the heavenly horse Harak to visit the heavens. But with all that, Mohammed spoke some wonderful truths. If you read the Koran, you will find the most wonderful truths mixed with superstitions. How will you explain it? The man was inspired, no doubt, but that inspiration was, as it were, stumbled upon. He was not a trained yogi and did not know the reason for what he was doing. Think of the good Mohammed did to the world and think of the great evil that has been done through his fanaticism! Think of the millions massacred through his teachings - mothers bereft of their children, children made orphans, whole countries destroyed, and millions upon millions of people killed!

Therefore, it would be incorrect to simply dismiss Muhammad as a charlatan or a crank; one such could not have inspired a civilization and religious world outlook that would survive him by many centuries. But, in a sense Muhammad is an almost tragic figure; a man of great personal gifts and enormous spiritual energy who fell onto what some have termed the "left-hand path" or in more recent popular imagery the "dark side". A deeper consideration of this is beyond the scope of this study but one student of these matters describes the phenomenon as follows:

> Finally there is a minute group of exceptional individuals that uses a fuel so powerful it can only be compared to dynamite.
>
> These rare individuals can exert very powerful effects on their fellow men. Depending on whether they use their power creatively or destructively, they can be for their fellows either a blessing or a curse.

The historian of religion Von Harnack refers to "diseases that only strike supermen who then draw from them new life never before suspected, energy that levels all hindrances in its path, and the zeal of the prophet or apostle." Philosopher of religion Jacob Needleman, quoting a Jesuit scholar of Christian spirituality, emphasizes the serious consequences when such a spiritual superman falls into "sin":

> He went on to explain that ... the traditional Christian teaching about mortal, or deadly, sin refers to a relatively developed individual. He enumerated the three characteristics of mortal sin: it must be of a serious nature; it must be done consciously with 'full knowledge'; and it must be deliberate. ... Inner psychospiritual discipline of any kind, certainly the reaching out for 'mystical experience' is an endeavor fraught with false directions - and a mistake in this sphere is of an immensely more serious nature than the usual so-called 'sins' or errors that we customarily suffer over in our everyday lives.

In addition it is surprising and, perhaps, significant that none of Muhammad's followers and admirers made any attempt to whitewash the Prophet's many shortcomings. "No other founder of a religion has been described from his human, indeed, all-too-human side without detriment to the idealized picture that people painted of him." The full extent of Muhammad's shortcomings, as derived from Islamic texts has been documented in numerous recent works. His participation in and encouragement of, or at least acquiescence in, slaughter, rape, plunder and assassination of critics; his Machiavellian political maneuvers and use of deceit and the frequent rationalizations accompanying the satisfaction of his numerous sensual whims, perhaps, characterize acceptable behavior of contemporary Bedouin chieftains. But they are certainly unworthy of a claimant to spiritual leadership. Historian Arthur Jeffery takes issue with the attempts by some modern scholars to whitewash the record of Muhammad's activities. He regards as 'the sheerest sophistry' attempts...made in some circles in modern days to explain away all the Prophet's warlike expeditions as defensive wars, or to interpret the doctrine of Jihad as merely a bloodless striving in missionary zeal for the spread of Islam...The early Arabic sources quite plainly and frankly describe the expeditions as military expeditions, and it would never have occurred to anyone at that day to interpret them as anything else...

It is, indeed, puzzling as to how the earnest, though perhaps annoying, Warner of Mecca metamorphosed into a bloody-minded and ruthless warlord. It is almost as if two different men went by the same name. During his Meccan period Muhammad acquired his knowledge slowly from various unorthodox sources:

His private thought during this period was quickened by persons ... A cousin of Khadijah, the blind Waraqah ... may have been a Christian, and although his information was apparently at many points misleading, Muhammad found him a useful source of knowledge concerning matters of faith and conduct. Less information was perhaps provided by a Christian slave boy called Zaid... In Medina Muhammad had a great turnaround in fortune, and after a series of setbacks he achieved remarkable success. An important turning point occurred at the battle of Badr:

The triumph at Badr was one of the most decisive moments in Muhammad's life. A new side of his personality came to the fore, and a new man was presented to the world ... The simple preacher and warner of Mecca turned into a vengeful warlord...

After Muhammad's victories "the attendant change of his personality did not escape the notice of his contemporaries."

And that change affected the nature of the revelations in the Koran. There is a "clear distinction between the two component parts" the revelations from Mecca and those written in Medina. As Noss observes:

> In the Meccan period, Muhammad was a long suffering prophet who, under the influence of Jewish and Christian teaching, proclaimed on the one hand God's purpose to bring the world to judgment, and on the other the wilful wickedness of man in rebellion against the will of God. ... The latest suras imply that men have the freedom of obedience only, since Allah wills all, both good and bad. Allah is a being beyond all human questioning – the inscrutable determiner of men's destinies, who acts according to divine ends which no man can clearly know ... Allah appears in the latest revelations, to use R.E. Hume's vivid characterization 'like an Arab sheikh glorified and magnified to cosmic proportions.'

Furthermore, it is significant that the Muslim scriptures, not only regard Muhammad as the "perfect man", but, in addition are devoid of any record that he struggled with temptation or was ever reprimanded by the Deity. This makes the Prophet very different from the prophets and other righteous figures from the Old Testament. The Hebrew Scriptures are full of tales of otherwise righteous kings yielding to temptations of various sorts and who are then condemned to divine punishment, of prophets condemned to suffering for attempting to evade their calling and righteous individuals inflicted with pain and sorrow as a test of faith. The greatest of the Hebrew prophets, Moses, was not permitted to enter the Holy Land because of the trespass he committed at the waters of Meribah-Kadesh. There is no record of any chastisement of Muhammad; on the contrary, Allah continually indulges all of His Messenger's whims.

The founders of the other great proselytizing faiths had to undergo and overcome temptation as a preparation for their ministries, or as a completion of their missions. Thus, the devil taunts Jesus in an attempt to make him use his powers and offers him all of the kingdoms of the world (Matthew 4.3 –

4.11). In the end Jesus must accept his death; a fate that he could easily have avoided. The temptation of worldly power, however, was too much for Muhammad. Similarly, Gautama the Buddha, sitting under the Bodhi tree, was tempted by Mara, the Evil One who paraded before him three voluptuous female divinities and their tempting female attendants. Mara follows with threats of death and destruction. Lastly, Mara offers Gautama immediate entrance into Nirvana.

The Buddha withstood all of these temptations and Mara was banished. The Buddha also willingly accepted his death by the "accidental" ingestion of poisoned food. However, the temptations of sex and personal gratification were not ones that Muhammad was able to resist. Finally, there was the example of Socrates, the great founder of the system of Greek philosophy that spread throughout the West and beyond. Socrates refused the means of escape that was offered to him and, like Jesus, elected to accept his execution in affirmation of his principles. Muhammad's principles, on the other hand, appeared to be rather more elastic.

Nevertheless, Muhammad's shortcomings did not prevent him from achieving considerable success in raising the level of civilization among the tribes of the Arabian Peninsula. The culture of the Arabs on the eve of Islam is described by the scholar of religious history Huston Smith as follows:

> The world into which Muhammed was born is described ... in a single word: barbaric. ... Scarcity of material goods and a fighting mood chronically inflamed by the blazing sun had made brigandage a regional institution and a proof of virility. ... Drunken orgies often ending in brawls and bloodshed were commonplace. The gaming impulse, always strong among nomads, was uncontrolled, with Meccan gambling tables busy the night through. Dancing girls moved from tent to tent inflaming the passions of the impetuous sons of the desert.

It is easily imagined how Muhammad, who in his early years in Mecca was strenuously and sincerely grappling with moral issues and religious concerns, regarded the behavior of his countrymen. There is no question that Muhammad ...was disturbed by the incessant quarreling in the avowed interests of religion and honor among the Quraysh chiefs. Stronger still was his dissatisfaction with the primitive survivals in Arabian religion, the idolatrous polytheism and animism, the immorality at religious convocations and fairs, the drinking, gambling and dancing which were fashionable and the burial alive of unwanted infant daughters...He must have been puzzled by the senseless bloodshed and inter tribal anarchy...

There can be no doubt of the extraordinary success of Muhammad's mission to the Arabs. It was the "genius" of Muhammad and his early successors to channel the violence, avarice and lust of "the impetuous sons of the desert" into a force capable of conquering a vast empire in a remarkably short time. However, the Prophet's success in improving the condition of his fellow Arabs and of introducing them to the benefits of higher civilization was purchased by the suffering inflicted on the neighboring peoples by these Arab conquerors; and with the consequent lowering of the high level of culture that the ancestors of the conquered had worked for millennia to attain.

The condition of women under Islam is a topic of contemporary concern and controversy. In this context a question that naturally arises is whether the new regime instituted by Muhammad resulted in an improvement in the situation of women. The condition of women in Arabia at that time was poor, and in all likelihood much worse than that in the neighboring territories:

In pre-Islamic 'Days of Ignorance,' marriage arrangements were as loose as to be scarcely recognizable. Conditional and temporary contracts were commonplace. Women were regarded as little more than chattel to be done with as their fathers or husbands pleased. Daughters had no inheritance rights and were often buried alive in their infancy.

In addition to a lack of legal rights and widespread female infanticide, marriage by capture was another common pre-Islamic Arab custom. Muhammad abolished this custom and instituted a whole series of reforms; the end result of which, however, was problematic according to Bernard Lewis:

In general, the advent of Islam brought an enormous improvement in the position of women in ancient Arabia, endowing them with property and some other rights, and giving them a measure of protection against ill treatment by husbands or owners. ... But the position of women remained poor, and worsened when, in this as in so many other respects, the original message of Islam lost its impetus and was modified under the influence of pre-existing attitudes and customs.

Lewis does not take into account that the subsequent decline in the position of women was one of the ultimate implications of Islamic law, which did not immediately follow the initial revelations, but took some time to be fully worked out. Nonetheless these implications are fully contained in the earliest Muslim texts. In this very early period, some Arab women, whether Muhammad's supporters like his first wife Khadija and the strong willed Aisha, or his female opponents in both Mecca and Medina, were still able to speak and act with a determination and fierceness that reflected the assertiveness of early Bedouin women; and this despite the many disabilities inflicted on them by Arab society. One such formidable woman was the acerbic wife of an early Meccan opponent of the Prophet:

The tenth-century Arab historian, al-Tabari's account of Hind bint Otba, the wife of Abu Sufyan, the head of one of the aristocratic families of Mecca, gives a vivid picture of the independence of aristocratic women before Islam. Women swore allegiance as much as men took part in negotiations with the new military chief of the city – that is, Muhammad himself – and were often frankly hostile to the new religion. When Muhammad arrived ... Abu Sufyan finally led out a deputation to make a formal submission and swear allegiance. The women led by Hind gave theirs only very reluctantly. Hind reproached Muhammad for having imposed obligations on women that he had not imposed on men.

However, it does appear that Islam somewhat ameliorated the lot of women in Arabia proper, although at the cost of curbing the spirited and free behavior of some upper class

Arab women prior to Muhammad's rule. But there is no doubt that an even larger price for that improvement was the deterioration of the condition of a much vaster number of women in the various conquered territories. Consider the following as an example of the high status of women among the Iranian tribes of the central Asian steppes before the coming of Islam; such assertiveness of women was characteristic of many nomadic societies:

> Of particular interest is the position of women in most Sarmatian tribes, but especially among the Sauromatians as described by Herodotus. ... their wives kept to the 'ancient Amazon mode of living, going out on horseback to hunt, and joining their husbands in war, wearing the same dress as men'. He also says that no virgin was permitted to marry until she had killed an enemy. ... The relatively large number of graves of armed women ... is usually looked upon as evidence of the survival of the ancient pre-Sauromatian social order based on a matriarchy. ... Hippocrates maintained that Sarmatian women were not only warriors, but also priestesses.

In the provinces of the Byzantine Empire, another area overrun by the Arab forces in the first years of Islamic expansion, the population consisted primarily of various Christian sects. Under the Roman Empire before the advent of Christianity women participated in business, social life and athletics. In various parts of the empire, opportunities for women were increasing over time:

> In Greece and Asia Minor, women participated with men in religious cults ... While the leading roles were reserved for men, women took part in the services and professions. Some women took up education, the arts, and professions such as medicine. In Egypt, women had attained, by the first century A.D., a relatively advanced state of emancipation, socially, politically, and legally. In Rome, forms of education had changed around 200 B.C., to offer to some children from the aristocracy the same curriculum for girls as for boys. Two hundred years later ... the archaic, patriarchal forms of Roman marriage were increasingly giving way to a new legal form

in which the man and woman bound themselves to each other with voluntary and mutual vows.

While orthodox Christianity ultimately rolled back many of these gains, early Christianity "showed a remarkable openness toward women." Some Christian sects went quite far in extending recognition to women. In fact among some "gnostic groups ... women were considered equal to men; some were revered as prophets; others acted as teachers, traveling evangelists, healers, priests, perhaps even bishops." Even in later centuries after the position of women deteriorated under Christianity, their subjugation was never nearly as complete as it was to be with the Muslim conquest.

Thus, the expansion of Islam was everywhere, outside of Arabia proper, marked by a severe loss of social status and legal rights for women. And this oppression of women instituted by the teachings of Muhammad was certainly morally reprehensible. However as will be shown in a later chapter, Culture of the Harem, it was also a key to the remarkable success of the Muslim faith and one of the primary factors behind Islam's enormous expansion. This fact, while implied by, is not usually explicitly stated in most historical narratives.

Muhammad brought the Arabian Peninsula under the rule of Islam. Immediately after the Prophet's passing his successors brought the greater part of the Near East into a new Arab empire. The following chapter outlines the Arab campaigns and illuminates the patterns common to these first and to all subsequent Muslim conquests.

9

Patterns of Islamic Conquest

In the first years of the Muslim expansion Islam was most concentrated among nomads or urban dwellers. The new religion lagged in its spread and appeal to sedentary agricultural communities. Nomads in the form of the Bedouin armies of the Prophet and his early successors were, of course, the initial carriers of the Islamic meme. The Arab leaders settled their army of occupation in large garrison towns which soon developed into cities. These pastoral conquerors quickly adapted themselves to urban environments. In addition, the conquerors attracted masses of camp followers from among the native population; these provided the Arabs with needed economic and administrative skills. These urban dwellers, in intimate contact with their Arab overlords were more susceptible to conversion than were the sedentary peasant masses. The second great wave of Islamic conquerors, the Turks followed a broadly similar pattern. While military conquest was the most important means for the expansion of Islam, there were minor additional factors. Historian Ira Lapidus sketches the different ways in which Islam expanded:

The expansion of Islam involved different forces. In North Africa, Anatolia, the Balkans, and India, it was carried by nomadic Arab or Turkish conquerors. In the Indian Ocean and West Africa it spread by peaceful contacts among merchants or through the preaching of missionaries. In some cases the diffusion of Islam depended upon its adoption by local ruling families; in others, it appealed to urban classes of the population or tribal communities. Even in areas where Islam spread by trade or conversion newly converted rulers, elites and clerics, invariably resorted to jihad to expand their territory or extend their new religion, at the expense of unconverted neighbors.

WORLD DISTRIBUTION OF ISLAM

The astounding success of Islam is evident in a cursory examination of population geography. A map of the world distribution of Muslim population in the middle of the last century shows Muslims predominating in a broad swath from the northwest bulge of Africa through Egypt and Sudan through the entire Middle East and Asia Minor into Pakistan and deep into Central Asia and Sinkiang. There are noncontiguous Muslim majorities from the horn of Africa extending down the east African coast; in Bangladesh and the Malay Peninsula extending through Indonesia into Mindanao; in the Balkans with pockets in European Turkey, Albania and Bosnia. In addition there are significant Muslim minorities in Sub Saharan west and east Africa, South Africa, the Caucasus and Central Asian fringes of Russia, north central and southern China and scattered throughout the Indian Republic.

The distribution of the Muslim population shows a striking correlation with a map of world climate. The broad expanse of land extending from Northwest Africa into Central and South Asia, and the horn of Africa contain the majority of the desert and semiarid steppe lands of the African-Eurasiatic landmass. This dry mass is only interrupted by large river valleys: the Nile, Mesopotamia, Oxus and Indus. A smaller portion of this area consists of dry-summer Mediterranean climates along the coastal fringes and extending along the fringes of the Caucasus Mountains into northern and western Iran; these make up a great part of the world's Mediterranean climates. In addition, most of the European territory once held by Muslims, the central and southern Iberian peninsula, Sicily, Cyprus and the southern Balkans also have dry Mediterranean climates. Noncontiguous areas with Muslim majorities or large minorities may, however, have radically different varieties of climates:

rainforest, tropical savanna, subtropical or High Mountain. There is an obvious advantage for Muslim armies, which consisted primarily of pastoral nomads, in maneuvering over dry treeless plains and subsisting in arid deserts and steppes.

CAUSES OF THE INITIAL ARAB EXPANSION

The unification of the Arab tribes and the end of their incessant inter-tribal raiding left the new Islamic rulers with the problem of containing or re-directing their warlike energies. The words of Muhammad were a useful, as well as profitable, instrument in channeling these energies. Now, it may be that these verses from the Koran were applicable only during the time of the Prophet and referred only to the wars against his Arab enemies; but they were certainly not interpreted as such by both his immediate and future political successors. Some of the calls to arms in the Koran are:

Fight against such of those who have been given the scripture as believe not in Allah nor the Last Day ... until they pay the tribute readily, being brought low. - Surah 9:29

And wage war on all the idolaters as they are waging war on all of you. - Surah 9:36

Go forth, light-armed and heavy-armed, and strive with your wealth and your lives in the way of Allah! - Surah 9:41

Then, when the sacred months have passed, slay the idolaters wherever ye find them, and take them (captive), and besiege them, and prepare for them each ambush. But if they repent and establish worship and pay the poor-due, then leave their way free. - Surah 9:5

There was an economic, as well as a social, imperative to the re-directing of the natural aggressiveness of the Bedouin:

There was an important material aspect to this militant doctrine. By forbidding fighting and raiding within the umma, Muhammad deprived the Arabian tribes of a traditional source of livelihood and drove them inexorably toward imperial expansion.

The motives of material advantage and providing the rambunctious Arab tribes with new outlets for their aggression were both nicely satisfied with raids outside of Arabia proper; raids that quickly and opportunistically became campaigns of conquest. As historian of the Arabs Philip Hitti notes:

Far from being entirely the result of deliberate and cool calculation, the campaigns seem to have started as raids to provide outlets for the warring spirit of the tribes now forbidden to engage in fratricidal combats, the objective in most cases being booty and not the gaining of a permanent foothold. But the machine so built soon got beyond the control of those who built it. ... It was then that the systematic campaigns began.

Some scholars, thus, emphasize the accidental nature of the first Arab conquests. Hitti sees it as a movement that "acquired moment um as the warriors passed from victory to victory" and views its creation as "due less to early design as to the logic of immediate circumstances." Noss, emphasizing the economic motive, agrees with that assessment:

It may be doubted whether the spread of Islam, at least in its early stages, was the result of calculation. ... Both religion and greed may be granted to have played their part as motivating impulses; but it would be closer to the mark to say that Muhammad unified the bedouins ... and thus made it possible for them ... to yoke together their economic need and their religious faith.

Other authorities contend that the religious imperative toward ever more expansion was present from the very beginning:

We know that before the end of his life Muhammad was in conflict with Christian populations in the north of Arabia, and even within the confines of the Roman [Byzantine] Empire. What would have happened if he had lived we do not know? But probably the policy which Abu Bakr carried on was the policy of Muhammad himself. There could have been no real compromise. He regarded himself as vicegerent of God upon earth. The true religion could only be Islam as he laid it down, and acceptance of it meant acceptance of his divinely inspired authority...

They believe that Muhammad envisioned jihad ...not as a limited defensive action to establish his religious community ... he saw it continuing far beyond his lifetime. 'Jihad will be performed continuously since the day Allah sent me as a prophet until the day the last member of my community will fight with the Dajjal (Antichrist).'

And even though ...it is unlikely that Muhammad had imagined the full scope of Islam's future expansion, let alone planned it in detail, 'his was the far-seeing mind which directed the Arabs' attention to the strategic importance of Syria for the new Islamic state.

However, the most likely event is that the "Arab conquests ... were in part the outcome of deliberate state policy and in part accidental." In the final analysis it might not make much difference; as Karsh observes:

Whether the conquests were an opportunistic magnified offshoot of small raiding parties or a product of a preconceived expansionist plan is immaterial. Empires are born of chance as well as design. What counts is that the Arab conquerors acted in a typically imperialist fashion from the start, subjugating indigenous populations, colonizing their lands, and expropriating their wealth, resources, and labor.

There can be no doubt that Arab appetites for further raids and even conquest were whetted once they were made aware of the immense and easily obtained booty available in the neighboring territories. And as it was that "in Arabia the result of victory had been booty, so at least for the tribes the Islamic conquests were great expeditions for riches." Indeed, as Goldziher points out:

It was precisely the prospect of tangible gain that made it possible to attract and hold the greater part of the Arab masses that joined him. ... A share in the spoils of war must have been among the preeminent inducements that enabled Islam to draw people to its banners. ... When one reads the ancient

> narratives ... one is truly astonished at the reports of magnificent distributions of plunder ...

The greed of the ruling aristocracy for plunder was almost insatiable. "Uthman ibn Affan ... the third caliph exploited expansion for unabashed self-enrichment. ... This fortune paled in comparison with the fabulous wealth amassed by some of Muhammad's closest companions." Zubair ibn Awam, Talha ibn Ubaidallah and the conqueror of Egypt, Amr ibn-al-As expropriated vast estates, villas and prodigious amounts of booty from the conquered peoples. The warrior elite, in general, also shared in the plunder:

> One cannot fail to be astonished when one reads lists, from as early as the third Islamic decade, of the great riches gathered by the pious warriors and men of prayer, of the vast pieces of land they called their own, of the well appointed houses they furnished at home and in the conquered territories, of the luxury with which they surrounded themselves.

The ideology contrived by Muhammad and his immediate successors, whether deliberately or by a fortuitous random evolution of doctrine was, certainly, an ingenious combination of worldly advantage with ascetic religious zeal. Hitti observes that the "passion to go to heaven in the next life may have been operative with some, but the desire for the comforts and luxuries of the civilized regions ... was just as strong in the case of many." And, as will be elaborated on in a subsequent chapter, in addition to material advantages there were immense sexual opportunities.

An additional factor underlying the Arab conquests was an increase in the population of the Arabian Peninsula relative to that of the adjacent areas:

> Demographic details give an approximate idea of the dimensions of the shift, and of the human resources which lay at the basis of Arab expansion ... while the populations of Anatolia, Syria, Lebanon, Palestine and Jordan stood at a mere 58 per cent of their AD 200 level in AD 600, that of Arabia and the Gulf states had nearly doubled. The clash of the giants, Byzantium and Persia, had favored a peripheral 'marcher' area.

The Arab conquests were, in fact, greatly facilitated by the exhausting wars between the Byzantines and the Persians. Only after the exhaustion of the Byzantine and Persian states was apparent "did calculated efforts to extend the spread of Islam make their appearance." Nor was it only the long rivalry between the empires that enabled the Arab armies to achieve quick victories; both Byzantium and Persia were rent by religious conflict and social unrest.

When the Arabs finally spilled out of the Arabian Peninsula they found the Byzantines not yet recovered from the Persian struggle and suffering from the internal convulsions of religious discord. The Persians, defeated by the Byzantines, had in addition suffered from a fossilized social structure that resulted in the jacquerie and communism of the Mazdakites.

For many years the Eastern Roman Empire had to cope with religious, social and ethnic conflict, corruption and inefficiency. According to the historian of Byzantium Vasiliev, "...the list of primary causes for Arabian success includes religious conditions in Syria, Palestine, and Egypt, the racial kinship of the population of the first two countries to the people of Arabia, the inadequacy of military forces, inefficient military organization and poor civil administration, and class relations in Egypt."

Similar conditions prevailed in the domains of the Persians. However, in the case of Persia, there was not only conflict between an established orthodoxy and heretical sects; there was also an inter-religious conflict pitting the Christian population of a major province, Mesopotamia, against the empire:

The welcome on the part of the Aramaean peasants was no less cordial than that rendered by the Syrian peasants and for much the same reasons. The Semitic Iraqis looked upon the Iranian masters as aliens and felt closer kinship with the newcomers. As Christians they had not been especially favoured by the followers of Zoroaster.

Social conflict, maladministration and heresy afflicted Persians as well as Byzantines. Bernard Lewis notes that,

...the Persian Empire at the end of the sixth century had just emerged from a revolutionary convulsion, in the course of which the old feudal structure was broken and replaced by a military despotism with a mercenary army. But the new order was far from secure and the many discontents of the population produced a series of dangerous religious heresies that threatened the religious and consequently the political unity of the Empire.

The weaknesses of the two rival empires made them exceedingly vulnerable to the tactical advantages naturally enjoyed, in all ages, by rugged and highly mobile nomad armies united under competent leadership:

The first instrument of victory was the exclusive use of horsemanship by a pastoral people genetically adapted and culturally trained for fighting. In this they were like all pastoral people. But they surpassed their predecessors in the rapidity of their movements carried out in a vast desert under conditions of appalling rigour. ... The Muslim expansion was led by commanders of the Koreish tribe ... whose commanding position at Mecca, at the centre of the great Arabian caravan industry, guaranteed that they would be supremely accomplished in controlling the force of 30,000 Bedouin and bandits whom they mobilized for their first attack. ... It was a success that was to be repeated from a Central Asiatic base by the Turks, the Tatars, the Mongols and the Moguls.

Hitti also observes how the Arab's "seemingly miraculous success was due to the application of a military technique adapted to the open steppes of Western Asia and North Africa – the use of cavalry and camelry." He cites one particular example of this blitzkrieg like campaigns conducted by the Arabs:

Ordered to go to the relief of Arab troops ... Khalid, 'the sword of Allah,' struck by forced camel marches from lower Iraq straight across the trackless desert with a body of veteran fighters and appeared with dramatic suddenness in the neighborhood of Damascus ... Water for the troops was carried in bags, but for the horses the paunches of the old camels, which were slaughtered for food served as reservoirs.

The difference in geography between the territories of the two empires may have resulted in the swift overthrow of Persia as opposed to the centuries of dogged resistance on the part of the Byzantines. Arab nomad armies, no doubt, found it easier to maneuver quickly over the arid plateau of Persia. And while the Arabs were able, subsequently, to overrun central Anatolia, the more heavily populated hilly and forested coastal areas slowed down their advance, enabling the Byzantine armies to regroup, to buttress the defenses of their formidable capital city and ultimately to drive the invaders out. The Muslim conquest of a debilitated Byzantium was only completed seven centuries later by another group of predatory nomads, the Turks.

In any event, in those very early days of Islamic expansion, the conquering Arabs were less than eager to share their religious insights with the conquered masses; it was only in subsequent centuries that the Muslims fully embraced the proselytizing implicit in the Prophet's universal message. To be accepted as converts it was necessary for non-Arabs to become "clients", second class citizens, of particular Arab tribes since "at first Islam was held to be a religion for the Arabs alone, or also for their clients."

Hitti emphasizes the ethnic exclusiveness of the early Arab conquests asserting that the "Arabians burst forth upon the unsuspecting world as members of a national theocracy. It was Arabianism and not Muhammadanism that triumphed first." Historian Richard Bulliet echoes that viewpoint:

The conquests of Islam are just as properly viewed as the conquests of the Arabs. Being an Arab and being a Muslim was so much the same thing that people in the conquered territories were sometimes unaware of the specific religious character of the invaders.

He also contends that the Arab conquerors at that time in history were not interested in creating a polity that would entice the conquered populations to abandon their own cultures and traditions. On the contrary, the early Arab leadership was exclusively concerned with reinforcing the new faith among the Arabs and establishing them as a permanent ruling class. For example, the Caliph "Umar's policy was to organize the Arabians, now all Moslems, into a complete religio-military commonwealth with the members keeping themselves pure and unmixed - a sort of martial aristocracy - and denying the privilege of citizenship to all non-Arabians." In pursuit of this goal and in violation of various treaties he expelled all Jews and Christians from Arabia proper.

However, this policy was doomed to failure; a fact that became increasingly obvious within a few decades of the conquest. For one thing, the universalism of the Prophet's message could not be permanently denied. A more important factor, which will be explored below in Culture of the Harem, was the system of polygamy and sexual slavery, which was one of the main tenets underlying the whole Muslim expansion. The combination of a numerous hybrid population combined with increasing numbers of converts made the goal of exclusion untenable; a development fraught with consequences for the future spread of the Islamic meme.

An additional factor assumed increasing importance over time in extending the initial territory seized by the Arabs, particularly against their Christian rivals in Byzantium and Europe. The Arabs, themselves an Oriental people, increasingly assumed the role as upholders of the east against the culture of Hellenism and the political ideology of Rome. The rapid Arab absorption of the territories of the eastern Mediterranean and Iran turned what was initially an Arab Islamic conquest into one more chapter of the century's old clash between East and West.

The clash can be traced back over a thousand years. During the first millennium BC, in an arc stretching from the west coast of the Levant through Anatolia, Greece and Italy a new consciousness, a dynamic individualism, arose in stark contrast to the static group psychology of the older river valley civilizations. Greece was the center and it was here that the critical breakthrough to a new mode of thought; a new conception of human destiny, a new civilization occurred.

From the beginning there was conflict between East and West as Greek civilization and its descendants clashed with the heirs of the ancient river valley civilizations. A series of armed conflicts began when in 490 BC, the Persians invaded mainland Greece. A century and a half later in his war of "revenge", Alexander conquered the Persian Empire. A century afterward, the Parthians revived the Persian Empire and struggled, first against the Greek kingdoms and later against Greece's Roman successors.

Religious conflict between the orthodox Christianity of the Hellenized Byzantine elite and the various heretical and schismatic movements in Egypt and Syria was one expression of this clash; an expression internal to the Byzantine Empire. Externally, the Sasanids were the standard bearers of Oriental culture. Then, early in the 7th century the Arabs imbued with a militant new faith, erupted from their desert home, overthrew the Persians, and Islam was to ultimately inherit and reinvigorate Oriental civilization. Philip Hitti observes that "the Moslem conquests may be looked upon as the recovery by the ancient Near East of its early domain. Under the stimulus of Islam the East now awoke and asserted itself after a millennium of Western domination." In fact, the Arabs at first and other Muslims later, assumed the role of defending Oriental civilization from the vanquished Sasanids. This became obvious when with the advent of the Abbasids "Arabianism fell, but Islam continued, and under the guise of international Islam Iranianism marched triumphantly on."

PRAGMATISM OF THE ISLAMIC CONQUERORS

The pragmatism of the Arab conquerors was one of the most important factors in consolidating the initial conquests and paving the way for future expansion. Though they fought with a fanatical intensity fueled by faith or by greed, once victory was achieved the early Arab conquerors, generally, exploited their new subjects with cunning practicality making a good show of tolerance or even benevolence. The Prophet himself was a model pragmatic political opportunist:

Yet being the astute politician and statesman that he was, Muhammad was prepared to content himself initially with a merely verbal profession of faith and a payment of tribute. He knew full well that paganism, as a social and political phenomenon, was virtually a spent force ... he could afford to wait and allow the socio-economic dynamics, which now favored Islam, to run their natural course.

Muhammad's successors were fortunate that the regulations devised by the Prophet provided for tolerating cooperative tribute payers in the conquered territories. Driving out of non-Muslims was an option "hardly available in the vast territories conquered by the Arabs, both because the populations involved were far too large to make their expulsion practicable and because their tribute was indispensable in enabling the Arabs to enjoy fully their privileges as conquerors." As Hitti, very succinctly, puts it "where the sword of Islam was not long enough to reach all the necks involved, technicality gave way to expediency." In those very early days, even spreading the faith took second place to considerations of expediency. As we have seen, the economic exploitation of the conquered territories was the primary concern of the Arabs and as "mass conversion would have threatened them with certain economic loss, they did not encourage conversion." Indeed, at times under the Umayyads converts were turned away since "they would attain the benefits of being a Muslim, which included a remission of paying the head or poll tax, or even in some instances the land tax."

Thus, Arab pragmatism even reached the point of discouraging conversions to maintain tax revenues. Another example of a practical concession made by the Arabs was allowing the continuing use of native bureaucrats and languages for a half century or more following the Arab conquests:

Although armed power was in new hands, the financial administration continued as before, with secretaries drawn from the groups which had served previous rulers, using Greek in the west and Pahlavi in the east. From the 690s the language of administration was altered to Arabic...

Pragmatic considerations prevailed in later waves of Islamic conquests. The Seljuk and Ottoman Turks tolerated the dhimmi populations for purposes of economic exploitation and even military recruitment; and continued the practice of employing native Greek officials for many years, at least until the time that Turkish speakers were able to assume these positions. However, by the time of the Turkish conquests the attitude of Muslims toward accepting converts had long since changed:

There is no indication that the Muslim rulers attempted to halt the conversions of Christians in Anatolia, and so it may be that satisfaction of a missionizing zeal may have outweighed losses from the head tax. Indeed, the conquests, commerce, and spoils of an entire empire may have served to soften the loss of such a considerable source of revenue as the djizye. The Ottoman Sultan Murad even considered the forcible conversion of Christian populations.

However, he "lacked the spare military resources to keep it [the Christian population of the Balkans] in subjection by police control. This ruled out a general policy of forcible conversion to Islam, which would in any case have served only to provoke and further to intensify any threat from the Christians."

The extension of Dhimmi status to Christians, Jews, Zoroastrians and other "people of the book" was provided for in early Islamic law. More problematic was the extension of such tolerated status to various pagan groups. However, after considerable struggle, pragmatic considerations led to granting such status even to the "idolaters" of India:

Recognizing that a newly conquered land is bound to have a substantial non-Muslim population, the Sharia provides for laws to govern them. They essentially become dhimmis. At first, it was meant only for 'People of the Book'- or Jews and Christians, soon including Zoroastrians because Iran was rapidly conquered by the Arabs.

Somewhat later, when Islamic rule came to parts of India, Hindus were given grudging recognition as dhimmis though, as idolaters, they were not entitled to it. But the expediencies of politics and governance forced Islamic rulers of India to bend the rules of the Sharia against the blandishments of the clergy.

In fact, the first Muslim general to penetrate Indian territory, the conqueror of Sind, al-Qasim "offered, in return for a peaceful surrender, to spare lives and guarantee the safety of temples ... Hindu and Buddhist establishments were respected ... The jizya ... was imposed; yet brahmins and Buddhist monks were allowed to collect alms, and temples to receive donations." However, the policies initiated by the far-sighted Governor were quickly repealed inaugurating a long and bloody period of persecution. In the early centuries of Muslim penetration "the Hindus were initially subject to mass execution and mass enslavement. Some of those enslaved converted. Others did not wait to be enslaved, but converted after witnessing the realities of life under Muslim rule." Eventually, grudgingly perhaps, the rulers of various far-flung Muslim territories had to come to a modus vivendi with their numerous Hindu subjects. In 14th century India "Muslim rulers, mostly far removed from the Islamic world, often at war with the sultan of Delhi or other co-religionists, and always dependent on the loyalty of a largely non-Muslim population, had perforce to compromise." In the end pragmatism led the final and greatest Muslim dynasty, the Moguls to formally extend the dhimmi contract to the Hindus.

But the Mughal rulers realized that if the only possible choices open to Hindus - as non-People of the Book (ahl al-kitab), they were not permitted to live and practice openly their religion - were death or conversion, then there would ultimately be no non-Muslims left to be exploited economically for the purposes of the Muslim state. This could end the fabled Mughal luxury, the famed Mughal magnificence... So the Hindus were accorded "honorary" status as dhimmis, not because of Muslim mercy, but because by so doing, the ruling Muslims could economically exploit them through the jizyah

Finally, it should be noted that the pragmatism which prevailed for much of Islamic history, once the subject populations meekly submitted to Muslim rule, gives an illusion of Muslim tolerance. Furthermore, in an analogy to the 'anthropic principle' of modern cosmology, one can say that if the conquerors had not shown at least a minimal amount of tolerance toward the conquered, Islam would not now exist in any significant form. They would have provoked the various factions of non Muslims into reconciling their differences and uniting in a desperate resistance. Moreover, there would have been no dhimmi population on which to parasitize both economically and culturally. The economic base of the conquered territories which provided Muslim rulers with resources for expansion would have been destroyed. Consequently, the Muslim polities in most areas of the world would have been stillborn.

Thus, today Islam, instead of being a powerful history shaping force, would be a relic; perhaps existing only in Arabia and a few scattered communities outside of the Peninsula. The system of dhimmitude and exploitation may not have been designed by any one man, but its cumulative effect over the years may be viewed as an ingenious social invention that facilitated Islamic expansion. Evidence bearing on this point is provided by Islam's ultimate failure in India. This failure is a likely consequence of particular ill treatment meted out to the "idolaters not of the book." The bitterness created, one that exceeds even the resentment felt by the conquered "peoples of the book" poisoned Islam's reception by the majority of Hindus.

THE ARAB EMPIRE IN THE CONTEXT OF ANCIENT IMPERIALISM

The Arabs were, certainly, not unique as empire-builders. They were both preceded and followed by a number of large empires in Eurasia and the Mediterranean. And although the Arabs had high motivation derived from a powerful ideological imperative; it was an advantage they shared with many other imperial nations:

Throughout history all imperial powers and aspirants have professed some kind of universal ideology as both a justification of expansion and a means of ensuring the subservience of the conquered peoples: in the case of the Greeks and Romans it was that of 'civilization' vs. 'barbarity,' in the case of the Mongols it was the conviction in their predestination to inherit the earth. For the seventh-century Arabs it was Islam's universal vision of conquest as epitomized in the Prophet's summons to fight the unbelievers wherever they might be found.

The Arab conquests, in their speed and extent were comparable to the conquests of Alexander the Great and Genghis Khan. However the Arabs had several unique advantages that made their empire more durable. Arab culture and Islamic religion developed deep roots in the conquered territories due, to a large extent, to their breeding system. Alexander also sought to encourage the spread of a fused Hellenic and Persian civilization through intermarriage. But the Arab breeding system, with a permanent system of concubinage and sexual slavery was more comprehensive and on-going than the Macedonian. Arab culture therefore penetrated deeply in the conquered territories while Hellenistic culture was never more than a thin surface on top of the oriental culture of the subject masses.

The lightning conquests of the Mongols are comparable to those of the Arabs, and the territory overrun was even more extensive. In addition, the Mongol warrior elite, like the Arabs practiced polygamy and concubinage. Indeed, recent genetic research points to Genghis Khan as having an enormous number of male descendants in Asia. However, the Mongols had nothing comparable to the strong religious motivation of the Arabs. In addition, they lacked the imperative to spread the ideology of Mongolianism; the Mongol chieftains were interested in power and in loot, they had no evangelical pretensions. Thus the Mongols, instead of absorbing, were absorbed by the culture of those they subjugated. The eastern Mongols were eventually assimilated by Chinese and Buddhist culture; the western Mongols became Muslims.

Rome had an empire comparable in extent to that of the Arabs. And like the Arab, Roman culture was deeply rooted and long-lasting. But, unlike the Arab empire, the Roman Empire was the result of a gradual slow accretion occurring over many centuries.

ISLAM'S NOMADIC SPEARHEADS

The expansion of Islam's borders by conquest was spearheaded by a series of barbarian nomadic or semi-nomadic peoples. Following the Arabs, it was primarily Berbers, Turks and Mongols that spread the sword of Islam into new territory. In contrast the more civilized Persians adopted a strategy of acceding to Islam and then infiltrating it from within, ultimately using it as a tool of vengeance against their longtime rival, the Greco-Roman civilization of the West. The ultimate triumph of Shi'ism as the state religion of Persia in the 16th century was another consequence of the Persian strategy of preserving their national identity. The Persians were instrumental in consolidating and administering the far flung Islamic possessions; even to the point of establishing their own dynasties which held sway over Persia, Transoxiana and a nominally Abbasid Iraq. But they formed only a subordinate legion in extending Muslim conquests west into Anatolia and east into India. The conquest of new territory was left mostly to the nomadic Turks and Mongols. It was the Turks who, falling under the sway of Persian civilization as well as that of the religion of Islam, administered the final blow to the Persians longtime rivals in Byzantium.

Of all the nomadic spearheads it was the Turks who became the most important champions of Islam. They along with their other central Asian cousins, the Mongols, eventually superseded even the Arabs:

A new race from Central Asia was now pouring its blood into the struggle of Islam for world supremacy. The story of these barbarian infidels setting their feet on the necks of the followers of the Prophet and at the same time accepting the religion of the conquered and becoming its ardent champions, was not a unique instance... the Mongols of the thirteenth century, as well as their other kinsmen, the Ottoman Turks of the early fourteenth century repeated the same process.

The Turks were the dominant Islamic Central Asian contingent. The Mongols entered the scene as avowed enemies of the Muslims, devastating large areas of Muslim territory and even sacking Baghdad. As Lewis observes regarding these people of the Asian steppes:

Unlike the Persians, the Greeks, and the ancient peoples of the Middle East, the Turks and Mongols were never conquered by Islam. On the contrary, they entered the Islamic world as conquerors, some of them freely converted in their homelands, some of them, the Mongols, arriving as pagan aliens and imposing a pagan domination over the Muslims.

Of course the Mongols eventually converted to Islam, and becoming indistinguishable from the Turks in language and culture, proceeded to spread their new faith further into both the steppe lands and India. These new converts from central Asia soon became even more "Muslim" than the Arabs. As Lewis notes:

Partly because of the simple intensity of the faith as they encountered it on the frontiers of Islam and heathendom, partly because their conversion to Islam at once involved them in Holy War against their own heathen kinsmen, the converted Turks sank their national identity in Islam as the Arabs and Persians had never done.

However, not all of these Turks came as conquerors. The first contingent entered the Arab world as recruits or even as slaves of the Caliph al-Mamun. In the far west another primitive tribal people, the Berbers, after a fierce but brief resistance, cast their lot with the Arabs and were instrumental in conquering Spain and spreading Islam to large areas of West Africa.

With every extension of Islamic territory the nomad vanguard was accompanied by Muslims of other ethnic groups. Some of these joined the original nomadic invaders in fighting the infidel, others simply followed in their wake as settlers or colonists. Thus, the Seljuk Turks were accompanied or followed by Persians, Kurds and Arabs in Anatolia. The Ottoman conquerors of Anatolia and the Balkans were joined by other

Muslim cohorts and by both converts and opportunistic mercenaries from many ethnicities. The Berbers joined with the Arabs in the invasion of Spain. In India the "Ghorid forces included Afghans, Persians and Arabs, but the most numerous and effective contingents were of Turkic stock."

Moreover, each of Islam's nomadic vanguards was usually followed at a later time by additional nomads from the same, or a closely related, ethnic group who were often extremely destructive to the newly pacified conquered territories and to the fragile social orders recently established by their preceding kin. Often, these unwelcome relatives would be diverted by the local Muslim authorities to attack rival Muslim rulers or to invade the territory of yet unconquered infidels. These secondary invasions were as important in expanding or consolidating Islamic territory as were the first invasions.

Following the conquest of the Maghreb and of Spain the still independent Berber tribes proved troublesome to the settled Muslim communities of Arabs and Berbers. While these tribes were often channeled into the continuing struggle against infidels in Spain or elsewhere in Africa, they also formed an opposition to established Muslim states which "took the form of schismatic and heretical Moslem sectarianism." In addition to this secondary Muslim Berber encroachment, the Maghreb in the eleventh century was ravaged by the "troublesome Arab tribes of the banu-Hilal and Sulaym".

The Fatimid caliph of Egypt, to rid himself of their bothersome presence, persuaded them "to move westward where for years they ravaged Tripoli and Tunisia." While these rapacious newcomers helped to bring about the Arabisation of many Muslim Berbers, they were, as the historian of Dhimmitude Bat Yeor, points out, even more devastating to the surviving non Muslim groups. "In the Maghreb, tribal wars which also decimated the Muslim populations were even crueler on the dhimmis living as they did under the protection of a monarch, whose assassination could cause their destruction." In fact, many Jewish merchants from the once thriving province of Ifriqiya "transferred to Egypt in the wake of the devastating Bedouin invasions that overwhelmed Ifriqiya between 1050 and 1057."

Another territory bordering Egypt, the Sudan, was also ravaged by Bedouin tribes, driven out or re-directed by the Egyptian Muslim authorities. The infiltration of these pastoralists was instrumental in the long process of Islamization of the Sudan. This infiltration gathered force "during the early disturbed decades of the third century of Islam" when "it seems that nomadic Arabs began to enter the Sudan in small parties".

While the Arab Bedouins were mostly directed toward the west and south (Sudan), there were continuing Bedouin incursions into the eastern Muslim domains, where they also wreaked damage on settled Muslims and non-Muslims alike. In Iran, although the destructive effects of nomadism occurred primarily as a result of the later Turkish and Mongol incursions "certain Arabs ... in the center and east, were pure Bedouins and frequently insufferable to the inhabitants of the agricultural fringes". And few areas were as continually ravaged as Palestine, no doubt due to the close proximity of the large reservoir of Bedouin tribes in the neighboring Arabian Desert. In Palestine, furthermore, "in the early Middle Ages ... the ravages which followed Arab tribal battles, resumed with the arrival of the Turkomans in 1071." In addition, the nomad traditions of feuding and raiding continued to plague settled populations, particularly non-Muslims, up to the twentieth century. According to Bat Yeor:

> Apart from the enslavement of rebels, there were episodic abductions of Christian and Jewish women and children by nomads in rural regions of Kurdistan, Mesopotamia, Iraq, Palestine, Syria, and the Maghreb. Although totally illegal according to Islamic law, this continued to be a regular practice during razzias and uprisings until the twentieth century.

The initial penetration of the Turkish Islamic vanguard was followed by subsequent migrations of closely related Turkish groups, usually known as Turkmen, and by, their more distant kin, the Mongols. The disruptions caused by these secondary

Turkish invasions to existing Muslim polities and to the hapless dhimmis, were as, or even more, severe than were the disruptions accompanying the secondary migrations of the Bedouin tribes. Both Bedouin and Turkmen nomads were a plague on settled Muslim populations and their rulers, as well as on Christians, but the latter as infidels had much the harder time.

Turkmen impact in Anatolia has been well documented by historians, particularly in the writings of Speros Vryonis. He notes that the conquest of the Byzantine borderlands in western Anatolia "was a long and destructive process that lasted for a century. ... The prolonged hostile relations of Byzantines and Turks in this part of Anatolia resulted in the destruction of Byzantine society and in the nomadization of large areas." As the later Bedouin migration altered the ethnic and linguistic balance in North Africa, so it was with the secondary Turkmen incursion into Anatolia:

> The invasions, settlements, and raids of the Turkmens played a crucial role in the fate of the Anatolian peninsula. The impact of this nomadic-pastoral-warrior society, which was at the height of its heroic age, upon the stability of the highly developed sedentary society of the Byzantine Christians was one of the principal factors in the cultural transformation of Asia Minor.

As the troublesome Bedouin were encouraged by local Arab dynasties to migrate out of their territories, so were the Turkmen directed to the borders by the Seljuk authorities:

> The appearance of the nomads on the borders is also connected with the fact that the sultans sent them there to carry on the djihad with the Christians. ... The report of the twelfth-century Arab traveler al-Harawi also bears out the ghazi character of these nomadic groups. ... It was also convenient for the sultans to send these tribes to the frontiers, for they were thus removed from the central regions of the Seljuk domains.

The displacement of the native Christians on the Byzantine frontier "along with the arrival of new Turkic and Mongol groups in Anatolia, resulted in an important demographic and ethnic alteration of the Anatolian population." The continuing disruption due to nomadic incursion along with the Islamic religion was instrumental in the Turkification of Anatolia; otherwise in the absence of continuing nomad migrations, the dense sedentary population might have absorbed them. Such had been the case, a few centuries before, when the Turkic Bulgarian ruling class was absorbed by the Slavic settlers in the province of Moesia. Vryonis specifies some of the many problems these additional nomads presented to an already burdened sedentary Christian population. After Emperor Manuel, ca 1175 drove the Turkmen out of the region of Dorylaeum the ...undeterred nomads ... reassembled with their flocks in the same area. This is quite characteristic of the struggle that the emperors had to wage against the Turkmens in western Asia Minor ... The incident of the rebuilding of Dorylaeum is one of the clearest chapters in the long struggle between nomadism and sedentary society in Anatolia.

As Vryonis points out: The very intrusion and physical presence of the tribesmen, their families and livestock in Anatolia, their status as pastoral military conquerors, and their continuing raids and banditry constituted a very serious disturbance to the sedentary, and especially to the Christian, groups.

These depredations compare with the original Seljuk invasions several centuries before. This second, late thirteenth century conquest according to Vryonis "was in many ways similar to the earlier conquest at the end of the eleventh century. That is to say, it was often accompanied by violent displacement of rural and urban populations, enslavement, and destruction."

These particularly primitive Muslim tribesmen were even less constrained by practical considerations or by Muslim law. Even dhimmi populations under the protection of settled Muslim rulers were subjected to enslavement, sexual slavery, and forced conversion. In Georgia "priests were immolated, virgins violated, young men forcibly circumcised, and children enslaved" by the Turkmen. Indeed, after the collapse of the once powerful Konya sultanate the Turkmen nomads resumed their depredations on the settled population, Muslim and

Christian alike. The end of the relatively enlightened Konya sultanate was the final blow to Greek culture and language in the major part of Anatolia:

> As they settled in the countryside, their language predominated in those areas where Greeks and Armenians had withdrawn, and even in those regions where the Christian groups remained, Turkish eventually prevailed as the language of the conquerors. ... when in 1276-78 the Turkmens of the Karamanids rebelled and entered the city of Konya one of their acts was to banish Persian and to proclaim the exclusive use of Turkish in the government and administration. ... When the Turks settled in towns and villages and intermarried with the converted Greeks and Armenians, their position as rulers and the official use of Turkish produced a gradual retreat of Greek and Armenian to isolated areas of non Turkish settlement, or to a few areas in which Christians remained compact...

Thus, there was considerable hybridization with the native population even of these nomads, as had been the case of the preceding Seljuks owing to intermarriage. Other factors adding to this hybridization were widespread concubinage and sexual slavery.

Even the states established by these nomads as successors to the Seljuks were disrupted by still additional nomadic invaders. Turkmen raiders were still active in the following century and were frequently reported attacking Byzantine territory and enslaving Christian children. Moreover, the hatred of both sedentary and town dwelling Greeks and Muslims for these barbaric nomads "left indelible traces in contemporary literature and historical deed". The descendants of one of these latter nomadic ghazi cohorts, the greatly hybridized Ottoman Turks, eventually established a stable state which absorbed the territories of all of the Seljuk successors. These new rulers faced the same problems with the Turkmen as had their predecessors. But they were ultimately strong enough to deal effectively with these raiders. The continuing depredations of the Turkmen nomads were such as to force "the Ottoman sultans to adopt a policy of partial extermination."

Islamic history is not unique with respect to the decisive effects of such secondary invasions on cultural change. The pattern exemplified by Muslim nomadic incursions is an example of a more general historical phenomenon whereby a particular group opens up a territory for conquest and is then followed by additional closely related invaders who war against the states established by the first cohort. One case cited by the historian of ancient Britain, John Morris, relates to the effect on the native British culture and the Welsh language of continuing invasions from northern Europe and Scandinavia after the initial Saxon conquest had settled down into a form of social stability. He notes that in "Britain, both the Norse invasions and the Norman conquest were upheavals severe enough to kill what remained of peasant Welsh in many parts of Britain."

India was also afflicted by successive waves of nomads starting in the eleventh century. One group of Turkic invaders after another entered the country, including the Moguls whose dynasty was Mongol in origin, but who had been Turkified over the centuries. And as was the case farther west, the Turks were joined by Muslims of other ethnic origins. Many of these migrants fled from the wrath of the Mongols. In fact, "it seems probable that far more Muslims entered India as refugees from the Mongol invasions than as warriors in the Ghaznavid and Ghorid armies combined." Also as for the western Turks, the more settled Muslims who followed in their footsteps imparted their higher level of culture to the newly conquered Indian territories. For example, in 14th century India, "Gujarat acquired a large community of African Muslims. Meanwhile the influx of Persians and Afghans into the Deccan would give to the Bahmanid sultanate ... a strongly Persian and Shi'ite flavour."

The effects of successive waves of ghazi nomads on recently conquered Muslim lands were devastating. *Dhimmi* populations, in particular, suffered acutely. The attrition to their numbers was due to continued slaughter, enslavement, forced conversion and plunder; in many cases these were in direct violation of the contract of protection under which they had lived for years. Many *dhimmis* "voluntarily" converted in order to preserve what little wealth and dignity remained to them. Established Muslim rulers usually attempted to protect their *dhimmis*. But as Bat Yeor observes, this was often ineffective:

The dynastic conflicts and tribal revolts brought the destruction of villages. ... The authorities strove to protect the dhimmis by dispatching troops, if only to preserve the state's source of finance. *Dhimmis* were exploited and despoiled by all parties. They were used as economic tools in political struggles which did not concern them.

In a process paralleling the experience of Jews in both Muslim lands and in Europe those *dhimmi* populations that managed to survive these pressures into modern times were often selected for cunning and intelligence. This is, undoubtedly one of the reasons for the comparative success and accomplishment exhibited by the Armenians, Assyrians, Copts, Parsees and other non-Muslim groups.

Finally, even the conquered Muslim populations in these areas were frequently singled out for oppression and discrimination. The military aristocracies arising from successive nomadic waves were quite happy to use the Muslim ideology as a means of conquest and control. However, they often held the preceding Muslim inhabitants, as well as the dhimmi populations, in contempt. For example, Stillman points out that:

Under the *Mamluks*, the sumptuary laws were taken more seriously than in earlier periods. After all, as the *Mamluks* did not allow the native Arabs to dress like Mamluks or ride horses as they did, they were not going to permit nonbelievers to dress like Believers.

Also it was observed that beginning with the 17th century in the Ottoman Empire the "ruling Turkish minority treated the average Arab Muslim almost as contemptuously as they did the *dhimmis*."

10

The Islamic Conquests A Survey

The following is a brief survey of the conditions leading to the conquest and Islamization of the territories that became subject to Muslim rule. It is not meant as a detailed history of the Muslim conquests; such histories are widely available. The dates are, of course, approximate. There were often incursions into a territory some time preceding the beginning of permanent occupation. Also, continued resistance in certain lands makes it difficult to affix an exact date to the completion of the conquest. In many areas, Islamization was a slow process of infiltration or of trade without any definite starting or ending points.

The following should, however, dispel any notion that Islam spread by peaceful means; it should also dispel the myth that the wars of Islam were "defensive." All the territories that Islam first appeared in, and most of the later Islamic territories were subdued by force of arms. Although, as we have seen, Islam was, at first, viewed by the conquerors as an Arab exclusive religion, ultimately it assumed the role of one of the world's great proselytizing faiths. Once the reluctance on the part of the Arab rulers to convert non-Arabs ended, and the unceasing pressure on the conquered populations eventually caused the large majority in most areas to become Muslim. By the time other ethnic groups became the carriers of the Islamic meme, conversion of the conquered peoples was eagerly pursued. Moreover, even in those areas where Islam was initially established by trade or through a slow migration of Muslims, local Muslim rulers used the martial virtues of Islam as a means of expanding their states through jihad.

It should also be noted that, while Islam had many attractions for nomadic tribes and other primitive peoples, the settled conquered population did not enthusiastically embrace the faith. In most instances Islam required as much time to become firmly rooted as had Christianity. The latter required about three centuries to emerge from a despised and persecuted faith to the official religion of the Roman Empire. In almost all of the conquered territories Islam required as much, and or even more time, to convert a majority of the natives. Given the obvious coercive advantages that a violent conquering faith has over a persecuted one, this observation is quite revealing of the fact that Islam did not have the same allure for more civilized and educated populations as had its chief competitor in the west, Christianity.

SYRIA

Greater Syria including Palestine and Lebanon was quickly and easily subdued during the first Arab conquests. Arab armies entered Syria in 633 and the final Syrian fortresses were reduced in 640. Hitti provides some reasons for this rapid conquest:

> This easy conquest of the land [Syria] had its own special causes. The Hellenistic culture imposed on the land ... was only skin-deep and limited to the urban population. The rural people remained ever conscious of cultural and racial differences between themselves and their masters. This racial antipathy between the Semitic population of Syria and the Greek rulers was augmented by sectarian differences.

However, it was only during the Abbasid caliphate, ca 800, that the conversion of the population passed the tipping point.

IRAQ

Iraq was conquered beginning in the year 634 and ending in 641 with the fall of Mosul. As was the case for Syria, the conquest was facilitated owing to the religious and ethnic differences between the population and the rulers:

> The welcome on the part of the Aramaean peasants was no less cordial than that tendered by the Syrian peasants, and for much the same reasons. The Semitic Iraqis looked upon the Iranian masters as aliens and felt closer kinship with the newcomers. As Christians they had not been especially favored by the followers of Zoroaster. ... As in the case of Syria ... an influx of fresh Arabian tribes, attracted by the new economic advantages, took place into the newly conquered territory.

Conversions also proceeded slowly. The population of northern Iraq "early in the tenth century was still ... 'Moslem in name but Christian in character'."

EGYPT

Arab armies first attacked Egypt at the beginning of the year 640. The second capture of Alexandria in 646 marked the effective completion of the conquest. Once again dissident religious factions among the native population were an important factor easing the way of the Arab conquerors:

> The native Copts ... were instructed from the very beginning by their bishop in Alexandria to offer no resistance to the invaders. This is not surprising in view of the religious persecution to which they as Monophysites had been subjected by the official Melkite (royal) church.

In Egypt the cities adapted easily to Muslim rule, however, the adjustment of the rural Coptic population, possibly because of their more pronounced ethnic differences with the Semitic Arabs, proved more problematic. Anthropologists Oliver Roland and Brian Fagan note this dichotomy between the cities and the country:

> During the eighth century it [Arabic] finally superseded Greek, and before long it was impinging on Coptic. ... As a result, the cultural transition for those who converted to Islam was greatly eased. The successful Egyptian of the early Islamic centuries was first an Arabic-speaker and only later a Muslim.

The movement began in towns and spread slowly to the countryside, where Arabic displaced Coptic ... only during the later Middle Ages.

Furthermore, the rural Copts proved willing to engage in violent insurrections "several times against their Moslem overlords before they finally succumbed in the days of ... al-Ma'mun (813-33)".

The Egyptian population, particularly the Christians, was hard pressed during Islam's early dynastic struggle. Bat Yeor notes that:

...the removal of the Umayyads ... created anarchy ... Marwan; the last Umayyad caliph ... operated a scorched earth policy when he fled from Abbasid troops. Towns, villages, and harvest were set alight and large numbers perished in the general exodus. The Coptic patriarch Michael ... was tortured daily ... to extort money from him.

The settled population of Egypt was also afflicted by later Bedouin incursions and without doubt these predations had a differential adverse effect on the remaining Coptic population. In the 15th century "marauding Bedouins in the Delta and the desert to the east repeatedly fell on the settled fallahin of the narrow agricultural valley and ravaged the land." The final blow to the rural Copts occurred in the Mamluk period. During this time conversions "to Islam, always a steady trickle, now became a flood, and even in regions like Upper Egypt, which adjoined the Christian region of Nubia and had long been a Coptic stronghold, became majority Muslim."

NORTH AFRICA

The conquest of the Maghreb began with the conquest of Libya in 643. After several decades halt to the Arab advance Carthage was permanently acquired about the year 698. Berber resistance in western Algeria and Morocco came to an end by 709.

A characteristic of this region was the extreme weakness of Byzantine civilization among the Berber masses. Unlike

Byzantium's eastern provinces, there was a considerable interregnum with respect to Roman rule. These western regions had been under barbarian control before being re-annexed by the Eastern Roman Empire. Nevertheless, the Byzantine authorities made strong, though not entirely successful efforts to integrate the barbarian Berber tribes into the Christian Roman system. Byzantine historian A. A. Vasiliev quotes Charles Diehl in L'Afrique byzantine:

> For two centuries the Byzantine Empire had conserved in these districts the difficult heritage of Rome; for two centuries the empire made the great and steady progress of these provinces possible by the strong defence of their fortresses; for two centuries it upheld in this part of North Africa the traditions of classical civilization and converted the Berbers to a higher culture by means of religious propaganda. In fifty years the Arabian invasion undid all these achievements.

This penetration of Byzantine Christianity and civilization was only strong among the town dwellers and settled Berbers of the coast. According to Hitti:

> At the time of the Moslem conquest most of the Berbers on the strip of fertile land bordering on the sea had become Christians. ... Otherwise the population was not deeply touched by Roman civilization, for the Romans and Byzantines lived mainly in towns on the coast and represented a culture that was quite alien to the mentality of these nomadic and semi- nomadic North Africans. On the other hand Islam had a special attraction for people in such a cultural stage as that of the Berbers.

It is also possible that the remnants of Carthaginian culture remained in remote areas, facilitating the Muslim conquest:

> Punic survived in country places until shortly before the Moslem conquest. This explains the seemingly inexplicable miracle of Islam in Arabicizing the language and Islamizing the religion of these semi-barbarous hordes and using them as fresh relays in the race toward further conquests.

Historian of the Maghreb, John Cooley also notes that the "Berbers were not the sophisticated bourgeois of the Syrian cities. Neither Latin nor Byzantine culture took root among them. This probably accounts for the total disappearance of Christianity." An additional factor in the extinction of Byzantine civilization and Christianity in the Maghreb was undoubtedly the intensity of the struggle for a region that was far from the central territories of Islam. The devastation of the towns and the mass enslavement inflicted on the inhabitants of the coastal cities by the invading Arabs and later on by Muslim Berbers would have exceeded that which took place in the more rapidly conquered eastern provinces. In fact, in "the dead cities of Tunis, which are today in most cases in the same condition in which they were left by the Arabian invasion, one still finds at every turn some traces of these formidable raids."

The conversion of the Berbers was an important part of the Arab strategy for consolidating their far flung African possessions. The reluctance of the Arabs under the first caliphs to proselytize non-Muslim populations was lessening at this time. And in any event the usefulness of adding a new group of large and warlike primitives to buttress their overextended ranks must have appealed to the early Arabs notable pragmatism. Thus, the "conversion of the Berbers ... was carried out in the following century after 70 according to a new plan of enlisting the Berbers in the Moslem army and thus winning them over by the new prospects of booty."

Despite "the rapid spread of Islam among the Berbers, however, Christianity still continued to exist among them, and even in the fourteenth century we hear of 'some small Christian islands' in North Africa." Hitti gives an example of one small group of Christian Berber holdouts as late as the beginning of the 16th century:

Here the final triumph of Islam was not achieved until the twelfth century, though certain Kabyls ... of Algeria had the Andalusian Moors driven out after the fall of Granada in 1492, to thank for their conversion.

In the final analysis, however, the Maghreb, unlike Arab territories to the east saw the complete destruction of Christianity. There appear to be a number of converging factors which made this disappearance inevitable. As noted above, the primitive level of culture among the Berber tribes, the dominant sector of the population was much more conducive to Islam. In addition their Christianity was superficial at best. While in the east, the national aspirations of the native populations, for several centuries at least, found an expression in Christianity, the Berbers quickly asserted their opposition to the Arab order through various Muslim schisms and heresies. Another factor was the greater destruction wreaked on the cities which were the strongholds of Christianity and Roman culture. During the time of the Aghlabid dynasty (800-909) the transformation of North Africa was "perhaps more complete than in any other region thus far reduced by Moslem arms."

Continuing tribal warfare and a lack of strong central governments for most of the first five centuries of Muslim rule in the Maghreb decimated the Christian population. Those centuries witnessed frequent uprisings and raids by schismatic Berber sectarians. Also of great importance was the migration of the destructive banu-Hilal Bedouins who, in addition to Arabizing the eastern regions of the Maghreb, caused the flight of both Jewish and Christian dhimmis.

The rise to power of fanatical Berber dynasties with the consequent abrogation of the contract of dhimmitude further decimated the remaining urban Christian communities. In 1159 the Almohad Abd al-Mumin destroyed the episcopate of Carthage and forced the native Christians who remained to convert. Final devastating blows occurred "with the beginnings of the Christian reconquest in Spain and Sicily and the Balearic Islands and with the crusade led by King Louis IX". It was then "that the Muslim rulers of North Africa faced their few remaining Christian subjects with the choice of conversion or death." It is instructive to observe that this preceded by a few centuries, and perhaps even inspired, the much better known Spanish expelling of its Jewish and Muslim populations.

Also of interest is the relative lack of intellectual activity in that part of North Africa as compared to periods of intense activity in the eastern provinces and in Muslim Spain. The continuing depredations of both Berber and Bedouin nomads and the deeper process of Islamization were, without doubt, important causes of the lower level of high culture in the Maghreb.

SUB-SAHARAN WEST AFRICA

In the large and heterogeneous territory of sub-Saharan West Africa, stretching from the western border of the modern nation of the Sudan to the Atlantic, Islam was introduced at widely varying times in different areas. A convenient start year is 1061 which marks the organization of the Maghreb Almoravid state by Ibn Tashfin. The Almoravids proceeded with an active program of spreading Islam to their non-Muslim or nominal Muslim trading partners in Ghana. The active period of Muslim expansion lasted many centuries only coming to an end, insofar as it can be said to have ended at all, with the termination of the West African jihads by the French in 1893.

While there had been a slow penetration of Islamic ideas south of the desert through the activities of Muslim traders, it was the zealous new Muslim sect of Almoravids (Murabits) who initiated a more violent and rapid spread of their militant faith. Hitti observes that:

Starting with about a thousand warrior 'monks', the Murabits forced one tribe after another, including some negro tribes, to accept Islam and in a few years established themselves as masters of all north-western Africa and finally of Spain. Their story serves as yet another illustration in Islam of what can be produced by the marriage of the sword to religion.

In 1076 the Soninke kingdom of Ghana suffered a defeat at the hands of the Almoravids resulting in the formal acceptance of Islam and payment of tribute. Oliver and Fagan contend that:

Probably the Almoravids ... merely helped the internal minority of Soninke Muslims to seize the positions of power. At all events, the written sources of the twelfth and thirteenth centuries are at one in claiming that Ghana was now a Muslim state, and that it was still the major power of the Mande-speaking region.

However, a violent invasion by Muslims external to the region was not generally the case in West Africa. As historian of Islam, Ira Lapidus notes, in "most of Africa, Islam was established by processes more closely resembling those of Southeast Asia than the Middle East and India." In West Africa he notes

...kings often turned to ... Islam, to acquire autonomous legitimization and to undermine the authority of competitors. In other cases kingship was not an indigenous institution, but grew out of the dominance of a foreign trading community. In the towns of Kano and Katsina monarchical rule was established by colonies of Muslim traders who either directly seized the state or converted a local ruler.

By 1260 the kingdom of Mali had been penetrated by Islam. The king at that time, "Mansa Uli was a pious Muslim, who made the pilgrimage to Mecca ... Mansa Uli was a conqueror ... during his reign ... Mali expanded its influence to the east ... subjecting the ancient kingdom of Songhay ..." and gained control of the northern routes through the desert. But along with "peaceful Muslim colonization there was a parallel tradition of militant determination to turn small colonies into Muslim states by defeating corrupt Muslim rulers, conquering the pagan populations, converting them to Islam, and ruling them according to Muslim law." In Mauritania jihad began with the resistance of Berbers to religiously lax Arab rulers. A later jihad in Senegambia, like other Muslim jihads in the 17th and the 18th centuries "had their origins in the efforts of small Muslim communities to overthrow local rulers and to establish states of their own." The "Futa Jallon jihad was the work of the settled Muslim communities allied with Fulani pastoralists." As late as the eighteenth and nineteenth centuries such jihads were numerous in West Africa and the central Sudan.

Islam's appeal to nomadic tribes is illustrated by the West African history of jihad. In addition, the experience of Muslim penetration into West Africa illustrates the danger of allowing the establishment of large immigrant Muslim communities and makes for an instructive lesson even today.

There were two more factors behind Islam's penetration into sub-Saharan Africa. One is the massive and lucrative slave trade which, along with other valuable commodities, attracted numerous Muslim merchants to establish outposts and initiate friendly relations with local rulers. The other factor was the understandable defensive reaction of local kings who through conversion could hope to deflect Muslim attack:

Accepting Islam would also give the king legal immunity from attack by other Muslims. Since raids by desert nomads upon the settled farmers were very frequent anyway, and raids by Muslims upon unbelievers was encouraged by religion, according to the common belief of Muslims, a Sûdân king would have strong motivation to become a Muslim as a pre-emptory defence against attack.

EASTERN AFRICA

Muslim rule in the coastal regions of East Africa was also a slow process of infiltration by settlers and merchants. A convenient start year is 850 by which time Muslim presence was well established on the Somali coast. However, Muslim forces had captured the Dahlak Islands in the Red Sea at the beginning of the eighth century, while Muslim merchants displaced the Greeks who for centuries held the trade of the city of Axum. The attractions Islam held for nomads was once again evident with its adoption by the pastoral camel herders of the coast. At the same time, the settled Christian populations of the nearby Ethiopian highlands, who have successfully resisted Muslim conquest, retain their religion to the present day. Muslim expansion along the East African coast continued under the aegis of various local rulers until the late 19th century ending with the establishment of European rule in the 1880s.

Between the ninth and thirteenth century most of the people in Somalia and the horn of Africa, under the influence of Muslim traders embraced Islam. "We have an illuminating glimpse of the situation around Berbera from Ibn Said in the early thirteenth century, who says that the people had mostly embraced Islam and were therefore no longer sold as slaves in the neighbouring Muslim countries." By the year 1200 a Muslim dynasty was ruling the East African islands of Mafia and Kilwa, some hundred miles south of Zanzibar. This was the "greatest and most civilized of all the East African settlements". In parts of East Africa, as elsewhere, local rulers converted to Islam for its military advantages:

In this region Arab and Swahili traders supplied local chieftains with firearms in exchange for slaves, and thus intensified the local struggle for power. Local adventurers, often supported by uprooted young men turned warriors, took advantage of the situation to conquer small kingdoms. Tippu Tip, a Swahili trader and warrior, set up a small Muslim state and in Buganda, King Mutesa I Islamized his regim.

SUDAN

Like Anatolia, the Sudan valiantly resisted repeated Muslim onslaughts for centuries, and remained predominantly Christian until the latter half of the 14th century. The beginning of Arab penetration into the Sudan can be conveniently dated to the same year, 651, that marked the conquest of Persia. In that year the Arabs besieged the city of Dunqula forcing the Nubian king to sue for peace and assent to the annual payment of tribute. Hitti notes, nevertheless, that for "centuries to come the Christian kingdom of Nubia ... stood as a barrier against the farther southward onrush of Islam." According to Oliver and Fagan:

What really happened in the seventh century was that the Arabs saw that the conquest of Nubia would not repay the effort involved. And during the six centuries that followed they saw no reason to revise that decision. As a result, the Sudan enjoyed during those centuries one of the most flourishing and vigorous periods in its long history.

The fall of Alwa, the last Christian kingdom in the Sudan at the end of the 15th century marks the effective end of the Muslim conquest of the Sudan. However, recent events make it apparent that the conquest was not complete in all of what constitutes modern Sudan. The process of Islamization continues in, a particularly vicious and racist form, in the southern Sudan.

The Islamization of the Sudan was, generally, one of slow invasion through migration rather than one of sudden conquest. Similar circumstances may well be occurring today in modern Europe. It was only in the "early disturbed decades of the third century of Islam" that small groups of Arab nomads migrated to the Sudan. This movement was apparently prompted by the policy initiated by the caliph al-Mu'tasim to replace his Arab army with one of Turkish slaves. An immediate consequence of this infiltration was the subjection of the Beja people living on the east coast of the Sudan to Arab rule. Here, in contrast to neighboring "Nubia, there was nothing to stop them from coming through the eastern desert into the Sudan." Sudanese historian Yusuf Hasan notes the importance of the slave trade in opening up the Sudan to Arab conquest:

The slave trade had influenced the penetration of the Arabs into the Sudan in two ways. In the first place … [slaves] obtained from Nubia and Alwa deprived those countries of their young elements and might in the long run have lessened their chances of standing in the way of the Arab tribes which were soon to submerge the Sudan. Secondly, the penetration of Muslim traders had increased the Arab knowledge of that country… Therefore, while in pursuit of trade they carried the frontier of Islam deep into the heart of the country …

The honesty of this modern Arab scholar, when compared to the denial and dissembling of many western historians is striking. The final phase of the Islamic conquest of the Sudan had to wait some five centuries and was brought about by the Mamluk dynasty of Egypt whose intervention overcame the last Nubian resistance and …let loose a migration of nomadic bedouin Arabs from Upper Egypt into the Sudan. … Immigrants poured south – first the Rabi'a and Juhayna Arabs of the cataracts … dispossessing and enslaving the Nubian owners; and then the camel nomads from the deserts of upper Egypt, who spread through the Nubian deserts…

As Hasan observes:

The Mamluk policy … aimed at the conversion of Nubia into a vassal kingdom. This design hastened the process of

Islamization. The Arabs who entered in large numbers with the Mamluk armies intermarried with the royal family and assumed power. Finally by the middle of the fourteenth century the Nubian kingdom was not so much overthrown as turned inside out - the royal family became both Islamized and Arabized. The collapse of Alwa was mainly due to the gradual ascendancy of the Arab tribesmen...

The end of Christian Nubia occurred on May 29, 1317 when a Muslim convert member of the royal family was raised to the throne by the *Mamluks*. Thus, in an interesting historical curiosity the ancient Christian kingdom of Nubia fell to the Muslims on the exact date that ancient Christian Byzantium was to fall one hundred and thirty six years later. Though Christianity lingered on for a few years, in the end "it could not withstand the impact of a vigorous Islam, sustained by the influx of marauding Arab tribesmen." The smaller Christian kingdom of Alwa continued in an enfeebled state of quasi independence for another century and a half; its extinction marked the end of Christian power in the Sudan.

PERSIA

Shortly after the occupation of Persian ruled Mesopotamia; the Arab invasion of Persia proper began. It was, essentially complete a decade later with the death of the Sasanid emperor in 651; however certain districts of the far-flung territory were to stubbornly resist Arab rule and the Islamic religion for a number of years afterward. For example, the revolt of Sunbad the Magian in 755 was based on the assertion of national feeling along with Zoroastrian religious sentiments. As was the case in Iraq and Syria, most Persians remained unconverted for several centuries.

In the neighboring provinces of Central Asia and Afghanistan, for centuries under Persian influence and often under Persian rule, the progress of the Muslim conquests and of Islamic religion was exceedingly slow. The ultimate victory of Islam in these regions was only achieved some centuries later under dynasties of Persian governors owing only nominal allegiance to the Caliph in Baghdad. The ninth century Persian Saffarids consolidated and extended Muslim rule in Afghanistan:

> One of the most important aspects of early Saffarid policy, of significance for the spread of Islam in Afghanistan and on the borders of India long after their empire had collapsed, was that of expansion into eastern Afghanistan. The early Arab governors ... had at times penetrated as far as Ghazna and Kabul, but these had been little more than slave and plunder raids.

In the year 900 Muslim powers in Afghanistan was still weak enough to allow two Indian princes to re-take Ghazna. "Yet though the power of the local rulers in eastern Afghanistan was not entirely broken, Islam did achieve a break-through ... it is probable that the Islamization of the region proceeded apace."

The Samanid dynasty, which eventually superseded the Saffarids, completed the Muslim conquest of the neighboring provinces of Tabaristan and Transoxiana. In 893 the Samanid Isma'il captured Taraz and converted its Nestorian church into a mosque. His conquest "enabled Muslim missionaries to propagate Islam into the steppes."

CENTRAL ASIA AND THE STEPPES

A convenient year to date the beginning of the conquest of that part Central Asia beyond the fringes of the Sasanid domains was 699 when an Arab army was sent against the ruler of the city of Kabul who refused the payment of tribute. Within a few years, the Arab armies crossed the Oxus River establishing themselves in the fabled cities of Balkh, Bukhara and Samarkand. The end of the first phase of the conquest of Central Asia occurred in the early tenth century when the Samanids subjected all of Transoxiana to Muslim rule. Islam slowly attained its full extent in Central Asia, East Turkestan and the Steppes. A convenient end date can be marked by the year 1513 when the peoples living in the Tarim Basin in Sinkiang accepted Islam.

During the 8th century direct Arab rule in western Transoxiana was confined to the cities where the Arab garrisons were located. "The Arab agents ... were merely military overseers and tax-collectors functioning side by side with the native rulers, who retained the civil administration." Ironically, the lack of a strong Arab central administration produced conditions that were to lead to the rapid Islamization of the population. However, these conversions were accompanied by the triumph, not of Arabic, but of the standard Persian language.

In Central Asia where the majority of the people were probably local Zoroastrians ... there was no strong religious community to hold their people together in the face of Islamic conversion. The much greater amount of fighting in Central Asia, as compared with Iran, also destroyed the links holding people together so that ... recovery of ancient traditions and culture was difficult. In addition, the vast number of slaves brought to the Near East from Central Asia in the conquests served to dilute the hold of local culture and tradition...

The end result was the vanishing of the "Bactrian, Khwarazmian and Sogdian languages ... together with their literatures, so that an all-Iranian culture and the Persian language dominated". The circumstances of internecine conflict and the isolation of local religious cultural institutions leading to rapid mass conversion, is strikingly similar to the later Turkish conquest of Anatolia.

While Islam in a Persian form made rapid progress in western Transoxiana, it was only in 893 that the Samanid ruler, Ismail, crossed the Syr Darya and established Islam in eastern Transoxiana. Islam was brought into contact with numerous nomadic peoples who were to be crucial to the future of the religion:

Western Central Asia, having recently accommodated itself ... to expanding Arab power, was about to enter into another period of ... contact with the Turkic societies to its north and northeast. ... it would serve as the transmission zone for the cultural fruits of one nomadic society to another. ... the Islamic culture which entered the steppe zone had been influenced and reworked by the Eastern Iranians.

Under the Karakhanid rulers the mass conversion of the nomadic Turks began. By 960 Islam had been accepted by some "200,000 tents of the Turks."This conversion was far from easy; it followed years of conflict between the Muslims and the Turkish tribes beyond the frontiers. When the conversion was finally effected, immense new energy was available for the subsequent Islamic expansions:

> The raids of the pagan Turks into the Samanid domains ... brought ghazis from all over the eastern Islamic world to fight in Transoxiana against the infidels. With the conversion of the Turks, however, the services of fighters for Islam were no longer needed in Central Asia, but still in Anatolia and the Caucasus regions. In 966 a host of 20,000 of them came from Khurasan and asked permission ... to go west and fight against the Byzantines. Among these freebooter warriors were ... many Turks, forerunners of the great movement of Turks to Anatolia in later centuries.

Islam made slow but steady progress in the lands toward the east. It was only at the end of the middle Ages that the Uighur stronghold of Turfan became Muslim. By the 14th century eastern Turkestan came into the domain of Turkish-Islamic culture. This was the result of a long, slow, and little-documented process in which Mongol peoples were converted to Islam and won over to the use of Turkish languages. Muslim rulers tried to use Islam as legitimization for warfare against non-Muslim peoples. ... in 1513, Sunni Islam was widely accepted in the Tarim basin ... Mosques appeared along the trade routes between Inner Asia and China. Muslim expansion, however, was checked by the Oirats (Mongols), who accepted Buddhism at the end of the sixteenth century. By then, however, much of the populace of Inner Asia outside Mongolia and Tibet was Muslim or under Muslim suzerainty.

In the northern steppes the progress of Islam was equally slow. The conquering Mongols merged with the Turkic speaking inhabitants and "evolved over time into the Turkic-speaking 'Tatar' population, and were eventually converted to Islam." The first Muslim ruler dates from 1257, but it was not until Uzbek Khan (1313-40) that all of the following the rulers were Muslim.

In remote steppe and mountain areas, the process of Islamic conversion required even more centuries. At about the same time as Islam was completing its South East Asian conversions, it also completed its conversions of the remote nomad tribes of the steppes north of Transoxiana. The first Kazakh converts were made in the 15th and 16th centuries; however conversion "made little headway until the eighteenth century". In the remote mountains of neighboring Afghanistan, pockets of infidels were still present at the end of the 19th century. As late as 1896," the rulers of Afghanistan launched a jihad for the conquest of the mountainous region ... known as Kafiristan, the land of the unbelievers." After the conquest the province was quickly Islamized.

SIND

Sind, the western boundary of India in the vicinity of the Indus River, marked the easternmost extent of the Arab conquests. At almost the same time as the Arabs entered the western limit of their conquests, Spain, the Arab general Ibn Qasim invaded Sind and captured the major cities of the province. Finally, in 713 the famous Buddhist center of Multan fell "where the invaders found a large crowd of pilgrims, whom they took captive." Sind set the pattern for the future Muslim experience in India. Slaughter, on a massive scale so characteristic of the behavior of Muslim armies in India began with that first invasion.

After the defeat and death of King Dahar according to al-Biladuri "the idolaters fled and the Mussulmans glutted themselves with massacre." Another pattern was that of.Indian resistance to Islam with feigned conversions followed by apostasy and rebellion as soon as central Muslim control was relaxed. Muslim law did not provide a contract of protection for "idolaters"; the only legal alternatives were conversion, enslavement or death. Accommodation by Hindus and Buddhists to the new religion was also quite difficult. Unlike the adherents of the monotheistic religions, Christianity, Judaism, even Zoroastrianism, the Indians found the Muslim creed totally alien. As the historian of South Asia, John Keay asserts:

> If conquest had been difficult, conversion was proving even more so. Yet the obstinacy of the idolaters ... always

afforded an excellent justification for pillage and plunder. So it was in Sind and so it would be in Hind (i.e., India).

Furthermore there was continued resistance for well over a century in Sind. "Baghdad's control of the entire province remained a rare phenomenon" until the year 870.

Despite the slaughter and oppression undergone by their fellow countrymen in Sind, most Indians remained blissfully unaware of the magnitude of the threat posed by these strangers. Invaders had entered the subcontinent for centuries, but as was the case with the Macedonians, when the battle ended some form of understanding and compromise was always possible. The very same naiveté that characterized certain Christian leaders regarding early Islam also characterized the Hindus in the first few centuries of the Muslim incursions. "There is no evidence of an Indian appreciation of the global threat which they represented; and the peculiar nature of their mission – to impose new monotheist orthodoxy by military conquest and political dominion – was so alien to Indian tradition that it went uncomprehended."

Indeed, the first native ruler to confront the invaders, King Dahar of Sind "never understood the nature of the war, never understood that more than his throne was at stake. There was for him, in war, an element of chivalry." For it had always been the case that warfare in India was constrained and chivalric. Keay quotes the ninth century Muslim traveler Suleiman: "When a king subdues a neighboring state, he places over it a man belonging to the family of the fallen prince who carries on the government in the name of the conqueror."

Moreover, civilians were traditionally held to be immune from attack. "Although the ploughmen may have had a stake in the outcome of the battle ... they were not expected to get involved. Warriors fought with warriors." Even the outsider, Alexander the Great, felt compelled to follow these rules in his conquest of India. The Indians were clearly unprepared to face the ruthless and implacable Muslim conquerors.

INDIA

For two centuries following the conquest of Sind, the rest of the subcontinent was spared the attention of the Muslims. The Arab empire, in addition to its overextended lines of supply and communication and enormous unassimilated conquered populations, fell into a period of civil strife beginning with the conflict between the Umayyads and Abbasids. It was left to a new race of Muslims from Central Asia to resume the invasion of India. The Turks, both free nomads and military slaves assumed the mantle of Islam in the East as well as in the West. It was still the case that "Muslim invaders were well aware of India's immensity, and mightily excited by its resources. ... The devout Muslim, although ostensibly bent on converting the infidel, would find his zeal handsomely rewarded." It was a Turkish former slave, Sabuktigin the Ghaznavid who swooped on the "luckless and ... undefended people of Lughman. In a taste of things to come, the Muslim forces butchered the idolaters, fired their temples and plundered their shrines; such was the booty, it was said, that hands risked frostbite counting it." Furthermore, the "Shahi forces had been routed and those not dead on the field of battle were being butchered in the forest or drowned in a river. No mercy was to be shown: God had ordained that infidels be killed 'and the order of God is not changed'."

Although Sabuktigin wreaked much slaughter and accumulated much plunder, his invasion was little more than a glorified raid. It was left to his son Mahmud of Ghazna to begin the permanent occupation of additional territory. He continued "the God-given duty of every Muslim to root out idolatry" and needing to "maintain and reward his large standing army" he instituted "a pattern of yearly incursions." He crossed into India "on what would be the first of perhaps sixteen blood-and-plunder raids, some time during ... the year 1000." Mahmud with his taste for booty and glory did not even spare his co-religionists. In 1005 "he determined to attack Multan, whose amir, though a Muslim was now a heretical Ismaili Shi'ah." The Hindu King Anandapala refused

Mahmud safe passage through his domains and duly felt "the hand of slaughter, imprisonment, pillage, depopulation and fire" once again. Then Multan fell, and after "heresy, rebellion and enmity were suppressed" Mahmud's fame reached "as far away as Egypt."

Mahmud's raids continued for many years. It would appear that the Sultan's "appetite for dead Indians, desirable slaves and portable wealth was whetted, but not satisfied." When the city of Thanesar fell, and "'the Sultan returned home with plunder that it is impossible to recount'. 'Praise be to God, the protector of the world for the honour he bestows upon Islam and Musulmans,'" wrote Mahmud's secretary al-Utbi. Mahmud looted and destroyed many Hindu temples including Mathura "whose colossally intricate stone structure, impressed even Mahmud."

Mahmud might have been impressed with the Mathura temple, though apparently not enough to keep from burning it. The "reputation of the uncompromising Ghaznavid and his blood thirsty zealots now preceded them" stirring up "Indian consternation at this new form of total warfare." At Somnath Mahmud slaughtered over 50,000. "Such was the resultant carnage that even the Muslim chroniclers betray a hint of unease." Mahmud, perhaps, recognizing that he lacked the means to garrison such extensive territory and control such a large population endeavored to reduce the local princes to a condition of vassalage. These "attempts to employ as feudatories Indian princes who had supposedly adopted Islam often proved as short-lived as their conversions."

It is no surprise that Mahmud's bloody career achieved so little in the way of permanent results. However, the devastation he wrought did pave the way for more permanent Muslim conquests. Frye sums up the results of Ghaznavid rule:

Islam made little progress in India during the Ghaznavid period; the succeeding periods of the Ghurids and the Slave Kings were more important for this. His main aim was to make the Indian princes his tributaries and to use them as milch-cows; the temples were despoiled primarily because of their great wealth. The sultan knew well that if he had tried to impose Islam on the princes as a condition of peace, they would have apostasized as soon as his troops left.

It was left to Muhammad of Ghor to resume the Islamic conquest. His 1192 victory over the Rajputs reversed the decline of Muslim power in India and began a new extension of Muslim territory. As in Anatolia after Manzikert, this victory enabled the Muslims to overrun large territories. "Kanauj, Asni and Varanasi ... had been overrun ... the Gujarati capital of Anhilwara ... had been sacked. The thirteenth century opened with even more sensational conquests as Muslim forces pushed further east into Bihar, Bengal and Assam". At Varanasi Muhammad was said to have returned with "fourteen hundred camel loads" of treasure. Another bloody-minded Muslim dynasty was the Khaljis. They pushed the Muslim conquests into Bihar and Bengal pausing only to put to death all of the inhabitants of the "famous Buddhist monastery-cum-university of Odantapuri." In general, the establishment of the various sultanates outside of Delhi appears to be a result of the diffusion of Muslim warrior elite in a manner analogous to the founding of Norman states in western and southern Europe.

It was the Mogul dynasty which, finally, achieved almost total Muslim dominion over India. This dynasty was noteworthy for its generally less fanatical, or at least somewhat more pragmatic rulers, notably the eccentric but tolerant Akbar, who was the one bright spot in an otherwise dreary succession of Muslim despots. However, it was one of their more fanatical rulers, Aurangzeb, who by extending Mughal dominion over much of southern India attained the greatest extent of Muslim power on the subcontinent. As Keay notes, this ruler was motivated by his piety to complete the conquest. "Twenty years of Mughal suzerainty over the sultanates had brought only disturbance and defiance. Additionally, their large Shi'ite communities and Hinduized ceremonial were deeply unacceptable to an orthodox Sunni as devout as Aurangzeb. Annexation rather than overlordship was the only solution" It was toward the end of his long reign that Muslim power in India peaked with a costly victory in 1700 over the Maratha rebels.

The great historian Will Durant succinctly describes the thousand years of Muslim warfare in India. "The Mohammedan Conquest of India is probably the bloodiest story in history." The slaughter and pillage committed by the invaders in an attempt to impose Islam on India's immense numbers backfired. One Hindu historian "writes of 'ceaseless resistance offered with relentless heroism' as warriors, 'boys in their teens', 'men with one foot in the grave' and 'women in thousands' fought and died 'to break the volume and momentum of the onrushing tide of invasion'" As the Hindu historian Rajaram puts it:

This brings up an interesting issue: the idolatrous Hindus, whose choice under Sharia was limited to 'Islam or death,' were much more successful in resisting the onslaught of Islam than the 'protected' Jews and Christians. Even the Zoroastrians of Persia, then a great empire ruled by the Sassanids, had to migrate to Hindu India to keep their faith alive. Hindus and Hinduism proved much more resilient than these 'Religions of the Book' and their adherents.

The Hindus never stopped fighting the imposition of Islam and finally defeated it though at great cost in terms of both land and people. It is a battle that still rages. It accounts also for the extraordinary hatred of Hindu India borne by Muslim 'leaders' in India and Pakistan for it is a living reminder of Islam's failure. This suggests that one is better off having Islam as enemy than 'protector'. The protector inevitably turns predator and eventually consumes its protected flock.

Eventually, however, the resistance offered by the large Hindu population induced later Muslim rulers to adopt the more pragmatic policy of fully extending the dhimma contract to the Hindus. "Not all temples were destroyed, although many were. The jizya tax on non-Muslims was not levied on Brahmans until ... 1351 ... and may never have been very effectively collected. Idolatry was condemned yet Hindus were not prevented from practising their religion."

The conquest of India exceeded all others in its relentless cruelty. The immense wealth of the country in riches and its large reservoir of potential slaves attracted wave after wave of Muslim tribes, Arabs, Turks, Afghans, Persians and Moguls. This was compounded by the religions of the inhabitants who lacked even the slight protection afforded to the peoples of the book. While the majority religion, Hinduism, proved more tenacious, Buddhism, unfortunately, was almost totally extirpated in India following the Muslim conquest. "The multitude of images used in Medieval Buddhist worship always inflamed the fanaticism of Muslim warriors to such fury that no quarter was given to the idolaters." The Muslim "invasions were fatal to the existence of Buddhism as an organized religion in northern India."

SOUTHEAST ASIA

Islam was brought to Indonesia and Malaya by Muslim traders. The exact date of the first permanent Muslim communities is not known, but Muslims in Sumatra were reported by Marco Polo in 1292 and there are records attesting to the existence of a Muslim ruler from the 1290s. There were, however, reports of Muslim traders in the East Indies as early as the twelfth century. These traders were from Indian trading centers in the province of Gujarat.

In any event, by the fifteenth century Islam made great strides in the islands prompted by the rise of the sultans of Malacca. The Dutch Indonesian scholar Bernard Vlekke notes that, The Malaccan ruler who visited China in 1419 bore the name of Muhammad Iskandar Shah which shows that the ruling family of Malacca either had gone over to Islam, or had been replaced by a new Moslem dynasty. ... Muhammad Iskandar Shah died in 1424. Islam had by that time spread along the northeast coast of Sumatra.

He also notes Islam's connection to the burgeoning spice trade. Even so Islam's "expansion was slow and did not gain momentum until the middle of the sixteenth century."

A question that naturally arises is why Islam was accepted in a territory beyond the reach of Muslim arms. Indonesia, like West Africa was characterized by many small rival states remote from the greater centers of civilization. In these areas where Islamic armies did not directly penetrate, certain local rulers found it advantageous vis-à-vis their rivals to adopt the militarist Muslim faith. It was analogous to a modern arms race. Those accepting Islam began to reap the benefits of its martial fanaticism and could expect aid from their co-religionists in waging jihad. In those countries, on the other hand, which directly confronted Islamic armies, the local aristocracy did not, generally, enjoy that option. The entry of a new military caste meant a loss of status and wealth by the local aristocrats, even with their conversion to Islam. One such area whose rulers found the new faith of great advantage was Atjeh on the island of Sumatra:

> Islam had come early to that part of the archipelago. The principality of Samudra, situated somewhat to the east of Atjeh, had already become Islamic in the thirteenth century. Atjeh had gone over to the new religion in the second half of the fifteenth century, and in the beginning of the sixteenth, its rulers started a series of 'holy wars' which gave them control over the pepper growing areas on Sumatra's northwest coast. Thus, they spread Islam while at the same time securing a firm control on the pepper trade. By the middle of the sixteenth century they had occupied the coast of ... Manangkabau and converted its princes and its people to the new faith.

In the early 1500s, another such ruler, the prince of Brunei converted "and was busily engaged in spreading his new religion and the extent of his rule in a northeasterly direction. He subdued the northern coast of Borneo and the Sulu islands, thus paving the way for the Islamization of the island of Mindanao."

The superiority of Islam with respect to other religions in providing military advantages was obvious to ambitious rulers. For the Javanese princes when confronted with a choice between Christianity and Islam were concerned with "which of the two religions would be more useful to them. From their point of view, Islam held a far greater appeal than Christianity." However, despite that, Christianity did succeed in gaining a foothold on some islands of the Moluccas.

Some of these rulers, in time became devout Muslims, while others remained simply nominal Muslims. The political situation in the Moluccas illustrates these two contrasting views of Islam by newly converted dynasties.

The villages of all those islands were grouped into two political alliances, one under the leadership of Ternate, the other under that of Tidore. On both islands Islam had become the official religion, but Ternate had been the first to accept the new faith and its kings were more fanatic. Ternate would not accept non-Islamic tribes or villages into its political group, while Tidore made no discrimination.

While some Muslim rulers were fanatical, for many "the acceptance of Islam was only a means to an end, and for a long time, many of them remained reluctant to recognize Islam in the way it ought to be recognized, that is, as being exclusive of all other beliefs."

Islam, with its long and triumphant history of conquest was bound to have a definite appeal for the primitive mind, in both Southeast Asia and Africa. As Vlekke bluntly states:

For many centuries, the Japanese princes had been accustomed to conceive of religious practices as a means of increasing their inner strength or magic force. Understandably they saw Islam in the same light. The growing influence of the new religion throughout Southeast Asia proved its powerful significance. Why should not the Javanese rulers accept Islam too? Why not add this new source of magic force to the ones they already knew? This would serve a double purpose: it would make them spiritually the equals of possible Moslem opponents and it might well secure the help of these same Moslems against their non-Moslem enemies. ... It would be unwise ... to exclude ... genuine conversions ... but Islam definitely did not cause a clear break with the past in Java.

However, as Vlekke also notes:

This does not mean that many of the Indonesian rulers who had outwardly accepted Islam did not become convinced Moslems in course of time. Once the more accessible parts of the archipelago were known to have turned Moslem, there began a continual influx of Moslem scholars from Arabia and India's west coast, who were readily given hospitality by the Indonesian princes in exchange for their advice in religious matters.

Religious factors were, inevitably, intertwined with external alliances and rivalries. A Hindu Javanese state, Sunda Kalapa, sought an alliance with the Portuguese against its Muslim neighbor. However, before assistance could be rendered, "it had been brought under the power of the Moslem king of Bantam."

In the 17th century to counter the growing Dutch power some of the Indonesian princes sought closer relations with the Ottoman sultan and with the Muslims of Persia and India. This led them to "bring the administration of justice into conformity with Islamic rules." But this "reform did not fully succeed."At this later time in history, when the European powers began their great expansions, Islam, in addition to its usefulness as a military motivating force in helping native rulers retain power, also served as an expression of local patriotism. "The struggle against the Portuguese and Dutch made Islam desirable as a bond of solidarity in resistance to the efforts of the Christian powers".

The Islamization of Indonesia, Malaya and other areas of Southeast Asia was a long drawn out process that continued even after European powers established dominance. In addition to proselytizing the remaining infidels, Islamic teachers devoted much energy to replacing the lax syncretistic religion that characterized much of the region with more orthodox forms. However, by the beginning of the 19th century the current pattern of Muslim dominance had substantially taken shape.

SPAIN

The Muslim conquest of Spain, like that of the eastern Arab conquests was quick. The conquest beginning in 711 attained its full extent within twenty years. The Arab and Berber invaders of Spain, as was the case further east, took full advantage of internal political and religious strife in the camp of their opponents. Hitti notes that the "natives included a considerable class of serfs and slaves ... which contributed to the success of the invasion and cooperated with the invaders ... Then there was the Jewish element in the population which was estranged ... through active persecution by the Gothic royalty."

However, Spain was never completely subdued. Continuing resistance by Christian states in the north was facilitated by ethnic squabbling between the two conquering ethnicities. For it was the case that the "Berbers never forgave their Arab superiors for appropriating to themselves the lion's share of the conquered land." Furthermore, dynastic rivalries served to weaken Muslim power in the Peninsula. Under the Umayyad prince Abd-al-Rahman, Spain was the first of the conquered provinces to split off from centralized Arab rule.

Unconverted Arabic speaking Christians known as Mozarabs drew inspiration from their independent co-religionists. The suspicion of the Muslim authorities inevitably fell upon the Christians, as well as upon Jews. Persecutions and expulsions, which were emulated by Christian rulers commencing in 1492, were the result. Both series of expulsions shared the same excuse – to prevent future treachery on behalf of external infidel rulers:

On a fatwa ... from his theologians, Yusuf in 1099 ordered a beautiful church ... possessed by the Mozarabs of Granada; to be leveled ... These same Granadans in 1126 were put to the sword or banished to Morocco because they had entered into communication with a Christian sovereign of the north. Eleven years later a second expulsion of Mozarabs left few of them in Spain.

These efforts on the part of the Muslim authorities, however, could not halt the Christian advance that gathered force in the thirteenth century. Hitti notes that many Moslems "were now forgetting their Arabic ... and becoming more or less assimilated to the Christians." He also observes how, even in the western Mediterranean, Islam had assumed the role as protector of Oriental civilization vis-à-vis the West:

After the middle of the thirteenth century two major processes were in operation: the Christianizing of Spain and its unification. ... The only part of the peninsula where Islam had struck root was that where the earlier Semitic, Carthaginian civilization had once flourished. The same was true of Sicily. In general the line of cleavage between Islam and Christianity coincided with the ancient line between the Punic and Occidental civilizations."

ANATOLIA

The Muslim conquest of Anatolia began in 1071 with the victory of the Seljuk Turks at Manzikert. The conquest was to last four centuries when the last Byzantine remnant, Trebizond fell to the Ottomans in 1461. Vryonis notes the longevity of the Turkish conquest which "subjected Byzantine society to repeated shocks and dislocations." In an all too depressing echo of almost every Muslim conquest from Spain to India, a long period of civic disorder paved the way for the invaders. "In the eleventh century the strife of the Byzantine bureaucratic class with the magnate-military aristocrats of ... Anatolia was the critical development. Not only did it paralyze Byzantine political life with its endless intrigues and rebellions but it destroyed the Anatolian armies and brought in the Turkmens as mercenary troops." Furthermore "the religious and political animosity of Greeks, Armenians and Syrians in the districts of eastern Asia Minor completed the disorganization of the Byzantine regions".

The crafty policy of Muslim rulers in deflecting the hostility of their primitive co-religionists was an important factor in advancing the Turkish occupation. As the Muslim rulers of Egypt diverted the Hilali Bedouin into North Africa and other Arab nomads into the Sudan so "the great Seljuk sultans of Persia made strenuous efforts to shunt the Turkmen tribes into Anatolia in order to spare their own domains from their ravages. Also it was the Turkmen element, an element devoted to raiding and plundering, which affected a great portion of the conquests and occupations."

Vryonis remarks on how the long extended period of warfare was fatal to Byzantine Christian civilization:

With the exception of the felicitous period during which the Nicean Empire and the Seljuk sultanate revived Anatolian society, the Turkish conquests and settlements ... fatally dislocated Byzantine society in Asia Minor. Inasmuch as the state apparatus was Muslim, the Christian community could not at any given time recoup its previous losses. ... Thus in spite of the stability and prosperity that characterized Anatolia in the first half of the thirteenth century, the Christians could do little about recovering all the ground that had been lost consequent to the decimating events of the late eleventh and the early twelfth century. Similarly, the Ottoman unification ... brought greater security and uniformity of conditions for the Christians, but it was of no avail in restoring the Christian communities to that position they had occupied in the thirteenth century.

However, Greek culture managed to survive in a new form for many years owing to extensive conversion and hybridization:

...the children of mixed marriages, as well as converts to Islam were very frequently Greek speaking or bilingual. Thus large numbers of mixovarvaroi in the Seljuk armies ... were both Greek-speaking and Turkish-speaking. ... The Seljuks, Ottomans, and house of Aydin, who ruled over large numbers of Greeks and had to deal with Greek states, all had Greek chanceries in their administration. John Cantacuzene remarks that the Ottomans themselves were familiar with the Greek language.

Eventually, the relentless pressure of the new virile religion and culture won the day. Kinross notes that in Ottoman times "through voluntary conversion to Islam, the Christian became automatically an Osmanli, with his origins soon forgotten, enjoying freedom from taxation, the right to hold land, opportunities for advancement, and a share in the benefits of the Moslem ruling elite."

BALKANS

The conquest of the Balkans can be dated to 1353 with the establishment of the first permanent Ottoman garrison in the Gallipoli peninsula. One century later, after defeating the Serbs and other rivals in the Balkans, the Ottomans achieved the long time Muslim dream of taking Constantinople. The empire which had held the Muslims at bay during eight centuries of unrelenting warfare came to an end. The high water mark of the Ottoman domains in the Balkans occurred in 1526 with the first siege of Vienna, following which the tide slowly receded.

In a number of respects the circumstances facing the Muslim conquerors in the Balkans were similar to those facing the invaders of India. Both areas were the home to large settled populations. In both India and the Balkans, the conquest was never unchallenged, large areas were frequently quasi-independent or even in open rebellion. Even at the height of Muslim power in India, unconquered territory continued to exist in the South as well as along the eastern and northern fringe. Similarly, in the Balkans the Ottomans were faced with independent and militarily powerful neighbors just across the frontiers in Russia, Austria and Poland, in addition to the always annoying naval power of Venice.

Kinross describes the occupied Balkan territories as follows:

The Ottoman conquerors were relatively few in number. Now here confronting them in Europe were populations far in excess of any of the conquered lands of Asia, moreover far more various and complex in their racial, religious and political character.

Lapidus describes the demographic situation and the progress of Islamization in the Balkans:

A census of 1520-30 showed that about 19 percent of the Balkan population was Muslim ... The Muslim population of Bosnia, one of the highest was 45 percent. In general, Muslims were concentrated in towns. ... The Muslim element was most numerous in Thrace, Macedonia, Thessaly, Bosnia, Herzegovina, and Silistria. A new wave of Islamization occurred between 1666 and 1690 in the Rhodope. Islam came to northern Albania and Montenegro in the seventeenth century. Greeks in southwestern Macedonia and Crete converted in the course of the seventeenth and eighteenth centuries.

Despite the brave resistance of the native peoples of both the Balkans and India, had Muslim rule continued uninterrupted in both regions, the slow process of conversion might, eventually, have produced Muslim majorities as it did elsewhere. But both the Mogul and Ottoman empires entered a period of decline and came under increasing pressure from technologically advanced Europeans. The Austrians, Venetians, Poles and Russians disrupted Ottoman rule and protected Christians in the Balkans; the British in India overthrew Mogul rule and, inadvertently perhaps, helped the Hindu majority revive their beleaguered culture.

OTHER ISLAMIC EXPANSIONS

There were, in addition to the major territories discussed above, a number of lesser Muslim invasions and settlements. Various islands in the Mediterranean and in the Aegean were seized by Arab Muslims, often more than once. These include the islands of Crete and of Rhodes which experienced periods of Arab rule prior to their final conquest by the Turks. Malta, Sardinia and the Balearic islands were also held at various times by Arabs or by Moors. Cyprus also passed back and forth a number of times between Muslim and Christian rule. Sicily was invaded by Arabs and Berbers from North Africa and Spain starting in 827. After a long drawn-out period of war, the conquest was finally completed in 902 by the Aghlabid ruler Ibrahim II. The Aghlabids also briefly seized a number of forts on the southern Italian mainland, an achievement repeated under the Ottomans. The Ottomans at the height of empire, in an extension of their Balkan conquests, established their rule over Hungary, Transylvania and Moldavia.

The westernmost extension of the Mongols, the Golden Horde, having converted to Islam, migrated from the northern steppes west into southern Russia and the Ukraine where they ultimately established the Khanate of the Crimea. The first Khan converted to Islam in 1257; however it was only from 1313 on that all subsequent rulers were Muslim. The

Crimean Khans ultimately became vassals of the Ottoman Sultans; the razzias of these Ottoman subordinates supplied the harems of the Ottoman world with many desirable European concubines.

Finally, in China proper, there were settlements of Muslim traders at various times. Their descendants, known as Hui, continue to exist in large numbers in parts of western and southwestern China. Being a small minority within the large Chinese population, they have led a comparatively peaceful existence.

The Muslims were the world's most successful imperialists. However, all empire-building eventually came to a halt, including those of the carriers of the Islamic meme. The following chapter describes the circumstances by which the various Muslim expansions were stopped.

11

Limits of Empire – Islam Contained

All imperial expansions, even those of the followers of the world's most warlike religion, eventually end. Supply lines are stretched too far. Panicked adversaries set aside their own differences and form alliances. Strong and skilful leaders arise in the enemy camp. Tribes as fierce as any of the Islamic vanguards prove resistant to Islam's call. Internal political or religious conflicts shatter Muslim unity. Geographic barriers divert or slow down even the most determined armies. When the advance of a Muslim empire slows, some of the yet unconquered peoples of the dar-al-harb have time to educate themselves about the threat and to apply effective countermeasures.

EARLY ARAB EXPANSIONS CONTAINED IN EUROPE

Arab confidence in their invincibility, following the quick victories in Syria, Egypt and the Sasanid lands, was doubtless at its highest point. They must have expected that the remaining Byzantine provinces would quickly succumb to the warriors of the Prophet. However, on three different occasions Arab attacks were broken before the formidable walls of Constantinople. They unsuccessfully besieged the city in the years 669, 674-680 and 716. Finally they were swept out of Anatolia when, in 740, the Greeks "won a decisive victory over

Arab invaders at Acrazas in Anatolia, and destroyed a major Syrian army." Thus was the direct road into Europe blocked for the Arabs.

However, the danger to Europe and Byzantium continued. In the north and in the far west Arab armies were poised to penetrate into Europe and surround Byzantium. But, the next blow to the advancing Muslims occurred in Spain where at the battle of Covadonga in 718 the Moors were first stopped by the Gothic chieftain Pelayo, and a northern enclave of Christian rule was preserved. Despite that setback, the Arabs were not ones to be easily deterred. Avoiding the remaining Christian strongholds in the north of the peninsula they advanced into France where they were finally turned back by Charles Martel in 732 at the famous battle of Tours.

At the same time, another formidable opponent awaited the Arab armies north of the Oxus River and north of the Caucasus. These were the Khazars, a Turkic tribe who slowed down the Arab advance into Transoxiana and actually counterattacked deep into Arab territory. In the year 730, The Khazars shattered the "Arab defenses, defeated them at Ardabil, invaded Armenia, and penetrated as far as Mosul". In 737 the Arabs counterattacked and were, again, defeated at the hands of the Khazars. Historian of Byzantium Dimitri Obolensky notes the significance of this Khazar victory:

The supreme trial of strength came in 737 when the Arabs marched up the Volga, destroyed the Khazar army, but were compelled to retreat south of the Caucasus. Five years earlier Charles Martel had, by his victory at Poitiers, halted the Arab thrust against Western Christendom on the line of the Pyrenees. The achievement of the Khazars in holding the Caucasus was of comparable importance.

Arthur Koestler notes, as well, that "the gigantic Muslim pincer movement across the Pyrenees in the west and across the Caucasus into Eastern Europe was halted at both ends about the same time." So it was that the Byzantines were spared from being outflanked on both sides of their stronghold. Also important in halting the Arab advance was the rejection by the Khazars of Islam in favor of Judaism around the year 740. Had the Khazars, like their fellow Turks, accepted Islam, the Muslim religion might have been swept into Eastern Europe by combined armies of Arabs and Turks as was, later, to occur in Transoxiana. Thus, the Khazar decision like the later rejection of Islam by the Russians and their conversion to Orthodox Christianity, once more prevented the Muslims from outflanking Byzantium and penetrating into the heart of Europe.

It was at this very time that religious dissension within Muslim ranks occurred in North Africa. While Charles Martel was campaigning against the Moors of Spain, Berber Khariji rebels "destroyed a Syrian army of 27,000 men." Taken together the above events mark the end of the Arab expansion after a century of triumph and the beginning of the end of the Umayyad dynasty. A later Arab attempt to penetrate into Europe, this time coming up through the Italian peninsula was, after considerable effort, thwarted. "The recapture of Bari by the Christians in 871 marks the beginning of the end of the Moslem menace to Italy and Central Europe".

CHINA: A WALL BLOCKING THE ARAB ADVANCE

Chinese rulers recognized early the nature of the rising Muslim threat and moved decisively to preempt it. In 713 the Muslims at the request of the Chinese Emperor sent ambassadors to the Chinese court to expound the Islamic faith. The "reception of the emissaries by the Chinese Emperor was by no means friendly, for he dismissed them with the threat that if his land were invaded the consequences would be terrible for the invaders. However that may be, it is certain that no regular invasion of China was attempted from the direction of Persia, and Qutayba's [Governor of Khurasan] incursion [into Chinese territory]marks the furthest limits to which Muslim troops advance into central Asia."

Furthermore, the Chinese were prepared to confront the Arab armies beyond the borders of China. However, they did not succeed in expelling the Arabs from Central Asia. The year 751 marked "the end of any serious resistance to Islam in western Central Asia. It also was the end of any Chinese intervention in the west ... Ziyad ibn Salih ...marched against a combined Chinese and Turkish army near Talas. ... At the battle the Karluks [Turks] deserted the Chinese who were defeated".

The 8th century Chinese assistance to Iranian refugees and local rulers in central Asia, against the Arabs, stands in sharp contrast to the behavior of various Christians who by endless squabbles and betrayals facilitated the advance of the invading Muslims. The Chinese, to the contrary, recognized the implacable nature and danger of the Muslim advance and were prepared to assist even those of vastly different cultures to resist. While the Chinese campaign in central Asia ultimately failed, by slowing the Arab advance and demonstrating their willingness and ability to resist they discouraged the Arabs from a military invasion of China proper. With its immense wealth and large population China must have presented a tempting target; a large reservoir of booty and slaves, as well as concubines to swell the ranks of the harems. However, the combination of the demonstration of Chinese doughtiness and the large route through inhospitable country inhabited by fierce tribes, made it clear to Arab commanders that such an expedition would be extremely costly and have no clear prospect of success.

SUDAN AND NORTHEAST AFRICA

Christian rulers in the Sudan and Ethiopia impeded and delayed the southward progress of Islam. The resistance of the strong Nubian kingdom blocked the Arab advance southward for many centuries and "Islam was denied its easiest line of access to black Africa. Muslim teachers, like Muslim traders, had therefore to cross the great deserts to the west." In Ethiopia "in the northern highlands at least, where Christianity had been the longest established, the strength and vitality of the Church were sufficient to prevent the merchants from spreading their religion, as they did elsewhere." After the fall of Nubian Christianity, Ethiopia came under increasing

Muslim pressure. However, with the assistance of an unexpected new Christian ally, Ethiopia avoided Muslim conquest. At Lake Tana, "in 1542, the Portuguese intervened to help Christian Ethiopia prevail over the Muslims." This victory "shattered the Muslim regimes."

GEOGRAPHIC BARRIERS

Geographic and climatic factors prevented or, at least slowed down, attempts at conquest or colonization by various Muslim vanguards. Great mountain ranges, such as the Caucasus, impeded the northern advance of both Arabs and Turks. The Himalayas proved to be a totally impenetrable barrier behind which the remnants of Indian and central Asian Buddhism was protected; this range also made a direct route into China impossible. Even in occupied Iran, as Frye points out, geographical factors prevented the Arabs from establishing an easy base for further expansion. "There never was any mass colonization of Iran by the Arabs, who did not care for the climatic conditions, except in the centre and in the south - the Arabian camel cannot endure cold winters - and their great waves of migration halted at the foot of the Zagros." What was true of Iran was even truer of the colder deserts and steppes north of Iran. In Africa the great Sahara desert made the movement of large armies impossible. Toward the east, Muslim armies were faced with the impenetrable jungles of south Asia.

In India, as we have seen, the resistance of the dense population once alerted to the bloody agenda of Islam, confined the Arabs to the conquered province of Sind. The Hindus finally realized that the Islamic meme was a not a force with which a permanent accommodation could be made. Other implacable warriors of the faith following in the footsteps of the Arabs were ultimately confronted with a number of insurmountable geographic barriers. In India it was the Himalayas that proved a quite effective barrier. "Howsoever, the Himalayas were certainly too physically challenging for the Khalji forces, [in an attempted invasion of Bhutan] most of whom perished in a swollen river." Under Muhammad bin Tughluq (d. 1351), in an attempt to bring the mountainous territory between India and China under Islam, an "expedition of at least sixty thousand duly headed off into the western Himalayas." It was "heavily defeated by 'Hindus who closed the passes and cut off the retreat.' 'Only ten horsemen returned to Delhi.'" The Moguls were also halted at the foothills of the mountains. A "Shan people from upper Burma ... pre-empted Mughal expansion in Assam and repeatedly rolled back Mughal incursions. In the north, along the foothills of the Himalaya, much was made of the capture ... in 1618 of the great fort of Kangra ... There followed minor conquests on the frontiers of Kashmir ... None of these places can have rewarded the expense of taking them".

Frigid steppes and fierce nomads blocked the Muslims from penetrating into northern Asia:

...the Dzungarian Confederation, the last of the great Inner Asian nomadic empires ... had its origins between 1400 and 1550, when Mongolian peoples were ... forced to move westward and northward into eastern Turkestan ... By the early seventeenth century an Oirat Khanate had come into existence ... and its leaders adopted Tibetan Lamaism as the religion of the confederation. Buddhism helped, as did Islam, to foster political unity among pastoral peoples, and to join them to sedentary populations. Expanding westward the Oirats attacked the Kirgiz and the Uzbeks ... and conquered the Tarim basin.

The Oirat conquest paved the way for the later Chinese expansion into Muslim areas of eastern Turkestan.

TURKISH ADVANCE HALTED

The later expansions of Islam under the Turks and the Golden Horde were halted by a series of military setbacks and by determined European resistance. Tamerlane's invasion of Turkish territory was an important factor leading to the eventual end of the Turkish expansion. By defeating the Ottomans and capturing their Sultan, he probably delayed their invasion of Europe by 50 years, during which time the nations in Western Europe advanced economically and technologically, so that they were better equipped to contain the Turks. Considering the speed and ferocity with which the Ottomans were to seize southeastern Europe, it is conceivable that without Tamerlane, much of Europe might have ended up under Islamic rule.

Another factor slowing down the Ottoman advance was the fierce and unexpected resistance that awaited them in the Balkans. After the defeat of Serbia on the fields of Kosovo and with the slow death and fall of Constantinople, a series of local Christian kings and commanders carried on the resistance for many years. The Hungarian general Hunyadi, the Albanian leader Skanderbeg and the Serbian Despot Brankovitch along with Venetian naval commanders mounted a futile but valiant resistance that harassed and delayed the Ottomans accustomed as they were to lightning quick victories. At the same time the notorious Rumanian ruler, Vlad the Impaler, who was to be immortalized as the fictional Dracula, invaded Ottoman ruled territory and executed en masse thousands of Ottoman soldiers. After Vlad's defeat Rumanian resistance was carried on by King Stephen of Moldavia, who before his own defeat, temporarily expelled the Turks from Wallachia.

Over the following two centuries the Ottoman advance was repeatedly checked by a series of desperate European actions. Belatedly, by this time, most western rulers awoke to the danger. In 1480 the Ottoman invasions of Italy and the island of Rhodes were thwarted. In 1529 the first Ottoman siege of Vienna ended in failure and a second attempt on Vienna was turned back three years later. The Ottoman failures at the siege of Vienna ended their advance into Europe. In 1565 the Turks were repulsed by the knights of St. John at the siege of Malta. This was to be followed, in 1571, by the battle of Lepanto which was the first major Ottoman maritime defeat. In 1683 the final siege of Vienna was followed by the rapid decline of Ottoman power in Europe.

In Russia, also, the Muslim tide was stopped by determined Christian resistance. The conquests by the Ottoman vassals of the Golden Horde represented the farthermost northern extension of the Muslim oecumene. Their advance toward the north was halted in 1380 when the Russians under Prince Dmitri Donskoi defeated the Tatars at the battle of Kulikovo. A century later in 1480 Ivan the Terrible turned back the last Tatar advance on Moscow.

At a later time, in India, Southeast Asia, and Inner Asia, in addition to the Balkans, Islam was contained by more technically advanced European, Russian and Chinese imperialists. Furthermore, the "spread of Islamic polities in both East and West Africa was checked at the beginning of the twentieth century by the sudden imposition of European colonial rule."

ISLAMIC DECLINE

Civilizations and empires rise and decline. However, the rise and decline of the various Islamic polities were particularly rapid. Even the long lasting Ottoman Empire quickly became a shadow of its previous self; its life being artificially extended by the continued existence of large numbers of non-Muslim subjects for the Muslim elite to exploit and by the jealous rivalries of the European states. Hitti describes the rapid rise and fall, which characterized Islam in general, with particular reference to the Arabs:

If anything parallels the astounding rapidity with which the sons of the Arabian Desert conquered in the first Islamic century most of the civilized world, it is the swift decadence of their descendants' domination between the middle of the third and the middle of the fourth centuries. About 820 more extensive authorities was concentrated in the hands of one man, the caliph in Baghdad than in those of any other living person; by 920 the power of his successor had so diminished that it was hardly felt even in his capital city.

One cause of the decline was the geographical dispersion of authority. This "decentralization was the inevitable consequence of such a far-flung domain with difficult means of intercommunication. In all local affairs the governor's authority tended to become supreme and his office hereditary." Another cause or, perhaps, simply an accompaniment of decline was the administrative dispersion of power exemplified in the office of the vizier. "The vizir acted as the caliph's alter ego and grew in power as his chief indulged increasingly in the pleasures of the harem." An additional factor, detailed in a subsequent chapter, was the harem intrigue resulting from the indulgence of those pleasures. Finally, the distrust of rulers for their own troops and the consequent employment of foreign mercenaries and slave soldiers was a development whose consequences for the political and social order were inevitably dire. The introduction of foreign units by al-Mutawakkil (847) "contributed to the destruction of the necessary conditions for the upkeep of the morale and esprit de corps."

Similar conditions marked the decline of the Ottoman Empire beginning in the 17th century. Kinross views the signal event of this decline being the assassination of the able vizier Sokollu, a victim of court intrigue, in 1578. Following this event, there was no check on the increasing dissipation of the Ottoman line; his murder "set the seal on a long period of Ottoman decadence." However, the factors described above may be only symptoms of the real underlying cause. Kinross summarizes the following as the real cause of Ottoman decline; it can just as easily apply to all Muslim empires:

> In part this derived from the fact that the Empire had ... exhausted both its field and its capacity for territorial conquest in Europe, which had served as its chief motive force. Centuries of war had inspired in the Ottomans unity of purpose; had provided wealth for them in the form not only of spoils but of territories for landed settlement. Now there remained few such outlets, few such rewards. In default of an enemy to plunder, men plundered one another; in default of land, they flocked to the cities or spread disorder through the countryside.

This point is expanded upon in the subsequent chapter on Islamic parasitism. When blocked, the energies released by the Islamic ideology must find another outlet or turn inward until even that is exhausted and the civilization settles down to the stagnation that has characterized Islam into modern times. The chapters to follow also go into more detail with respect to the reasons for political, social, economic and intellectual decline.

THE COUNTER JIHAD

It was inevitable that the followers of other traditions, viewing with a fearful fascination the inexorable advance of Islam's inspired warriors, should seek to imitate those militarily useful aspects of the Prophet's militant faith. The most famous of the non-Muslim holy wars was, of course, the Crusades. The Crusades, despite the notoriety attached to them in certain historical circles, were just one of a number of "counter jihads" by Christians. There were also instances of such counter-jihads among Hindus and even Buddhists. Bernard Lewis draws the following important distinction between jihad and its' non-Islamic imitations.

The idea of holy war - a war for God and the faith – was not new in the Middle East. It suffuses the books of Deuteronomy and Judges, and inspired the Christian Byzantines in their wars against Persia and in their struggles to repel the Arab and later Turkish invaders. But these were wars with limited objectives – the conquest of the Promised Land, the defence of Christendom against non-Christian attack. Even the Christian crusade, often compared with the Muslim jihad, was itself a delayed and limited response to the jihad and in part also an imitation. But unlike the jihad it was concerned primarily with the defence or reconquest of threatened or lost Christian territory. It was, with few exceptions, limited to the successful wars for the recovery of southwest Europe, and the unsuccessful wars to recover the Holy Land and to halt the Ottoman advance in the Balkans. The Muslim jihad, in contrast, was perceived as unlimited, as a religious obligation that would continue until all the world had either adopted the Muslim faith or submitted to Muslim rule. In the latter case, those who professed what Muslims recognized as a revealed religion were allowed to continue the practice of that religion, subject to the acceptance of certain fiscal and other disabilities. Those who did not, that is to say idolaters and polytheists, were given the choice of conversion, death or slavery.

Centuries before the Crusades, various Christian leaders envious of the advantages conferred on their Muslim opponents by the militant doctrine of jihad, suggested instituting a similar doctrine. The late ninth century Byzantine Emperor Leo VI "speaks with some respect of the doctrine of the holy war and of its military value, and even suggests that Christians might be well advised to adopt something of the same kind." In the following century Byzantine Emperor Phocas (ca 964) stated that for "the Muslims the jihad ... was a duty enjoined by Islam. Phocas, highly religious and an ascetic, wished to have every soldier who fell in the wars declared a martyr for the faith, but were frustrated by the disagreement of the patriarch."

Furthermore, the Byzantines had a number of "military saints" to lend an aura of divine sanction and protection to their campaigns. Doubtless, the almost continuous assault by the Islamic jihad led to an increased emphasis on these divine warriors. "St. Demetrius was, with St. Theodore Stratilates, St. Theodore of Tyre and St. George, one of that great quartet ... of warrior saints who protected Byzantine armies in battle." There can be no doubt that the Russians, who inherited the mantle of Byzantium, pursued the Tatars and Turks through the steppes and into central Asia with the same Byzantine religious fervor.

Leaders of the Christian west, long before the Crusades, also advocated imitating Muslim theology as a means of motivating Christian warriors. In 846, when an Arab fleet raided the coast of Italy and sacked Rome, a synod sent an appeal for help to the various Christian monarchs. Pope Leo IV "offered a heavenly reward to all those who died fighting the Muslims." A similar promise was made thirty years later by John VIII "offering forgiveness of sins for those who fought" in defense of Church and faith and "eternal life for those who died fighting the infidel."

The most famous of these counter-jihads, the Crusades originated with Pope Urban II who 'borrowed' the Muslim idea of earthly riches, or else martyrdom and a heavenly reward for those who die in battle, in the service of their faith. Urban is quoted as saying at the Council of Clermont in 1095:

You, who sell for vile pay the strength of your arms to the fury of others, armed with the sword of the Machabees, go and merit an eternal reward. If you triumph over your enemies, the kingdoms of the East will be your reward. If you are conquered, you will have the glory of dying in the very same place as Jesus Christ, and God will never forget that he found you in the holy battalions. Not to be outdone, shortly afterward, Peter the Hermit promised his followers, in a very Muslim-like way, that "for all those who took part in the expedition the gates of Paradise would open."

A direct consequence of the ideology of the Crusades was the religious fervor fueling the Reconquista in Spain. As early as "the eleventh century the northern armies of la reconquista were filled with monks who had become soldiers. ... The three great military orders created during the crusade against the Moors were called Calatrava, Santiago, and Alcantara." Indeed, like the Byzantine military saints, Santiago "was transformed in Spain from a peaceful apostle into a fierce warrior, capable of panicking the Moors ... Santiago, the Moor-slayer ... fortified the soul of the reconquest. ... If Santiago was on our side, then so was God, and our war was every bit as holy as the other side's." These military orders were to soon imitate those created to battle the Muslims in the Holy Land. "In the second half of the twelfth century the reconquest became institutionalized. Religious-military fraternities, such as the orders of Calatrava and Santiago, financed by landed estates, conquered and colonized Muslim territories."

The newly unified Spanish absorbed the attitudes of their erstwhile Muslim masters well. "Yet another facet of the identification between war and religion, between sword and cross, to be determining in the conquest of the New World, had been established. The militant religious orders were founded to conciliate a warring clergy with holy aims. ... The armies of la reconquista were also the seed of the future Latin American armies." Naipaul discussing the Arab conquest of Sind also emphasizes the relationship between the experience of Spanish Christians under their Muslim masters and their later conquests in the Americas.

There are resemblances to the Spanish conquest of Mexico and Peru, and they are not accidental. The Arab conquest of Spain, occurring at the same time as the conquest of Sind, marked Spain. Eight hundred years later, in the New World, the Spanish conquistadores were like Arabs in their faith, fanaticism, toughness, poverty, and greed.

An additional parallel between the Spanish conquistadors and the Arab jihadists was that the one fifth of the booty after conquest reserved for the caliph, as specified in the Sharia, is reflected in the institution of the Spanish "royal fifth" of the proceeds from the American conquests.

Another spillover from the ideology of holy war that the Christians copied from Islam occurred in northeastern Europe when Christian crusaders were redirected against pagan Slavs and other Baltic tribes. "The Teutonic Knights ... were one of the militant orders founded during the crusades to further the conquest of the Holy Land from the Infidel. In the early thirteenth century the Order was granted wide uninhabited districts in Transylvania to found a frontier march against the heathen" Kuman tribes. In 1225 "a new field of activity was opened ... in the lower valley of the Vistula. ... Farther to the east ... the Prussians ... fiercely resisted the spread of Christianity. Against them crusades were proclaimed." Also "the Knights Templars and the Hospitallers took a very active part in the colonization of the east." Christianity had generally spread among pagan areas through a slow process of conversion. Subsequent to the Crusades, in the remaining pagan areas of Europe and in the New World, Christianity was deliberately spread by force of arms.

Christian Europe was not the only area of origin for counter-jihads. In India the Rajputs were a military caste of knights who emerged in the 12th century to oppose the march of Islam. As Keay describes them:

Although perjured and persecuted during centuries of Islamic supremacy, they were in fact the native aristocracy of India ... They had ... shown a bold front in the face of Muslim aggression. And for whatever that defiance had lacked in the way of coherence, they had amply compensated with a stalwart perseverance unequalled in the annals of mankind.

The religious zeal exhibited by the Rajputs was in no way inferior to that of their opponents. In the Rajput hill forts when "all was lost ... the womenfolk hurled themselves into the flames, the men rode out in a still brighter blaze of glory to kill until they were killed. Fanaticism was not an exclusively Islamic prerogative."

Later centuries saw the rise of other militant religious orders in India who were aroused by the fanatical Mogul emperor Aurangzeb. The Islamist policies of Aurangzeb "to non Muslim groupings of a more martial disposition like the Sikhs, Rajputs and Marathas ... furnished both pretext and support for outright defiance." The Sikhs under their leader Guru Govind established themselves in the Punjab hills where they metamorphosed from "a movement for religious and social reform into an embryonic political and military formation." In the 1660s, another militant group the Marathas under Shivaji revived "Hindu kingship at a time of awesome and markedly orthodox Muslim supremacy. ... they have also" encouraged Hindus "in the belief that martial prowess is ... part of their tradition".

In the northern reaches of Central Asia, the normally pacific Buddhists also found militant defenders. The Oirats, founders of the Dzungarian Confederation adopted Tibetan Lamaism. Using Buddhism as a means of establishing tribal unity the Oirats defeated the Kyrgyz and the Uzbeks and established themselves as masters of the Tarim basin. Here was a belated Buddhist counter jihad under the aegis of a militarily adept tribal people practicing a more militant and primitive form of the religion.

Thus, in all instances, the formidable advance of Islam came to a halt. There is, however, one additional factor that helped to fuel almost all of the remarkable military campaigns of the warriors of the Prophet. The next chapter describes the great skill with which Muslim commanders exploited the political, religious and ethnic rivalries present within the ranks of the infidels.

12

Patterns of Treason

Muslim conquerors were able to avail themselves of a remarkable and extensive pattern of treachery, opportunism and collaboration from elements among their opponents. The forces of the dar-al-harb were always plagued at the most inopportune times by rebellion, civil war, religious conflict, schism and heresy. Renegades ready to join the Arabs or to "turn Turk" abounded just before or immediately after the warriors of Islam invaded. Often, non-Muslim technicians, mercenaries and scholars seemed to queue up in seeking patronage from Muslim caliphs and sultans. Ambitious non-Muslim rulers and politicians sought alliances against their co-religionists with the Muslims. Many of these were eager to make use of the fierce military energy of Islam and turn it to their own purposes. Suffice it to say that those who played with fire usually themselves ended up burned.

Of course, the long history of treason and betrayal includes many examples of Muslim renegades turning on their own people and of Muslims entering into alliances of convenience with non-Muslims. Thus, such maneuvering for advantage by seeking alliance with infidels was not all one sided. Muslim rulers and rebels certainly engaged non-Muslims as allies against their fellow Muslims. However, these appear to occur with less frequency. In general, the Muslims were much better at this game for most of Islam's early history. This may well be due to the greater individualism characterizing non-Muslims, as compared to the greater conformity and religious solidarity of the Muslims. Only at times of Muslim retreat, as occurred during the crusades or in modern times, were western powers able to use intra-Muslim rivalry with any degree of success.

Bat Yeor provides the following useful overview of this sad history of treason, betrayal and collaboration skillfully utilized by Muslim leaders:

> After the Arab conquest, Muslim caliphs and governors knew how to play on the inter-Christian dissension in order to impose Islam irrevocably on Christian countries. The Monophysite wish to be rid of the Chalcedonian Greeks had facilitated the Persian, and then the Arab, conquest of Egypt, Mesopotamia, and Syria; the conquest of Spain was organized by princes and dissident bishops. The Arab advance into Armenia and then the Turkish conquest of Anatolia and the Balkans were based on the same alliances and betrayals in high imperial and ecclesiastical circles. The alliance between the turban and the tiara constituted a major factor in the Islamic progression, the patriarch under Islam regaining the legislative and economic power which the Christian state had disputed. In fact, the rallying of the Eastern Churches to the Arab-Islamic government reflected the power struggles between the Christian state and the Churches.

Early Arab Conquests

One of the earliest traitors "Mansur ibn–Sarjun (Gr. Sergius), who figured in the treacherous surrender of Damascus ... was the scion of a prominent Christian family some of whose members had occupied the position of financial controller of the state in the last Byzantine period." Indeed, treason was common during the Arab conquest of Greater Syria. "In some cities and towns the Jews, Samaritans, and Monophysite Christians openly collaborated with the invaders. In Emesa (Hims), the local Jews and Christians barred the gates of their city before the Byzantine army. In Hebron and Caesarea, the Muslims were able to penetrate the defenses with the aid of Jewish collaborators." However, it should be noted that there were instances in which religious dissidents recognized that the invaders might turn out to be a greater problem than the Byzantine rulers. For example, in Gaza "the Jews actually may have fought alongside the Byzantine troops, who were badly outnumbered ..., in a vain attempt to defend the city."

In Egypt there was a notable instance of collaboration by high Church officials. The Patriarch of Alexandria, Cyrus "returned to Alexandria in order to conclude peace. Hoping to administer the country for the Arabians independently of Constantinople, the bishop signed with 'Amr ... a treaty ... accepting the payment of a fixed tribute of two dinars per adult head and a land tax payable in kind and agreeing not to allow a Byzantine army to return or attempt to recover the land."

Persian traitors were also active in helping the first Arab conquerors. In the Arab invasions "of Iraq and Iran the sources tell us of units of the Sasanian army joining the Arabs, after seeing that their government had collapsed. This means that the Arab armies included not only experienced cavalry, but also engineers conversant with sieges."

In the west, as well as the east, the Arab armies advanced along a path paved by treachery. After the fall of Carthage in 698 the Berbers were "led by a prophetess ... who exercised a mysterious influence over her followers. The heroine was at last defeated by treachery and killed." The Spanish resistance to the Moorish assault was riddled with treason and betrayal. The ships for the invasion were "provided by a certain semi-legendary Julian, count of Ceuta." The city of Cordova, "after holding out for two months ... was delivered to the besiegers through the treachery of a shepherd ... who pointed out a breach in the wall." The city of Toledo was betrayed to the Moors by resentful Jewish residents..Finally, "the Visigothic army was utterly routed owing to the treachery of the king's political enemies, headed by Bishop Oppas." All throughout the peninsula "the Jews rose up en masse in armed revolt against their Visigothic persecutors, and in city after city were organized by the overextended Muslims into garrisons." Treason at high levels of society continued as the Moors of Spain attempted to establish a foothold across the Pyrenees. In 759 some "Christian potentates in southern France sided with the Muslim invaders" against their Carolingian overlord Pippin.

In the following century, the Muslims began a series of major assaults on Italy. Treason, often at high levels, also marked these campaigns. In Sicily in 825, "Euphemius, the Byzantine admiral, finding himself threatened with imperial punishment for some offence ... rebelled ... and seized the island. Later, when defeated ... he fled to Tunisia and sought the aid of ... the Aghlabid ruler ..." that sent a fleet to conquer the island. Karsh describes how treachery on the part of local Christian rulers and city-states marked the subsequent Islamic Italian campaigns:

> In 837 the duke of Naples appealed for Aghlabi support against a local potentate besieging his city ... The thankful Neapolitans reciprocated by assisting the Muslim attack on the Sicilian city of Messina ... Naples was joined by the cities of Amalfi and Gaeta, which allowed the Muslims to use their ports for raids on Sicily and the Italian mainland and served as markets for the disposal of the booty obtained in these raids.
>
> In 876-77 the southern cities participated in the Muslim raids on the Roman littoral, with Naples serving as a base of operations. ... As a result, the Muslims entrenched themselves along the road to Rome, plundering and ravaging substantial parts of the countryside at will. It was as late as 915 that the pope finally managed to assemble an effective war coalition that routed the last remaining Muslim forces on the Italian mainland; even then, Amalfi refused to join the campaign while Naples and Gaeta connived to help the enemy escape. ...attacks from Sicily and North Africa continued for another century, with the ad hoc connivance of local Italian cities.

Later Byzantium

The centuries of Turkish conquests culminating in the fall of the Byzantine Empire was accompanied by a plethora of treason, betrayal and collaboration from within the Christian ranks. At the fateful battle of Manzikert "Romanus was an emperor with vast military experience ... commanding a hundred thousand well-trained troops ... There was, however, treachery among his officers; orders were not obeyed." Having learned nothing from the experience of their fellow Christians to the south who, at first, welcomed the Arab armies, various groups of religious dissidents and political rebels welcomed the invading Turks. According to Vryonis:

> One theory holds that the Christians largely welcomed the Turks. ... the Turks were welcomed first of all because Byzantine taxation in Anatolia was oppressive.
>
> This theory ... seems to receive further confirmation from the fact that Christians often cooperated with the Turkish conquest. Tzachas could never have built his fleet ... without the aid of the anonymous Smyrniote who undertook the construction of the ships. The naval arsenal ... erected ... under the orders of Abu'l-Kasim must also have been the work of local Christians.

There were also Christian "contingents in the Turkish armies."

With the death of the emperor Manuel the "last semblance of vigorous defense disappeared and the Turks raided even more frequently, on occasion being brought in by Greek rebels." Vryonis documents a number of instances of Byzantine aristocrats who employed Turkish contingents to support their acts of rebellion. Pseudoalexius employed 8,000 Turkmen followers of Emir Arslan in 1192. Michael, a rebellious official, obtained troops from Sultan Rukb-al-Din. Manuel Maurozomes obtained Turkish troops to ravage the valley towns of Bithynia. Theodore Mangaphas commanding Turkish troops sacked Caria and enslaved its population. Also Kir Farid and Cassianus delivered the towns over which they were governors to Turkish commanders in return for lands and positions among the Turks.

Conversions to Islam by high Byzantine aristocrats were a frequent occurrence. The following are examples of some Byzantine and other Anatolian aristocrats who converted in order to preserve their lands and social status: Philaretus, members of the Gabras and Comnenus families, Armenian governors of Seveverek and a number of Georgian chieftains.

In addition to keeping their estates many of the high-born renegades were rewarded with positions of great power:

...a number of Greek Christians as well as Greek renegades appeared side by side with Turks, Arabs and Persians in the Turkish court, administration and army. ... A number of Greeks appear with the title emir...

There are a number of instances where Byzantines fought for the sultan against other Muslims or against the Mongols. Even though that may not, qualify as treason against their countrymen it does indicate a mindset of collaboration, accommodation and the pursuit of personal interest with the end result being the strengthening of the Muslim hold on Anatolia. The following are instances of Byzantines serving as officers in the sultan's armies at times against their fellow Christians, at others against Muslims or Mongols. A Greek Emir by the name of Maurozones served in an expedition against Cilician Armenia in the early 13th century. Five brothers, the Awlad I Ferdahli from the empire of Nicaea served in a Syrian expedition. Michael Palaeologus served as kondistabl in charge of the sultan's Christian troops. A Frankish mercenary named Istankus defended Erzerum for the sultan against the Mongols.

The rapidly diminishing Byzantine domains did not see any diminishing of treachery. "The collapse of Byzantine rule in Bithynia and Paphlagonia [late 13th and early 14th centuries] was accelerated and facilitated by the religious and factional strife among the Byzantines there, some of whom went over to the side of the Turks." One of these was Evrenos the governor of Bursa who "with other leading Greeks, surrendered the city and embraced the Moslem faith." In addition, in these provinces a number of Akritai, the "Greek frontier warriors ... were induced to change sides." Kinross notes how the Turks, "united as they were in the holy warfare of Islam", were well equipped to take advantage of such disunity and betrayal.

Probably the greatest single act of treachery occurred in the Fourth Crusade. The act of betrayal by the crusaders toward the empire they were pledged to help protect was "a perfidious attack by the Latin knights of the Fourth Crusade, not against the Moslems of the Holy Land as first projected, but against their fellow Greek Christians in Constantinople." Also worth noting was that Venice the principal mover of this act of civilizational treason "became the largest slave market in Central Europe, selling even Christian slaves to the Muslims." Historian of the Crusades Robert Payne writes of the deplorable Latin conquest of Constantinople:

> The sack of Constantinople can be explained only by sheer lust for conquest, at whatever the cost in lives and treasure. It was accomplished by treachery in the modern manner, in cold blood, without any regard for the consequences, which inevitably included the weakening of the Byzantine Empire, an empire that had for so long been a bastion against the Turks. ... They did not even have an interest in recovering the Holy Land; they wanted loot.

The final chapter in the fall of Byzantium was ushered in by the self-serving aristocrat John Cantacuzene. In 1345 six thousand Ottoman troops crossed into Europe "on the invitation of John Cantacuzene ... who had proclaimed himself Emperor and required Turkish support in the civil war which followed." In both 1350 and 1352 Cantacuzene called in another 20,000 Ottoman troops to aid him against his Balkan rivals. In 1353 the Ottomans established themselves permanently in Gallipoli. It must be noted, however, that Cantacuzene's opponent the empress Anna also sought Ottoman aid, promising sultan Orhan that he could carry off into slavery her defeated opponents. A century later, it was a Christian military engineer who by selling his services to the Ottoman Sultan delivered the coup de grace to the embattled Byzantine capital. In 1452 a Hungarian cannon founder named Orban built the enormous cannon with which Mehmed the conqueror battered the walls of Constantinople.

Some Greeks in the following century appeared to have learned nothing from the history of decimation of their fellows at the hands of the Muslims. In the year 1563 "a number of

Cypriots, led by their priests, contacted the Ottomans and asked them to put the island under their rule." Nor were Western Christians, even after the fall of the great Orthodox capital, immune from the temptation of trying to make use of Turkish might in their petty dynastic disputes. Allying himself with the Ottomans against his fellow Christian rulers Francis I found the Muslim alliance to be a peculiar double edged sword.

In 1543 the Sultan sent Barbarossa westward ... in command of a fleet of a hundred galleys, with a French envoy on board. ... Barbarossa ... was granted as his naval headquarters the port of Toulon, from which a portion of the inhabitants was evacuated, and which the French were presently describing as a second Constantinople ...The port indeed presented a curious spectacle, humiliating to the French Catholics, with turbanned Moslems pacing the decks and Christian slaves ...even some Frenchmen chained to the benches of the galleys. To replenish their crews ... the Turks took to raiding French villages, carrying off peasants to serve in the galleys, while Christian captives were openly sold in the market. Meanwhile, as in a Moslem city, the muezzins freely chanted their own call to prayer ... Francis I, having asked for Turkish support soon grew disturbed at the overt nature and extent of it, and its unpopularity with his subjects. ... In 1554 Francis I rid himself of his embarrassing ally through bribery, making substantial payments to the Turkish forces and presenting precious gifts to the admiral himself.

The parallel of the 16th century French-Ottoman alliance, to circumstances in parts of the contemporary West, ought to be a lesson the present leadership in both Europe and America would do well to heed.

The seduction of susceptible Europeans continued for many years. In the early 18th century a major role in the restructuring of the Ottoman armies was "played by European experts. Some came as individuals and threw in their lot completely with the Ottomans, to the point of embracing Islam and entering the Ottoman service." By then Europe was too strong relative to the Ottomans to be in any danger. However, such skills would have been used, of course, to attack Europe if the Ottomans were able to reverse their decline.

India

In India, as in the west, the Islamic invasions were aided by numerous occurrences of native treason. When ibn Qasim invaded Sind some Buddhists of the city of Nerun "were reminded of their vows on non-violence and came to terms with the invader. Thanks to these 'Buddhist fifth columnists' ... Nerun capitulated." During Qasim's siege of Debal "a Brahmin comes out of the town. He tells the Arabs that the town is guarded by ... four long flags of green silk that hang down ... the flagstaff ... of the great temple ... While the flagstaff stands the ... people of Debal will fight." When Qasim had the flagstaff knocked down the defenders surrendered. The pattern of betrayal for the Arab conquest of Sind was set at Nerun and Debal. The "betrayal by nobles or Brahmins or Buddhist priests who do not believe in killing" paved the way for the Arab occupation. Naipaul remarks of these Sind traitors, in words that apply to many of the betrayers in all the lands invaded by the Muslims; they "understand only that power is power, and believe they are only changing rulers; they cannot conceive that a new way is about to come."

A famous instance of Indian treason occurred centuries later at the beginning of the Mogul regime. When the rajputs, under their leader Sangha, opposed Babur's invasion of India at the battle of Kanga "defeat resulted not from tactical naivety but from treachery. 'The Tomar traitor who led the [Rajput] van went over to Babur, and [Rana] Sangha was obliged to retreat.'"

RELIGION OF CONQUERORS

As shown above there was reluctance on the part of the early Arab Muslims to convert non-Arabs. The fact is that the Arab conquerors were far less interested in the mass conversion of the vanquished peoples than in securing their tribute. Not until the second and third Islamic centuries did the bulk of these populations embrace the religion of their latest imperial masters, and even this process emanated from below in an attempt to escape paying tribute and to remove social barriers, with the conquering ruling classes doing their utmost to slow it down.

In its' initial expansion Islam was not a proselytizing faith for other than Arabs. Only after more than a century did the Arab ruling elite become seriously interested in converting non-Arabs. From that point on, the succeeding Muslim vanguards were interested in conversion from the first days of their conquests. This accounts for the rapid spread of Islam in Anatolia and for the tragic and bloody experience undergone by the Hindu "idolaters". However, the tribute that even the first Arab conquerors were interested in included slaves and concubines as well as material possessions. Many of these slaves converted to Islam and the children of the concubines were brought up as Arabic speaking Muslims. This was, in part, a consequence of the nature of the initial conquests:

> Far from a mass migration of barbarian hordes in desperate search of subsistence, the Arab invasions were centrally organized military expeditions on a strikingly small scale. ... There is no evidence of whole tribes migrating into the Fertile Crescent ... or of warriors taking their own families and herds with them (apart from a few isolated cases). It was only after the consolidation of the initial conquests that substantial numbers of Arab colonists arrived in the newly acquired territories. ... This makes the conquests first and foremost a quintessential expansionist feat by a rising imperial power, in which Islam provided a moral sanction ...

In Egypt, as well, the number of Arab conquerors was small, although not known with any certainty. According to Hasan, "Amr b. al-As came with an army of three or four thousand, al-Zubayr b. al Awwam followed him with five or twelve thousand, and Abdullah b. Sa'd had twenty thousand in his first campaign against Nubia!" And as in Iraq and Syria, it was at a later time that large numbers of colonists followed when Arabs of the Qays tribe migrated to Egypt and practiced agriculture. These settlers were to be important in the eventual Islamization of the Copts. "The sedentary occupations of these Arabs encouraged their intermixing with the Egyptians, and were an important factor in the spread of Islam among the Egyptians. The Copts were gradually induced by social and financial privileges to be converted to Islam and to adopt the Arabic tongue."

The following template set by the earliest Arab conquerors was copied by later invaders; the Moors in Spain, the Turks in Anatolia, the Turks, Moguls and Iranians in India. Warrior elite seize territory and co-opt local women to create a hybridized population. This opens up the territory for subsequent nomadic infiltration, often against the wishes of the now settled hybridized Muslim population. These new invaders are then diverted to the frontiers where they can engage the infidels. Over a period of centuries, the conquered population slowly accepts the religion and sometimes the language of the invaders. That happened with the Arab infiltration in North Africa and the Sudan, with the Turkish frontier ghazis in Anatolia and with the extension of Islamic sultanates into unconquered areas of southern and eastern India.

TRIUMPH OF PROSELYTISM

Islam with its clear pretensions to universality could not long remain an Arab exclusive religion. The urge to spread the new faith on the part of its zealous adherents was matched by the ease with which a non-Muslim could adopt the new religion. This was in keeping with the pragmatism demonstrated by the early Muslims. All that was required was a simple declaration of faith. No complicated ritual or painful initiation rites were required. The temptation to convert must have been great to those most severely affected by the conquests - prisoners, slaves, concubines and those dhimmis living in close proximity to their new overlords. Eventually the temptation to convert with its consequent increase in legal rights, enhancement of economic opportunities and avoidance of ruinous tax and tribute obligations induced masses of non-Muslims to, at least verbally, profess the conquering faith. Furthermore, the conversion process was to turn into a positive feedback loop; the converts themselves induced still further conversions among their countrymen. Trifkovic gives a capsule summary of the long conversion process typical of many Muslim conquests:

> Muhammad's pragmatism in demanding only verbal submission to start with was a very useful device in spreading Islam throughout the conquered lands from Bosnia to India. St. Paul's 'Let each be convinced in his own mind' could not apply to the conquering faith that depended on the power of the sword, not that of the word. In the longer term, as it turned out, the formal submission of the first generation of converts inevitably led to the irreversible change of identity and belief system of those that followed. Lingering suppressed guilt at the original act of betrayal turned Muslim converts of the Balkans, in particular, into zealous oppressors of their Christian kinsmen who had retained their identity.

Even in the early days of the Arab conquests, some of these converts were motivated by religious zeal as well as by hoped for social advantages. Some of them even, "proved religiously 'more royal than the king', and their zeal for the new faith made them persecute non-Moslems. Among the most intolerant early Moslems were some of those converts from Christianity and Judaism."

It was under the caliph Umar II (717-720), that a more deliberate policy of conversion was adopted. Umar rescinded the taxes that were re-imposed on Muslim converts by his predecessors with an inevitable and unfortunate fiscal consequence. "Though inspired by the best of intentions, Umar's policy was not successful. It diminished the revenues of the state and increased the number of clients in the cities. Many Berbers and Persians [and Iraqis] embraced Islam to enjoy the pecuniary privileges thus accorded them." He also sought to promote conversion by imposing humiliating restrictions on non-Muslims; a precedent that was to be repeated by many future Muslim rulers. It is interesting that Umar was regarded by Muslims in succeeding years as being particularly noted for piety and righteousness.

In addition, the conversions of non-Muslims advanced by Umar and other proselytizers backfired in yet another way:

Non-Arabian Moslems in general and Persian Moslems in particular had good reasons for dissatisfaction. Far from being granted the expected economic and social equality ... they were ... reduced to the position of clients and were not always exempted from the capitation tax paid by non Moslems. What made them more disconnected was the consciousness that they represented a higher and more ancient culture ... It was among such discontented neophytes that the Shi'ite-'Abbasid seed found fertile soil.

Following the Abbasid revolution Islam's proselytizing imperative was fully in effect. According to Hitti:

During the first century of 'Abbasid rule the conquests entered upon their second stage, the victory of Islam as a religion. It was in the course of this stage that the bulk of the population was converted... such a country as Syria continued to present the aspect of a Christian country throughout the whole Umayyad period. The situation now began to change. The intolerant legislation of al-Rashid and al-Mutawakkil undoubtedly contributed its quota of fresh converts. Cases of individual and collective conversion added to their numbers ... But the process of conversion in its normal working was more gradual and peaceful, though also inescapable. ... To escape the payment of the humiliating tribute and other disabilities, to secure social prestige or political influence, to enjoy a larger measure of freedom and security, these were the strong motives in operation.

Abbasid officials, however, experienced many of the same problems with these neo-Muslims as had their Umayyad predecessors. The decline in state revenues accelerated as the numbers of Egyptian, Persian and Aramaean converts exceeded the number of Arab Muslims. Furthermore, the increased financial burden this placed on the still unconverted population, undoubtedly, had a positive feedback effect leading to still more conversions. Finally, the entire fiscal basis of the Muslim state had to be overhauled:

Escape from oppressive taxation and social inferiority was certainly a great inducement to conversion. ... Many mawali were sorely disappointed when they discovered they were not to be permitted to go from being tribute bearers to pension receivers by the ruling Arab military elite. Eventually, however, there were enough converts to undermine totally the old tax base and necessitate fundamental changes in the economic system of the empire.

In addition, the Abbasid revolution did not diminish the unrest endemic to the converts. Most of "these neophyte Moslems formed the lowest stratum of Moslem society, a status which they bitterly resented." This explains why many of them found Shi'ite or Kharijite causes so appealing. Some converts, however, entered the ranks of the social elite; among them were those Persian officials who continued the traditions of the Sasanian bureaucratic class under the new regime.

CONVERSION OF THE NATIVES

The Muslim nomadic conquerors, in almost all instances, formed a small elite minority amongst a large vanquished population of non-Muslims. Yet, over time, the conquered populations in most of these territories accepted Islam, so that the Muslim proportion in modern times is overwhelming. There were, of course, both major and minor instances of territories where the native populations held on to their old faiths despite long periods of Muslim domination. The two most prominent such territories were India and the Balkans. In India Hindu majorities generally prevail although the Muslims, through a recent exchange of populations, became the overwhelming majority in what are now Pakistan and Bangladesh. In the Balkans, Christian majorities prevail, although aided by similar population displacements; the Muslims form a large majority in Bosnia, Albania, Kosovo and Eastern Thrace. The Caucasus and the mountains of Lebanon are two lesser territories where non-Muslim populations remained a majority, at least until very recent times.

Professor Richard Bulliet has derived a set of conversion curves for those territories that were conquered in the initial wave of Arab conquests. These are obtained by fitting data from various biographical dictionaries onto a mathematical function called the logistic curve; a device commonly used by statisticians and economists who study the spread of technical and social innovation. The Bulliet curves are reproduced below. These show the percent of conversion to Islam over time.

The conversion curve for Egypt also applies to Tunisia and most likely, the rest of the Maghreb. Conversion times for parts of central Asia, Afghanistan and western India are probably similar to that for Persia, although other parts of these territories were much more resistant to Islam. The conversion curve for Spain is more problematic due to the slow expansion of Christian held territory. As historian of the Spanish reconquista Harvey points out, Bulliet's curve for Muslim Spain "is not replicated exactly in the history of the peninsula" and leads to estimates that are too high. Therefore, the above reproduction of the curve for Muslim controlled territories of Spain is scaled down somewhat from the original Bulliet estimated curve. Indeed, the reconquest of Spain by Christians was a mirror in reverse of the Turkish conquest of Anatolia with a demoralized Muslim population, mass conversions to Christianity, displacement and the entry of large numbers of new immigrants.

Based on the shape of the above logistic curves as fitted to conform to historical accounts of the Muslim expansions, the following approximate conversion curves are drawn for the two other major territories with current Muslim majorities. Islam was, of course, established in Anatolia and Indonesia (including Malaya) by later groups of non-Arab Muslims.

The rapidity of conversion in Anatolia may partly reflect the fact that Muslim rulers subsequent to the initial Arab conquerors were no longer reluctant to promote the spread of Islam.

The small numbers, usually less than ten percent of the population, who still resisted conversion, marked by the leveling off of Bulliet's curve , consisted of a disproportionate number of artisans and craftsmen. The reason for their survival is given by Darlington as follows:

They continued to follow their hereditary trades and professions. They continued also to follow their equally hereditary religions. There were Jews, Samaritans and

Mandaeans. And there were the diverse Christian sects, Greek or Maronite, Coptic, Assyrian or Armenian. These different faiths continued in the cities of Islam. They maintained themselves by their rejection, not only of interbreeding with Muslims ... but also of interbreeding with one another.

Hence, the non-Muslims were the most pure descendants of the ancient peoples while most Muslims, particularly those living in the towns and cities, underwent considerable interbreeding with peoples brought in from all over Islamic territory. Furthermore, while "the peasants of Egypt, the shepherds of the Maghrib and the minor artisans of the cities escaped hybridization and resisted change, each new conquest or revolution threw urban society into some disorder."

Bulliet in constructing his curves emphasizes that, as previously indicated, in the early years of the Arab conquests "one must conclude that those who converted to Islam during the period when the mawali were so heavily stigmatized must have been people for whom being second class Arabs was superior to any other options. ...prisoners of war who might seek through conversion to escape slavery and people ... from the very lowest classes."

FERTILE CRESCENT

For Iraq and Syria the curves support Hitti's contention that not "until the second and third centuries of the Moslem era did the bulk of the people in Syria, Mesopotamia and Persia profess the religion of Muhammad." However, in parts of Syria, especially in the north "Christian majorities survived through the twelfth century, until - compromised by their sympathies with and assistance to the Crusaders - they were put under severe pressure." Many of these even held out until the thirteenth and fourteenth centuries.

IRAN

In Iran, as seen in the above graph, by the 10th century a major part of the population had become Muslim. It was under the Muslim national Iranian dynasties that conversion to Islam became universal, although it proceeded at varying rates in different parts of the country. The dhimmis "were not forced to convert, but they suffered from restrictions. ... How seriously such rules were applied depended on local conditions, but even in the best circumstances the position of a minority is uneasy and the inducement to convert existed." According to Lapidus, the remaining non-Muslims of both Iran and Iraq, soon after Islam became the majority faith, came under intense pressure. "Only with the breakdown of the social and religious structures of non-Muslim communities in the tenth to twelfth centuries did the weakening of churches, the awakening of Muslim hostility to non-Muslims, sporadic and localized persecution and the destruction of the landed gentry of Iraq and Iran destroy the communal organization of non-Muslim peoples."

The Abbasid ascendancy opened up the top ranks of the aristocracy to talented and energetic non-Muslims, particularly Iranians. In Iran under the new Abbasid order:

> The Shi'ites considered them avenged. The clients became emancipated. ... Khurasanians formed the caliphal bodyguard and Persians occupied the chief posts of government. The original Arabian aristocracy was replaced by a gamut of nationalities under the caliphate. The old Arabian Moslems and the new foreign conquerors were beginning to coalesce and shade off into each other.

Members of the Old Persian aristocracy found that this Abbasid open door policy made taking the Islamic profession of faith quite advantageous. Petty tributary rulers at the far reaches of Persia, such as Mazyar the early ninth century king of Tabaristan converted. The famous Barmakid family of officials and viziers who ruled the Islamic empire under the early Abbasids was originally a "Buddhist priestly family from Balkh".

In western Central Asia, Islam was overwhelmingly the religion of the masses by the end of the ninth century while Zoroastrianism still lingered in many parts of the Iranian countryside. Moreover, the new west Central Asian converts, in contrast to the Iranians, became staunch upholders both of Islam and Arabism. "When non-Arabs converted to Islam they were given Arabic names and ... were said to have become Arabs. As frequently happens with new converts, many became more fanatic than the Arabs."

EGYPT

In Egypt, as in the Fertile Crescent, the first Arab conquerors had little desire to promote Islam to the conquered population. And the latter found little of appeal in Islam. Eventually, as in Iraq when the Umayyad dynasty declined and with the ascension of the Abbasids, circumstances changed. "The Arabs in Egypt were a privileged minority. ... Only towards the end of the Umayyad rule did they start to mix with the Egyptians. In a few hundred years Egypt was turned into an Arab and Muslim country." As in Iraq, the number of conversions accelerated in the 10th and 11th centuries with increasing persecution and weakening of Christian institutions. The conversion curve for Syria, Iraq and Egypt shows an increase in the converted fraction of the population over these two centuries from about one quarter to three quarters. In the following centuries, Egyptian dhimmis were subject to sporadic persecution and Islam continued its steady progression. Under the repressive Mamluks "large numbers of Copts and Jews, especially among the professional classes who found the institutionalized humiliation too burdensome, converted to Islam."

Native Syrian, Iraqi and Egyptian converts never attained the degree of prominence within the Islamic state as that attained by the Iranians. Nevertheless, there were instances where some western converts reached positions of great power. For example the Jew Ya'qub b. Killis "who still maintained close ties with his former coreligionists" was brought to the attention of the Fatimid Caliph al-Mu'izz. He helped plan the conquest of Egypt and helped prepare "Egypt to become the center of the greater Fatimid Empire."

Spain

In Muslim Spain, as in Iran, Iraq, Syria and Egypt many non-Muslims adopted the Islamic faith in the hopes of improving their status, only to be disappointed and resentful at their continued second class status. As Hitti observes, in Spain

> Christians flocked to Islam. ... In the course of time these neophytes became the most discontented body in the population. Their ranks were recruited mainly from serfs and freedmen ... Some of them were 'secret Christians'; but they all knew well the clear and inexorable law of apostasy from Islam, which prescribed death. The Moslem Arabs treated all ... as inferior, though some were of noble descent.

These converts became the majority in several cities "where they were the first to take up arms against the established order."

MAGHREB

North Africa illustrates a type of conversion to Islam that was typical of nomadic or primitive cultures when first engaged by Islam. It is reported ... that various North African Berber tribes converted to Islam and subsequently fell away. This type of conversion, although the words of the confession of faith might actually have been mouthed by the tribesmen, would not qualify as social conversion. ... Apostasy probably had little significance because formal conversion alone meant very little in any social sense. The same could be said at a later period for the conversion of various Turkish tribes...

TURKISH CONQUESTS

The Turkish conquest of Anatolia and later of the Balkans, taking much longer and being better documented than was the case for the early Arab conquests, illustrates many details of the conversion process. The Seljuk annexation of the central Anatolian plateau amounted to the introduction of a small Turkish military elite ruling over a large Christian population. In this respect it was rather similar to the earlier Arab conquests of Byzantine territory. Vryonis notes that there "has been a tendency to exaggerate the number of the original Turkish settlers, but the sources seem to suggest that ... the Turks who came at this time very definitely constituted a minority." And as was the case with the Arab conquests, in the first century following the Turkish occupation of the plateau, only a small percentage of the population embraced Islam so that the left side of the conversion curve probably looks very similar to that of Syria and Iraq. As Vryonis contends

...in the eleventh and twelfth centuries, conversion also had the effect of decreasing the number of Christians while increasing the Muslim population. ...there seems to be some indication that in this period conversions to Islam were numerically significant, though not as extensive as they later were to become.

Furthermore, despite "migrations, displacement, massacres, plagues, famine, and enslavement, it is highly probable that the majority of the Anatolian Christian population remained in Asia Minor fifty years after Manzikert." Vryonis emphasizes that the Turks at this time were a small minority and that during the "first half century of occupation of Anatolia they formed a small governing and military caste and appear from time to time in the sources as the administrators and military garrisons of areas otherwise inhabited by Christians." A number of contemporary sources attest to the continuing Christian majority in the early decades of the Seljuk ascendancy; in fact Christians appear to constitute a significant portion of the population for over two centuries following the first arrival of the Turks:

There are other indications that the Christian population of Asia Minor was still quite extensive in the twelfth and even in the thirteenth century. The History of the Patriarchs of Alexandria asserts that the majority of the subjects of the sultan Mas'ud I (1116-56) were Greeks, and there is the testimony of the thirteenth and fourteenth century travelers. ... Marco Polo implies that the urban classes contained a large Christian element. A contemporary William of Rubruque, remarks rather exaggeratedly ... 'that not one man in ten there is a Saracen; rather they are all Armenians and Greeks.' ... Both Sanuto and Ibn Battuta noted the presence of considerable numbers of Christians in western Asia Minor as late as the early fourteenth century. ...the single largest source of revenue in Muslim Anatolia during the latter half of the thirteenth century was the tax that they paid.

Thus, the pattern of conversion appears to be broadly similar to that which took place in the Arab Byzantine territories. However, there seems to be a slight acceleration in Anatolian, as compared to Syrian conversions, since at the time of the Turkish conquests, Muslims were fully committed to the conversion of infidels. The Turkish epic Danishmendname attributes a strong proselytizing zeal to the Muslims ... There are conversions of individuals, bodies of soldiers, and whole towns and the conversions that occur in the poem break down into two categories: voluntary and forced. Those who convert voluntarily do so as a result of a religious vision, or for romantic reasons, or because of some material advantage to be obtained.

Muslim proselytizing zeal was strongest among the various Sufi sects that eventually followed the Seljuk warriors. Vryonis believes that it was "only in the thirteenth and fourteenth centuries that the conversionary activities of these orders become manifest." The dervish contribution to the conversion of the Anatolian population was considerable and extensive as subsequent territory came under Muslim rule. In the 14th century dervish missionaries roamed the newly annexed territories in western Anatolia and "so successful were they that ... the western traveler ... von Suchem ... in the mid fourteenth century ... remarked that the Turks as a people were in part Christian renegades." The demoralization of the Christian population and the collapse of Byzantine institutions under unceasing Muslim pressure paved the way for the spread of the dervish teachings. These brotherhoods were instrumental in "transforming the majority of the Greek and Armenian Christians into Turkish Muslims." Sufi missionary activities, so extensively documented in Anatolia, were an important factor in most conversions subsequent to the first Arab expansion. Central Asia and India were also scenes of mass conversions brought about through the efforts of various Sufi brotherhoods.

The continued depredations of nomadic Turkmen were an important factor in the demoralization of the Byzantine population. This is one more, well attested example, of a process common to the other Muslim expansions. Vryonis gives an example of the way the nomads affected the settled population on the Byzantine frontier. "The inability of the Byzantines to retake Konya and to retain Ankara, and the partial removal of the Greek population from southern Phrygia are not the only indications of the comparative density of the Turkmens in these regions. The sources refer specifically to the fact that the Turkmens were present in large numbers." This example is indicative of a higher rate of infusion of Turks in the central plateau than in western and coastal Anatolia; it is plausible that a third of the population on the plateau consisted of the original Turkish invaders and the following nomadic Turkmen. Byzantine chroniclers write, with approval, of various benevolent Turkish rulers. However, as Vryonis points out these "very authors who praise Malik Shah and others as the clement protectors of the Christians make it quite obvious that the element against which the sultans had to protect the Christians was the Muslims themselves."

Thus, the migration of Turkmen tribes into Anatolia disrupted the order established by the Seljuks. The descendants of these Turkmen continued their unrest into Ottoman times. In their period of decline the Ottomans were confronted with agitation from a group known as Jelalis who "drew their strength ... from Turcoman, Kurdish, and other Asiatic tribesmen ... and...from the dispossessed feudal sipahis." These Jelalis controlled whole provinces and extracted tribute from towns in Central Anatolia. Their leader "Deli Hassan was induced by the central government to lay down his arms, and as condition was made governor of Bosnia. This enabled him to use his wild troops in Europe. In a new invasion of half-naked, long-haired Asiatic 'barbarians,' they ravaged Rumeli, slaughtering Moslems and Christians alike."

These well documented instances in Anatolia illuminate an important factor in the decimation of non-Muslim populations in most of the Islamic conquered territories.

Continued pressure on dhimmi populations as a result of subsequent nomadic migrations also characterizes Muslim conquests prior to the great Turkish expansion. The Hilali invasion of the Mahgreb in the 11th century was decisive in the almost total extirpation of the Christian religion in North Africa. Other Arab Bedouin tribes afflicted the settled populations of Iraq, Syria, Iran and Egypt with severe impact on surviving non-Muslim communities. The Christian kingdoms of the Sudan were under pressure from nomadic Arabs for centuries. At the same time Anatolia was being ravaged by new migrations of Turkmen, these kingdoms came under renewed Bedouin pressure which was finally fatal. In about the year 1324, Bedouins from Upper Egypt were forced by the Mamluks to flee into Nubia. "Those who migrated to Nubia were already famine stricken and could do nothing but continue their rapacious behavior - plundering the Nubian Christians and quarrelling with the new Muslim rulers or among themselves."

Furthermore, since the new Muslim nomads evinced the same yearning for a more comfortable settled existence as their immediate predecessors, a series of petty Muslim emirates followed in the wake of the migrations. In Anatolia, for example, the "disappearance of political unity attendant upon the Turkish invasions not only brought considerable upheaval but often placed the Anatolian populations under the onerous burden of supporting a large array of courts, administrations, and armies."

Other key factors leading to Islamization: slavery and the forced conversion of non-Muslims were well illustrated in the history of Asia Minor. The effects of these, according to Vryonis, were quite significant over long periods of time.

It is difficult to give the number of Christians [youths] who were taken into the system [of slave administration] and thus Islamized. Obviously the number was comparatively small at any given time, but the system must have had some affect on the conversion of Christians over a period of several centuries. We are told that after the capture of the city of Chiliat in about 1231 a troop of 1,000 royal gulams was left to settle the affairs of the city, and in another instance there is mention of 500 serhenk. When Trebizond fell 800 Greek youth were taken, and 100 were levied from New Phocaea.

Furthermore, "Scholarius' writings bear extensive testimony to the large scale conversions that were emptying the Christian ranks. ...sieges, massacres, enslavement, famine, taking away of children, dishonoring of priests, and above all conversion to Islam, both voluntary and involuntary."

By the year 1500 the conversion of Anatolia was essentially complete. Thus, the right-hand side of the above conversion curve can be drawn as asymptotically approaching a maximum close to 90%. As Vryonis asserts:

The evidence as to the remaining Christian populations in the fifteenth and sixteenth centuries contrasts greatly with the testimony of the twelfth and thirteenth century sources indicated that the Christians were probably still the majority. ... The critical transformation of the population, prepared by the events of the eleventh and twelfth centuries was consummated in the late fourteenth, and the early fifteenth century. But the absorptive process had been a long one, stretching over four hundred years.

Furthermore the "basic farming stock of Seljuk Anatolia up to the mid thirteenth century consisted of Greek, Armenian, and Syrian peasants. After the thirteenth century, the majority of these farmers converted to Islam and these converts, with the sedentarized nomads, came to constitute the Turkish farming population of most of Anatolia." However, under more settled Ottoman times, pragmatic sultans permitted significant re-colonization of the western Anatolian coastlands by Greek Christians; a situation that was reversed early in the 20th century. Moreover, descendants of converted Byzantines make up the major part of the population of modern Turkey. "The numbers of the Muslim population were increased by the emigration of Arabs, Persians and Turks ... but especially by the mounting tide of religious conversions."

The first Abbasids owed their success, in large part to the talent and energy of Iranian converts. Similarly, Greeks and other converts energized the states established by the Turkish conquerors. The long run success of the Turks and the longevity of the Ottoman Empire were due to these neo-Muslims. Numerous examples of such converts are mentioned in the historical accounts for the case of Turkey; it is undoubtedly the case that this was an important characteristic of most Muslim expansions. There were two distinct categories of talented converts. One consisted of many prominent aristocrats, high officials, scholars, soldiers or mercenaries who, through self interest or genuine conviction joined the Turkish ranks. The other category consisted of "upwardly mobile" slaves who through sheer ability rose to the upper echelons of the Turkish state.

Vryonis remarks on the existence of many socially prominent Byzantine collaborators and converts:

The appearance ... of a number of the representatives of these Anatolian aristocratic families in the services of the Turks during the centuries of Seljuk and Ottoman rule indicates that a significant portion of the Greek aristocracy came to a mutually profitable understanding with the Turks. ...many retained their Christian faith for a considerable period of time, while others apostatized to Islam early.

And of somewhat lower rank were the many soldiers of Christian origin employed by Turkish rulers:

There are also indications that the Seljuk rulers frequently employed Christian troops, those specifically mentioned being Greeks, Franks, Georgians, Armenians, Russians and Germans. ... The Greek troops were drawn ... from the Byzantine lands and from the sultan's domains. ... Upon the worsening of conditions in Bithynia in the latter half of the thirteenth century, the acrites sought service with the Turks. ...it seems to have been customary to recruit military units for the Seljuk armies from among the Greek Christian subjects of the sultan, and it is quite possible these soldiers were eventually converted to Islam.

The history of the Ottoman state is replete with instances of prominent converts. The early Ottoman sultan Osman held power in the province of Bithynia. Among his "closest companions were the Greek families of Michaelogli and Marcozogli ... As a result of their association with him, they adopted the Moslem faith." Mehmed the Conqueror employed numerous converts from the high Byzantine aristocracy. His general Hass Murad Pasha was a descendant of the Palaeologus family. Another scion of the Palaeologus family, the last Byzantine dynasty, was his admiral Mesih. In addition, Mehmed's grand vizier Mahmut Pasha was a Byzantine from a noble Greek and Serbian lineage. In the century following, the famous Ottoman admirals, the Barbarossa brothers were from a lower rank of Greek society, but still respectably middle class. These were the "red-bearded sons of a potter, a Christian renegade retired from the Janissaries and married to the widow of a Greek priest ... from the island of Lesbos."

Another variety of converts profitably employed by the Ottomans were from distinctly lower strata of society, often slaves. The genius of Ottoman administration, which undoubtedly was crucial to the longevity of the dynasty, was the scope given to talented slaves and converts of humble background to rise to the top rungs of Ottoman society. After the execution of his vizier Halil, Mehmed "had around him only advisors of the growing renegade class, Christian converts to Islam whose careers depended directly on the Sultan's favor and on whom he could thus count to do his bidding. His new Grand Vezir was his general Zaganos Pasha, an Albanian in origin." Mehmed's replacement of Turkish officials with lower class converts was the final blow to the old nomadic Ottoman ideal of egalitarianism among the conquering warrior elite. And the Ottoman conquest of the Balkans opened a whole new base on which to draw lower class or slave converts into the ranks of the administration.

In the centuries after the reign of Mehmed, Balkan converts continued to staff the highest positions of the state. Ibrahim Pasha, Suleiman's Grand Vizier was born a Greek Christian. Ibrahim's successor was "Rustem Pasha, the Bulgarian, who as an economist skillfully handled the Ottoman treasury". Rustem's successor was Sokollu Pasha "a Slav from

Bosnia who in boyhood had served as an acolyte in a Serbian church, and who was to uphold for a crucial period the power and prestige of his late master." Sokollu who continued in power under Suleiman's dissolute son Selim, "set indeed a precedent for the pattern of centuries to come when from time to time a strong vezir, often Christian in origin, would emerge to counterbalance a weak Sultan, and help guide the state through its periods of crisis." The strength of Christian institutions in the Balkans coupled with a moderating of the Turkish impulse to convert in the Ottoman period preserved a large Christian population from which the Sultans could draw slaves or other humble converts for the military and administration; converts who had no problematic power base but were completely dependent on their Ottoman patrons. The continuance of a large Christian "reservoir" was, undoubtedly, the reason that the Ottoman dynasty lasted much longer than other Islamic regimes. It may well be that the more far-seeing Ottoman rulers were willing to curb the zeal of their Muslim subjects for converting non-Muslims, in order to maintain this advantage.

The Ottoman search for talented converts was wide ranging. "The first grand vizier of definitely Caucasian slave origin seems to have been Hadim Mehmed Pasha, a palace eunuch of Georgian birth ... in 1622-3." Hadim was one of many officials of slave or humble backgrounds from remote mountainous areas. The founder of the Koprulu dynasty of Grand Viziers was Mehmed Koprulu an Albanian of humble origin who began his career as a cook.

"His appointment stimulated a growing process of recruitment and conversion to Islam of Balkan Christian mountain tribesmen, both in Albania ... and Bulgaria, which was to infuse the army and the administration with new sources of energy and loyalty." The increased susceptibility of the 'mountain tribesmen' to conversion shows, once again, the greater appeal of Islam to more primitive societies. Even in the later centuries of the Ottoman state the continuing large Balkan Christian populations enabled the Ottoman dynasty to continue appropriating human resources not yet stultified by Islam and, thus, to renew the life of their Empire.

INDIA

India proved much more resistant to conversion than were the Levant, Central Asia and Anatolia. However, there were many instances of Hindu soldiers joining the Islamic invaders to avail themselves of the greater material and sexual opportunities available to warriors of the Prophet. "In fact there is good evidence that the superior prospects on offer to the champions of Islam induced some Hindus from the north-west frontier to switch both religion and allegiance and to fight for the Ghaznavids."

Despite the conversion of some Hindu auxiliaries, India was a tough nut to crack. Unlike the dry plateaus and desert areas, there was a large dense population; the towns were not few and scattered, but close by and well fortified. Also the Hindus faced a much starker choice. Since they were not "people of the book", those Muslim leaders who were more fanatical and less pragmatic than the first Arab governor, Qasim, could offer them only conversion, slavery or death. This undoubtedly stiffened the resistance of those committed to their beliefs. The large dense population necessitated the use of native vassals, and these would often apostatize as soon as their overlords left the area. There were similar conditions in the Balkans, although there the Christian inhabitants could not lawfully be forcibly converted; a fact of which Sultan Selim the Grim was reminded by his qadi when he schemed to implement a policy of forced conversion.

Historian of India John Keay writes of the difficulties faced by some of the bloody-minded Muslim invaders of this vast and populous land:

> Mahmud, seemingly, ravaged only to revive. Even as he was demolishing some of the north's greatest temples, others were being built; even as he carted away their wealth, more was accumulating elsewhere. ... For every fifty thousand idolaters that were massacred, fifty thousand equally unregenerated devotees swarmed to some other place of pilgrimage ... or politico-religious significance.

Moreover, if "temple-building was indeed 'a political act', there could be no more eloquent testimony to the ... defiance of ... the Muslim invader." It was not until the time of Muhammad of Ghor and the Delhi sultans that many temples of northern India were destroyed by the fanatical Muslim iconoclasts. Indeed, the modern day destruction of Buddhist monuments in Afghanistan is a continuation of the Muslim commitment to destroying pagan temples and icons. In India pagan temples, unlike Christian churches, were generally destroyed wholesale. In conquered Christian territories, the best churches would be converted into mosques, but lesser ones were permitted to continue in use by jizya paying Christians.

Lapidus compares and contrasts the experiences of India, Anatolia and the Balkans under these later Muslim conquests:

> In Anatolia, as in the rest of the Middle East, the conjunction of Muslim state power, the decline of organized Christian societies, and the social and cultural relevance of Islam facilitated mass conversions to the new religion.
>
> In the Balkans, however, the spread of Islam was limited by the vitality of the Christian churches. It came at a later stage of the Turkish conquests, at a time when Ottoman policy favored Christian nobles and churches as vehicles of Ottoman administration ... Most Balkan peoples, buttressed by the continuity of organized Christian community life, remained loyal to their faith.
>
> The history of Islam in India most closely resembles that of the Balkans. ... In most of India ... as in the Balkans, the appeal of Islam was relatively restricted. Only in the Northwest Frontier, the Punjab, Sind, and Bengal were populations converted en masse. In these regions the transition from hunter-gatherer and pastoral activities to settled agriculture was the occasion for a total reconstruction of society under Muslim leadership and for the development of new Islamic identifications. Conversion to Islam on a mass scale was most likely among disorganized populations.
>
> However, in some parts of India as in Anatolia, with fragmented and demoralized populations, conversions were

abundant. It is also interesting that the northwest India frontier peoples were, like certain mountain peoples of the Balkans, notably, Albanians and Bosnians attracted to Islam. Moreover, in parts of India as in Anatolia "the adaptability of Sufism to traditional religious cultures was important in the transition ... to Islam."

MERCHANT PROSELYTIZERS

Since it is the duty of all Muslims to spread Islam, traders carried the Islamic religion to those peripheral territories not under effective government control and to foreign nations beyond the borders of the Dar-al-Islam. The periphery of the Muslim world, consisting largely of tribal peoples at a lower level of civilization was resistant to direct or permanent conquest by Islamic armies. Despite raids capturing numerous slaves, the Arabs found it impossible to subdue another nomadic group entirely by military means. Hence mercantile missionary activity was needed to complete the process of Islamization.

The Berber tribes inhabiting the hinterland of the Maghreb were defeated by Arab armies. Nevertheless, continuing resistance and apostasy made an accommodation with these tribes necessary. The Berbers were induced by the prospect of conquest and booty to join forces with their nominal Arabian overlords. At a later date these very Muslim Berbers faced similar circumstances as, following trade routes across the desert, they spread Islam through much of West Africa. Along the East African coast Islam was spread by Arab traders who found it necessary to come to an accommodation with local power holders to spread Islam beyond a few fortified trading posts.

Similarly for most of the Central Asian steppes:

> The major impetus for conversion to Islam, despite the evidence of considerable military activity, does not appear to have been the jihad. Rather, Islam penetrated the steppes in a more pacific fashion through Muslim merchant caravans and settlers.

Of course, in these peripheral areas local converts in later years would take up jihad to conquer and convert their neighbors. The easternmost conquest of Islam in Central Asia occurred during the reign of a local Muslim ruler, Mansur (1502-43) who "took up the jihad, aimed chiefly at eastern Sinkiang." It was at that time "that formerly Buddhist places like Turfan definitively entered the Dar al-Islam."

Indonesia and adjacent areas of Southeast Asia had been exposed to the ideas of higher civilization carried by Hindu traders and Buddhist missionaries. Nevertheless, the inhabitants were primarily tribal or else lived in geographically isolated areas divided into numerous petty states. Seas and impenetrable jungles prevented any direct Muslim conquest. However, seafaring Muslim merchants abetted by converted local rulers slowly Islamized most of the islands in the archipelago. The process of Islamization lasting some seven centuries is not as well documented as the one in Anatolia. Nonetheless a hypothetical conversion curve for Indonesia is shown above modeled on the general shape of the other logistic curves.

In China, with its long history of civilization, Islam made little progress despite extensive trading relationships with Muslim merchants. Some natives in certain regions of China intermarried with Muslims and adopted Islam. The first penetration of Islam into China occurred in the early days of the Abbasid dynasty:

> Eastward, Moslem traders ventured as far as China, which ... was reached from al-Basrah as early as the days of the second Abbasid caliph. ... In the mid eighth century a number of Moslems settled in China ... under the name Ta-shih (a Persianized form of the Arab tribe Tayyi) and later under the title Hui-Hui ...

A second wave of Islamic penetration occurred when Turkish subjects of Chingis Khan, who was indifferent to religious matters, imported Islam into China. Sociologist Reuben Levy notes that, Islam had relatively little appeal to the average Chinese even when the road was thus left open, and although Muslims are now to be found in every Chinese province, they only achieved considerable numbers in the west and north, i.e. in Kansu, Sinkiang, Shensi, Shansi, Chuhli and Yunnan. He also notes that the Muslims in China "are said to be indistinguishable from their fellow countrymen ... and have long been cut off from Muslims elsewhere". That may account, at least in part, for the relative peacefulness of Chinese Muslims up to the present day.

It is not surprising that Islamic conversion achieved its greatest success in the conquered territories, for in those circumstances Muslims related to non-Muslims as superiors. Islamic conversion was also reasonably successful in unconquered areas where Muslim traders encountered the inhabitants on the basis of equality. With respect to one group, the Mongols, Muslims were in the unaccustomed position of inferiors. The Mongol converts were a result of the unique case where non-Muslim conquerors were absorbed into the culture of, and adopted the religion of, their Muslim subjects. As the Romans conquered the Greeks only to be conquered by Greek civilization, so it was that the rude Mongol tribes were assimilated into the more sophisticated civilization of their subjects. In the western part of their domains that civilization was Islamic. One group of western Mongols, the Ilkhanids in Iran was Islamized under Ghazan Khan who ruled from 1295 to 1304. Another group, the Batuids, who came to be known as the Golden Horde, converted under Uzbek Khan between 1312 and 1341. The conquests of the Golden Horde, as we have seen, represented the farther most northern extension of the Dar-al-Islam before being halted in 1380 by the Russians under Prince Dmitri at Kulikovo.

INTERMARRIAGE

Interbreeding was a crucial factor in the Islamization of the vast Muslim conquests. It is difficult to disentangle the effects of hybridization from those of conversion in the growth of Muslim populations. Since the laws and customs of the conquerors forbade marriage or concubinage of a Muslim woman to a non-Muslim male, in most cases the father would be a member of the Muslim military elite. However, there were, undoubtedly, very many instances where a new Muslim convert would enter into marriage with a Muslim female.

The Turkish conquests provide the most abundant

documentation of intermarriage and its relation to conversion. Kinross refers to the ease with which such intermarriage occurred in Anatolia. He notes that a number of Christians became Moslems from choice ... in a realistic spirit, preferred the relative order and security of Osmanli rule, together with its greater freedom of opportunity for Moslems and exemption from onerous taxes. ... Socially they did not differ profoundly from their frontier neighbours the Osmanlis in their background and habits of life. ... Intermarriage became common between Turks and Greeks.

The sons of these mixed marriages known as mixovarvaroi as well as converts formed a large part of the Turkish armies. "The mixovarvaroi came to play a significant role as a further source of military manpower ... and so did the converts. The Turks resorted to taking Christian children and converting them" to meet their demand for military manpower.

And, of course, the intermarriage of the conquerors with the Dhimmi population was an important factor in Islamization, Arabization and Turkification. "Though this phenomenon of intermarriage [in the 12th century] and the appearance of a new generation of mixovarvaroi is only briefly mentioned by the sources, one must assume that it was no rare or isolated occurrence." Vryonis, like Kinross, also notes the ease and frequency with which such unions occurred in the early days of Turkish rule:

There is every reason to suppose that intermarriage took place rather extensively from the very beginning of the Turkish occupation ... and for several centuries afterward. ... Nicephoras Gregoras passed through Bithynia ... in the middle of the fourteenth century ... he observed that the population consisted of Greeks, mixovarvaroi ... and Turks. Thus intermarriage of Muslims and Christians at every level of society played a very important role in the integration and absorption of the Greek Christian element into Muslim society.

The importance of intermarriage, conversions and slavery in forming the present day Anatolian population is emphasized by Vryonis:

...a significant portion of the Muslim population in

Anatolia represents the 'invisible' physical residue of this Byzantine past. The mass conversions, intermarriage, gulam-devshirme, and slave systems resulted in the fusion of the majority of the Byzantine population with the Turks and, consequently, made of the Turks a people with origins as mixed as those of the Greeks, Serbs, Armenians, and Bulgars.

The addition of other racial elements absorbed by the Turkish nomads occurred at a very early stage in their migrations. Geneticist C. D. Darlington notes that the "first Turkish conquerors, the Seljuks, were gradually changed, diversified, and multiplied by hybridization with Greeks and Armenians, Persians and Arabs." Vryonis observes how such hybridization, occurring at a very early period with groups such as the Kurds continued in later Turkish history as the tribesmen fused with Christians and with recently converted Muslims. Therefore, such interbreeding was of crucial importance in the expansion of Turkish Islam.

Kinross notes a number of prominent instances of intermarriage at the highest levels of both Ottoman and Byzantine society. The Byzantine statesman Cantacuzene gave his daughter in marriage to Sultan Orkhan as did the tsar of Bulgaria. John Palaeologue gave his daughter in marriage to Orkhan's son Halil. Also the Serbian ruler Stephen gave his sister in marriage to Sultan Bayezid I. The latter also married the daughter of Greek aristocrat Helen Cantacuzene. Vryonis notes an instance of the marriage of a high Byzantine aristocrat who converted to Islam. "John Comnenus, the nephew of the emperor John II Comnenus, took to wife a daughter of the sultan and turned Muslim."

While Turkish history is especially rich in documented instances of intermarriage, this was a widespread occurrence in all Islamic territories as noted by other historians. In Iran "before long a large proportion of the Arabs yielded to their environment and, as a result of mixed marriages, were using a language with Iranian words; conversely, Islamic influence was particularly strong in the zones where Arab penetration was most concentrated." In parts of West Africa Muslim traders "married local women and raised families, which were tied to the Muslim community through the father and to the local pagan community through the mother. The offspring of such marriages often inherited chieftainships and brought about the conversion of local peoples." Often these chiefs "tried to maintain elements of both pagan and Muslim ritual in order to satisfy the cultural interests of their double constituencies." Since in instances such as the latter where the Muslim outsiders did not enter as conquerors, the Islamic indoctrination of their mixed-breed offspring was less complete. The result was a syncretistic religion and a hybrid culture.

WHIMS OF THE RULERS

The Dhimmi population was always subject to the whims of particular rulers. Some Muslim rulers were relatively benevolent, others were scrupulous in carrying out Muslim law in protecting Dhimmis, but often these would be followed by less well disposed successors or rivals. One such occurrence took place in the Byzantine city of Melitene which was captured in the early days of the Seljuk incursions. "Kilidj Arslan took it in 1106, and though he was kind to the inhabitants, on his death the citizens were subjected to financial oppression by his successors." Vryonis emphasizes the fact "that the very chroniclers who praise individual Turkish and Arab rulers for their clemency to the Christians ... make them the exceptions to the more general rule."

Some Muslim rulers either through an excess of religious zeal or simple ignorance of their obligations under the contract of dhimmitude decreed the forced conversion of dhimmi populations:

> Periods of forced conversion interrupted the protection-persecution rhythm which alternated throughout history within complex parameters and was governed by imponderable factors, combining individual personalities and political contingencies. As protection was guaranteed by the highest political authority - caliph or sultan - orders for conversion emanating from this source eliminated the possibility of any recourse. ...such orders were decreed under

the Umayyads, Abbasids, Fatimids and Mamluks – from Spain and the Maghreb to Yemen and Persia. Even if they could be revoked by payment of heavy ransoms, they decimated whole communities...

THE ISLAMIC WELFARE STATE

Another reason for the rapid spread of Islam, as well as the Arabic, and subsequently the Turkish, language, was the attractiveness their concept of society held for many Syrian, Greek, Egyptian and Persian rural peasants and urban proletarians previously oppressed by rapacious bureaucrats and greedy aristocrats. Islam had a well developed charitable structure; a sort of primitive welfare state. In addition, the class structure of medieval Islam was somewhat less rigid, at least for males, than that of their Byzantine and Persian rivals. As we have seen this allowed young men of energy and ability to rise more easily in the social structure. Similarly, in India, Islam was attractive to numerous Hindus as an escape from the oppressive caste system. Of course, the very disruption of non-Muslim religious and social institutions along with mass impoverishment created by the Muslim attacks was an additional factor that impelled many non-Muslims to embrace Islam and its charitable institutions.

Vryonis notes how the Islamic welfare state discriminated in favor of Muslims at a time of great hardship for the Christian community:

> The Muslim state ... supported and favored Islam in every way, and Christianity was tolerated only as the religion of its second-class citizens. The sultans and officials built mosques, medresses, imarets, zawiyas, hospitals, caravansarays, and fountains for the Islamic associations and endowed them with lands, serfs, and revenues. Consequently, the ulema and dervishes had the economic wherewithal to perform their spiritual functions with elegance and their socioeconomic tasks with great efficiency.

These wakfs (endowments) account for a considerable "part of the history of Christian decline and Muslim expansion." Also important is the fact that the burden of financial support for these religious and charitable institutions were often imposed on nearby Christian communities. These Muslim charitable endowments, "by harnessing much of the land, manpower, and revenues of Anatolia to Islamic institutions, enabled the latter to achieve preeminence at the expense of Christianity."

In addition, some Sufi sects were quite amenable to using their considerable charitable endowments to bribe impoverished Christians to convert. "The Bektashis ... appear as a group that dispenses charity and food to all the needy ...this dervish community along with others was able to furnish to Christians, as well as Muslims, the charity and sustenance that the Christian church was no longer able to provide."

Thus, often the resources of Christian subjects were directed toward the support of their fellows who were converting to Islam. Nor was it only Christian apostates who were the beneficiaries of these resources extracted from their former co-religionists. Jews who were in the process of converting, as well as pagans among the Mongol and Tatar tribes accompanying the invading Turkmen were also the beneficiaries of such largesse. Vryonis gives an example of one establishment outside of the city of Konya that was dedicated to these new converts. "One-fifth of the income from an eighteen-room khan ... was to provide for the teaching of the Koran and prayers, the performance of circumcision, provision of shoes, clothes and food to Christians, Jews and pagans who apostatized to Islam."

The Ottomans extended the Islamic welfare state inherited from their Seljuk predecessors. Mehmed the Conqueror endowed a number of charitable institutions, wakfs, in his newly conquered city. "When Mehmed built his own great mosque, there were eight medresses around it ... a children's school, a library, two hostels for travelers, a refectory, kitchens where the poor were given food, and a hospital ... Here was the free education and health service of a medieval Islamic welfare state." Under Suleiman the mosques' "precincts ... included also treasuries, banks, hospices for travelers, refectories, libraries, bathhouses, fountains, and other such charitable amenities of the Ottoman 'welfare state' as soup kitchens, hospitals, and madhouses."

The Islamic welfare structure in combination with the destruction of existing institutions was an important reason for the spread of Islam in all Muslim conquered lands. In Abyssinia, for example, "among the causes given for the spread of Islam among the common people in later times, one is that the Christian priesthood was corrupt and ignorant, and another that the Church had abandoned large tracts of territory and was therefore unable to fulfil its charitable obligations."

Finally, one additional factor facilitating conversions to Islam is the lure of theological simplicity. Reuben notes how in Africa Islam by providing the tribesman "with a way of life which, though not by any means easy, is yet simple and clearly defined, ... frees him from the numerous vague terrors inseparable from a primitive state of culture." Such simplicity was undoubtedly a factor advancing Islam among the less educated and sophisticated in all lands penetrated by Muslims.

13

Culture of the Harem

Polygamy Concubinage and the Spread of Islam

Islam for most of its existence was carried forward by the sword. Two nomadic tribal peoples, the Arabs and the Turks were responsible for most of this expansion. The question to be answered is how these primitive and thinly populated nomadic tribes expanded so explosively into large and densely populated civilized regions.

One important answer to the question lies in an ingenious social invention arising among the early Muslims. This was a breeding system that motivated successful warriors with a great incentive to spread their faith and their culture. Bloom puts this motivation in stark terms as "the restless effort of human males to find more wombs to carry their seed." Islam has the remarkable advantage of being highly patriarchal and polygamous with great sexual benefits for those warriors able to conquer in its name; Islam was and remains a great male racket.

Furthermore, these advantages are not the temporary kind that have always been associated with warfare, but continue to exist within the peacetime new order. Wherever the warriors of Islam went they were able to commandeer large numbers of native women as wives and concubines. And unlike their counterparts in the West, they were able to do so with full religious and legal sanction. Their warrior sons, the mixed offspring of these matings, in turn zealously spread their new religion and culture as they conquer still more territory and the process is repeated through several generations. Of course, such a permanent system also meant deterioration in the status of women; the latter lost even the limited rights they had managed to acquire under the preceding Greek and Roman civilization.

Indeed, Islam was, until the West developed its technological edge, the civilization most successful at both expansion and tenacity. In a remarkably short time the Arabs burst out of their peninsula to encompass the entire Middle East, Persia, North Africa and Spain. Later on, Muslim Turks and, ultimately, Mongol convert extended Islam into Asia Minor, the Balkans and South Asia. Other empires, such as those of the Macedonians and early Mongols expanded rapidly, but within a few centuries they were pushed back or assimilated by the cultures they had conquered. Rome also had a vast empire but its growth was a long drawn-out process requiring centuries. Furthermore, in contrast to the religion of Islam the other two great proselytizing religions, Christianity and Buddhism, grew very slowly and, at least in their initial stages, peacefully.

Historians have enumerated a number of reasons for Islam's success but have ignored or, perhaps have not understood, the unprecedented way in which Islam evolved as an engine for harnessing the aggressive energy of young males. Nor have they acknowledged how the usual and temporary sexual advantages accruing to successful warriors in a time of war were extended into a permanent institution sanctified by religious law. This part of the Islamic meme, expressed by the institution of polygamy and concubinage, may be termed the culture of the harem. This institution was not limited to that of the large harem complexes of the Abbasid caliphs, Ottoman sultans and other high officials of Muslim society. These large harems were most prominent at certain periods and were limited to powerful and wealthy elites. However, the more general institution of polygamy was fairly common in Islamic history and is still widespread in certain parts of the Muslim world. And sexual slavery was a frequent occurrence, even among lower levels of society throughout much of Islamic history, particularly during the periods of the great Islamic conquests.

For, during those times of conquest, a Muslim warrior was motivated by more than religious fanaticism to achieve success. He had the prospect of confiscating as his permanent property many of the most attractive females among the conquered population as concubines or wives. These women, now stripped of their cultural moorings provided numerous half breed sons who were acculturated into Islam as well as into the Arabic, and later the Turkish, language. These sons, in their turn, extended Islam and its harem culture to new territories. In this way, a relatively small number of Arab and, at a later period, Berber and Turkish warriors imprinted Islamic religion and culture on vast areas with large populations.

Warriors were not the only Muslim males sexually rewarded for advancing Islam. As seen above, Islam was also spread by trade and mercantile activity. The wealth accumulated by a successful merchant could be considerable. Thus, those responsible for promoting Islam beyond the borders of the Dar-al-Islam could also obtain the means of purchasing concubines and of affording multiple wives. Muslim officials and administrators who successfully defended and consolidated Islamic gains would also obtain the ability to acquire such advantages.

A requirement of this harem culture is the grinding down and degradation of even free Muslim women. For they are required to accept all of the concomitants of that institution: polygamy, ease of divorce and concubinage. During Islam's frequent wars they are obliged to resignedly accept their husbands returning from the campaign with captive concubines for his own use as often as for sale. In other traditions, particularly in the West, wives were a little more assertive as shown by some famous examples from Greek mythology. Hera was not inclined to look on placidly while Zeus consorted with his numerous mortal mistresses. The fate of Agamemnon at the hands of his wife, Clytemnestra, showed what danger a warrior might expect after sacrificing a daughter and dragging home a concubine. Similarly, the formidable Medea did not meekly acquiesce in Jason's infidelity. Under Islam such an ideology and expression of female assertiveness had to be suppressed.

An additional consequence was that the misogynistic harem culture became deeply embedded within Islamic civilization as it spread from the warriors to the general male population. A successful merchant or religious pundit was also able to partake in these sexual advantages. The result is the peculiar degradation of women as well as many of the other sexual oddities, i.e. the sexual abuse of young boys by older men, which have become almost institutionalized. To be sure, misogyny and oppression of women is not confined to Islamic culture. But it appears to be much more persistent in Islam. When the British abolished the Hindu custom of suttee, there was much agitation among Hindu traditionalists. Yet, Hindu culture adapted to the change without any great upheaval. But Islam seems peculiarly resistant to altering its established sexual attitudes. The reason may lie in the fact that the very existence of Islamic culture over wide regions is due to these attitudes. Winston Churchill wrote of the consequences of Muslim attitudes toward women: "A degraded sensualism deprives this life of its grace and refinement; the next of its dignity and sanctity. The fact that in Mohammedan law every woman must belong to some man as his absolute property - either as a child, a wife, or a concubine - must delay the final extinction of slavery until the faith of Islam has ceased to be a great power among men."

SCRIPTURAL LEGITIMIZATION OF SEXUAL SLAVERY

In addition to allowing polygamy and permitting easy divorce to his male adherents, the Prophet also provides ample verses promoting the rape of captives and the institution of sexual slavery:

O Prophet! We have made lawful unto thee thy wives unto whom thou hast paid their dowries, and those whom thy right hand possesseth of those whom Allah hath given thee as spoils of war... Surah 33:50

It is not allowed thee to take (other) women henceforth ... save those whom thy right hand possesseth. Surah 33:52

Save with their wives and those whom their right hands possess... Surah 70:30

And if ye fear that ye will not deal fairly by the orphans, marry of the women, who seem good to you, two or three or four; and if ye fear that ye cannot do justice (to so many) then one (only) or (the captives) that your right hands possess. Surah 4:3

And all married women (are forbidden unto you) save those (captives) that your right hands possess. Surah 4:24

And marry such of you as are solitary and the pious of your slaves and maid-servants. Surah 24:32

Successful indeed are the believers; who are humble in their prayers; ... And who guard their modesty; Save from their wives or the (slaves) that their right hands possess, for then they are not blameworthy. Surah 22:1-6

And all married women are forbidden unto you except those captives whom your right hand possesses. It is a decree of Allah for you. Lawful unto you are all beyond those mentioned, so that you seek them with your wealth in honest wedlock, not debauchery. Salih Muslim, Book 8:3371

After the battle with the Bani Al-Mustaliq, Muhammad is presented with a question by his men of whether they could have sex by means of coitus interruptus with the captive women so as to avoid impairing their ransom value. "When Muhammad said 'It is better that you should not do it.' He was referring to coitus interruptus, not to raping their captives. He took that for granted." Indeed, no other major world religion puts it quite as bluntly as the Prophet does in Surah 2:223. "Your women are a tilth for you (to cultivate) so go to your tilth as ye will". Commentator Jamie Glazov remarks on the singular reversals of morality present in Islamic doctrine regarding sex with captives:

Since it emphasizes the importance of Muslims conquering all non-Muslims, Islam bestows some intriguing sexual incentives. While it is a sin for a male to have sex with an unmarried woman, Allah makes an exemption for the Muslim male who rapes the women of the infidels that he kills. Muhammad did just that.

This explains why any time Islamic warriors defeat another nation, they call the inhabitants kafir (the one who, according to the Qur'an, is ungrateful to the blessings showered by Allah) and rape their women. Pakistani Muslim soldiers raped a quarter of a million Bangali women in 1971 after they massacred 3 million unarmed civilians. This atrocity is not considered a sin in Islam, because the religious leader of the soldiers decreed that Bangladeshis were infidels.

Moreover, it may sound harsh, but the distinction between "fertilizing" and "punishing" a woman is evident. On the one hand you have sexuality as a tool serving the expansion of Islam, and on the other hand there is sexuality as a weapon against disobedient and non-Muslim women, both categorized as "unbelievers". Against them jihad is the duty, and what to do with women "conquered" in jihad, this may be read in the Qur'an: they become slaves to be used by the victors.

The rape of enemy women in war has been widespread in all cultures and at all times. However, the institutionalization of sexual slavery in Islam when combined with the downtrodden condition of Muslim women made the continuation of legalized rape in time of peace a commonplace of Islamic society and puts an indelible mark on the Muslim character. According to historian Stanley Lane-Pool the

> ...female slave in the East ... is at the entire mercy of her master, who can do what he pleases with her and her companions; for the Muslim is not restricted in the number of his concubines. ... The female white slave is kept solely for the master's sensual gratification ... The Muslim soldier was allowed to do as he pleased with any 'infidel' woman he might meet with on his victorious march. ... And this cruel indulgence has left its mark on the Muslim character, nay, on the whole character of Eastern life.

Bernard Lewis also notes the "generous provision" Islam makes for male sexual needs while enforcing a puritanical code regarding sex in general. He observes that while polygamy was confined to the upper classes, concubinage was common throughout all strata of Muslim society. In addition, he acknowledges that non-Muslim female slaves occupied the "bottom of the social pile".

HEAVENLY DELIGHTS

For the Muslim warrior Islamic heaven offered rather more robust delights than did its competitors. There was no floating on clouds and playing harps for male jihadists. Neither the Jewish nor the Christian concept of the afterlife could compete with the Prophet's paradise. Moreover, the best way to merit eternal bliss was by slaughtering enemy infidels; a method not generally endorsed by the other monotheistic faiths. The other religions that Islam encountered in its expansion, Zoroastrianism, Hinduism and Buddhism also suffered a competitive disadvantage in the rewards offered to warriors.

With respect to Hinduism, Keay observes how the Ghaznian, Mahmud's, forces "were powerfully motivated by religious zeal, plus the prospect of booty and women in this world or something equally agreeable in the next. ...for Hindus no particular merit attached to the massacre of mlecchas." The Prophet offers his warriors these agreeable delights in a number of verses. The following surahs promise sexual delights as a reward for pious Muslim men and martyred warriors:

"Lo! For the duteous is achievement - Gardens enclosed and vineyards, and maidens for companions" Surah 78:31-33

"Reclining upon couches lined with silk brocade, the fruit of both gardens near to hand. Which is it, of the favours of your Lord that ye deny? Therein are those of modest gaze, whom neither man nor jinni will have touched before them. ... (In beauty) like the jacynth and coral stone." Surah 55:54-7

"Fair ones, close-guarded in pavilions ... whom neither man nor jinni will have touched before them" Surah 55:72-74

"And (there are) fair ones with wide lovely eyes, Like unto hidden pearls, Reward for what they used to do." Surah 56:22-4

"Lo! We have created them a (new) creation and made them virgins, Lovers, friends, for those on the right hand." Surah 56:35-8

"Reclining on ranged couches. And we wed them unto fair ones with wide lovely eyes." Surah 52:20

"And with them are those of modest gaze, companions. This it is that ye are promised for the Day of Reckoning." Surah 38:53-4

"Lo! Those who kept their duty will be in a place secure amid gardens and water-springs ... And we shall wed them unto fair ones with wide lovely eyes." Surah 44:51-4

So it was that even the unsuccessful warrior, who died in the service of Islam, would be compensated in heaven with the sexual advantages he failed to win on earth. The Koran's promised "fair ones with lovely eyes" was eventually multiplied into a harem of some seventy perennially virginal heavenly concubines. Paradise became a veritable orgasm factory with one accommodating virgin after another on the heavenly assembly line. Glazov describes these virginal prizes:

The Islamic temptation to wage violent war against non-Muslims also involves the sexual incentive of the houries (the 72 eternal virgins in paradise that are given to the Muslim warrior who dies in battle). The houri makes earthly women even more redundant. Yet even the individual houri herself is not sacred or special in any way. As Fatna Sabbah notes, she "has no spiritual dimension; she is a thing because she has neither will nor any possibility of development.... [she] has no intellect; she does not think. She is a thing that awaits consumption."

The houri is a manifestation of the ultimate misogyny...

Warraq describes how later Muslim commentators enhanced the lurid aspects of Muhammad's Paradise.

In these utterly childish and sensual fantasies, the woman once again has been created to serve man – there are no fantasies of dark eyed gigolos serving reclining sensual women. The Koranic paradise was further elaborated with much glee by Muslim commentators. As Suyuti, for example wrote: 'Each time we sleep with a houri we find her virgin. Besides, the penis of the elected never softens, the erection is eternal. The sensation that you feel each time you make love is utterly delicious and out of this world and were you to experience it in this world you would faint. Each elected will marry seventy houris, besides the women he married on earth, and all will have appetizing vaginas. 'Thus eternal erections and appetizing vaginas, not harps and wings, are the distinguishing characteristics of the Prophet's paradise.

HAREM CULTURE AND THE GROWTH OF THE MUSLIM POPULATION

Polygamy and widespread legal concubinage was the prime factor underlying the success of Islam's nomadic vanguards. The conquerors were driven by religious zeal to ensure that Islam be imposed on the numerous half breed children resulting from these matings. These offspring formed the nucleus of Muslim elite which assisted in the conversion of native populations and enabled Islamic culture to crystallize over vast territories. The Macedonian Greeks shared with Muslims a desire to spread their way of life. However, Greek culture, lacking the institution of polygamous marriage and the extensive peacetime concubinage that characterized Islam, was unable to establish deep roots in the very lands that ultimately became Muslim. The Mongols, like the Muslims, also had widespread polygamy and sexual slavery. However, lacking a strong cultural imperative, the Mongols were ultimately absorbed by those they conquered.

Geneticist C. D. Darlington comes to very similar conclusions in his study of the breeding system established by the Arab conquests. He notes that the Arab governing elite ...were derived at the beginning ... from the commanders of the conquering armies ... They had killed in battle or driven into exile the rulers and commanders of the defeated states. The widows and daughters of these enemies they generously took into their harems. ... In this way they created in one generation a new governing class, undoubtedly Muslim, assertedly Arab and unmistakably both able and diverse in their abilities. They also became exceedingly numerous. The original armies issuing forth from Arabia in the seventh century may have numbered no more than a hundred thousand men. The survivors of war, including civil war, must have been fewer. But their descendants in two or three generations numbered millions; they populated the Muslim world.

At once we can see that polygamous conquerors must always be selected for a high rate of propagation. ... But certainly the genetic effect of the Arabs was enough to influence the whole Islamic world. It was enough to beget in a few generations, at each successive expansion, a vast hybrid population.

Thus the vast hybridization plan of Alexander, frustrated by his caste-forming successors was now ... carried to a fruitful issue. A consequence of this hybridization was the spread of the Arabic language in which converts had to affirm their Muslim faith. ... This continuity of language and religion, reinforcing the continuity of race, created the triple-bound network in space and time for the lack of which military empires have promptly fallen to pieces.

Furthermore, the continuing vitality and solidarity of Muslim society required a large influx of captive concubines. When the conquests ceased and the razzias were contained, the frustrated energy of young males needed to find other outlets in crime and outlawed sexual practices.

...the polygamy of the conquering Muslim warriors could be genetically effective only when their conquests gave them large numbers of female slaves. At other times only a small section of society could indulge in a harem. And as a rule the propagation that resulted was compensated for by a high death rate either from war or murder. ... And homosexual and other perversions ... became the fashionable cult of all the governing warrior castes.

Historian Hitti joins with Darlington in affirming the importance of this breeding system. "Between the master and the female slave concubinage, but not legal marriage, was permissible. The children...belonged to the master and were therefore free". Furthermore, in "the melting pot process which resulted in the amalgamation of Arabians and foreigners, the slave trade undoubtedly played an extremely important role." Hitti, like Darlington, shows how the diffusion of the Arab bloodline among the more numerous conquered peoples was accompanied by the grafting of Arab culture onto the conquered lands. "In bringing about this fusion of the Arabians with their subject peoples polygamy, concubinage and the slave trade proved effective methods. As the pure Arabian element receded into the background non-Arabs, half-breeds and sons of freed women began to take their place."

In distant Spain, as in other conquered lands, the same process of the spread of Muslim culture through hybridization took place:

From the beginning ... the real Arabians in the army of conquest and among the colonists were comparatively few, limited to those in command and in high office. The number of women accompanying the army and first immigrants was necessarily small. Disease and fighting decimated the early conquerors and settlers. After the fourth generation the Arabian blood must have become greatly diluted by intermarriage with native women. Concubines, slaves and prisoners of war helped the process of amalgamation, as in other lands. The researches of Ribera have shown that even the Moslems of Spain, the so-called Moors were overwhelmingly of Spanish blood.

The Turkish conquests were followed by the same process of sexual slavery and hybridization. The confiscating of vast numbers of native women by conquering nomads led to the genetic absorption of the Turks by the conquered races and the simultaneous impressing of Turkish religion and language on that population. Ottoman historian Kinross observes:

Women ... whether war widows or the young daughters of Greeks, Serbs, and Bulgarians, were generally enslaved as wives and concubines for the conquerors, who had brought virtually no women of their own. The eventual result of this was the development of an Ottoman race vigorous and rich in the mixture of its blood. Eastern blood - Tatar, Mongol, Circassian, Georgian, Persian and Arabian - which already flowed through Turkish veins was now mixed with the blood of the Balkan races and those of Europe beyond ...

This insight of Kinross is echoed by Darlington:

But owing as much to the prestige of the Greeks as to the polygamous habits favored by Islam, the new governing class of the Turks seems to have been more deeply transformed than that of the Christians in Spain. As the Turks advanced they converted the Christians and they also interbred with them. The conquered agricultural peoples constituted a new hybrid Turkish-speaking nation governed by hard-riding pashas also somewhat hybrid...

SIZE AND EXTENT OF THE SYSTEM OF SEXUAL SLAVERY

Numerous historical references to the sheer number of native women enslaved by the Muslim invaders, as well as the vast extent and diversity of lands in which these occurred, support the assertions given above. The enormous numbers of female slaves possessed, like the immense wealth expropriated, by members of the Muslim elite is astounding.

The importance of the Islamic female slave trade is evident from the beginning of the Arab conquests. Arab historian Abun-Nasr describes circumstances in Cyrenaica a decade after the followers of the Prophet burst out of Arabia:

Human tribute was a means through which the conquerors obtained slaves, especially slave girls, to cater for the pleasures of the Arab ruling class. ...upon conquering Cyrenaica in 642 or 643 'Amr b. al-'As fixed the jizya to be paid by the Berber tribes ... From the Lawata tribe he demanded that they should 'sell' to the Arabs a number of their 'sons and daughters' to the value of their share of the total jizya. ... Ibn 'Abdul Hakam ... reports that during his term as amir of Ifriqiya his son and nephew, each commanding a column of troops, raided Berber settlements and took captives who were treated as war booty and taken into slavery.'

There was, of course, a learning curve for some of these early Arab conquerors, lacking experience in the intricacies of the sex slave market. "When an Arabian warrior at al-Hirah [Iraq] was blamed for selling a nobleman's daughter who fell as his share of the booty for only 1000 dirhams, his reply was that he 'never thought there was a number above ten hundred.'"

After the Muslim armies conquered Persia and the Near East, their addiction to sexual slavery led them to raid lands far from their centers in Arabia and the Fertile Crescent. In 652 the first Muslim attack on Sicily took place. "The delights of Syracuse, ravaged in this first attempt consisted of women, church treasures and other valuable booty which invited repeated returns by Moslems in the course of the second half of the seventh century." Similarly, after the pacification of Andalusia, the Moors satisfied their perpetual need for slave women by repeated raids across the Pyrenees. The Muslim historian Ibn-al-Athir describes a Moorish incursion into southern France in 793. "Abd al-Malik b. Abd al-Wahid b. Mugith ... traversed this land in every direction, raping women ...burning and pillaging everything... He returned...dragging behind him God knows how much booty." God also knows how many of the raped women were dragged back to harems as part of the booty.

Huge numbers of female slaves were widely available for satisfying the lust of Arab males of all classes in Umayyad times. Musa ibn Nusayr is said to have forwarded 30,000 virgins to the Umayyad caliph al-Walid. These were, presumably, not destined for work in the mines. Of course, the Caliph undoubtedly sold many of these, as even the prodigious appetite of a caliph would not be up to copulating on such a mass scale. Included among virgins sent "as an adornment to Caliph Walid's seraglio" were the two young daughters of King Dahar, a present sent by ibn Qasim the conqueror of Sind? Another Umayyad aristocrat, Al-Zubayr ibn-al-'Awwam, "bequeathed among other chattels one thousand male and female slaves." Even middle and lower class Arab males partook in the bounty. "The famous Makkan poet of love 'Umar ibn-abi-Rabi'ah (ca 719) had many more than seventy slaves. For an Umayyad prince to maintain a retinue of about a thousand slaves was nothing extraordinary. Even the private in the Syrian army at the battle of Siffrin had from one to ten servants waiting on him".

Women slaves were invariably required as part of the tribute exacted by conquest or by treaty. In the invasion of Sind "what was required of the conquered people was not conversion to Islam, but tribute and taxes, treasure, slaves and women." The tributary states of the Sudan were required by treaty to provide the Arabs with a quota of women since "attractive Nubian and pretty Bejawi girls ... were valued as concubines."

Under the Abbasid dynasty, there was no diminishment of the voracious appetites of Muslim males for sex slaves. In Abbasid times there "are few indications of the numbers of women who might be found in a harem ... Harun al-Rashid is said to have had more than two thousand singing and servant girls in his huram, and records suggest that there were around twenty four concubines who bore him children. ...it was claimed that the mid-ninth-century caliph al-Mutawwakil had four thousand concubines and had sexual intercourse with every single one of them." The latter reportedly, at one time received a present of "two hundred slaves from one of his generals. It was customary for governors and generals to send presents, including girls received or exacted from among their subjects, to the caliph or vizir; failure to do so was interpreted as a sign of rebellion."

Furthermore, the "girls who formed the Abbasid harem came from many different lands and cultures ... almost always procured from outside the empire." Some were of aristocratic or even royal origin captured as prizes in war. Many of these came from Iran, central Asia or Afghanistan. "None of these women was married to the caliphs or other notables to whom they belonged, but their aristocratic origins were certainly part of their appeal". Women destined for the harems of the caliphs also came from far beyond the neighboring provinces. "Some of the most beautiful slave-girls were sent to the harems of the Baghdad Caliphs from Europe, particularly from Spain."

In the Abbasid court all pretensions of religion were discarded such as the prohibition against drinking and the disapproval of music and poetry. Thus, the underlying reality of the male pursuit of sexual advantage is shown in its unvarnished form. The early Abbasid period saw the rise of the singing girl as a desirable commodity. "They were sexually available, at least to their owners and patrons." The most desirable were often procured by courtiers who "would make it their business to send out talent scouts. Large sums of money were involved. ...girls could be traded up, gaining value at each transaction." The top tier, of course, would usually reach the caliph's harem.

In addition to pimping for their caliphs, Arab generals would wisely make certain that the common soldiers under their command should have no cause for complaint. Michael the Syrian wrote that after the capture of Amorium in 838 "there were so many women's convents and monasteries that over a thousand virgins were led into captivity, not counting those that had been slaughtered. They were given to the Moorish slaves, so as to assuage their lust."

The trade in sex slaves continued to flourish after the Abbasid Empire fragmented into a number of regional dynasties. In 1291, when the Mamluks captured the city of Acre from the Crusaders the harems of the Muslim world were replenished:

> Soon the Moslem soldiers penetrated right through the city, slaying everyone, old men, women and children alike. A few lucky citizens who stayed in their houses were taken alive and sold as slaves, but not many were spared. No one could tell the number of those that perished...Some prisoners were freed and returned to Europe after nine or ten years of captivity...Many women and children disappeared for ever into the harems of Mameluk emirs. Owing to the plentiful supply the price of a girl dropped to a drachma a piece in the slave market at Damascus.

During the Turkish conquests, also, there was often a plentiful supply of female slaves. At times, concubines were so ubiquitous and hence cheap that they could even be given as a casual gift to a passing traveler. "Ibn Battuta reported that the ruler of ... Aydin had twenty Greek slaves standing at attention at the entrance to his palace; indeed he gave the traveler a Greek slave woman as gift." Greek female slaves were extensively employed in both domestic and commercial slavery. Battuta also remarks on the use of Greek slave girls in the brothels of Laodicea.

The early Ottoman sultans, with their recent history as nomads from the steppes, found the Muslim institution of sexual slavery quite congenial. The Ottoman experience is but one more example of how an Islamic institution invented by nomads, inevitably conformed with and, appealed to similar nomadic cultures. Historian Leslie Peirce notes that the "stories of Osman's village wife, Orhan's bride from Bilejk, and Murad's consort Gulcicek suggest that the practice of acquiring women through raid and conquest, familiar to the early Ottomans from their nomadic heritage, overlapped in important ways with the Muslim institution of slave concubinage."

The later Ottomans certainly proved themselves worthy of living up to both their religious tradition and nomadic ancestry. At the fall of Constantinople in the great Hagia Sophia cathedral, "most of the worshippers were tied together ... herded through the streets to the bivouacs of the soldiers who quarreled fiercely for possession of the comelier girls and youths". Shortly thereafter, the Byzantine historian Doukas tells how Mehmed left Constantinople taking back "in wagons and on horseback all the [Byzantine] noblewomen and their daughters."

Two centuries later the Ottoman Grand Vizier Kara Mustafa (ca 1680) had a harem that "was reputed to house fifteen hundred concubines and as many female slaves, with seven hundred Black Eunuchs to attend them." This indicates that large harems were common among the Ottoman elite and were, by no means, limited to the famous seraglio of the Sultan.

A serious problem arose for the Ottoman upper classes as a consequence of the halt to the expansion of the Empire into the lands of the infidels. Such lands had, in the past, been the source of nubile sex toys for the pleasure of the Sultan and other notables. With the end of the Turkish advance that supply dried up necessitating the seeking out of alternative sources. One of these sources was the region of the Caucasus, for "Caucasian women had always been appreciated in the harems of the Middle East". The Caucasus continued as a source into the nineteenth century. "Georgians and Circassians were greatly appreciated both in Persia and in the Ottoman lands ... the women for pleasure." The Sultan Ibrahim (ca 1640) had a rather more direct solution to the concubine shortage. He simply had his soldiers scour the baths of Constantinople "to find beauties for his pleasure".

The Muslim invaders of India also had a copious demand for slave concubines. "According to Ferishta, Mahmud's [Mahmud Khalji (1431-69)] successor was able to assemble a harem of ten thousand maidens." Even accounting for a tendency to exaggerate on Ferishta's part, it still must have been a formidable number.

Another Muslim ruler with a prodigious sexual appetite was the Mogul ruler Shah Jahan who "had 5,000 concubines in his harem, but nevertheless indulged in incestuous sex with his daughters". Furthermore, when the Moguls took the Portuguese enclave of Hugh four thousand inhabitants "were taken to Agra where they were offered Islam or death. Most refused and were killed, except for the younger women who went to harems."

Mass enslavement of young women was not confined to the jihads and razzias of the distant past. There have been a number of equivalent examples in the modern age. As late as 1860 during Muslim-Christian strife in Lebanon and Damascus, Christian women were consigned en masse to harems. "Between twenty and twenty five thousand Christians were brutally slaughtered ... and another hundred thousand were forcefully dislocated. Women were seized for harems; mothers were forced to sell their children."

During the Armenian massacres of 1916, female "slave markets were established in the Muslim agglomerations through which the Armenians were driven, and thousands of young Armenian women and girls were sold in this way. Even the clerics were quick to avail themselves of the bargains of the white slave market."

DEGRADATION OF WOMEN

Besides the indignities visited on the captives, the harem system had the more general effect of lowering the position of all women, Muslim as well as non-Muslim, free as well as slave. The large harems, made possible by the large number of eunuchs and numerous child slaves, all contributed to the degradation of women at every level of society. To be sure, in early Islamic times there was a general looseness of behavior amongst the Arab elite and a degree of freedom for women, which was later to be curtailed as the system of concubinage and sexual slavery inevitably led to the oppression of free and even aristocratic Muslim women. In those first days of the Arab Empire the "ladies of the royal household seem to have enjoyed a relatively high degree of freedom." The first establishment of harems guarded by eunuchs did not appear until the reign of the Umayyad caliph al-Walid II (743-4).

Levy contends that the institution of the harem attained its full form in the reign of Harun and was no longer only the prerogative of the caliph. Upper class males in imitation of the caliph, frequently built their own harems.

It is not possible to say when the harem system and the seclusion of women began to be general. The early interpreters of the Koran were men who originated in Persia, a land in which the women had long been secluded, and it is probable that their authority began to make itself felt after the close of the rule of the Umayyad Caliphs of Damascus. By the time of Harun al-Rashid ... the system was fully established, with all the appurtenances of the harem, in which among the richer classes, the women were shut off from the rest of the household under the charge of eunuchs.

The ideology of the harem soon affected all classes of society, even among those who could not afford elaborate secluded quarters guarded by a staff of eunuchs. By "the end of the tenth century ... the system of strict seclusion and absolute segregation of the sexes had become general." And with that followed a "period of decline, characterized by excessive concubinage, laxity of sex morality and indulgence in luxury" so that "the position of women fell to the low level we find in the Arabian nights."

Other social ills followed as the system of sexual slavery began to permeate most of Muslim society. The increasing demand for eunuchs, for instance, was prompted by the growth of the harem system. As Lewis observes:

The recruitment by natural increase to slave parents within the empire was never sufficient for the insatiable needs of Middle Eastern society ... The price of slaves, especially of young female slaves, was high, and despite the perishable character of this merchandise the trade was well worth the risks. The price of young male slaves could be greatly increased by castration to meet the demand for eunuchs to serve in palaces, in the wealthier homes, and in some religious sites.

As the possession of concubines became widespread, a class distinction developed even within the ranks of sex slaves:

Slave women of every ethnic origin were acquired in great numbers to staff the harems of the Islamic world – as concubines or as menials, the two functions not always clearly differentiated. Some slave girls received education. Some were trained as performers ... A few even have an honoured place in literary history. These belong to the elite rather than to the commonality.

In addition, to the earthly rewards and heavenly delights promised to the young male warrior, Islamic sexual ideology created a more negative incentive driving youths to violent behavior which could only be diverted through participation in holy war. The existence of polygamy and massive slave concubinage when combined with the puritanical sanctions against illicit sex kept young males in a state of heightened frustration. For these practices entailed a severe restriction in the available sexual outlets. The wealthy and powerful monopolized the supply of young women and enforced their property rights with drastic penalties. One consequence was the growth of potentially disruptive factions among young men such as had existed in ancient Persia, another society with widespread polygamy. "Polygamy had been practiced in pre-Islamic Iran as under Islam, and the shortage of women resulting from it fostered the recruitment of bachelor societies". The other outlets for youthful male energy, of course, jihad or razzia, held the promise of quicker and more effective relief for frustration.

HOMOSEXUALITY

A number of authors note one additional result of this bottling up of male sexual energy. In Muslim nations, the suppression of liaisons between men and women has produced frustrated sexual tension that has sought and found release in homosexual intercourse through the centuries. Those denied access to licit sexuality have sought and obtained outlets that have produced chronic contradictions between normative morality and social realities. Male and female prostitution and same-sex practices - including abuse of young boys by their older male relatives - have been rampant in Islamic societies from the medieval to the modern period.

It should be emphasized that those societies stress a distinction between the sexual act itself, which was deemed acceptable, and emotional attachment, which was unpardonable: 'Sexual relations in Middle Eastern societies have historically articulated social hierarchies, that is, dominant and subordinate social positions: adult men on top; women, boys and slaves below.'

Thus, in spite of its condemnation by religious authorities, homosexuality persisted in a subterranean manner. For the great accumulation of wealth and power in a few hands combined with the continuance of and regularization of polygamy and concubinage must have severely restricted the sexual opportunities available to young men, even with the prohibition of female infanticide. Such opportunities were only opened via jihad and razzias or through some form of illicit sex.

Darlington observes that in pre-Islamic Arabia the practice of homosexuality was common; there was "a caste of dancers whose boys before marriage act as male prostitutes. ... The excess of women arising from the slaughter of men was compensated by female infanticide. If it was over-compensated, male homosexuality was in the past ... no less common than it is now." However, the formal Islamic prohibition against female infanticide was accompanied by scriptural injunctions against homosexuality. These were both the means by which Islam reversed the "immemorial system of population control" necessitated by the life of the desert, in favor of increasing fertility. But, once the Islamic system was fully in place and young men found their licit sexual outlets extremely restricted, homosexuality returned in a surreptitious form.

Homosexual activity existed and was, undoubtedly, frequent during times of conquest when the pent-up exuberance of Muslim males was explosively released. Such acts inflicted on a vanquished and enslaved population could be quite open. In fact, members of the elite could continue to indulge their varied tastes long after the heat of battle subsided, as shown by the actions of one particularly renowned warrior. Mehmed the Conqueror "who was known to have ambivalent sexual tastes, sent a eunuch to the house of Notaras, demanding that he supply his good looking fourteen year old son for the Sultan's pleasure. When he refused, the Sultan instantly ordered the decapitation of Notaras, together with that of his son and his son-in-law; and their three heads ... were placed on the banqueting table before him." Another youth Mehmed found attractive, and who was presumably more accommodating, was the brother of the famous Vlad the Impaler, "Radu, a hostage in Istanbul whose good looks had caught the Sultan's fancy, and who was thus singled out to serve as one of his most favored pages." After the defeat of Vlad, Mehmed placed Radu on the throne of Wallachia as a vassal ruler.

ENORMOUS PROGENY

Polygamy, sexual slavery and the oppression of women provide substantial reproductive opportunities for favored Muslim males. Monarchs, high officials and wealthy merchants have, since the beginning of Islam and up to the present day, sired incredible numbers of children. Following are some of the more notable examples. Undoubtedly, the most extreme case is that of the documented world record holder in paternity, "Moulay Ismail, Emperor of Morocco, who is alleged to have had 700 sons (so presumably as many daughters) by the time he was forty nine in 1721. He died in 1727 – so there was another six years to have some more."

There were other somewhat less prodigious, but still impressive, documented examples of fatherhood. The Spanish Umayyad Abd-al-Rahman II fathered 45 sons. It can be presumed that he sired an equal number of daughters. The Ottoman Sultan Murad III was "known chiefly for his 112 children." That feat is even more astounding "in that fifty-four of these children were born in the last twelve years" of his life, during which "he seems to have done little other than serve as the royal stud." Many Ottoman sultans would regularly father large numbers of children, though short of Murad's record. For example Mahmud II (1808-39) had eighteen concubines who "bore him nineteen boys and seventeen girls." Abdul Mecit was also no slacker, having fathered eighteen sons and twenty five daughters."

The logical outcome of this system was, indeed, the degeneration of the person of the Ottoman sultan solely into that of a stud whose role was to produce male sons to continue the dynasty lest the empire fall into civil strife and fragmentation. The Sultan Ibrahim, a shadowy figure who was raised to the throne directly from the Cage, had lost all of his sexual inclinations. The Queen Mother Kosem took it upon herself to remedy this by finding beautiful concubines for Ibrahim's harem, which were supplied to her from the slave market by a confidant named Pezevenk, or the Pimp. But when her son at first showed no interest in these women she consulted the sultan's tutor and confidant, Cinci Hoca, who dosed Ibrahim with aphrodisiacs and brought him illustrated pornographic books ... The treatment worked, and Ibrahim soon began enjoying the company of his concubines as well as the other pleasures of life that had been denied to him...

Such instances of prodigious paternity are by no means confined to the distant past. The modern conqueror of the Arabian Peninsula, Ibn Saud started his career as a desert raider. His sexual payoff was equally impressive. He sired forty-five official sons by twenty-two mothers. He fathered at least an equal number of daughters by a bewildering variety of women that included concubines, slave girls and 'wives of the night'. As of 1981, roughly five hundred royal children, grandchildren and great-grandchildren could trace their origins back to Ibn Saud's loins.

There are other modern examples of ardent Muslim males, of somewhat lesser renown, who have taken up the challenge of fruitfully multiplying. In Saudi Arabia, "133 year-old Hussein Rashid al-Sowaikat al-Baqami died on May 8, 2002, leaving behind the last of his nine wives, 23 sons and 113 grandchildren." In the Gaza Strip the oldest resident "Haj Abdullah Kadurah, died ... at the age of 128. ... Kadurah is survived by more than 240 children, grandchildren, great-grandchildren, and great-great-grandchildren."

THE HAREM LEGACY: SOCIAL PATHOLOGIES OF MODERN ISLAM

As the culture of the harem degrades women and by restricting the availability of sexual outlets leads to the frustration of large numbers of males. This system has been good at producing and motivating warriors for jihad; for only those successful at spreading Islam could have their frustrations relieved and that in quite an abundant way. However, the consequent pathologies produced by this system afflict Muslim society even today.

In pursuit of this sexual imperative Islamic societies have evolved a number of child rearing practices. One unfortunate consequence noted by all "those who have made first-hand observations of Arab family life" is "that the incidence and severity of corporal punishment administered to Arab children is much greater than is the case in the Western world." Bloom observes that an Arab boy at puberty ...is expelled from the loving world of his mother and sisters into the realm of men. There, hand-holding between males is still allowed, but physical affection between men and women is frowned upon. A vengeful masculinity stands in its place. The result: violent adults.

Social psychologist Patai notes the effect of the cognitive dissonance created by the vast discrepancy in the treatment children receive in the two realms:

> The harsh, disciplinarian father is thus counterbalanced by the compassionate loving mother. Accordingly, the budding personality of the boy develops a twofold aspect; one expressive of his self-image and his position in the larger male world; and the other presented to him by the small world of the women...

The similarity of child rearing practices in "even two such widely separated cultures as those of Morocco and Iraq" show the power of Islamic Arab culture in impressing itself on originally quite diverse ethnicities. Moreover, the effects of such practices on the political life of the Muslim world are grave.

In much of Arab society, the unmerciful approach of fathers to their children continues, and public warmth between men and women is still considered an evil. Perhaps this is why a disproportionate number of Arab adults, stripped of intimacy and thrust into a world in which vulnerable emotion is a sin, have joined extremist movements dedicated to wreaking havoc on the world.

It is undoubtedly the case that Muslim sexual mores creates a greater obsession with sex than occurs in other cultures. It is the Muslim view that both men and women have little or no control over their sexual appetites, and will always copulate given even the slightest opportunity. According to Patai "intense and uncontrolled sexuality is the assumption that underlies the segregation of the sexes ... and of the entire strict code and rigid Arab code of sexual conduct." Furthermore, as another example of the bottling up of male sexual energy:

> ...the average Arab, unless he happens to live in a larger town ... has no sexual experience with women until he marries. If we add the fact that the average Arab does not marry until his middle or even late twenties ... we find that usually years pass between sexual maturation and the beginning of licit heterosexual activity.

Homosexuality, although condemned in Muslim law, is a frequent outcome of the Islamic sexual system. As shown above, historically it occurred during periods of raiding and conquest, but it is also common in times of peace. Moreover, in certain parts of the Muslim world, as in the Egyptian Siwa Oasis, it is quite openly practiced "with the shaykhs and the well-to-do men lending their sons to each other." Reconciling behavior strongly condemned by religious stricture with a common social practice is accomplished by some deft rationalization on the part of many Muslims. Patai points out that among Arabs and Turks homosexuality is justified as an expression of power. The "active homosexual act is considered as an assertion of one's aggressive masculine superiority, while the acceptance of the role of the passive homosexual is considered extremely degrading and shameful because it casts the man or youth into a submissive, feminine role."

Glazov emphasizes the utilization of the homosexual act as an expression of the domination of the strong over the weak. Older and stronger unmarried males seek their sexual outlet in "victimizing younger males just the way they were victimized."

Socially segregated from women, Arab men succumb to homosexual behavior. But, interestingly enough, there is no word for "homosexual" in their culture in the modern Western sense. That is because having sex with boys, or with effeminate men, is seen as a social norm. Males serve as available substitutes for unavailable women. The male who does the penetrating, meanwhile, is not emasculated any more than if he had sex with a wife. The male who is penetrated is emasculated. The boy, however, is not, since it is rationalized that he is not yet a man.

In this culture, a male sexually penetrating male becomes a manifestation of male power, conferring a status of hyper-masculinity. It is considered to have nothing to do with homosexuality. An unmarried man who has sex with boys is simply doing what men do. As the scholar Bruce Dunne has demonstrated, sex in Islamic societies is not about mutuality between partners, but about the adult male's achievement of pleasure through violent domination.

This cycle of frustration, humiliation and rage has consequences for all members of society. It is an important factor in the abusive child rearing practices detailed above. It is also a cause of violence against, and humiliation of, Muslim women. Patai describes the underlying violence toward women which is always present just beneath the surface of Arab society.

> Thus sex is both prohibited, and therefore feared, and desired, and therefore sought after. Both emotions are experienced with considerable intensity, which can be taken as an indication of the intensity of the childhood repression of the sexual interest. After adolescence this repression creates a strong sense of frustration. If, however, the social controls break down, or are eliminated, the repressed aggression engendered by the frustrated sex drive breaks through to the surface and seeks its expression in sexual as well as other aggression. ... In an environment where he is unknown, the individual feels that the old taboos with their built-in threat of punishment can be infringed with impunity. A third type of occasion ... is at an accidental encounter between a man ... and a woman in a place where there are no witnesses. In such a situation, and especially if the woman is not a member of the ingroup, or is a member of a hostile group, her sexual abuse is quite likely to occur.

Glazov emphasizes the denial that surrounds the issue of violence against women and the resulting poisoning of the relations between the sexes.

> There is silence around this issue. It is the silence that legitimizes sexual violence against women, such as honor crimes and female circumcision. It is also the silence that forces victimized Arab boys into invisibility. Even though the society does not see their sexual exploitation as being humiliating, the psychological and emotional scars that result from their subordination, powerlessness and humiliation is a given. Traumatized by the violation of their dignity and manliness, they spend the rest of their lives trying to get it back.
>
> In all of these circumstances, the idea of love is removed from men's understanding of sexuality. Like the essence of Arab masculinity, it is reduced to hurting others by violence. A gigantic

rupture develops between men and women, where no harmony, affection or equality is allowed to exist. In relationships between men, meanwhile, affection, solidarity and empathy are left out of the picture. They threaten the hyper-masculine order.

Another consequence of this syndrome is that women are required to devalue their own worth and deny their own sexuality. Women are viewed as instruments of the devil; lures placed to tempt and deceive Muslim men. Thus from an early age women are required to accept their moral and social inferiority. "Within a few months after weaning, the female infant is well on the way to internalizing the role she will play in life as a woman: a subordinate, a person of little importance, destined to remain most of her life in a servile position in relation to the menfolk who will dominate her life: her father, brothers, husband, sons." She is also required to acknowledge that only males are allowed sexual privileges. She must accept polygamy and the ease of divorce, as her forbears were required to meekly accept sexual slavery. "Thus, a man does not have to invest in one woman. The concept of "the couple" is shattered; the individual woman is seen as useless and expendable."

Glazov points to the prevalence of female circumcision in many parts of the Muslim world as being one additional probable consequence of the deep seated misogyny rooted in Islamic culture.

To add to this tragedy: whenever the genital mutilation holocaust is raised, the first chorus that comes from the Muslim community is that this genocide is not rooted in Islam and predates Islam. Well then, why are Muslim girls this genocide's greatest victims? And why do so many Muslims spend more of their time and energy arguing that female genital mutilation is non-Islamic than campaigning to stop this "un-Islamic" barbaric practise from violating their women and defaming their religion?

The answer is simple: female genital mutilation produces the oxygen that Islamic fundamentalism needs to breathe. It helps militant Islam keep intact the foundation on which its life depends: the subjugation and enslavement of women under a rigid system of gender apartheid.

LURE OF THE HAREM

In addition to the payoffs that Islam's harem culture provided its warriors, it gave a powerful incentive to potential male converts. Vryonis notes that in Anatolia "there is some evidence that the hedonism attendant upon polygamy and concubinage appealed to some converts." Of course, some cultures were more predisposed than others to embrace Islam owing to its system of polygamy and concubunage. In parts of Africa, for example, Islam "finds the readier acceptance ... amongst the men of the native tribes by recognizing polygamy as necessary, both as satisfying sexual demands and as according with the indigenous system of family life."

Furthermore, the harem system even appealed to some dhimmis still clinging to their religious traditions. In Spain during the reign of Abd-al-Rahman II "the lure of the language, literature, religion and other institutions of the conquerors - including the harem system - had become so strong that a large number of urban Christians had become Arabized." The Norman conquerors of Muslim Sicily were, likewise seduced by Islamic culture in general, and the institution of the harem, in particular. "The strange and fascinating Sicilian-Arab line started by Roger I culminated in his son and successor, Roger II" who "dressed like a Moslem and his critics called him the 'half-heathen king." Roger II's grandson the Emperor Frederick II, who invited philosophers from Baghdad to reside at his court, "kept a harem and was semi-Oriental." The harem provided an endless source of titillation even for Europeans far from Muslim lands. Legends of harem life were fueled by the reports of travelers. "European visitors to the Islamic lands were intrigued by what they ... heard concerning the harem system and some of them speak with ill-concealed ... envy of what they imagine to be the rights and privileges of a Muslim husband and master of the house."

The lure of concubinage would also be used by Muslim rulers as a bribe, inducement or reward for useful or favored individuals, even including non-Muslims. One such case was that of the English craftsman Thomas Dallam, sent by Queen

Elizabeth to install an organ as a present for Mehmed III. Dallam was reportedly asked to stay on permanently in the palace and that "the sultan would set him up there with two women for his own harem." Dallam politely refused the offer. Presumably many favored non-Muslim males were less strong in their resistance to temptation. Another documented case was that of the Jewish Exilarch Bustanay b. Haninay who was honored by the Arabs because he was considered to be a descendant of King David, whom they revered as a prophet. ... Bustanay was given the captive daughter of one of the last Sasanian shahs for a wife. The gesture was clearly to emphasize his own noble lineage ...Caliph Ali (656-61) gave another Persian princess to his son Husayn, who was the grandson of the Prophet Muhammad. Bustanay must have rendered the conquerors important services and... acted as a trusted adviser on native affairs. After Bustanay's death ... his sons by Jewish wives attempted to repudiate the offspring of the Persian princess, claiming that she had never been properly manumitted and thus her issues were merely slaves ...

HAREM INTRIGUE

Although women may have been beaten down under Muslim culture, sheer ambition and ability could not always be extinguished. The intrigues of the harem were an outlet for those ambitious and energetic women who were situated in proximity to the levers of power. Favored wives and concubines often exercised great influence over their husbands and jockeyed for position and power on behalf of their own sons. A trusted wife or concubine might be given considerable power by a ruler despite the generally poor position of women in Islamic law. This was due partly to the general distrust male relatives had for each other combined with the limits placed on ambitious women by the Islamic prohibition against women holding high offices in their own names.

However, strong-willed women wielding power occur rarely. Therefore, as would be expected with any curiosity, these are extensively documented in Muslim chronicles. While the same is also true of the West, "outside Islam the obstacles deliberately and officially put in the way" of women "have not been so formidable." Lewis notes how "the slave women of the royal or imperial harem ... as the favorites, or still more as the mothers, of the reigning sultans, were sometimes able to play a decisive if largely hidden role in the course of public affairs."

Another factor playing a part in the politics of the harem was the tendency in those Islamic states of long duration for the ruler to resort more frequently to concubinage than to legal marriage. After the death of the Abbasid Harun-al-Rashid, the caliphs apparently only rarely married relying instead on their concubines to produce children. "The change is connected with the emergence of the queen mother, rather than the wife or favourite, as the leading figure in the huram." This situation was mirrored seven hundred years later in the Ottoman court with marriage for sultans becoming rare and the harem now ruled by the Valide Sultan (Queen Mother). Thus harem intrigue became closely connected with the problem of the succession. With numerous sons by numerous mothers, each of which could be considered a valid candidate for rule, strife, assassination and even civil war was the consequence. This problem, conveniently solved by the Ottomans through mass fratricide, afflicted almost every Muslim dynasty. For example, in India, when the Khalji Sultan Ala-ud-din died, "in the space of four years two of his sons, plus a Hindu convert occupied the throne and quickly paid the price ... invariably lethal. So did ... Kafur who briefly acted as king-maker; half a dozen other pretenders were either blinded or murdered."

The price paid by the wives, concubines, eunuchs and other denizens of the harem, as well as by the contending sons of the monarch, for their close proximity to power was considerable. There were the inevitable fratricides, assassinations and mutilations which awaited those who lost the game of power. But even more common were the psychological costs. As Kennedy puts it the "social and emotional lives of the harem" involve "stories of bitter jealousies", enmities, sexual frustration and ubiquitous lesbianism.

Harem intrigue was costly to Islamic society in general and played a major role in the decline of many Muslim states. Hitti, in particular, lists the harem system and its intrigues as one of the reasons for the decline of the Arab empire. The "unlimited concubines and numberless half brothers and half sisters in the imperial household with their unavoidable jealousies and intrigues ... all these ... sapped the vitality of family life and inevitably produced the persistently feeble heirs to the throne." The very same pattern was reproduced by subsequent Islamic conquerors.

It was in the Abbasid dynasty, under which the royal harem institution reached its full development that harem intrigue first surfaced.

In the sphere of practical affairs it was not often that women's capacity was openly recognized. In the harem and behind the throne it obviously existed very frequently ... during the Abbasid Caliphate several instances are known of royal ladies whose influence extended beyond the throne. ... the name of the Sitta Zubayda, wife of Harun al-Rashid, acquired such renown that to this day great reverence is paid to the tomb which ... is said to be the depository of her remains. ...the mother of the Caliph Muqtadir, who was a weakling, ruled the empire of Islam - somewhat shrunken by that time. It was said that she held public audience ... summoned governors and qadis ... and ... signed and issued state edicts.

Another powerful lady of the Abbasid harem was Khayzuran whose son the Caliph Hadi "resented the fact that his officers continued to visit his mother to ask for favors ... After a barrage of ... none-too-subtle hints, courtiers stopped going to Khayzuran and she was left lonely isolated and powerless. ... in mid September ... the young caliph was dead". It was whispered that his mother "had ordered one of her slave girls, with intimate access to the caliph, to place a pillow over his face and sit on it until he suffocated. ... Whatever the cause of the caliph's death, Khayzuran ... summoned Yahya the Barmakid and other allies, who moved fast." Hadi's young son Ja'far was arrested and Harun al Rashid, Khayzuran's other son was proclaimed caliph. These women accumulated great wealth, exercised power, and helped make or unmake caliphs ensuring the succession for a favorite son, and sometimes dominated a weak or underage caliph.

There was another famous incident showing that slave girls who were singers, dancers and concubines could exert considerable influence over their masters. Dhat-al-Khal whom al-Rashid "in a fit of jealousy bestowed on one of his male servants", ultimately extracted from the caliph a governorship for her new husband. "In order to wean him from another singing-girl to whom he became attached, al-Rashid's wife Zubaydah presented her husband with ten maidens one of whom became the mother of al-Ma'mun and another of al-Mu'tasim." The tale of Tawaddud in the Arabian Nights "illustrates how highly cultured some of these maids must have been." In the following century there was "the case of the weak and vacillating al-Musta'in (862-6), who eventually fled to Baghdad pursued by his guard after he had been besieged and forced to abdicate, his slave mother shared with two Turkish generals the supreme power."

Islamic Spain was also the scene of intrigue and treachery in the royal harems. Abd-al-Rahman II's favorite wife Tarub was "a consummate intriguer. The eunuch was his gifted slave Nasr, the royal chamberlain and favourite with the queen." This favorite "entered into a conspiracy with Tarub to poison her royal husband; Tarub's motive was to secure for her own son ... the succession to the throne to the prejudice" of his elder brother. Another able intriguer was the mother of the Spanish caliph Hisham II, "a beautiful and able Basque named Subh" who "was the real power in state affairs." Her protégé and lover al-Mansur "started life as a humble professional letter writer and ultimately became virtual ruler of the kingdom." Hisham who was totally incapable of rule as a result of a life spent in enforced seclusion was forced to abdicate. Another famous and talented concubine who wielded much influence in the state was the beautiful I'timad. She became the wife of Al-Mu'tamid (1068-91) ruler of Seville, a rather liberal and cultured ruler. With I'timad's help he made his capital a center of art and learning before being overthrown and imprisoned by the intolerant and fanatical Almoravids.

The Fatimids of Egypt also experienced their share of, often deadly, harem intrigues. In 1021 Caliph al-Hakim was killed in a conspiracy organized by his sister whom he had accused of behaving unchastely. The mother of the long-reigned caliph al-Mustansir (1035-1094), was a Sudanese slave purchased from a Jew. His mother along with her one time vendor ruled the Fatimid domains in the early part of al-Mustansir's reign. The darkest days of the Fatimid dynasty in the 1140s and 1150s were rife with jealousy and intrigue. The murder of one vizier and the attempted assassination of his son and successor at the behest of the caliph were followed by the murder of the caliph himself.

But the greatest influence of the women of the harem occurred under the Ottomans. These descendants of central Asian nomads still maintained some of the attitudes of their ancestors who held women in relatively high status. The high position of women on the central Asian steppes goes back thousands of years. Russian archeologist T. Sulimirski observes the power and prestige of women among the ancient Iranian tribes inhabiting the steppes before the coming of Islam. Women of the ancient Sarmatian tribes, one of the inspirations, no doubt of the legend of the Amazons, were expected to take up arms and join their husbands in war. Sarmatian women also exercised important religious functions as priestesses.

An echo of the ancient status of the Iranian women of the steppes persisted in Central Asia even under Islam. "So also in central Asia the women of the nomad tribes are not restricted in their social intercourse with men by the veil, and the harem system is unknown." The Arab traveler Ibn Battuta also suggests that "Turco-Mongol political traditions were very much alive in the public roles of these fourteenth century women." Two centuries later these "Central Asian models and traditions had lost much of their overt force. Nevertheless, the idea persisted that a woman of the royal dynasty, especially in her capacity as mother, had a vital role to play in ... the protection and preservation of the dynasty." Vryonis notes how the ancient female military tradition of the steppes persisted even under some of the early, nominally Muslim, Turkish invaders of Anatolia:

> ...the Turkmen women ... assumed along with their maternal tasks military duties. The Dulgadirogullari in east Anatolia are said to have had 30,000 such women-soldiers ... and the subject is so frequently mentioned ... that one assumes it to have been a regular aspect of Turkmen organization and life.

Therefore, it is quite possible that the greater prominence of Sultanas among the Turks may be a reflection of the higher status of women in the early Turkish tribes, as compared to the patriarchal Arabs. This higher status was also, certainly, due as well to Byzantine influence since Byzantium was noted for its powerful and influential royal women. Darlington observes how European and Byzantine attitudes may have influenced the position of Ottoman royal women:

> While the Dynasty trembled on the verge of extinction, the Empire stumbled on, ruled by the mothers and the grandmothers of its puppet princes. These women were themselves in a strange situation. For the sultans' concubines were themselves largely European. But they were trapped in an institution, the harem, adapted by its origins and customs to an oriental and patriarchal submission of women. They did not submit. On the contrary they often thought they could manage the state; and they usually succeeded in managing the Sultan.

The most famous of the Ottoman women was Suleiman the Magnificent's favorite concubine, an ambitious and formidable woman of Russian birth, Roxelana. She conspired in the overthrow in 1536, of her rival for the sultan's counsels, the Grand Vizier Ibrahim. Her next target was Suleiman's former favorite concubine, Gulbehar. Following the birth of her child "Roxelana contrived to become in terms of Moslem law his acknowledged legal wife ... as no concubine of an Ottoman Sultan had been for two centuries past." Finally, she contrived to have her son-in-law and protégé Rustem Pasha appointed Grand Vizier. "As the Sultan increasingly relinquished the reins of government to Rustem, so did Roxelana approach the zenith of her power." Finally Roxelana achieved her ambition by contriving the murder of the Sultan's son Mustafa whose mother was Gulbehar. A few years after the strangulation of Mustafa, Roxelana herself died. But, by then she had ensured that one of her sons would succeed Suleiman.

A few decades later the Valide Sultan Nurbanu, a woman with a reputation for wisdom, along with the Vizier Sokullu kept her husband Selim's body "in an icebox to conceal his death until her son Murat could be summoned ... Murat finally arrived in Istanbul twelve days after Selim's death." Shortly thereafter he ordered his five brothers strangled to secure his position as Sultan Grand Vizier Sokullu; having dutifully assisted Murad's accession to the sultanate was now "continually at the mercy of the capricious intrigues of his new master's slave favourites and the women of his harem, who sought maliciously to influence the Sultan against him." Murad, who was under the influence of his many courtiers allowed several women to rule over him. One was his mother, another one was his sister, Sokullu's wife. Still another "was a Venetian beauty named Safiye. She had been captured by a Turkish corsair ... Disturbed at Safiye's ascendancy, his mother did her best to direct his desires into more promiscuous channels, and he plunged into a life of license, requiring the services of two or three concubines in a single night."

Safiye, following what was now a family tradition kept Murad's death a secret to give her own son Mehmed time to return to the capital. "She took him to see the body of his dead father, which presumably had been preserved in the same icebox in which the corpse of Selim II had been kept twenty-one years before." The following evening he had his nineteen surviving brothers strangled. Then he had all of his father's pregnant concubines drowned. This extension to the tradition of fratricide by the drowning of concubines shows that Mehmed was determined to introduce his own innovation into the family custom; clearly, he was not one to be upstaged by his forbears. Mehmed, in turn fell under the domination of his formidable mother. Safiye obstructed and delayed the plans of his ministers to have the Sultan command in Hungary "fearing to let the Sultan out of Istanbul, hence beyond the sphere of her influence. She preferred instead to provide him with distractions in the form of well-chosen concubines." Mehmed was finally persuaded to take command of his forces in Europe.

Following their victory at Mezo-Keresztes, Mehmed returned to Istanbul where "he relaxed as before amid the pleasures of the harem, leaving the direction of affairs to his ...mother." Mehmed's own son Ahmed I "was forever changing his Grand Vezirs, largely at the behest of the harem ... which now spread its corrupting influence everywhere. A Sultan Valide participated in the regicide of Ahmed's son, the Sultan Osman who she then had replaced by her mad son Mustafa. As proof that the murder took place one of Osman' ears was cut off and sent to the Sultan Valide. Mustafa was soon replaced and the Sultana took control of the administration of government, making and unmaking Grand Viziers, "When Janissaries and sipahis together momentarily turned against [Grand Vizier] Hussein, the Sultana fully veiled but nonetheless in contravention of the laws of the Koran, appeared before them to ask which of these candidates they would now prefer as Grand Vezir." This Sultan Valide, Kosem, with her young son Murad IV now on the throne exercised authority with vigor and ability until he came of age.

The intrigues, rivalries and jealousies of the powerful women of the harem continued into the next generation:

When the Sultan Ibrahim refused a demand to appear before his troops, a deputation from the army and the ulema approached his mother, the Sultan Valide, who had been removed from the Seraglio through the intrigues of the favourites and was now threatened with exile. ... The Sultana had alienated Ibrahim through endeavouring, without success, to persuade him to mend his ways. She now pleaded for him, insisting that he was a victim of bad ministers, begging that he should be allowed to retain his sovereignty but placed under the guardianship of the ulema and the new Grand Vezir.

Following the accession of the boy sultan Mehmed IV to the throne in 1648, "sedition continued at home in a partisan spirit among the Janissaries and sipahis, playing off against one another the two Sultanas Valide: Mehmed's mother, Turhan, and his once powerful grandmother, Kosem, who in due course was murdered at the instance of her rival." The career of the remarkable Kosem marks a milestone, of sorts, in Ottoman harem intrigue. Here was a woman so formidable that not only could she conspire in assassinations, but would, herself, require assassination as the only means of ending her grip on state power.

The Mogul dynasty was also marked by the inevitable Muslim distrust between male members of the ruling family. Such distrust here, as elsewhere in the Muslim world, was a factor engendering harem intrigue. Its exacerbation was also a consequence of that intrigue. "Distrust between father and son, as also between brothers, would be a recurring theme of the Mughal period, generating internal crises more serious and more costly than any external threat." One such intriguer was Jahangir's favorite wife Nur Jahan who "acted as co-ruler and, during periods of imperial incapacity, as the supreme sovereign." She attempted to secure the succession of her son-in law Prince Shariyar, "one of Shah Jahan's brothers and rivals, who were duly married to Nur Jahan's daughter by her first marriage." Shariyar was ultimately defeated and murdered by his rival Shah Jahan, putting an end to Nur Jahan's career.

Thus, political maneuvering within the royal harem was the only means by which aristocratic women in Islam could assert themselves. This fact illuminates the contrast in the status of women between Islam and the West. To be sure, Christian states were no paradigms of female equality. However, in the West there was a definite elevation in the freedom and status of women when compared to that of Islam. In Islam powerful women able to exercise authority openly, as the Sultana Kosem was able to do, were quite rare. Female power brokers generally remained hidden within the harem walls. As Lewis observes:

> But even the free Muslim woman was at a considerable disadvantage and was virtually excluded from the political process, except by what was seen and condemned as palace intrigue. There are no queens in Islamic history … There are a few instances where Muslim dynastic thrones were briefly occupied by women, but this was perceived as an aberration and condemned as an offense.

In Western Europe and the Byzantine lands, high-born women were expected to be visible and in many cases were able to wield sovereign authority in the absence of eligible royal males. In Byzantium there was the example of Empress Theodora wielding almost as much authority as her husband Justinian. At a later time the empresses Irene (797-802) and Zoë (ca 1057) ruled in their own names. In the West, there were, among others Marie de Medici, Eleanor of Aquitaine, Elizabeth I of England, Isabella of Castile, Mary Queen of Scots, Christina of Sweden and Catherine the Great who wielded power openly or even held outright sovereignty. Oftentimes these women proved themselves abler sovereigns and more cunning politicians than their male contemporaries.

Even under Islam, however, exceptions are bound to occur. There were two instances of Muslim women bold enough to rule in their own name. As Lewis indicates, Muslim opinion found the sovereignty assumed by these women to be an abominable violation of religious law. In addition, both of these queens came to unfortunate ends. Undoubtedly the most daring and successful of the female harem intriguers was Shajar-al-Durr. This Islamic version of the female Pharaoh Hatshepsut began her climb to power when her husband, the Ayyubid sultan of Egypt al-Salih died in November 1249. She, like some of the Ottoman sultanas afterwards, kept his death a secret until the sultan's son Turan-Shah returned to Egypt. However, "Turan failed to make himself agreeable to the slaves (mamluks) of his father and with the connivance of his stepmother was murdered in 1250." Shajar then proclaimed herself Sovereign. Hitti summarizes the life and unfortunate fate of this remarkable woman who initiated the rule of the Mamluk dynasty:

The foundation of Mamluk power was laid by Shajar-al-Durr ... originally a Turkish or Armenian slave. Formerly a bondmaid and member of the harem of the Caliph al-Musta'sim, Shajar entered the service of al-Salih, by whom she was freed after she had borne him a son. On her assumption of sovereign power her former caliph-master addressed a scathing note to the amirs of Egypt saying: 'If ye have not a man to rule you, let us know and we will send you one.' For eighty days the sulatanah, the only Moslem woman to rule a country in North Africa and western Asia, continued to function as sole sovereign in the area which had once produced Cleopatra and Zenobia. ... And when the amirs chose her associate.... Aybak for sultan she married him. ...the queen was not only sharing her consort's power but keeping him in subordination. Finally, on hearing that he was contemplating another marriage, she had him murdered ... Immediately after she was herself battered to death ... by the slave women of Aybak's first wife ...

The other instance of a Muslim "queen" occurred in India. In Delhi the slave sultan Iltumish was succeeded by an "ineffectual son" with a "vindictive and detested" mother as the power behind the throne. They were ultimately toppled by Iltumish's strong willed daughter Raziya. Despite her acknowledged wisdom and justice "Raziya's reign lasted barely four years (1236-40). Perhaps her decision to dispense with the veil" and dress "in mannish garb of coat and cap ... was unnecessarily provocative to Muslim sensitivities."

THE CONQUERORS HALF BREED SONS

The mixed progeny resulting from the harem culture was an important component in the population of every land conquered by Muslims. The sons resulting from such matings, acculturated as Arabs or Turks, indoctrinated into Islamic religion and following in the footsteps of their fathers were instrumental in pushing the bounds of Islamic territory outward. These sons were warriors, merchants, scholars, administrators and even rulers. The examples given by Muslim historians or recorded in official chronicles, of course, are only given for the top tier of Muslim society. However, the system of polygamy and sexual slavery was common among all Muslims. Thus the historically cited cases among the elite are an indication of more general social circumstances.

It is true that during the first Arab conquests and into early Umayyad times only "true Arabs ... of pure Arab descent on both sides were admitted to the highest levels of power and privilege. Half-Arabs, sons of an Arab father and of a non-Arab, usually a slave mother, could ascend part of the way, but were still excluded from the highest levels." That the class of "Half Arabs", generally the offspring of the conquerors and enslaved concubines, is specifically enumerated as a social class shows how numerous these must have been. In Umayyad times there are a number of prominent cases of "Half Arabs". The distinguished general, Prince Maslama being the son of a concubine was barred from the succession. The Umayyad governor of Iraq, Abdullah al-Qasri had a Christian mother. It was toward the end of the Umayyad dynasty that the offspring of concubines became eligible for the highest office. By the year 744 in the reign of the caliph Yazid III the eunuch system, which made the harem institution possible, was now fully developed. Indulgence in luxury due to increased wealth and a superabundance of slaves was rife. Even the reigning family could no longer boast pure Arabian blood. Yazid III was the first caliph in Islam born of a slave mother. His two successors were also the sons of such freed women.

It is true that Yazid III's mother was no ordinary slave. She was a descendant of the last Persian emperor who was captured by the governor al-Hajjaj and sent to the Caliph al-Walid. However, the last Umayyad caliph Marwan II's mother was a Kurdish slave of no particular distinguished background.

The Umayyads of Spain, like the last of their line in

Damascus and like their enemies in Baghdad, were also not fastidious in allowing the succession to their half-breed sons. Abd-al-Rahman's mother was a Berber slave. His namesake, Abd-al-Rahman III's mother was a Christian slave. The mother of the caliph Hisham II (976-1009) was a Basque. The powerful vizier and general al-Mansur had a son nicknamed little Sancho, since his mother was a daughter of the Christian King Sancho.

The Abbasid dynasty is filled with half breed caliphs. The following is a list of Abbasid caliphs whose mothers were slaves:

Caliph	Origin of Mother
al-Mansur	Berber
Harun al-Rashid	Foreign (unspecified)
al-Mamun	Persian
al-Wathiq	Greek
al-Mu'tasim	Soghdian
al-Muhtadi	Greek
al-Muntasir	Greco-Abyssinian
al-Musta'in	Slav
al-Muktafi	Turk
al-Muqtadir	Turk
al-Mustadi	Armenian

In addition, it is recorded that the second Abbasid caliph Mansur had at least two concubines who bore him sons. One was a Kurdish and the other a Byzantine slave girl.

In Egypt and the Maghreb, many of the rulers were also sons of concubines or of non-Muslim wives. Among the Fatimids, al-Hakim's Russian mother was the sister of the Melkite patriarch and al-Mustansir's mother was a Sudanese slave.The Almohad ruler abu-Yusuf Ya'qub al-Mansur (1184-99) "like many other Berber rulers, was the son of a Christian slave." The mother of the famous 16th century Ottoman pirates and rulers of Algiers, Uruj and Khayr al-Din Barbarossa, was Greek. Moreover their father was either a Turkish soldier stationed on the island of Mytilene, or else a Greek Muslim convert. The sultans of Morocco had a long tradition of sons born of slave mothers, sometimes from Spain. "Rashid's son and successor, Mawlay Ibrahim" in the 1520s reportedly had a Castilian mother. Known as a half Spaniard, Ibrahim felt it necessary to go on raids regularly in order to establish his reputation as a holy warrior. Another common source of slave mothers of Moroccan rulers was sub-Saharan Africa. "The Moroccan sultan, Ali b. Uthman b. Ya'qub (d. 1351) was the son of a Nubian slave girl." Mawlay Ismail (1672-1727) who "himself was half-Negro" created an army consisting of black slave soldiers.

In general, the Turkish ruling families were even more hybridized than were Arab rulers:

A sultan's father would naturally be the previous sultan, but his mother might be a concubine or a slave, possibly not a born Muslim, and from one of a dozen subject peoples. This genetic inclusiveness was to provide the Ottomans with extraordinary resources.

The dilution of the Turkish strain among the Ottoman sultans, as well as other Turkish rulers, was to such a degree that they can scarcely be said to be Turks at all. A mixture of Greeks, Slavs, Italians, Caucasians and others constituted most of the blood line. Such was undoubtedly the case with the rest of the Turkish elite families, many of whose founders were themselves slaves; and also of all classes of Turkish society. Yet such was the power of the Islamic meme that this population of diverse origins was of undoubted Turkish culture and Muslim religion.

Intermarriage was frequent among the Seljuk conquerors of Anatolia. Sultan Ghiyath al-Din Kaykhusraw had a Greek Christian mother. Ala al-Din I Kaykubad took the daughter of a Christian governor into his harem and Rukn-al-Din Kilidj Arslan IV had a Christian wife. Two of the sons of al-Din II Kaykhusraw had Christian mothers: Izz-al-Din's mother was

Greek, while al-Din Kaykubad's mother was Georgian. Moreover, Vryonis notes that:

This history of intermarriage of the Seljuk sultans with Christian women is incomplete, but the process is discernible among the Ottoman sultans while they were still resident in Bithynia, as well as among the Karamanid and Dulgadirogullari dynasties and the Turkish princes who had close relation to the Greek state of Trebizond. There is occasional reference to intermarriage in the ranks of the Muslim and Christian aristocracy.

Furthermore, the Conqueror Mehmed II's, mother "was a slave girl of undetermined but probably Christian origin." His son Bayezid II's mother was a "slave girl, Gulbehar, presumed to be of Albanian or Greek Christian" birth. In addition, Mehmed's opponent in eastern Anatolia, the Turcoman nomad prince Uzun Hassan had a Syrian Christian mother.

Many of the Ottoman sultans of the sixteenth through the nineteenth centuries were of mixed birth, almost always to harem slaves. Sultan Selim II's mother, the famous Roxelana, was a Slav. Murad III's mother was the Graeco-Venetian Nurbanu and Mehmed III's mother was the Venetian Safiye. Osman II's mother was Hadice, a concubine reported to be of Greek origin. Murad IV's mother, the formidable Kosem, was Greek. Mustafa II's and Ahmed III's mother was a Greek girl captured during the Turkish invasion of Crete. Osman III's mother was of Russian parentage and Selim III's mother was a Georgian slave girl. Three of Abdul Mecit's sons and successors were the offspring of Circassian slave girls.

In India also, many of the sons of the rulers were of mixed parentage. One notable example was that of the Mogul Emperor Jehangir, whose mother was a Hindu princess.

DEMOGRAPHIC EFFECTS OF HAREM CULTURE

In the 9th century a Turkish tribe encounters Muslims from newly conquered Iran and is slowly converted to the new religion. Islam has the remarkable advantage of being highly patriarchal and polygamous with great sexual advantages for successful warriors. In the 11th century a chieftain named Orkhan leads a group of these nomad Turks into the territories of the decaying Byzantine Empire. Becoming ghazis they spread their language and religion, as they establish themselves in Byzantine territory. Orkhan, who is appointed governor of a small town and its adjacent area, takes two wives and four concubines from among the conquered sedentary Greek and Armenian inhabitants. Three of his sons, in the early 12th century, follow in their father's footsteps and become ghazis. One son, Iskender, whose mother is a Greek peasant captured on a raid into adjacent Byzantine territory, leads a Turkish war party into that territory. Although, raised as a Muslim Turk, Iskender is also bilingual and is recognized as "cousin" by his mother's relatives. They help him consolidate his new fiefdom. Iskender takes a wife from among his Greek kinfolk, as well as two concubines, one being a Slav originally from Bulgaria who was captured and enslaved by Muslim corsairs. The second son, Ibrahim, whose mother is half Syrian Christian and half Greek, enters the service of the Seljuk sultan as a bodyguard. Rising in the service of the sultan, Ibrahim is given the governorship of a territory in southern Anatolia whose inhabitants are primarily Armenian.

He takes two wives and two concubines from the local population, and also purchases an additional two concubines, a Georgian woman from the Caucasus and a Greek woman captured from the Aegean coast. The third son, the dervish Bayazit, becomes the religious and military leader of a small group of newly converted Turkmen ghazis. After two decades spent raiding and plundering he settles down with his eight Greek concubines, on an estate purchased from a newly converted Byzantine aristocrat.

These three sons have between them thirty eight surviving children including twenty three sons. Eight of these sons, themselves, become highly successful Muslim warriors and take numerous local indigenous women as concubines as well as mixed Turkish-Greek Muslim women as wives. Some of the offspring of these matings, in turn, zealously spread their new religion and culture as they conquer still more territory further west, and so on into the following generations. Eventually, Orkhan's hybrid descendants aid the Ottomans in their conquest of Constantinople and their expansion into Europe.

The following demographic simulation of a hypothetical area conquered by nomadic Muslim warriors gives a reasonable quantitative illustration of the way in which a newly conquered territory becomes Muslim. It shows a possible path for the process of Islamization in intervals of twenty five years over a period of four centuries by tracing the various bloodlines. Initially the territory is assumed to contain one million native inhabitants who survive the war of conquest. The surviving warrior elite among the Muslims consist of 50 thousand men; these are joined by 25 thousand Muslim women. In the year of conquest 10% or 50 thousand of the infidel women are appropriated by the Muslim warriors as wives or sex slaves.

The following demographic parameters yield plausible results which approximately conform to the progress of Islam in a conquered region as described by various historians. Pre-modern societies have both high fertility and high death rates. The death rate for both Muslims and non-Muslims is assumed to be 1.6% annually which means that roughly 40% of the existing population will die over a quarter of a century. The total fertility rate for non-Muslim women, the average number of children they will have throughout their childbearing years, is assumed to be 3.8. Muslim women and concubines are given a slight reproductive advantage resulting from polygamy; this TFR is assumed to be 4.0. It is also assumed that each quarter century interval encompasses 90% of the average reproductive life of females. Another factor driving the growth in the Muslim population is a steady flow of concubines. In the second quarter century 30 thousand concubines are added as a result of continued war on the borders of the province. For each quarter century thereafter, 20 thousand concubines are added from more distant lands. Finally, a conversion rate of 25% a century or 6.25% for each 25 year interval, roughly following some of Bulliet's conversion curves, are applied to the remaining non-Muslim population.

Under these assumptions the following tables show the numbers and percents of the various groups. The population of the territory increases three and a half fold over four centuries. The Muslims steadily increase as a percent of the population to almost ninety percent. This conforms to Bulliet's findings for Muslim conquered lands.

There are four components of the population. Of course, this simulation is an idealization; in fact, there are no sharp divisions between these groups; all of the bloodlines have blended to varying extents. The Original Muslim category represents the bloodline of the original invaders. These might, in reality, be represented by the Bedouin and Turkmen nomads who still exist in the Arab and Turkish speaking lands and make up a very small fraction of the population.

The Concubine Hybrid group consists of the descendants of the original invaders and their female slaves or indigenous wives. The original invader bloodline, however, has thinned out considerably for this group. The Convert group consists of the descendants of those natives who voluntarily or through force accepted Islam. These could well be concentrated in certain cities and rural parts of the province. The last two groups have, in reality, greatly mixed with each other; they constitute the great majority of the population. The non-Muslim group represents the ancient pre-Islamic bloodline in its purist form. Their adherence to the old religions has prevented extensive hybridization from taking place.

It can be seen that under the assumptions of this simulation it takes about a century and a half for the Muslims to become a majority and two centuries for them to become an overwhelming majority and the actual experience of the different lands conquered by Muslims.

The enormous demographic assimilative power of

nomadic Muslim conquerors is clearly shown by early Ottoman history. Three generations after the founding of the Ottoman state in Bithynia by the end of the reign of Sultan Orkhan, "the population of his state had increased ... to some half-million souls - a far cry from Ertoghrul's legendary four hundred horsemen." In three quarters of a century, a relatively few tribesmen were able to co-opt a large indigenous population; using their skills and exploiting their economy to create a powerful state.

The mass enslavement of non-Muslims, as well as the institution of concubinage, was important to the ability of Islam in the assimilation of large populations and the extension into large territories.

14

The Slave Society

THE INSTITUTION OF ISLAMIC SLAVERY

The institution of slavery, in general, was a key element in that growth. All Muslim empires, from the early Arab expansions to the Ottoman conquests were addicted on a massive scale to the institution of slavery. Slavery, of course, was widespread in the ancient world. But nowhere was it as intractable and long-lasting as in the Dar-al-Islam. Slaves were one of three classes of social subordinates specified in Islamic law.

All three adult inferiors, the slave, the woman and the unbeliever, were seen as performing necessary functions, though there were occasional doubts about the third. ... Slavery, in the Islamic lands, was more often domestic than economic, and slaves as well as women thus had their place in the family and in home life. ... The position of the non-Muslim ... was not, as with the slave and the woman, to preserve the sanctity of the Muslim home, but to maintain the supremacy of Islam in the polity and the society which the Muslims had created. Any attempt to challenge or modify the legal subordination of these groups would thus have challenged the free, male Muslim in two sensitive areas – his personal authority in the Muslim home, his communal primacy in the Muslim state. ... It is the more noteworthy that none of these movements [revolutionary or reform movements within the context of Islam] ever questioned the three sacrosanct distinctions establishing the subordinate status of the slave, the woman, and the unbeliever. Although Lewis uses somewhat different language, he recognizes that the oppression of women and the enslavement or other parasitical exploitation of non-Muslims forms the core structure of Muslim society. Such oppression and exploitation became stronger with time since the expansion and very existence of the Islamic conquests depended on them. Moreover, the disdain shown by modern Arabs for physical labor might well be a result of the long continuous Muslim institution of slavery. Patai observes how an aversion "to manual labor, in particular work that involves dirtying one's hands is another Bedouin attitude that has widely influenced the Arab mind."

At the time that chattel slavery was dying in Christian domains, it was thriving under Islam. Kinross notes how at a time that the "Byzantine emperors had gone far toward the emancipation of slaves", Turkish law, i.e. Sharia, provided for the enslavement of infidel captives. The desire to avoid enslavement, "precipitated a certain degree of conversion to Islam" among the conquered Greeks. The Byzantines, as was typical of other Europeans in that age, and in contrast to the Muslims, were in the process of terminating the institution of slavery. Islamic conquest, therefore, constituted a definite reversion of society to a more primitive economic and moral level.

Muslim slaves originated from a variety of sources. Almost all slaves were "recruited from non-Moslem peoples and captured by force, taken prisoner in time of war or purchased in time of peace." Spencer expands on the various methods of slave procurement:

> The jihad slave system included contingents of both sexes delivered annually in conformity with treaties of submission by sovereigns who were tributaries of the caliph. ... However the main sources ... remained the regular raids on villages within the dar-al-harb ... and the military expeditions which swept more deeply into the infidel lands, emptying towns and provinces of their inhabitants.

The slave trade quickly became very important and lucrative. There were slaves from throughout the conquered territories, as well as those captured in raids, sent as tribute or purchased from beyond the borders. Hasan observes how the numbers and sources of slaves varied during the different phases of Muslim history:

> During the early period of Muslim expansion the Muslim world was flooded by slaves from different origins ... when the wave of conquest was spent the flow of captives was very much reduced. Consequently the majority of the slaves required were obtained by commercial as opposed to military means from outside the Muslim world. Large caravans were busy transporting slaves mainly from central Asia and Africa to the slave markets in the major cities of the Empire.

Slaves were commonly employed in domestic tasks within Muslim households. There were also instances, particularly in Iraq, of large numbers of agricultural slaves. Frye observes, for example, that in Iran, in contrast to neighboring southern Iraq with its Zanj revolt, the slaves "were essentially domestic - including concubines - and were limited almost exclusively to the towns" except for Turks in the army. Other slaves were assigned to the household of the ruler or other high officials as clerks, scribes or soldiers.

And, as we have seen, large numbers of female slaves were concubines. One particularly imaginative use of slaves was invented by the caliph al-Amin. This was the ghilman institution, which was the use of youthful eunuchs "for the practice of unnatural sexual relations." Lewis also notes that, with certain exceptions, most slaves were used for domestic purposes and contends that the "medieval Islamic economy, unlike that of the ancient world, was not primarily based on slave labor." However, even if slaves were not directly employed in the most important economic activities, their massive importation must have freed substantial labor resources among the free population for those very activities.

The primary source of slaves in the initial stages of a Muslim conquest was the vanquished population itself. Persia in the early years of the Arab expansion is typical of this variety of enslavement.

In the wars between the Iranians and the Arabs ... The numbers of these male and female captives ... were excessive. ... The battle of Jalula and the expeditions into Khuzistan were particularly productive of captive slaves. ... The condition of these slaves ... was not at all pleasant, although the majority of them by becoming Muslim gained their freedom. It was a qualified freedom, for they became mawali ... who as second-class citizens, could be exposed to ill-treatment and the contumely of the Arab Muslims.

In times of peace - more precisely during lulls in the Islamic expansions – the insatiable Muslim demand for slaves was met by the activities of traders. The Sudanese slave trade, subsequent to the first Arab invasions, is an example of how Muslim merchants added slaves to their line of imported commodities. In the al-Muqarra and Alwa regions of the Sudan Arab merchants "took back ivory, ostrich feathers, cattle and slaves. It is probable that the last item constituted the main activity of the Arab merchants who sought to satisfy the great demand for slaves in the Muslim world." Large numbers of purchased slaves were required to replace those previously obtained as booty during the active period of conquest. In the 9th century the recently pacified Maghreb became the destination and transshipment point for the new trade in Sudanese slaves. "From the Sudan came also slaves in large numbers, who were either kept in Ifriqiya itself or were exported to the Mashriq [Arab East], thus replacing the slaves obtained during the eighth century from the Maghrib itself."

Purchase of slaves was supplemented by tribute. During the first Arab empire pragmatic caliphs and governors, realizing the uncertainty and expense of annexing additional territory to their overextended domains, were content to leave local rulers on the frontiers in place. Tribute was, of course, required from these autonomus rulers as the price of peace. One of the most famous instances was the treaty entered into between the Arabs and the Christian rulers of Nubia. The treaty with Nubia requiring an annual supply of slaves "was used to justify a mutually convenient arrangement" whereby Nubia served as a channel for the supply of slaves and castration of eunuchs, the latter prohibited within Muslim territory. Hasan points out that owing to this treaty between the Muslims and Nubian kings, "Muslim legal opinion seems to regard the stealing or capturing of Nubians by Muslims as unlawful." But, in a masterpiece of understatement he then notes: "However Muslim law was not strictly enforced." Indeed, a "Christian source states that as early as 747-8 Muslims were in the habit of stealing Nubians and selling them in Egypt."

This stealing of infidels from beyond the frontiers was characteristic of the small, and often, large scale raids undertaken throughout Muslim history, whose primary purpose was feeding the Islamic slave machine. These "razzias" constituted a third means by which slaves were obtained. Nubia and its neighboring province of Beja was just one of many lands raided under the pretext of holy war. The Nubians, in turn to avoid depopulation, would raid neighboring territories for slaves to meet the requirements of their tribute. "Unfortunately Arabic sources do not tell us much about the areas from which these black slaves were obtained. Al-Istakhri states that the black slaves ... were not Nubians, Beja, Abyssinians nor Zanj but a darker people who came from beyond Bilad al-Nuba and who lived in a vast stretch of land that extended to the great ocean." Thus, the mass enslavement of people from tropical Africa was initiated by Muslims and had its origin seven centuries before it began in the European colonies of the new world. Reuben notes this massive importation of black Africans purchased or captured from throughout Central Africa. "Egypt, South Arabia and North Africa were the chief markets for Negro slaves from the centre of Africa, and Islamic rulers never legally abolished the trade." Moreover, as Lewis acknowledges, it was only in recent times that this trade was impeded. "The massive importation of black slaves dates from the advance of the Muslim armies into the African continent." This trade in slaves was finally abolished by European colonial rulers.

It is a fact little acknowledged by modern historians, that white Europeans were also victims on a large scale of the massive Muslim slave trade. The conquest of Spain, of course, was accompanied by large numbers of enslaved captives. However, this was followed by frequent razzias over the Pyrenees in search of plunder and slaves. Furthermore, for many centuries after the arrival of Arabs in North Africa, the coasts of Western Europe were raided by Muslim mariners. One particularly large-scale raid occurred in the tenth century when the Fatimid ruler of Tunis al-Qa'im (934-946) "sent a fleet which ... harried the southern coast of France, took Genoa and coasted along Calabria, carrying off slaves and other booty." The raids did not cease after the Spanish reconquista. On the contrary, they expanded in geographic scope beyond Italy and the other coastlands of the western Mediterranean. "Between the sixteenth and eighteenth centuries Christian Europe was ravaged by the Turks and Barbary corsairs, who not only enslaved the crews and passengers of ships sailing to the Mediterranean and Spanish ports, but sacked parts of Ireland and threatened Bristol as well as carrying off hundreds of British captives." Lewis describes how these increasingly daring mariners even ventured quite far out into the Atlantic:

> A smaller but not unimportant supply of West European slaves was provided by the activities of the Barbary corsairs, who by the seventeenth century extended their raids from the Mediterranean shores and shipping to the Atlantic coasts and sea-lanes. In 1627 they raided Iceland, and carried off 242 captives for sale in the slave market of Algiers. On 20 June 1631 Barbary corsairs raided the fishing village of Baltimore, in Ireland. A report sent at the time to London lists the Baltimore people 'carried away' by the raiders, with their wives, children and maidservants – 107 persons in all, to which were added forty seven 'captured from other sources'.

Foreshadowing the poignant tales later told by American abolitionists, a visiting French priest described the sad spectacle of European families being broken up with wives, husbands and children sold separately.

Eastern Europe was an even larger source of slaves for the Muslim world. "In the tenth century the most valuable commodity imported into central Asia from the Volga lands" were slaves. "At Samarra, on the Tigris, the slave bazaar invited the special interests of the geographer Ya'qubi" who observed the facilities provided for the housing and selling of slaves from the region of the Volga. At this time slaves from Eastern Europe were also imported in large numbers to Andalusia and the Maghreb. At a later century in "Eastern Europe, the Ottomans ... were able to cut out the middlemen and get their Slavic slaves direct from the source." During this period "the Tatar rulers of Eastern Europe raided the villages of Russia. Poland, and the Ukraine, and each year carried off thousands of young slaves ... who were shipped to Istanbul and sold in the cities of the Ottoman Empire."

This massive and continuing trade in slaves from Eastern Europe was known as "the harvest of the steppes". The lands of the Caucasus were another fruitful source of slaves for the Muslim world. When the Turkish nomads of the steppes converted to Islam the Arabs found an alternate supply "in the Caucasian lands from which Georgian and Circassian slaves, both male and female" were imported. This trade in Caucasian slaves continued during the later Ottoman and Persian empires. These slave trades from the steppes and the Caucasus only ended in the 18th and early 19th centuries during the Russian conquests.

The termination of the Caucasus trade, however, simply impelled Muslims to look elsewhere to satisfy their slave addiction. Historian of Shi'ite Iran Thomas Ricks observes how the Safavids substituted African slaves for their diminished supply from the Caucasus:

Under Shah Abbas I (1588-1626 C.E.), the Safavid Shi'ite theocracy of Iran expanded its earlier system of slave razzias into the Christian Georgian and Armenian areas of the Caucasus. Georgian, Armenian, and Circassian inhabitants of the Caucasus were enslaved in large numbers, and converted, thereby, to Shi'a Islam. The males were made to serve as (primarily) military or administrative slaves, while the females were forced into harems. A transition apparently took place between the 17th and 18th centuries such that fewer of the slaves came from the Caucasus, while greater numbers came via the Persian Gulf, originating from Africa. As discussed by Bat Yeor, the Islamic slave system had enormous demographic and social consequences for both conquered and conquerors. The demographic disparity between the vanquished and the Muslims after the conquest and during the ensuing centuries represented a considerable danger, threatening the permanence of Islamic power. A collection of measures – including deportations and transfers – were employed to reduce the ethnoreligious gap. The planned emigration and settlement of many waves of Arabs and Turks in the conquered territory was accompanied by forced conversions in frontier zones. This was supplemented by abductions of women and children ... and enslavement for insolvency.

Many of these subsequent waves of settlement were unplanned secondary incursions of Bedouin tribes in the Middle East and North Africa and Turkish tribes in Anatolia, some time after the initial conquests. The insolvency afflicting the conquered was often brought about by the jizya, confiscations and demands for tribute. The inability of the Dhimmis to pay the jizya resulted in enslavement; children, in particular would be seized as payment for taxes and tribute owed to the Muslim authorities. "Inability to pay taxes, offenses in respect of individuals or troops, razzias by rebels - there was scarcely a place or period when slavery did not claim its harvest of dhimmis: men, women and children."

Therefore, slavery was an important factor in changing the language, religion and culture of the vast population of the vanquished. As Yeor observes, slavery "constituted the most effective channel of Islamization." However, there was also considerable feedback from the culture of the slaves on that of the Islamic society:

The slave system which determined the whole social, political, and military structure of the dar al-Islam permanently introduced Christian influence at every level. Placed in harems, in the army, and the government, or kept in the countryside, Islamized Christian slaves of both sexes formed a considerable population. The workforce they provided was essential to maintain Islamic domination, while it fed a constant current of Islamization. Children, adolescents and adults - these human waves endlessly renewed by razzias and wars - kept all the social wheels in motion.

SIZE AND EXTENT OF MUSLIM SLAVERY

The scope of slavery in Muslim conquered lands was enormous. The following are just some of the many accounts documented by both Muslim and non-Muslim historians. The full extent and numbers can never be known for certain since throughout the history of Islam there was an almost continuous series of razzias and a flow of slave caravans of various sizes. The modern focus of scholars concerns the Muslim slave trade in sub-Saharan Africa which has continued into very recent times. However, African slavery "important as it is, ignores other vast domains of jihad slavery: throughout Europe (Mediterranean and Western Europe, as well as Central and Eastern Europe, involving the Arabs [Western/ Mediterranean], and later the Ottoman Turks and Tatars [Central and Eastern Europe]); Muscovite Russia (subjected to Tatar depredations); Asia Minor (under Seljuk and Ottoman domination); Persia, Armenia, and Georgia (subjected to the systematized jihad slavery campaigns waged by the Shi'ite Safavids, in particular); and the Indian subcontinent (razzias and jihad campaigns by the Arabs in the 7th and 8th centuries, and later depredations by the Ghaznavids, during the Delhi Sultanate, the Timurid jihad, and under the Mughals)."

The first Arab commanders, under the early caliphs and the Umayyads, were determined to make their mark on the history of this baneful institution. "An idea of the number of slaves flooding the Moslem empire as a result of conquest may be gained from" the following "exaggerated figures". Musa ibn-Nusayr took 300,000 captives from the Maghreb. Qutaybah brought back some 100,000 captives from the central Asian province of Sogdiana. Boastful Arab chroniclers may be prone to hyperbole; the modern historian Abun-Nasr estimates the number of slaves taken during ibn-Nusayr's invasion to be somewhat lower. "The caliph's share of the Berber slaves captured during Ibn Nusayr's amirate, according to the rule that he was entitled to one-fifth of the booty won by the Muslim army, is said to have amounted to 20,000." Such numbers, whether 100,000 or 300,000 from just one campaign, exceeded the grasp of even the most ambitious Roman general. The extent of Muslim slavery dwarfed that in contemporary Christian lands and, undoubtedly, that in the Far East as well.

Other accounts of the mass enslavement practiced by the early Arab warriors are given by eyewitnesses and documented by historians:

An eyewitness of the Muslim conquest of Armenia in 642 tells what happened when they took the town of Dvin: "The enemy's army rushed in and butchered the inhabitants of the town by the sword.... After a few days' rest, the Ismaelites [Arabs] went back whence they had come, dragging after them a host of captives, numbering thirty-five thousand."

On the island of Cos a few years later, the Muslim general Abu l-A'war, according to another contemporary account, "laid waste and pillaged all its riches, slaughtered the population and led the remnant into captivity, and destroyed its citadel."

According to the Syrian Orthodox patriarch, Michael the Syrian (1126–1199), Muslims conquered Cilicia and Caesarea of Cappadocia in the year 650 in this way: "They [the Taiyaye, or Muslim Arabs] moved into Cilicia and took prisoners... and when Mu'awiya arrived he ordered all the inhabitants to be put to the sword; he placed guards so that no one escaped. After gathering up all the wealth of the town, they set to torturing the leaders to make them show them things [treasures] that had been hidden. The Taiyaye led everyone into slavery - men and women, boys and girls - and they committed much debauchery in that unfortunate town; they wickedly committed immoralities inside churches."

Following the Moorish conquest of Spain, enormous numbers of Spaniards were sent east as slaves. The conqueror of Spain, Musa made his way back to Syria "followed by an endless retinue of slaves and prisoners of war loaded with enormous treasures of booty."

The impressive numbers of captives taken in warfare and boasted about by Arab chroniclers were just part, and possibly a small part, of the numbers of slaves flooding into the early Arab empire. There were additional numbers of slaves, less spectacularly delivered as tribute and by purchase which took place on a continuing basis. One example is given in the case of the Sudan where in 652 Amr b. al-As concluded a treaty with the Nubians requiring them annually to "deliver 400 slaves: 360 to the treasury and 40 to the governor of Egypt."

Despite the fact that the Arab expansion essentially ended with the accession of the Abbasid caliphs, there was no end to mass enslavement; only the means of acquiring slaves, and the regions from which slaves came changed:

> ...the prime economic factor here was ... the traffic from the Central Asian steppes in Turkish slaves for which demand ... rose sharply in the course of the 9th century. ... on his accession in 847 al-Mutawakkil received a gift of 200 slaves of both sexes from the Tahirids ... amongst the tribute sent by the Shah of Kabul during Abd-Allah b. Tahir's governorship were 2,000 Oghuz slaves...

Moreover, under the Abbasids, the numbers of slaves did not appear to drop. "An idea of the prevalence of slavery may be obtained from the high figures used in enumerating those in the caliphal household. The palace of al-Muqtadir (908-32), we are told, housed 11,000 Greek and Sudanese eunuchs."

The twilight of the Abbasids and the rise of local Arab dynasties saw no weakening of Muslim slavery. In Amorium in Asia minor in 838, according to the Christian chronicler Michael the Syrian, "there were so many women's convents and monasteries that over a thousand virgins were led into captivity, not counting those that had been slaughtered." These unfortunates were fated to satisfy the lust of Muslim slave soldiers. In 904 the Arabs under the renegade Leo of Tripoli "sacked Thessalonica and carried off into slavery 22,000 of its inhabitants." In 977, the governor of Dahlak delivered to the ruler of Yemen "a tribute of one thousand slaves, half of which were Nubian and the other half Abyssinian girls." Thus, even the prince of Yemen, a relatively minor Muslim ruler, was able to command a large slave tribute. Another example of massive enslavement occurred in the era of the crusades. When Crusader held Antioch "fell to the Muslims, 16,000 Christians were put to the sword, and 100,000 are recorded to have been sold as slaves."

In the vaunted enlightened land of Andalusia, the degrading institution was as strong as in any other Muslim society. At the height of the Umayyad dynasty in Spain under Abd-al-Rahman III (912-61) the royal palace had "four hundred rooms and apartments housing thousands of slaves and guards." Muslim chroniclers of the time make no secret of the Andalusian slave trade. The Muslim historian Ibn al-Athir (1160-1233), in his world history includes the following account which was representative of eighth and ninth century Muslim razzias into France for plunder and to replenish the Moorish slave markets:

> In 1777 Hisham, [Muslim] prince of Spain sent a large army commanded by Abd al-Malik b. Abd al-Wahid b. Mugith into enemy territory, and which made forays as far as Narbonne and Jaranda [Gerona].... For several months he traversed this land in every direction, raping women, killing warriors, destroying fortresses, burning and pillaging everything, driving back the enemy who fled in disorder. He returned safe and sound, dragging behind him God knows how much booty.

The Turks, themselves at one time subject to razzias and mass enslavement, when their turn came proved to be apt pupils of their erstwhile Arab masters. In his long and depressing account of the Turkish conquest in the 11th and 12th centuries Vryonis frequently notes the deportation of entire populations of towns. In the region of Edessa and Melitene in 1120 "Artukhid Ilghazi burned the villages, enslaving and massacring the populations, from Tell Bashir northward to Kaisum. Shortly after 1134 Afshin pillaged the regions of Kaisum only to be followed by Mas'ud who in his first raid pillaged and took captives in the neighborhood. ... Finally in 1179 Kilidj Arslan destroyed its walls and carried off the inhabitants into captivity."

The ultimate demographic effects of mass enslavement by Muslim Turkish nomads was as severe as anything that had previously taken place in the lands conquered by the early Arab nomads. "A further contributing factor to the decline in the numbers of the Christian inhabitants was enslavement. Throughout antiquity and the Middle Ages slaves constituted one of the most important items of wealth in the East. This was particularly true of Islamic society. Since the beginning of the Arab razzias into the land of Rum, human booty had come to constitute a very important portion of the spoils." When the Turks assumed the Anatolian jihad they "enslaved men, women and children from all major urban centers and from the countryside where the populations were defenseless. In the earlier years ... the captives were sent to Persia and elsewhere, but after the establishment of the Anatolian Turkish principalities, a portion of the enslaved were retained in Anatolia for the service of the conquerors. They were employed ... as domestic servants, as intimates of harems, and of course many of the youths were set aside for special training for the ghulam [military slave] bodies."

Some of the numbers reported for the twelfth century give a further idea of slavery's magnitude. As noted by Vryonis 16,000 slaves were taken at the fall of Edessa. Another 16,000 enslaved by Nur-al-Din in Cilicia were sold at Aleppo. In 1176 a large Turkmen raid in western Anatolia enslaved Greeks by the thousands. In 1185 26,000 inhabitants of Cappadocia, Armenia and Mesopotamia were sent to the slave markets. A hundred years later in 1282 when the city of Tralles was captured and destroyed for a second time, of "its inhabitants who had survived, some 20,000, were taken off into slavery."

The Ottomans continued the Muslim Turkish tradition of mass enslavement. The decimation of the Christian population of Constantin ople was merely the most spectacular act of mass enslavement. The enslavement of whole Christian populations was a routine occurrence in the chronic jihads waged by the Ottomans. Under the 14th century Sultan Orhan's incursion into Thrace "large numbers of slaves were marched back to

Ottoman territory." Mehmed the Conqueror, a whimsical despot typical of the early Renaissance, easily moved back and forth from benevolence to treachery and cruelty. When Trebizond fell, despite its peaceful surrender, "the people of the city were less generously treated" than were those in other surrendering cities. The entire population, males and females alike, were enslaved and divided between Mehmed and his nobles. The Ottomans, like their Arab predecessors ranged far and wide in search of slaves. One spectacular raid took place in 1535 when the Ottoman admiral Barbarossa captured and enslaved thousands of Christians during the sack of the Minorcan port of Mago.

Barbarossa's successors, the corsairs of the Barbary coast, not only raided the Christian lands of the Mediterranean in search of slaves, but ventured out into the North Atlantic, as far as Britain and even Iceland. The cumulative numbers of slaves taken was immense.

From the early seventeenth to nineteenth centuries, thousands of British men women and children were kidnapped by Arab corsairs and sold into slavery in Morocco where they were kept in conditions of unspeakable barbarism. The astounding thing is that these British victims were not merely seized at sea where they ran the gauntlet of such pirates in places such as the Straits of Gibraltar. They were actually abducted from Britain itself.

Corsairs from a place in Morocco called Sale - who became known in Britain as the 'Sally Rovers' - sailed up the Cornish coast in July 1625, for example, came ashore dressed in djellabas and wielding damascene scimitars, burst into the parish church at Mount's Bay and dragged out 60 men women and children whom they shipped off to Morocco. Thousands more Britons were seized from their villages or their ships and dispatched to the hell-holes of the Moroccan slave pens ... this assault upon the British people (and upon Europeans and Americans who were similarly seized) was a jihad.

In Iran and Central Asia, the later Persian dynasties also zealously pursued the Islamic religious impulse of jihad and mass slavery. Frye observes how the Turks were one of the prime targets of slavers from Persia:

> One of the reasons for the efforts of the early Samanids to expand their boundaries to the north and east was much more to obtain slaves than to spread Islam. The missionaries who followed the Samanid armies ... did convert many pagans in the course of time. ... On these expeditions the ghazis or warriors for the faith were an important factor in Samanid successes. ... Turkish slaves were highly valued for their martial qualities and the Samanid amirs maintained schools for slaves who prepared for military or for administrative service. It is probable that the amirs used Turkish slaves ... because they were more reliable ... and were well trained for their positions from childhood. ... One Arab geographer says that in the year 985 ... the Samanids had made so many prisoners ... so the prices dropped because of the glut on the market.

Indeed, as we seen, these same Turks were so well schooled in the Islamic slave ideology that they found it perfectly natural to adopt the exact same system of military and administrative slavery, a few centuries hence, when they became the ghazis overrunning Anatolia and the Balkans.

Under the later Safavid dynasty, the large numbers of female slaves and white and black eunuchs at the royal court indicates the large scale of slavery still practiced in 18th century Iran. "According to a contemporary historian, Shah Sultan Husayn (d. 1722) made it a practice to arrive at Isfahan's markets on the first days of the Iranian New Year (March 21) with his entire court in attendance. It was estimated by the contemporary recorder that 5,000 male and female black and white slaves including the 100 black eunuchs comprised the royal party."

Later Muslim invaders carried on the slave trade in Indian "idolaters" pioneered by the Arabs in Sind. From his campaign of 1018 "Mahmud [of Ghazni] returned with booty valued at twenty million dirhams, fifty-three thousand slaves and 350 elephants." He "sometimes ... spared the population of the ravaged cities, and took them home to be sold as slaves; but so great was the number of such captives that after some years no one could be found to offer more than a few shillings for a slave." Some centuries later when Timur sacked Delhi the Muslim quarters "were spared; everywhere else was sacked, and the entire Hindu population was either massacred or enslaved." Timur's sack of Muslim ruled Delhi was just one more example of the disaster befalling an infidel population when in times of war or disorder the established Muslim authorities were incapable of carrying out their obligations under the dhimmi contract. The intensity of enslavement in densely populated India was quite possibly greater than in any other Islamic ravaged land. Durant notes the typical case of the Sultan Aibak "a normal specimen of his kind - fanatical, ferocious and merciless." In just one of this ruler's victories "fifty thousand men came under the collar of slavery, and the plain became black as pitch with Hindus."

Even into the 19th century, when the slave trade, though not slavery itself, was abolished in the U.S. and in British colonies, vast numbers of slaves could still be captured in jihad. "After the Serb revolt had been crushed in 1813, one thousand eight hundred women and children were sold in a single day in Belgrade. The repeated revolts by the Greeks replenished the slave markets."

Africa may not have matched India in the intensity of Muslim slavery, but owing to the much longer time period over which the slave trade was active there, the numbers victimized exceed that of any other Muslim ravaged land. In addition, as Bostom points out, Muslim slavery in Africa was larger than the entire trans-Atlantic slave trade:

The scale and scope of Islamic slavery in Africa are comparable to the Western trans-Atlantic slave trade to the Americas, and as Willis has observed (somewhat wryly), the former "...out-distances the more popular subject in its length of duration." Quantitative estimates for the trans-Atlantic slave trade (16th through the end of the 19th century) of 10,500,000 (or somewhat higher), are at least matched (if not exceeded by 50%) by a contemporary estimate for the Islamic slave trade out of Africa. Professor Ralph Austen's working figure for this composite of the trans-Saharan, Red Sea, and Indian Ocean traffic generated by the Islamic slave trade from 650 through 1905 C.E., is 17,000,000. Moreover, the plight of those enslaved animist peoples drawn from the savannah and northern forest belts of western and central Africa for the trans-Saharan trade was comparable to the sufferings experienced by the unfortunate victims of the trans-Atlantic slave trade.

Lower in duration, but equal in intensity to the African slave trade was the "harvesting of the steppes."

Fisher has analyzed the slave razzias conducted by the Muslim Crimean Tatars against the Christian populations of southern Poland and Muscovite Russia during the mid-15th through late 17th century (1463-1694). Relying upon admittedly incomplete sources ("...no doubt there are many more slave raids that the author has not uncovered"), his conservative tabulations indicate that at least 3 million (3,000,000) persons - men, women, and children - were captured and enslaved during this so-called "harvesting of the steppe".

THE SLAVE MENTALITY

Accompanying the physical institution of slavery are the psychological attitudes enshrined in Islamic teaching and internalized by devout Muslims. The noted authority on Islamic law, Ignaz Goldziher expresses this as follows:

Islam means submission, the believer's submission to Allah. The word expresses, first and foremost, a feeling of dependency on an unbounded omnipotence to which man must submit and resign his will. It expresses, better than any other, Muhammad's idea of the relation between the believer and the object of his worship. Submission is the dominant principle inherent in all manifestations of Islam: in its ideas, forms, ethics, and worship. Submission is the distinguishing feature that determines the specific character of the education of man that Islam intends to accomplish.

Similarly, Trifkovic observes that: The entire world is by definition obedient to Allah and his laws. The whole creation must be in a state of Islam – submission to Allah – to be itself. ... 'Freedom' is incompatible with this relationship; in Islam any notion of freedom distinct from that implicit in the complete submission to the will of Allah is not an ideal, but a perilous trap.

Thus it is that Islamic political theory regards the populace as being the slaves of the ruler and the ruler as the slave of God. "The duty of obedience to legitimate authority is not merely one of political expediency. It is a religious obligation, defined and imposed by Holy Law and grounded in revelation." The ruler "is bound no less than is the humblest of his slaves." Muslims regarded slavery as a normal condition of all people. "The sultans had none of Aristotle's belief that some men are born slaves ... They were themselves sons of 'slaves,' for their harems were likewise made up chiefly of daughters of Christians." Their denial that some men are born slaves was due to a belief that all men are born slaves – to Allah or to his representative, the sultan or caliph; the latter was himself the slave of Allah. The Muslim conception of freedom may be summarized as follows:

Hurriyya "freedom" is - as Ibn Arabi (d. 1240) the lionized "Greatest Sufi Master", expressed it - "being perfect slavery." And this conception is not merely confined to the Sufis' perhaps metaphorical understanding of the relationship between Allah the "master" and his human "slaves." The late American scholar of Islam, Franz Rosenthal (d. 2003) analyzed the larger context of hurriyya in Muslim society. He notes the historical absence of hurriyya as "...a fundamental political concept that could have served as a rallying cry for great causes". An individual Muslim "...was expected to consider subordination of his own freedom to the beliefs, morality and customs of the group as the only proper course of behavior..." Thus politically, Rosenthal concludes, "...the individual was not expected to exercise any free choice as to how he wished to be governed...In general, ...governmental authority admitted of no participation of the individual as such, who therefore did not possess any real freedom vis-à-vis it."

Lewis notes the effect of this pervasive institution on the very speech of Muslims. "The Islamic languages developed a rich vocabulary of terms for 'slave,' denoting the whole range of the vast slave population, from the humble toilers in fields, mines, and kitchens to the sultan's slaves who commanded armies, governed provinces, and controlled the central administrations." Furthermore, he notes that neither of the words "free' or 'slave' was used in a political context, and the familiar Western use of the terms 'freedom' and 'slavery' as metaphors for citizen's rights and oppressive rule is unknown to the language of classical Islamic discourse."

Even the highest officials of an Islamic state could be literal, and not simply metaphorical, slaves. Among the Ottomans the personnel of the Sultan's court "were former Christians, as indeed were all the civil and most of the military officials of the Ottoman state, from the Grand Vezir and his fellow vezirs down to provincial governors, fief holders, tax collectors, and executives of different grades. For all were members of the Sultan's 'Slave Household,' of which the Seraglio provided the prototype - personal slaves of their master, who remained so throughout life, regardless of any level of preferment and power to which they might attain."

Not all Ottoman officials, however, submitted to the expected obsequious and slavish behavior, often meeting a violent end as a result. Ibrahim's (ca 1640) Grand Vizier Kara Mustafa "warned ... by the Mufti to take care what he said" to the Sultan replied "Surely it is a service to him that I should tell him the truth? Must I flatter him? I would rather die free then live as a slave." Sure enough Kara Mustafa was soon afterward put to death and was succeeded by Sultanzade Pasha "a flatterer so obsequious as to prompt his master's question: 'How is it that you always approve of my actions, good or evil?' To this he received and accepted the reassuring reply: 'Thou art Caliph. Thou art God's shadow upon earth. Every idea which your spirit entertains is a revelation from heaven. Your orders, even when they appear unreasonable, have an innate reasonableness which your slave always reveres though he may not always understand it." Clearly Sultanzade was much more in tune with, and understanding of, the essence of Islam than was his unfortunate predecessor.

One particularly interesting, albeit bizarre, expression of the slave mentality, which exemplifies how it afflicted even the top levels of Muslim society, was the Ottoman institution of the Cage. Once the custom of royal fratricide was allowed to fall into disuse, male relatives of the sultan were confined to a cell in the Seraglio, from which new Sultans were drawn as needed. These, of course, often suffered from acute physical or mental disabilities. "Sultan Mahmud died in 1754, to be succeeded by his brother, Osman III, a victim of the Cage so deformed as to be almost a hunchback." Nor was this Ottoman institution of enforced seclusion of royal males unique. The Spanish caliph Hisham II was elevated to the throne after having spent thirty years in seclusion. The pitiful Hisham was rendered so totally incapable of rule as a result, that he was forced to abdicate.

MILITARY SLAVES

One peculiar Islamic custom that typifies the pervasiveness of the slave mentality was the institution of military slavery. Lewis notes that "the military history of the Muslim states shows something new and distinctive - the slave soldier constituting the slave army, commanded by slave generals" and, eventually, leading to the rise of slave kings and dynasties. Previous societies made limited use of military or quasi military slaves as was the case with the famous Scythian archers employed as policemen in ancient Athens. But no non-Islamic polity had such a widespread employment of massive numbers of slave soldiers. Military slavery came into prominence under the Abbasid caliphates, when large numbers of slaves from Central Asia were acquired specifically for military use. The process of 10th century military slavery in Central Asia was also present in the far western provinces of the Islamic world. Such slavery, "also characteristic of other parts of the Islamic world and of other periods, and drawing in other ethnic groups, may seem contradictory or paradoxical to us; in Islam, however, it played an at times crucial role, even to the point where these slave soldiers seized power and formed their own ruling dynasties. During the period under consideration, Turks and Slavs – the latter mainly western Slavs acquired by the Umayyads of Spain and Fatimids of Tunisia – were the two main sources of military slaves."

In fact, instances of whole regiments and even armies made up of slaves occur in all regions of the Islamic world. One example is that of the Abbasid al-Mutasim (833-842) who created "a new division made up of Turks, originally his slaves, from Farghanah and other regions of Central Asia." Shortly thereafter in Egypt when Ibn-Tulun seized control in 868 he "depended upon an army of a hundred thousand whose core consisted of a bodyguard of Turkish and Negro slaves." In tenth century Spain the caliph Abd-al-Rahman III surrounded himself with over 3000 slaves and prisoners referred to as "Slavs" but including all purchased foreigners "who as a rule were secured young and Arabicized. With the aid of these ... the caliph ... reduced the influence of the old Arab aristocracy." Slavic and Black slave soldiers were also commonly used in the Maghreb at an early date. Ibrahim b. al-Aghlab, about the year 797 in Ifriqiya, "surrounded himself with ... a bodyguard of black slaves. His successors took into their service also European slave troops called Saqaliba who had been bought from the merchants of Naples and Venice."

The following centuries saw still further increases in the employment of slave soldiery by Maghrebi rulers. "With the collapse of the Almohads ... North African states increasingly moved toward the Saljuq (and Egyptian Ayyubid-Mamluk)" model of a military heavily dependent on slave troops and mercenaries. As late as the 18th century, for example, the Moroccan ruler Mawlay Ismail built an enormous army of black slaves. The black slaves recruited into his army "were provided with Negro women and encouraged to have children so that at the end of his long reign, Mawlay Ismail had a black army estimated at 150,000 men."

Indeed, other local Arab dynasties were not to be outdone by the Abbasids in employing massive slave armies. "The majority of Sudan slaves were ... recruited for military use, especially in Egypt." The Tulunid and Ikhshidad rulers of Egypt "in their bid for independence ... the need for a strong trusted personal bodyguard was keenly felt: Ahmad b. Tulun recruited 7,000 freeborn fighters ... 24,000 Turkish slaves and 40,000 Sudan."

Certain pragmatic Muslim rulers, realized that conquest and conversion would diminish the supply of infidel slaves on which their society and military was strongly dependent. Thus, they preferred the procurement of slaves from beyond their borders through trade, tribute and raids, rather than through direct rule. "Nubia and the lands beyond were a large market, from which large numbers of slaves were procured" by the Tulunids, the Ikshidids and the Fatimids.

The descendants of the very people who provided the Abbasids, and local Arab dynasties with large numbers of slave soldiers, were to make good use of this institution at a later date. "The use of gulams-devshirmes by the Seljuks and Ottomans resulted from the fact that they inherited the traditional Islamic forms of government and further, from the fact that Christian youths were plentifully available to them in Anatolia, whether from their own domains or from the neighboring lands of the Greeks and Armenians." The large and conveniently at hand Christian population of Anatolia continued as a source of military slaves until the time that Christian numbers became insignificant. "By the sixteenth and seventeenth centuries, the Ottoman devshirme seems to have been levied rather extensively in Anatolia. ... The system of slave administration and slave soldiery apparently experienced an unbroken continuity in Anatolia from the first appearance of the Turks well into the Ottoman period." The Ottoman slave military institution, however, did change with the passage of time. "In 1568 Selim II ... agreed to allow the janissaries to enter their sons on the army payrolls as cadets. By 1592 these 'sons of slaves' made up the majority of the corps.

Generals, governors and even rulers were eventually drawn from the ranks of the slave soldiery. An Abyssinian eunuch slave abu-al-Misl Kafur, for example, even succeeded in becoming de facto and then sole ruler of Egypt (946-968). At a very early date in the Muslim conquests, upwardly mobile slave soldiers were making their mark. Tariq ibn Ziyad the Berber general who invaded Spain was the freed slave of the governor of North Africa, Musa ibn Nusayr. Another military slave superstar was Jawhar al-Siqilli, originally a Greek slave from Sicily, who in 969 wrested Egypt from its Ikshidad rulers on behalf of the Fatimids. "Jawhar thus became the second founder ... of the Fatimid Empire." The Fatimid state was dependent for its survival on yet another one-time Christian slave. "In 1073 the vacillating [Fatimid] caliph summoned the Armenian Badr al-Jamali, a former slave, from his military governorship ... to act as vizir." Al-Jamali took command with such vigor that he temporarily revived the declining Fatimid dynasty.

The Ottoman sultans utilized a long line of administrators and governors chosen from the ranks of the military devshirme. Thus, enslaved Christians effectively governed large areas of the Ottoman Empire and "played an active part in the continuing campaign ... in the Balkans and in the subsequent pacification" of newly conquered territory. Muslim rulers in India were also quick to discover and utilize talented slave soldiers. Among the Khalji sultan Ala-ud-din's booty "was a Hindu captive who would add particular lustre to the Khalji sultanate. A eunuch and a slave, he quickly espoused Islam ... Ala-ud-din trusted him implicitly and appointed him a ... senior commander." This captive, Kafur, carried out a series of extremely profitable raids through the south of India. Another talented slave general was the African Malik Ambar ...who had been sold in Baghdad as a slave, brought to the Deccan, and after speedy advancement as a result of numerous military exploits, now undertook the restoration of the Ahmadnagar sultanate ... Throughout Jahangir's reign ... Ambar harassed and occasionally routed most of the many Mughal expeditions launched against him.

So pervasive was the notion of slavery in the Muslim world, that it was considered perfectly acceptable for even rulers to be of slave origin. As we have seen, many of the Abbasid caliphs and Ottoman sultans were the offspring of slave mothers. Moreover, some lesser Muslim polities were actually ruled by the sons of slave soldiers. One local ruler was Zangi, the son of a Turkish slave and founder of the Zangid dynasty (1127-1262) which ruled the cities of Aleppo, Harran and al-Mawsil. Indeed, in some Islamic lands the institution of the ruler of slave origin was pursued to its logical conclusion - that of an actual slave dynasty. The peculiarity of this institution to Muslim polities is noted by Hitti who writes regarding the famous Mamluk dynasty of Egypt.

> In other than Moslem annals the rise and prosperity of such a dynasty as the Mamluk is hardly conceivable. ... The Mamluks were ... a dynasty of slaves, slaves of varied races and nationalities forming a military oligarchy in an alien land.

India was another Muslim ruled land which, like Egypt, carried the slave mentality to the same logical conclusion with whole dynasties of slave sultans. "In 963 Alptigin an ambitious ... Samanid general, crossed the Hindu Kush and seized Ghazni. He once a Turkic slave, Alptigin was succeeded in 977" by Sabuktigin another Samanid slave. The latter "was able to acquire a large tract of territory and found the dynasty of the Ghaznawids ... Aybak, the favourite slave of the chieftain Muhammad Ghuri ... was the first of the Slave Kings of Delhi, and the Mamluk Sultans of Egypt were of similar origin. Whole series of dynasties were founded ... during the twelfth and thirteenth centuries by the Turkish Atabegs." These Atabegs were originally slave bodyguards of the Seljuk sultans.

Thus, the formidable slave general, Aybak, founded the famous 'Slave Dynasty' of Delhi". Like the nearly contemporary Egyptian Mamluks, these 'Slave Kings' were hardly servile. They may even have found their slave origin to be advantageous:

> In a court awash with intrigue ... India's Turkish conquistadors regarded a slave's loyalty as ...dependable ... Purchased, rapidly promoted, eventually freed and still highly trusted, the erstwhile slave of a royal patron was ideally placed

to act as either power-broker or pretender. Aybak would be succeeded ... by...Iltumish, another ex-slave of Turkic extraction. That no stigma attached to either of them is clear from Aybak's recognition as sultan by his titular superior in Ghazni, and from Iltumish's ... recognition by the caliph himself.

The Delhi slave sultans were followed by another dynasty of slave origin. In 1320 in the Delhi sultanate "Ghiyas-ud-din Tughluq, the son of one of Balban's slaves, emerged as the founder of a new dynasty." The Sharqi kingdom of Jaunpur was another dynasty founded by a slave. The sultan Feroz (d. 1388) conferred the provinces of Uttar Pradesh and Bihar on Malik Sowar "a eunuch-slave ... who proving exceptionally able, was given the title of Sultan-ush Sharq" and was the first ruler of the Jaunpur sultanate.

SLAVERY, RACISM AND ISLAM

It is a popular belief that Islamic societies are free of the racism that has prevailed in the West. The practice of slavery clearly demonstrates that the idea of the absence of racism under Islam is just one among many myths. Even free black Muslims were subject to prejudice and discrimination. According to sociologist Levy:

Faith, if not logic, therefore demanded that the Negroes should be permitted to regard themselves as the peers of other Muhammadans. But those Arabs who had been brought up in the older tradition, which was reluctant to concede equality even to free men of their own kind and colour, were still more reluctant to recognize the parity of a people foreign in origin and, in their eyes, of definitely inferior status.

The case of the deposition of the female Sultan of Delhi, Raziya illustrates the difficulty many Muslim societies have with black Africans as well as with assertive females. One additional cause of her overthrow "may have been the appointment as 'personal attendant to her majesty' of Jamal-ud-din Yakut, an 'Abyssinian' who was probably once a slave and very definitely an African."

One illustration of the racism infecting even the everyday social relations within Muslim societies is provided by the case of Ibn Musajjih, a renowned Black poet and musician in the time of the Umayyads. Brought to the house of a singing girl in Damascus as the guest of some youths he was met by the following uproar:

When the singing-girl and her friends appeared, he recited a complimentary verse, whereupon she flew into a rage at what she regarded as his presumption. "Shall a negro like this be permitted to utter parables about me?" she cried, causing the company to look at him disapprovingly. Their anger, however, did not restrain him from applauding as before when a second girl appeared and sang. This time it was the owner of the girl who was enraged at his presumption. He cried out: "Shall a Negro like this embolden himself toward my slave-girl?" For the sake of peace the youth who had first offered hospitality to the Negro poet suggested that he should go home to his lodging, but the rest of the company regarded this as unnecessarily discourteous, and the poet was finally permitted to stay, being warned to better his manners.

While Muslims engaged in mass enslavement regardless of race, Africa was regarded as a particularly legitimate area for the procurement of slaves. This is well illustrated both by the sheer numbers caught up in the web of the African slave trade and by the particularly brutal treatment meted out to black slaves.

Over ten million Africans were taken to the Americas during that period, while the number of captives taken to the heartlands of Islam - while impossible to establish with precision - is many times greater. Nevertheless, there are tens of millions of descendants of slaves in the Americas, and practically none in the Moslem world outside Africa. For all its horrors, the Atlantic slave trade took place within a capitalistic context in which slaves were expensive pieces of property not to be destroyed. In the Moslem world slaves were considerably cheaper, far more widely available, and regarded as a dispensable commodity.

Indeed, not only was the treatment of African slaves more brutal in Islamic lands than in the American colonies, but it was Muslim slave traders that supplied a lot of the demand of the colonial Atlantic trade. Nigerian scholars have documented this Muslim sale of African slaves to Europeans:

> Many slaves were exported through the Atlantic market. No doubt the profits and value of this trade in the late 18th century were well known in commercial circles of the north, since northern Muslim traders constantly frequented the routes to the coast. The same traders could report the advantage of securing control of these trade routes and integrating them into the Sokoto caliphate once this was established.

There are a number of reasons for the relatively few descendants left by African slaves in the larger Muslim world as noted by Trifkovic. Geneticist C. D. Darlington summarizes these factors:

> On the other side we see millions of Negro slaves have been carried off from tropical Africa to Arabia, Egypt, Turkey, Persia and the Maghrib. But they have left very little trace among living people. ... Certainly Negro slaves have been bred on a small scale and the effects of hybridization may be seen in the villages of Arabia and North Africa. But in general it is clear that the Negro slave has been sterilized. Castration in meeting the demand for black eunuchs has been one factor. Infanticide, abortion, perversion ... are other factors.

Castration was carried out on a massive scale with devastating results:

> ...when the castration was carried out in sub-Saharan West and West-Central Africa...a figure of 90% [mortality is] often mentioned. Even higher death rates were occasionally reported, unsurprising in tropical areas where the danger of infection of wounds was especially high. At least one contemporary price quotation supports a figure of over 90% mortality: Turkish merchants are said to have been willing to pay 250 to 300 (Maria Theresa) dollars each for eunuchs in Borno (northeast Nigeria) at a time when the local price of young male slaves does not seem to have exceeded about 20 dollars...Many sources indicate very high death rates from the

operation in eastern Africa.. Richard Millant's 90 general figures for the Sudan and Ethiopia are 90%.

Ironically, as Sudanese historian Hasan observes, young black male slaves may have been victimized twice owing to Muslim law. Sharia permits and encourages mass slavery; however it also forbids castration. Nubian males were the slaves most favored "as custodians of wealth and families. The eunuchs among them were particularly suited for this last type of work. The operation of castration was apparently carried out outside the boundaries of the Muslim world as it is condemned by Muslim law." Thus, Muslim law required that the operation of castration be carried out in particularly dangerous locations and circumstances; the prohibition against castration proved to be no favor to the ultimate victims.

The slave system illustrates the racism afflicting Muslims in yet another way. The value of slaves in the Muslim world was a function of ethnicity. For instance "Spanish slaves fetched about a thousand dinars each, while Turkish slaves fetched only six hundred apiece." Distinctions made between slaves show that Muslim racism extended far beyond that of color. While Blacks may have been at the bottom, Muslim slave masters seemed to have a preference for Europeans in general. As we have seen, the Turkish invaders of the Byzantine lands showed a peculiar preference for the very Greeks that they dispossessed.

Muslim racism is also revealed in the history of rebellion by Black slaves or former slaves. "One of the most spectacular and sanguinary episodes ... was the rebellion of the Zanj slaves. These were negroes imported from East Africa and employed in the saltpetre mines on the lower Euphrates."0 Karsh notes how this uprising exposes the racist attitudes held by the contemporary Arab population and future Arab historians. "Religious resentment of the heretic Zanj, together with deep contempt among the indigenous population toward black Africans (nearly five hundred years later ... Ibn Khaldun would describe them as 'close in their character to dumb animals') left the rebels isolated."

Other Arab versions of a contemporary race riot, large enough to be recorded by chroniclers, took place in Egypt. "The increasing power and misbehavior of the black soldiers in ... the reign of al-Hakim (997-1021) angered the Turkish and Berber troops and induced them to take common action." Ultimately, after a period of conflict, the Blacks "were defeated in 1062 by a combined force of Turkish and Berber troops, who drove about 50,000 of them to Upper Egypt." About the year 1168, there was further conflict. "In the bitter struggle that followed the black troops were ruthlessly hunted down and their living quarters, in Cairo, were burnt to the ground."

In conclusion, all of the evidence indicates that Islamic slavery was larger in extent and scope than those of such ancient societies as pre-Islamic Persia, Greece and even Rome. Muslim slavery was also larger than that practiced by other invaders of one-time Roman territory. The number of Christian slaves taken by the first Arab invaders was even larger than the number of Roman subjects taken captive by the invading Germanic, Slavic and Hunnish barbarians. The Muslim traffic in African slaves exceeded that of the Atlantic colonial trade; indeed Muslim traffic in slaves of all races was many times greater than African slavery in the Americas. Moreover, the treatment meted out to African slaves by their Muslim masters was even more deplorable than that suffered by slaves in America. Also, at a time that chattel slavery was dying out in Europe, it was thriving in the Islamic world. Europeans, prompted by the moral teachings of Christianity, were the ones who ultimately suppressed the institution, often over the vehement opposition of believing Muslims.

Oppression and slavery were important factors in the extirpation of pre-Islamic cultures. However, the process of Islamization was never total. The different peoples absorbed into the Dar-al-Islam had varying degrees of success in preserving and passing on their ancient customs. The following chapter describes the indigenous cultural traits that survived the coming of Islam.

Bibliography

Abraham, A. J. *Islamic Fundamentalism and the Doctrine of Jihad.* Lima, OH: Wyndham Hall Press, 2002.

Abu Khalil, As'ad. *Bin Laden, Islam, and America's New 'War on Terrorism'.* Open Media Pamphlet Series. New York: Seven Stories Press, 2002.

Ahmed, Nafeez Mosaddwq. *The War on Truth: 9/11, Disinformation and the Anatomy of Terrorism.* Northampton, MA: Olive Branch Press, 2005.

Aho, James. *Politics of Righteousness: Idaho Christian Patriotism.* Seattle, WA: University of Washington Press, 1995.

Alexander, Yonah. *European Terrorism Today & Tomorrow.* Brassey's Terrorism Library. Washington, DC: Brassey's, 1992.

Alexander, Yonah. *Middle East Terrorism: Current Threats and Future Prospects.* International Library of Terrorism; 5. New York: G.K. Hall & Co., 1994.

Alexander, Yonah. *Middle East Terrorism: Selected Group Profiles.* Washington, DC: Jewish Institute for National Security Affairs, 1994.

Alexander, Yonah. *Palestinian Religious Terrorism: Hamas and Islamic Jihad.* New York: Transnational, 2002.

Alexander, Yonah. *Terrorism in Europe.* New York: St. Martin's Press, 1982.

Alexander, Yonah. *Usama bin Laden's al-Qaida: Profile of a Terrorist Network.* Ardsley, NY: Transnational Publishers, 2001.

Alexander, Yonah; Latter, Richard, editors, *Terrorism and the Media: Dilemmas for Government, Journalists and the Public.* Washington, DC: Brassey's, 1990.

Bartholomeusz, Tessa J. *Buddhist Fundamentalism and Minority Identities in Sri Lanka*. New York: State University of New York Press, 1998.

Barton, Greg. *Indonesia's Struggle: Jemaah Islamiyah and the Soul of Islam*. Sydney, Australia: University of New South Wales Press, 2004.

Cateura, Linda Brandi. *Voices of American Muslims: 23 Profiles*. New York: Hippocrene Books, 2005.

Catholic Institute for International Relations, *Guatemala, Never Again*. Maryknoll, NY: Orbis Books, 1999.

Davies, Barry. *Terrorism: Inside a World Phenomenon*. London: Virgin Books, 2003.

Devji, Faisal. *Landscapes of the Jihad: Militancy, Morality, Modernity*. Ithaca, NY: Cornell University Press, 2005.

Devji, Mantoshe Singh. *The Mad Messiah: Osama bin Laden and the Seeds of Terror*. Scottsdale, AZ: Inkwell Productions, 2002.

Emerson, Steven. *American Jihad: The Terrorists Living Among Us*. New York: Free Press, 2002.

Esposito, John L. *Islam: The Straight Path*. 3rd edition. New York: Oxford University Press, 1998.

Esposito, John L. *The Islamic Threat: Myth or Reality?*. New York: Oxford University Press, 1992.

Esposito, John L. *The Oxford Dictionary of Islam*. New York: Oxford University Press, 2003.

Esposito, John L. *Unholy War: Terror in the Name of Islam*. New York: Oxford University Press, 2002.

Etzioni, Amitai. *How Patriotic is the Patriot Act? Freedom Versus Security in the Age of Terrorism*. New York: Routledge, 2004.

Fandy, Mamoun. *Saudi Arabia and the Politics of Dissent*. New York: Palgrave, 2001.

Farah, Douglas. *Blood From Stones: The Secret Financial Network of Terror*. New York: Broadway Books, 2004.

Gardell, Mattias. *Gods of the Blood: The Pagan Revival and White Separatism.* Durham, NC: Duke University Press, 2003.

Gerges, Fawaz A. *The Far Enemy: Why Jihad Went Global.* New York: Cambridge University Press, 2005.

Habeck, Mary R. *Knowing the Enemy: Jihadist Ideology and the War on Terror.* New Haven, NY: Yale University Press, 2006.

Hoffman, Bruce. *Holy terror: The Implications of Terrorism Motivated by a Religious Imperative.* Santa Monica, CA: RAND, 1993.

Howard, Russell D. *Defeating Terrorism: Shaping the New Security Environment.* Guilford, CT: McGraw-Hill, 2004.

Jaimoukha, Amjad M. *The Chechens: A Handbook.* New York: Routledge Curzon, 2005.

Karawan, Ibrahim. *Islamic Impasse.* New York: Oxford University Press, 1997.

Miniter, Richard. *Losing Bin Laden: How Bill Clinton's Failures Unleashed Global Terror.* Washington, DC: Regnery, 2003.

Mishal, Shaul. *The Palestinian Hamas: Vision, Violence, and Coexistence.* New York: Columbia University Press, 2000.

Napoleoni, Loretta. *Modern Jihad: Tracing the Dollars Behind the Terror Networks.* Sterling, VA: Pluto Press, 2003.

Noorani, A. G. *Islam & Jihad: Prejudice versus Reality.* New York: Zed Books, 2002.

Nusse, Andrea. *Muslim Palestine: The Ideology of Hamas.* Amsterdam: Harwood Academic Publishers, 1998.

O'Ballance, Edgar. *Islamic Fundamentalist Terrorism: 1979-95.* Basingstoke: Macmillan, 1997.

Ojeda, Auriana. *Islamic Fundamentalism.* San Diego, CA: Greenhaven Press, 2003.

Randal, Jonathan C. *Osama: The Making of a Terrorist.* New York: Knopf, 2004.

Rapoport, David C. *The Rationalization of Terrorism.* Frederick, MD: University Publications of America, 1982.

Scheuer, Michael. *Through Our Enemies Eyes: Osama bin Laden, Radical Islam, and the Future of America.* Rev. ed., 2nd ed.. Washington, DC: Potomac Books, 2006.

Taheri, Amir. *Holy Terror: Inside the World of Islamic Terrorism.* Bethesda, MD: Adler & Adler, 1987.

Venske, Ben. *The al-Qaeda Threat: An Analytical Guide to al-Qaeda's Tactics & Targets.* Alexandria, VA: Tempest Publishing, 2003.

Venzke, Ben. *The al-Qaeda Threat: An Analytical Guide to al-Qaeda's Tactics & Targets.* Alexandria, VA: Tempest, 2003.

Waardenburg, Jacques. *Muslims and Others: Relations in Context.* New York: Walter de Gruyter, 2003.

Wiktorowicz, Quintan. *Global Jihad: Understanding September 11.* Falls Church, VA: 2002.

Zacharias, Ravi K. *Light in the Shadow of Jihad.* Sisters, OR: Multnomah Publishers, 2002.

Index

H

I

K

L

M

N

P

R

S

T

W